The Idea of History
in Early Stuart England

Title-page from Sir Walter Ralegh, *The History of the World* (1614)

D.R. WOOLF

The Idea of History
in Early Stuart England

Erudition, Ideology,
and 'The Light of Truth'
from the
Accession of James I
to the Civil War

UNIVERSITY OF TORONTO PRESS

Toronto Buffalo London

© University of Toronto Press 1990
Toronto Buffalo London
Printed in Canada

ISBN 0-8020-5862-0

Printed on acid-free paper

Canadian Cataloguing in Publication Data
Woolf, D.R. (Daniel R.)
The idea of history in early Stuart England

Includes bibliographical references.
ISBN 0-8020-5862-0

1. Historiography – Great Britain – History – 17th century.
2. Great Britain – Intellectual life – 17th century.   I. Title.

DA1.W66 1990   907'.2042   C90-094644-X

The frontispiece is reproduced by permission of
the Thomas Fisher Rare Book Library,
University of Toronto.

This book has been published
with the help of a grant from the
Social Science Federation of Canada,
using funds provided by the
Social Sciences and
Humanities Research Council of Canada.

To

Margaret Mary Woolf

and

Cyril Isaac Woolf,

my earliest teachers

Contents

Preface

This book has had several previous incarnations. My interest in the history of historical writing and in the sense of the past in Tudor and Stuart England dates back to an undergraduate essay on Shakespeare's history plays. Curious as to the origins and eventual destination of the various intellectual streams feeding into and emerging from the Tudor chronicle play, I made a general study of early Stuart historical writing the subject of my 1983 Oxford D Phil thesis which, in revised form, has become the present volume.

Historical *writing* and what is sometimes called historical *thought* are related but not synonymous terms. The former, and more narrow term, I take to be the formal historiography produced in a particular era, understood as such by contemporaries. The latter, of course, is far broader and less socially exclusive. It involves perceptions of, reflections on and utterances about virtually any aspect of the past, and it can be found in just about any written document of any period, as Arthur B. Ferguson's *Clio Unbound* has demonstrated.[1] Although Ferguson's book is over a decade old, further discussion of the broader issues of historical thought and perception which he raised is really only now getting underway. I have examined aspects of the perception of the past elsewhere and I hope to do so at greater length in a future book.

The present work, much more limited in its aims, is a study of narrative accounts of the past and, where related, those poetic works which influenced prose writers or which, in some cases, form part of a prose historian's general corpus. It is not intended as a comprehensive survey of all forms of historical writing, and even less of all modes of historical thought. I devote little space here to history plays, believing these to be well served by an abundance of literary studies.[2] The same may be said for historically oriented poetry, though it is impossible to treat a historian such as Samuel Daniel without reference to his poetic works or to examine views of ancient Rome without discussing Fulke Greville's verse *Treatise of Monarchy.*

Nor in the present book do I discuss at great length – except, as will be seen, where it impinges directly on formal history-writing – the development of the antiquarian movement, which from the point of view of modern scholarship may have been the most significant Renaissance contribution to historical study. My earlier studies of English antiquarian writers have convinced me that while the activities of the narrative historian and the antiquary were related by a common humanist parentage and a common focus on the past, they were nevertheless not the same thing and, more important, were acknowledged to be different in the late sixteenth and seventeenth centuries *even when the same individual was simultaneously both an antiquary and a historian.*[3] That very distinction and the various exceptions to it are, indeed, one of the central issues to be discussed here.

The subject of this volume is not a new one. A number of well-known books have been written over the past thirty years on various aspects of Tudor and Stuart historical writing. J.G.A. Pocock's *The Ancient Constitution and the Feudal Law,* first published in 1957, has recently been reissued with a retrospect.[4] Pocock's book has become a classic for its subtle analysis of the 'common law mind,' and its impact on Stuart antiquarian and legal scholars' discussions of such issues as the timelessness of English law and of the significance of such epochal events as the Norman Conquest. Pocock was concerned primarily with this single aspect of the development of politico-historical thought, and his book was never intended as a general survey of historical writing.

The two books that come closest to filling that bill are F. Smith Fussner's *The Historical Revolution,* published in 1962, and F.J. Levy's *Tudor Historical Thought,* which appeared five years later.[5] Fussner studied the development of Renaissance historiography in England with little reference to intellectual breezes blowing from across the channel. He also pigeonholed the five major authors in his work – Ralegh, Camden, Stow, Bacon, and Selden – under anachronistic chapter headings such as 'territorial history,' 'local history,' and 'problematic history.' Not surprisingly, Fussner's general thesis that the period 1580–1640 (roughly the years we are here concerned with) witnessed a 'revolution' in historical writing, a decisive break with the past as sharp as the contemporary revolutions in science and political thought, has been disputed, though it was endorsed incidentally by so influential a voice as Christopher Hill.[6] Although Fussner's book remains useful, few scholars would now agree that there was anything terribly revolutionary about the developments in English historical writing, and I have deliberately avoided reopening that question here. But a lack of revolutionary change should not be equated with stagnation. Perhaps the most pernicious consequence of the whole debate over Fussner's thesis has been to obscure his point that substantial change and growth in the research and writing of various types of historical discourse occurred in the late sixteenth and early seventeenth centuries.

F.J. Levy's widely read *Tudor Historical Thought* begins with the late medieval chronicles and ends, as we shall, in the early Stuart period. Its wider lens makes even clearer just how much things had changed between Polydore Vergil's arrival in England in 1502 and Camden's death in 1623, though Levy, more sensitive to contemporary attitudes and conventions than most commentators, stresses the gradual and slow character of change rather than positing a sharp break at any stage. Since the 1930s, a number of even more specialized articles and books have appeared on minor antiquaries such as Laurence Nowell and Joseph Holland, and on such better-known scholars as John Bale and William Lambarde.[7] May McKisack and Joseph M. Levine, following on the earlier works of T.D. Kendrick and D.C. Douglas, have furnished us with guides to the antiquarian movement in the sixteenth, seventeenth, and early eighteenth centuries.[8] We know a great deal about the origins of historically minded literary criticism, about post-Reformation concepts of fortune and providence, and on the relation of these to literature, politics, and historical consciousness.[9] Kevin Sharpe, Linda Levy Peck, and the late David S. Berkowitz have reminded us of the political implications of history, antiquarianism, and scholarship in their respective books on Sir Robert Cotton, Henry Howard, earl of Northampton, and John Selden.[10]

It has become clear that one cannot usefully study English historiography without reference to European developments. Since Felix Gilbert's monograph on *Machiavelli and Guicciardini* appeared in 1965, knowledge of Italian historiography in the fifteenth and sixteenth centuries has grown steadily.[11] Similarly, for the last two decades we have been able to reap the rewards of scholarship on the place of history in the French Renaissance, most notably in the studies by Donald R. Kelley and George Huppert.[12] England was much less isolated from the main currents of continental legal and philological scholarship than was once supposed; as early as the fifteenth century, European books were being imported and foreigners were making visits to Britain for extended periods. The continuing life of Latin as a scholarly language cemented an international community of letters, despite the barriers of religion and physical problems of communication and transportation. It is true that the active members of this literary realm, from Thomas More to John Selden, were a small group. But far greater numbers of the literate population would by 1640 have had at least some exposure to foreign books; and many less well known historians, as we shall see, were indebted to earlier and contemporary continental authors in one way or another.

Given all this, why the present book? Two issues seem not to have been confronted yet. The first, alluded to above, is that antiquarianism and history, two related but not identical activities, gradually came to a *modus vivendi* of sorts. It seems beyond dispute that the eighteenth century witnessed a separation between so-called technicians of history like Mabillon, Muratori, Du Cange, Wanley, and Hearne, and imaginative *philosophes* like Voltaire and Gibbon. But intellectual history does not proceed in straight lines, and what may be true of the sixteenth and eighteenth centuries need not necessarily hold true for the period in between. I suggest that beginning in the early seventeenth century, history as a literary form on the one hand, and that type of philological or antiquarian knowledge which can broadly fit under the rubric of 'erudition' on the other, grew more familiar with each other, both in practice and in theory.[13] Furthermore, somewhere along the way an intellectual leap was made which converted the meaning of the very word 'history' into something more recognizably modern. A large portion of this work is therefore devoted to exploring exactly what early seventeenth-century authors thought they were doing when they wrote 'history,' how they defined that subject, and how the meaning of the word changed between 1600 and 1640.

The second point concerns the public structure of the discourse known as history in the early modern period, the nature of its connection with attitudes toward then-current political and religious issues, and in particular the relative absence in the early seventeenth century of systematic debate and argument, except on a small number of issues. I will suggest that a catalyst was required for a structural change which shifted historical discourse from its pre-1640 focus on rhetorical *restatement* of the past to its post-1640, and more modern, structure involving controversy, dispute, and debate.

That catalyst was ideology, or more precisely the conflict of multiple political ideologies whose differing views of the present necessitated the articulation of differing views of the past. An ideology may be defined as a set of beliefs about the way one's community – which, depending on the context of discussion, may be the nation itself, the family, or the church – and the individual who belongs to it, should be governed; it is also at the same time an articulation of the discrepancies between ideals and realities and the source of potential solutions to those discrepancies. Within any given political or religious community (and in the 'ecclesiastical polity' of late sixteenth- and early seventeenth-century England, the two overlapped to a great extent) there are likely to exist differences of belief among individuals or subgroups, which may lead to the formulation of slightly different visions of the world.[14] These will often conform in their essentials, as they did, with some exceptions, in the Elizabethan and early Stuart periods. If pushed by events, however (as had happened in the Reformation and would happen again in the 1640s), previously minor differences of outlook will deepen; the result will often be the erosion of a broad consensus and the exacerbation of conflicts, to the point that a single ideology (or if one prefers, a narrow band of highly congruent ideologies) dissolves into a much broader spectrum of beliefs. In short, the existence and dominance of a collective, socially accepted set of political, religious, and social beliefs – rather like one of Thomas S. Kuhn's scientific paradigms – in no way presupposes the concurrent existence, within the same political context, of other belief systems more radically opposed to it; yet its internal contradictions and anomalies, and its failure to satisfy all interests equally well, may eventually give rise to these if the appropriate circumstances arise.

Since its invention in distant antiquity, the written representation of the past has, in one way or another, always been affected by present concerns, many of which can be considered to spring from the ideological disposition of the author. All Tudor and early Stuart historical writing thus reflects a conservative ideology of obedience, duty, and deference to social and political hierarchy. Historians used the past to sanction certain types of behaviour and to deplore others; they also used it to justify the authority structures of their present, structures which in turn shaped and coloured what they said about the past.

It would take the civil war to shatter what by the 1630s had become a relatively monochromatic, and almost universally shared, image of the national past. Lest this be misinterpreted, I would like to be absolutely clear from the start on one point: that the presence before 1640 of a number of shared beliefs about the past – or, if the reader will excuse a second use of Kuhnian terminology, of an authoritative paradigm of concepts of history – in no way precluded the possibility of early Stuart historians saying different things about various episodes in the past.

This they surely did; and while there is only limited space in the present book for a discussion of the actual political context of historical writing, the following chapters should at least bring out the nuances that distinguish one historian's view of the past from another, within a range of socially and politically acceptable opinions.

Early Stuart political thinking, never quite as single-stranded as some (but not all) recent revisionist works have suggested, permitted a range of opinions on questions such as the relationship of monarch and law, of prince and parliament, and of church and state, without ever challenging assumptions about the need for political order, the importance of social hierarchy, and the dangers of rebellion.[15] So, too, did contemporary historians, many of them inspired by these questions, find ample room to dissent on points of detail without having to make a radical departure from the broad consensus on the past. This type of agreement in historiography could only be sustained for as long as the national consensus on the adequacy and appropriateness of traditional forms of religion and governance from which it derived and which it supported. When that consensus on the present broke down, as it would do in the 1640s, the way was cleared both for the emergence of radically distinctive interpretations of the past, and for much more heated disputes among the defenders of such interpretations.

The movement from an atmosphere of historiographical 'consensus' to one of debate is itself not a single phenomenon, attributable only to the period under discussion, and this is therefore not an account of *the* transition to a dialectical historiography, but a description of one such transition. In fact, historical writing since the seventeenth century has shifted back and forth from relatively consensual atmospheres (for instance in the mid-eighteenth, the late nineteenth, and the early twentieth centuries) to more divisive, contentious environments. This has been ably demonstrated, in the case of the American historical profession over the past century, by Peter Novick's brilliant study. This charts the movement of American historiography from the genteel professionalism of the end of the last century (combined with an apparently bottomless faith in the 'objectivity' of the historian and in the existence of historical truth which could have been written, *mutatis mutandis*, in the Renaissance) to the relativist challenge between the wars, back to a general agreement in the 1950s, and finally to the era of historiographical fragmentation which began in the sixties and from which we have yet to emerge. Novick's description of the way in which American historians first began to question 'the traditional assumption that "conflicting conclusions" were an anomaly, and that authoritative, objective consensus could be expected on important historical issues' applies very well to the mid-seventeenth century.[16] Though of course they had no concept of 'objectivity' or of history as a science, the English historians of the 1640s (and in the earlier tithes controversy of 1618 to 1622) were to be rudely awakened by the differences in interpretation of the past that a civil war could produce, as the final chapter of the present book will show.

What follows is a study not only of how English historians viewed their own national past and the past of the wider world (and especially of ancient Rome, which serves as a kind of 'mirror' for attitudes to English history) but of how they perceived the meaning of the word history itself. It can be taken as given that history in the seventeenth century was conceived of as a form of literature (a term which itself is not coterminous with 'fiction'), not as a 'discipline' or, still less, a 'science'; it did not really become a discipline before the late eighteenth century and – depending on one's point of view – it may never have grown into a science. But if we wish to understand how history developed in the hands of greats such as Hume, Gibbon, Macaulay, and Stubbs, we must first grasp precisely what it meant to their predecessors, and how their ideas of its purpose, scope, and form differed from those of later times. And in order to do this, we must pay close attention to both the content and the style of individual works, as well as to the context within which each author wrote.

This approach creates certain problems of presentation. It has proven necessary to provide 'plot summaries' of individual histories, particularly in the case of works which have had less attention from earlier scholars; I ask the reader's indulgence if these from time to time seem to repeat one another, since that is largely a function of the degree to which many works covering similar territory *do* in fact concur on most points. Faced with the further problem of whether to discuss the works chronologically or topically, I have opted for a mixture of the two approaches. Broadly speaking, the account proceeds chronologically from the accession of James I to the personal rule of Charles I and, more briefly, its wartime and Restoration aftermath. In most chapters, works are discussed in the order in which they appeared (which is not always the same as the order in which they were written); in others, such a sequence has proven impractical. A strictly chronological approach would blur other relationships, notably those of subject or genre. With that in mind, several works devoted to the task of providing political instruction to the prince have been treated separately, in chapter 5, from the biographical histories, studied in chapter 4, which in many ways they closely resemble. The study of Roman history, hitherto a relatively neglected subject in the secondary literature, similarly seemed to lend itself to topical treatment in a separate chapter; so, too, did the writings of Samuel Daniel and John Selden, the one because of the close connection between his poetry and his prose, the latter because of his critical place in the double dialectic between politics and scholarship, erudition and history. The reader may also find in these pages discussions of less familiar historians which seem lengthy in comparison with the treatment given to such acknowledged 'greats' as Ralegh, Bacon, and Camden. I have opted for relatively brief treatments of the better known figures partly because so much has already been said about them, and partly because I believe their modern claim to 'classic' status has had the effect of obscuring, even obliterating, the achievements of their less famous contemporaries.

Since I began this project I have incurred many debts. G.E. Aylmer supervised the original thesis with his characteristic blend of erudition and sympathy, demonstrating limitless patience with an amoeba-like topic which, at least in its early stages, changed its size and shape with the frequency of the Oxford weather. My examiners, Sir Keith Thomas and Professor Quentin Skinner, offered many helpful suggestions while forcing me to rethink some of my conclusions. Parts of chapters 1 and 7 appeared as 'Erudition and the Idea of History in Renaissance England' in *Renaissance Quarterly*, 40 (1987). Chapter 3 is an expanded and revised version of my essay 'Community, Law and State: Samuel Daniel's Historical Thought Revisited,' *Journal of the History of Ideas* 49 (1988). I am grateful to the editors of both journals for permission to reprint this material, and to the Social Sciences and Humanities Research Council of Canada, which awarded me a post-doctoral fellowship between 1984 and 1986, during which period much additional research was done. I am also greatly indebted to the staffs of the various libraries, on both sides of the Atlantic, who answered my inquiries, assisted me during visits, and gave me permission to cite and reproduce material in their care, in particular the staffs of the Bodleian Library in Oxford and the Killam Memorial Library at Dalhousie.

It is impossible to thank all those individuals who have helped me in some form or another, either by suggesting avenues of inquiry or by reading various parts of the book in their earlier incarnations. A few debts, however, must be acknowledged. Paul Christianson has been an unfailing source of good advice and information, and a close friend, for over a decade; in addition to reading both the original thesis and the manuscript, he allowed me to see in typescript his forthcoming major study of John Selden. F. J. Levy, whose own *Tudor Historical Thought* has provided the most solid of foundations upon which to build, has offered advice and encouragement at various stages. David Wootton read the penultimate draft of the book and was particularly helpful on theological issues. Kevin Sharpe, who helped me to define the scope of the original study a decade ago, also read the book in draft and offered several suggestions for further revision. Penelope Gouk, Louis Knafla, Robert Tittler, and Thomas Mayer have similarly provided me with valuable feedback at various times over the last decade. My colleagues in the Department of History at Dalhousie University, above all John Crowley, have tolerated my frequent references to Daniel, Camden, and their ilk with good humour, as have my students. Sharon Earle typed the manuscript into machine-readable form with precision and speed. At University of Toronto Press, Prudence Tracy has proven a model editor, without whose encouragement the book would not have been written. William Barker copy-edited the text with thoroughness and sensitivity, saving me from several gaffes. Finally, my wife, Jane Arscott, has been the soul of good humour over several years and has provided the happiest of environments within which to put this study into its present form. Any errors or omissions, it hardly needs adding, are my responsibility alone.

Citations and Conventions

Dates are given in old style, except where indicated new style (ns). The year is taken to begin on 1 January; in some instances, dates are written 21 February 1628/9, in order to avoid ambiguity. Spelling in all quotations from original sources has in general been retained. The seventeenth-century usage of the letters 'i' and 'j,' and 'u' and 'v' has, however, been modernized, as has capitalization for all prose sources. Punctuation has occasionally been altered for the sake of clarity. Translations of Latin and other foreign expressions are mine except where otherwise noted. I have referred to European scholars by their vernacular names, except where an individual has become known primarily by the Latin form: thus Jacques-Auguste de Thou rather than Thuanus, but G.J. Vossius instead of Vos.

In cases where a single book has been used very extensively within a section, references have been given parenthetically in the text to avoid repetition of notes. References to works given briefer treatment appear in notes in the normal fashion. The bibliography lists manuscript and printed primary source material and the large majority of articles, books, and theses cited in the notes. References to printed primary material (works published in the seventeenth century as well as modern editions of those works and collections of documents) are cited in full at the first citation and thereafter in abbreviated form. Rather than duplicate references to secondary authorities, I have opted (except in the preface) to cite all important secondary works by author's surname and abbreviated title in the notes, providing full title and bibliographical details in the bibliography. Page references to articles will be given in the notes only when a specific page or section is intended;

beginning and end page numbers will, however, be found in the bibliography. Works referred to only incidentally are cited in full in the note in which they first appear; they are not included in the bibliography.

Abbreviations

The following abbreviations are used in the text and the notes. For full details of secondary sources, the reader is referred to the bibliography.

Alum Cant	Venn, J., and J.A. Venn *Alumni Cantabrigienses* (Part 1 to 1715, 4 vols, 1922–7)
Alum Ox	Foster, J. *Alumni Oxonienses: The Members of the University of Oxford, 1500–1714* (4 vols, 1891–2)
Arber	Arber, E. *Transcript of the Registers of the Company of Stationers of London, 1554–1640* (5 vols, 1875–94)
Bacon *Works*	Bacon, Francis *Works* ed J. Spedding, R.L. Ellis, and D.D. Heath (7 vols, 1858–61)
Bacon *Letters and Life*	*Lord Bacon's Letters and Life* ed. J. Spedding (7 vols, 1861–74)
Cal sp Dom	*Calendar of State Papers Domestic*
Camdeni epistolae	*Gulielmi Camdeni et illustrium virorum ad G. Camdenum epistolae* ed T. Smith (1691)
Collection	Daniel, Samuel *The Collection of the Historie of England* (1618)
Civil Wars	Daniel, Samuel *The Civil Wars* ed Laurence Michel (New Haven 1958)

DNB   *Dictionary of National Biography* ed. L. Stephen and S. Lee (24 vols, rpt 1921–2)

Hearne *Curious Discourses*   Hearne, Thomas *A Collection of Curious Discourses* ed J. Ayloffe (1775)

Hist Mss Comm   Historical Manuscripts Commission, *Reports*

ns   new style date

PRO   Public Record Office, Chancery Lane

STC   Pollard, A.W., and G.R. Redgrave *A Short-Title Catalogue of Books Printed in England, Scotland and Ireland and of English Books Printed Abroad, 1475–1640* (1926; 2nd ed, revised by W.A. Jackson, F.S. Ferguson, and K.F. Pantzer, 1976–86)

SP   State Papers

Wing   Wing, Donald G. *Short-Title Catalogue of Books Printed in England, Scotland, Ireland, Wales, and British America and of English Books Printed in Other Countries, 1641–1700* (3 vols, New York 1945–51)

Wood *Ath Ox*   Wood, Anthony *Athenae Oxonienses* ed P. Bliss (4 vols, 1813–20)

The Idea of History
in Early Stuart England

Happy those English historians who wrote some sixty years since, before our civil distempers were born or conceived ... seeing then there was a generall right understanding betwixt all of the nation.

But alas! Such as wrote in or since our civil wars, are seldome apprehended truely and candidly, save of such of their owne persuasion ...

Thomas Fuller *The Appeal of Injured Innocence* (1659)

The Structure of Elizabethan and Early Stuart Historiography

Fortune, Providence, and the Irrational

In 1574, eight years after the French philosopher Jean Bodin had published his important *Methodus* on the reading of history, another such *ars historica* appeared in England. Thomas Blundeville, one of the earl of Leicester's followers, abridged and translated into English two Italian discourses on the correct manner in which histories should be both read and written. *The True Order and Methode of Wryting and Reading Hystories* was the first completely theoretical statement on the issue by an Englishman, though Blundeville added little to his sources, Francesco Patrizzi and Giacomo Aconcio. Both were sixteenth-century Italian humanists; the Protestant Aconcio had himself spent his last years in Leicester's service. Blundeville's ideas were all entirely representative of humanist historical theory, and *The True Order* provides a particularly clear statement of Tudor ideas of history and of the domain of the historian.[1]

Drawing first on Patrizzi, Blundeville asserts that politics is the proper province of the historian. The history of a city or country should proceed from its beginning to its end, 'bycause every thing hath hys beginning, augmentacion, state, declinacion, and ende.' Historical change, like life, occurs in cycles: the state is a body and the history should be its biography, dealing with 'the trade of lyfe, the publique revenewes, the force, & the maner of governement' (155). Blundeville does not advocate a complete history in the sense of one that takes cultural and social change into account. His mind is fixed firmly on the political life cycle of the organic *civitas*. 'Hystories bee made of deedes done by a publique weale, or agaynst publique weale, and such deedes, be eyther deedes of warre, of peace, or else of sedition and conspiracy' (156). This is to be the history of great men, for their lives help one understand the six kinds of government into which mankind, according to Aristotle, has organized itself: monarchy, aristocracy and polity and their perversions, tyranny, oligarchy, and democracy.

> All those persons whose lyves have beene such as are to bee followed for their excellencie in vertue, or else to be fledde for their excellencie in vice, are meete to be chronicled. And if they were publique personages or governours, then they are to be considered in as many divers ways, as there be divers kindes of governement. Whereof according to Aristotle, there be six. (159)

A historical event occurs in the finite dimensions of space and time, and the historian should, therefore, be precise as to both. He must also be accurate and truthful, or he is no historian, but a storyteller. He must accurately describe the causes and outcomes of events, 'without either augmenting or diminishing them, or swarving one iota from the truth.' The writer should even avoid the long-accepted practice of constructing fictional speeches for his characters (157, 164).

Aconcio, whose *Delle osservationi* forms the second part of Blundeville's treatise, presents three reasons why histories are worth reading. Though it may be argued that histories 'winne fame' for the writer and provide a pleasant pastime for the reader, their 'chiefe & principall' functions are didactic:

> First that we may learne thereby to acknowledge the providence of God, wherby all things are governed and directed. Secondly, that by the examples of the wise, we maye learne wisedome wysely to behave our selves in all our actions, as well private as publique, both in time of peace and warre.
>
> Thirdly, that we maye be stirred by example of the good to followe the good, and by example of the evill to flee the evill. (165)

At this point, Blundeville's tract becomes much more interested in the providential aspect of history, departing somewhat from Patrizzi's focus on the worldly life cycles of the state (150).[2] The reader should learn, by past example, how to act on this earth, and he should note the role of God in events, 'for what causes and by what meanes hee overthroweth one kingdome & setteth up an other' (165). The two interlock, for the deeds of man are ultimately also those of God. Nothing new takes place under the sun, and nothing is mere accident. 'God by his providence useth, when he thinketh good, to worke marveylous effects ... Nothing is done by chaunce, but all things by his foresight, counsell and divine providence' (ibid).[3] Blundeville is equally emphatic that one does not study historical facts for their own sake. 'I can not tell whyther I may deryde, or rather pittie, the great follie of those which having consumed all theyr lyfe tyme in hystories, doe know nothing in the ende, but the discents, genealogies, and petygrees of noble men and when such a king or emperour raigned, & such lyke stuff ...' (170).[4] Again, this was nothing more than his readers expected to hear.

History is the record of the process of change over time, as it occurs in nature, of which society is part. All nature is beneath God and subject to mutability, a general tendency to change. Only God, above nature, escapes the corrosion of time. As Spenser put it, 'nothing here long standeth in one stay.'[5] Embedded in the Elizabethan mind were two seemingly contradictory notions of the movement of time. Through Revelation the Judaeo-Christian tradition taught that all events proceeded *sub specie aeternitatis*, in a more-or-less straight line from Creation to Apocalypse. But classical writers had asserted a different pattern, based on the cycles observable in nature. Types of government not only grew and declined: one type tended to change into another, said the Greek historian Polybius, in a predictable *anacyclosis*.[6] Humanists like Blundeville had no difficulty synthesizing these two streams: the Judaeo-Christian view was itself not strictly linear; and the very concept of divine judgment rewarding and punishing individuals, and of the rise and fall of empires and cities, reveals the Christian time scheme as a spiral rather than a straight line. Nor was the idea of historical recurrence confined to classical writers. Renaissance practitioners of history like Sir Walter Ralegh, as much as theorists like Blundeville, drew eclectically on Moses and Polybius, *Fortuna* and providence.

Both systems of time were, to different degrees, deterministic. Events were fixed and unchanging, points pre-plotted on a timetable. Whether one adhered to a view of time as proceeding from Creation to Apocalypse, during which period God foreknew and ordained the death of every sparrow, or to a view according to which the same events and even specific *personae* recurred, time and time again, there was little room for the irrational, though it is true that the Greek historians allowed more play to the contingent and unpredictable than did their Roman successors. In the form in which they came down to the English Renaissance, however, the Christian and classical views of time, as much as of space, are both 'closed systems' in which man's actions affect only man and not the ultimate outcome of events, except insofar as they are immediate instruments of a higher plan.

Put simply, history in sixteenth-century England, particularly after the advent of a protestant metaphysics through such reformers as Melanchthon, was not in the realm of the contingent or the irrational. Even the completely unexpected was foreshadowed, if one could but read the signs.[7] 'It may seem to you that there is contingency in human affairs,' argued Melanchthon, 'but in this idea, rational judgement must be over-ruled.' The great reformer believed that 'all things come to pass according to divine purpose.' Nearly a century later, the puritan scholar Thomas Gataker, writing on the use of lots, distinguished between events which were necessary, those which were contingent on some deliberate human action, and those which appeared to happen by random chance. Yet, like most early seventeenth-century writers, he agreed that even the apparently random could take place only by God's decree.[8]

The omnipotence of God did not – as yet – conflict with the routine operations of nature, or with the unpredictable course of human affairs, but neither did notions of providence offer an entirely satisfactory explanation for these events. Just as English protestants could look to the individual 'providences,' either judgments on or mercies granted to themselves and to their contemporaries by the Lord, so they could look into the past for examples of such harsh judgments and miraculous deliverances over the finite course of man's time. And there could be no question that strange, inexplicable things did indeed seem to happen in history. Why did Alexander the Great and Henry v sicken and die at the peak of their powers? How was Henry vii able to defeat a skilful and ruthless usurper? Why did men like Thomas Wolsey and Thomas Cromwell, on top of the wall at one moment, suddenly pitch over and shatter at its foot? The manifest occurrence of unpredictable, unlikely events offered a Sphinx's riddle.

Generally, the irrational was rationalized as 'fortune,' 'fate,' or 'chance,' or even personified as the unpredictable medieval goddess *Fortuna*, whose feminine whims determined the rise and fall of men and nations, and the outcome of battles. Yet fortune herself was, if unfathomable by man, essentially rational, and could occasionally be mastered, as Machiavelli put it, by a strong man who knew not to rely on her.[9] As Philosophy had told Boethius, fortune is always, by nature, 'constant to her own inconstancy.'[10] The medieval and Renaissance conceptions of fortune and chance did not carry the modern sense of an existential randomness of events; they were simply man's admission that human faculties could not grasp all the data necessary to predict outcomes. One could easily deny the mere accident by ascribing the apparently contingent event to an external force which could humble the mightiest at the bat of an eyelid.

'Fortun's a right whore,' complains Lodovico, opening Webster's *The White Devil*. 'If she gives ought, she deales it in smal percels, that she may take away all at one swope.'[11] Fortune provided a mode of explanation of events which could easily be reconciled with and subordinated to her Christian counterpart, providence. The Tudor chronicler Edward Hall, addressing the deposition of Richard II, asked, 'But O Lord, what is the mutabilitee of fortune?' A rhetorical question, plainly: every reader knew that 'fortune' was simply another word for the divine instrument which determined Richard's fall, and that she was fickle only in the eye of the human beholder. Similarly, Henry V was 'a capitaine against whom fortune never frowned nor mischance once spurned.' Hall figuratively blamed Henry's untimely death on 'cruel Atropos' but had the pious warrior thank God for having 'called him out of this miserable life at suche tyme when he was of most perfite remembraunce both towarde God and the world.' In the anonymous play *Edward III* (1596), King John begs 'Sweet Fortune' to turn. Edward III, victorious over him, thanks

> Just-dooming Heaven, whose secret providence
> To our gross judgment is inscrutable.[12]

Raphael Holinshed could speak both of 'the Lords vengeance' on the house of York, and of Richard III's 'misfortune and unluckinesse.' Fortune's fickleness is the unifying theme in the stories making up the popular *Mirror for Magistrates*. The ghost of the earl of Salisbury, 'chaunceably slayne with a piece of ordinaunce,' muses that 'this Goddes gideth al the game.' Henry VI, imprisoned after his fall, subordinates fortune to God:

> Woulde god the day of birth had brought me to my beere,
> Than had I never felt the chaunge of Fortunes cheere ...
> But god doth gide the world, and every hap by skill.
> Our wit and willing power are paysed by his will.

Map-maker and antiquary John Norden similarly asserted that 'naught befalles, but by supernall hest.'[13]

To subordinate fortune or chance to God or providence was not simply a matter of intellectual convenience; it was positively necessary in the context of a Christian cosmology in which God was accepted as omnipotent First Cause. It is significant that Guicciardini, amid the turmoil of sixteenth-century Florence, probably came closer than anyone to a theory of history in which fortune really was Polybius' random *Tyche*, but his English translator still turned fortune into the rational Christian providence.[14] Henry Carey, Lord Leppington, scrupulously explained the intent of the Italian historian he was translating: 'Where the author names princes in wicked actions, he means tyrants; and where he writes of Fortune, he understands her to bee a cause unknowne to us; which as all others depend upon God, the cause of all causes.'[15]

The Elizabethans and their early Stuart successors took it for granted that the sins of the wicked were punished on earth as they were in heaven. Providence, even more than pagan fortune, was the instrument of God, by which his will was done. Holinshed had described the fall of the House of York as the product of divine revenge on its bloodshed in the Wars of the Roses. 'For such is Gods justice, to leave no unrepentant wickednesse unpunished.' The archdemon of Tudor historical mythology, Richard III, was almost unanimously believed to have perished in a lost cause. God *wanted* the tyrant dead, and in the words of lawyer and antiquary Sir John Dodderidge, 'raised up Henry Earle of Richmond ... to [execute] justice upon that unnaturall and bloody usurper.' The Jacobean historian Edward Ayscu similarly ascribed the English victory over the Scots at the battle of Musselborough in 1550 to divine intervention. 'God gave the victory to the Englishmen, onelie by the working of his divine power, and not by either power or pollicie of man.'[16]

Whether a writer used fortune, fate, providence, or any combination of these to explain the causes and the outcome of historical events, the result was the same. The course of history was predetermined. Every cycle of nations and dynasties from the Ptolemies to the Plantagenets was foreknown by God. In most cases, this determinism was simply assumed to a degree that it rarely occasioned elaborate discussions of free will, though now and then historians might pause to acknowledge fundamental truths: Edward Ayscu, for instance, explicitly adopted Boethius' idea of the *nunc stans*, the 'eternal now,' to explain how God perceives all time at a glance. 'But he, that seeth the state of all things and time at one instant, knoweth what is fittest to bee admitted in every season, and disposeth of the successe, of all that man purposeth, to the best advantage of such as serve him.' Sir Walter Ralegh applied the same idea in his *History of the World*, and it underlies most late Tudor and early Stuart historical narrative.[17]

The Causal Framework

Like their European precursors of the early Renaissance, Tudor historians worked within a framework of concepts which, despite the revival of Platonism and the development of new logics such as Ramism, remained fundamentally Aristotelian. According to the Aristotelian scheme, as modified by Christian scholasticism in the later Middle Ages, causes are of four types. An event has efficient, material, formal, and final causes. In the case of a great historical event, such as a war or peace treaty, the material cause is 'the matter wheron the doer worketh, the deede of peace, of warre, or of sedicion.' The formal cause is 'the meanes and maner of doing'; the 'cause efficient is the doer himselfe.' The final cause was particularly important to Patrizzi/Blundeville as the motive or end for which an event takes place: 'and note here, that by the cause, I meane the ende.' These causes are the animating forces in the world, and hence in history. Behind them, for the post-Thomist Christian, lies the first cause of everything, God; it is ultimately by 'the providence of God [that] all things are governed and directed.'[18]

Important as was the efficient cause, historians were equally concerned with the final cause of events, the end or purpose for which they were ordained, and the consequences to which they led. Thus the victory of Henry Tudor at the battle of Bosworth Field had four sorts of subordinate causes. God, the first cause, wished the usurper Richard III destroyed. He accomplished this through secondary efficient causes, like Henry himself. Material causes included Stanley's defection to Richmond's side, and 'accidental' events like Richard's legendary fall from his horse. The formal cause was the battle itself, the scene in which all the matter was given shape. The final cause was the purpose for which the victory had been ordained, the union of the two houses.

English historians seldom delineated these causes as explicitly as Blundeville in practice, but this is essentially the way they perceived history. That is to say, their view of history, like Aristotle's view of nature, was teleological, since it ascribed motion and change to a final cause; and they wrote history accordingly, from its outcome back to its beginning. Edward Hall entitled his chronicle *The Union of the Two Noble and Illustre Famelies of Lancastre and Yorke* because the union itself, the restoration of order, was the focal event, the natural point towards which the conflicts of the fifteenth century progressed.[19] Neither Hall nor any other Tudor historian ever asked the question, 'What if Henry VII had *lost* the battle?' because such a question was absurd.

The fates of Henry VII and Richard III had long been laid down, and they worked to God's purpose, which was the restoration of order in England after a chastening century of anarchy. For the Tudor historian and playwright alike, Henry VII's victory and the Tudor dynasty appeared as inevitable as the coming of spring after a harsh winter.

The Reasons for Studying History

It is well known that Tudor historians saw their primary function as educative. Histories taught God's presence in time, and they taught men how to behave in all kinds of situations. Thus the Elizabethan printer and chronicler Richard Grafton urged the rising Robert Dudley in 1563 to read history for two reasons:

> Beside many profitable causes ... for which histories have bene written, the chiefest in polecie is this, that the examples in tymes passed are good lessons for tyme to come: But the principall com- moditie in the highest respecte is the settynge foorth of the course of Goddes doinges, and in disposing the estates of men to the advauncement of his glorye.[20]

Cicero, the much-quoted classical source of the purposes of reading history, had called history the *magistra vitae* and *lux veritatis* because from history one learned by example what philosophers taught only by precept.[21] Throughout the sixteenth century, what might be called the 'Ciceronian tradition' of history as a morally educative 'light of truth' dominated discussions of its scope and practice. Sir Thomas Elyot, for instance, believed history was an excellent medium for the communica- tion of man's past experience. 'The knowledge of this experience is called example, and is expressed by historie, whiche of Tulli is called the life of memorie.' Once again, secular history was seen primarily to consist of the fluctuation of states and the lessons derived therefrom:

> For it nat onely reporteth the gestes or actes of princes or capitaynes, their counsayles and attemptates, entreprises, affaires, maners in lyvinge good and bad, descriptions of regions and cities, with their inhabitants, but also it bringeth to our knowledge the fourmes of sondry publike weales with their augmentations and decayes and occasion thereof.

Roger Ascham similarly asserted that 'surely one example is more valuable, both to good and ill, than twenty precepts written in books.' Because similar situations tend to repeat themselves, histories are instructive, 'and breed staid judgment in taking like matter in hand.'[22]

Time after time this didactic function was stressed, and it had not in the least declined by the beginning of the seventeenth century. The gradual emergence of an interest in history as a source not of morals, piety, and manners but of models for emulation in the world of affairs merely shifted the focus of readers and writers from the realm of moral behaviour to that of practical action. Beginning late in Elizabeth's reign, one can detect a harder edge on the didacticism of historical writers, as such authors as Tacitus, Machiavelli – in spite of his odious reputation – and Guicciardini (and, a little later, Giovanni Botero and Justus Lipsius) began to offer a politically oriented rival to the Ciceronian tradition. Yet this was little more than a change of emphasis, the exchange of one didactic mode for the interpretation of the past for another. An anonymous writer recommended in 1619 that the courtier be a 'well-red historian,' for history was more instructive than philosophy. The early Stuart miscellanist Richard Brathwait offered the earl of Southampton a statement almost indistinguishable from Blundeville's forty years earlier, according to which history was 'the compendiarie director of affaires.' It should concentrate on principal events, not 'impertinent circumstances' and 'frivolous tales,' and in Brathwait's opinion it was particularly instructive for statesmen, teaching them principles of justice and law. Robert Powell, the Caroline biographer of King Alfred the Great, used biblical rather than classical examples of 'the lives of good and bad subjects,' and he intended that his work be of use principally to the powerful, but he still managed to quote Cicero's old saw: 'History is the herauld of antiquity and the life of time, and well deserves Cicero his appellation, magistram [sic] vitae.'[23]

Any characterization of historical writing as divided into a 'political' and a 'moral' school (or, perhaps, into Machiavellian and Ciceronian traditions) is at best a schematization which would have been lost on contemporaries, but it does serve to distinguish the types of attitude different writers could take to the past as they prepared to recount it. I shall suggest below that early Stuart historical writing is fraught with tensions, ambiguities, and uncertainties, and that among these is an ambivalent attitude on the part of even the most politically motivated historians to Machiavelli and his teachings.

If histories could teach the present about the past, so too could they inspire the men of the present to emulate their predecessors and achieve lasting fame for themselves. The prospect of being remembered by future historians, of enjoying great reputation, decades or even centuries hence, in the eyes of posterity, would spur the Tudor and early Stuart gentry and aristocracy on to greatness, as Fulke Greville observed:

For else, what Governor would spend his dayes,
In envious travell, for the publike good?
Who would in bookes, search after dead men's wayes?
Or in the Warre what Souldier lose his blood?
  Liv'd not this FAME in clouds, kept as a crowne;
  Both for the sword, the scepter, and the gowne.[24]

Equally, histories had the potential to deter evil deeds, for the historian would ensure that these outlived the doer. *Fama mala*, depicted as a foully spotted trumpeter in the wonderfully graphic frontispiece to Sir Walter Ralegh's *History of the World*, was a creature to be feared by those who wished to be celebrated rather than excoriated by posterity.[25] In this way, as the medium of fame, history maintained the connection between a mortal and the future, rescuing him from oblivion or condemning him to perpetual infamy. As Sir John Hayward pointed out, great men might expect, in addition to their lives on earth and in heaven, a 'life of fame' bestowed through history.[26]

The principal consequence of this utilitarian theory of historiography was a lack of interest, at least by modern standards, in establishing the precise truth of the past for its own sake, through a cumulative process of research, selection, interpretation, and argument. When the historian spoke of the 'truth' of histories, he meant their moral as much as their factual verity; he never had in mind the kind of precise, literal truth denoted in the nineteenth century by Ranke's famous phrase 'the past as it actually happened.' The silky rhetoric of the Italian and French historians who imitated Livy in the fifteenth and sixteenth centuries was calculated to inculcate 'true' principles of behaviour in readers by entertaining and persuading them, and these writers in turn were emulated by English historians in the late sixteenth and early seventeenth centuries. In these terms, such a practice as inventing fictional speeches for characters in a narrative was entirely permissible, and was a device endorsed by that reputed 'modern,' Francis Bacon.

That the lesson to be drawn from the event was more important than the event itself is a point driven home by the glosses to Simon Goulart's *Admirable and Memorable Histories* which highlighted 'ruines, strang, pitifull and wonderfule' and the desperate fate of traitors, thieves, and vagabonds.[27] Even if one eschewed the set speech, as did William Camden, and sought, through diligent research in records and manuscripts, to paint the picture of the past as accurately as possible, the end was not historical truth *per se,* but some external purpose: panegyric of a dead or living king or nobleman, entertainment, or the edification of the reader.

Antiquities and History

Late Elizabethan and early Stuart historical writers recognized in theory, even if they did not always observe in practice, a fundamental distinction between history proper and the newer antiquarian and philological explorations which became increasingly attractive toward the end of the sixteenth century. Professor Arnaldo Momigliano once observed, in a now famous essay, that Renaissance students of the past, and especially of the ancient world, were remarkably reluctant to write new narrative accounts of Greek and Roman history.[28] Since the ancient historians had usually lived in or shortly after the times of which they wrote, and since they had collectively covered the subject both exhaustively and – of more importance – elegantly, any attempt by modern men to imitate them would be regarded as an act of hubris. With this restriction in mind, many sixteenth-century writers eschewed altogether the narrative of great events for a topical, often topographically organized, account of their nations' antiquities.

Nowhere was this more true than in Tudor England. There was no good ancient example of an antiquarian treatise available (the much-praised Varro had vanished into oblivion, leaving only a few scraps), so those students of the non-political past who soon came to be called 'antiquaries' were forced by default to turn to geography as a model. In organizing their accounts of the past they followed Strabo, Ptolemy, and Pliny, rather than Thucydides, Caesar, and Tacitus, partly because there were adequate medieval precedents for doing so (for example, the writings of Gerald of Wales), but principally because they and the historians were writing about different sorts of things. It was one thing to describe England's Roman past and its surviving remnants, and quite another to attempt to supplant Tacitus. The former was a useful and reverent casting of light upon buried ancient culture; the latter was a pretentious waste of time. As a result, Momigliano argued, no one before Gibbon saw fit to construct a fresh narrative account of ancient history, based on a thorough re-examination of all available sources.[29]

This pious dread of the ancient masters did not, of course, prevent the writing of historical narratives of the non-classical past. It may even have encouraged such projects. What better burden could the admirer of Livy take up than to do for his own nation what the Paduan had done for the Roman republic? In early modern England, as elsewhere in Europe, narrative history commonly took two forms. A moribund medieval chronicle tradition lingered through the sixteenth century to breathe its last in the seventeenth. Meanwhile, the influence of humanist rhetoric triggered the development in the Elizabethan era of a more sophisticated and elegant political narrative, the authors of which confined their gaze principally to medieval and modern times; they emulated the practice of the ancients without stealing their material. In the seventeenth century, this tradition would spawn such classic histories as Bacon's *History of the Reign of King Henry the Seventh*, Clarendon's *History of the Rebellion* and Burnet's *History of His Own Time*.[30] These were literary masterpieces of a kind, though, it is generally agreed, devoid of the minute erudition gradually being amassed by antiquaries, archivists, and philologists from Leland in the 1530s to Hearne, Madox, and Rymer in the early eighteenth century. Change would come, but not until the late eighteenth century, when Gibbon synthesized his vast learning into the polished phrases of *The Decline and Fall of the Roman Empire*, a work of history which unashamedly addressed issues of the social and cultural past with the same care and interest with which it narrated imperial politics.

Momigliano concerned himself primarily with historical investigations of the classical world, and his comments on the distinction between antiquaries and historians of the non- or post-classical world are, understandably, less full. But it is clear that he did not ascribe such importance to this distinction with regard to the non-classical past:

While the student of Latin and Greek antiquities did not feel entitled to consider himself a historian, the student of the antiquities of Britain, France and the rest was only formally distinguishable from the student of the history of those countries – and therefore was inclined to forget the distinction. In the sixteenth and early seventeenth centuries there were both antiquarians and historians (often indistinguishable from each other) for the non-classical and post-classical world, but only antiquarians for the classical world.[31]

While it is true that there were indeed both sorts of writers on the medieval past, where there was (usually) only the one kind for antiquity, it is less clear whether the student of the British, French, or German past really could 'forget the distinction' with the ease which this statement implies. Other writers, though following Momigliano's lead, have been less sanguine on this score, and it seems probable that, as far as the theory of history-writing is concerned, much of what Momigliano holds for studies of the ancient past can be extended to medieval history as well. J.G.A. Pocock states the case with particular force:

> It is one of the great facts about the history of historiography that the critical techniques evolved during the sixteenth and seventeenth centuries were only very slowly and very late combined with the writing of history as a form of literary narrative; that there was a great divorce between the scholars and antiquarians on the one hand, and the literary historians on the other; that history as a literary form went serenely on its way, neither taking account of the critical techniques evolved by the scholars, nor evolving similar techniques of its own, until there was a kind of pyrrhonist revolt, a widespread movement of scepticism as to whether the story of the past could be reliably told at all.[32]

Not only did historians and antiquaries remain virtually oblivious of each other's existence, or perversely unwilling (as it seems to us) to help each other in writing what the French historian La Popelinière had craved at the end of the sixteenth century, an 'histoire accomplie'; they did not even recognize that they were all essentially doing, in different ways, a subject called history.

Men who wrote histories were called historians (*historici* in Latin) in Elizabethan England, or historiographers, or sometimes 'historicians.' Occasionally they were called chroniclers even if, like John Speed, they thought that they were superior to the medieval and early Tudor chroniclers whose accounts they plundered remorselessly for the materials with which to construct their own.[33] The meaning of the word *history* (Latin, *historia*) itself is much more problematic and fluid. Different writers used it in different contexts to mean different things. At its most fundamental level, however, it almost always meant either a *story* (the two words are often used interchangeably) of some sort or, less commonly, an *inventory* of factual knowledge, for example, a 'natural history.'[34]

Both these senses have respectable classical pedigrees. The latter does not immediately concern us, since it does not typically involve an account of the past. Natural history began with Herodotus' ἱστορία (an inquiry which included matters of the past as well as of geography and nature) and continued in the works of Aristotle, Pliny, Theophrastus, and others.[35] The natural historian was one who surveyed and drew up an inventory or list of natural life and of the composition of the world or the cosmos. Since there was as yet no notion of evolution, such an inventory inevitably depicted a world of stasis, not one of long-term change; it made no distinction between past and present. The absence of a temporal dimension is reflected in the synchronic – that is, non-narrative – form of all natural histories of the period. Robert Fludd's 'history of the greater and lesser cosmos' provides a good example of history-as-inventory, while Thomas Hobbes similarly considered history as the register of all factual knowledge, distinguishing it from philosophy (or science) which deals with matters *conditional*.[36] Bacon's list of projected 'histories' (of the winds, of life and death, etc) is largely devoted to the composition of such inventories, a pursuit which manifestly has little to do with the exploration of the past, though Bacon often dabbled in this also.[37] His awareness of the confusion caused by the fact that one word, *historia*, which he equated with 'experience,' signified two really mutually exclusive types of discourse led Bacon, following a long line of continental *artes historicae*,[38] to construct an elaborate taxonomy of histories which in its final form neatly divided history into two major categories, civil and natural.

History as 'story' is more complex. In common parlance, a play could be a history, or a 'tragical history,' or a 'historical comedy,' or even, somewhat redundantly, a 'chronicle history.'[39] Poems were also often considered histories, especially but not exclusively when they versified events generally accepted as having actually occurred. Samuel Daniel's *The Civil Wars* was considered a history both by its author and by his sternest critic, Ben Jonson, who complained that for a history of civil wars it was remarkably devoid of battles.[40] A variety of prose forms was also called history. Besides the obvious candidates – Bacon's *Henry VII* (1622), Camden's *Annales* (1615–27) and the like – narratives of current events, which would now be deemed journalism, were commonly referred to as histories: for example, the newsbooks and corrantoes which reported events on the continent.[41] So, too, were works which dealt with a romanticized and atemporal past, didactic pieces such as the venerable allegories, the *Gesta Romanorum* and the *Seven Wise Masters of Rome*, and works for entertainment such as the chivalric romances: the *History of Guy of Warwick*, *Palmerin of England*, and a dozen similar tales.[42] All these genres have two features in common: they tell stories, true or false, about real or imaginary men and women who lived in the remote or the recent past; and they take the form not of a synchronic *inventory* of information but of a diachronic *narrative*.

During Elizabeth's reign, certain conventions of usage began to develop. It became more common to distinguish between history proper, a truthful account of real events, and poetry or fable, the account of the verisimilar or fabulous. Aristotle had made a rigid distinction between history and poetry (which defenders of poetry such as Sir Philip Sidney were quick to exploit), while Cicero, the touchstone on most matters of good form, had developed the literary concept of history still further. In *De inventione,* he listed *historia* as one of three branches of *narratio* – the other two being *fabula* and *argumentum. Historia* dealt with the true account of things done in the remote past, *argumentum* with a fictional but plausible action of the sort found in tragedy or comedy, and *fabula* with the completely imaginary.[43]

This nomenclature, primarily a rhetorical one – for history in the classical tradition was conceived of as a branch of oratory – was reinforced by Cicero's own defence of *historia* and its moral virtues in *De oratore.* In this extremely influential work, history was defined as a book (or speech) about the past, not as the past in its totality, a sense of the word current today. But it would be going too far to say that for Cicero, *historia* was simply another kind of literature, for it was more than this: it was a source of correct action and human wisdom. The well-known passage in *De oratore* which praises history for its didactic effectiveness acquired the status of a topos in Elizabethan historical theory, soon becoming an incantation chanted in preface after preface. By 1581, it had grown so familiar that John Marbeck could define history in a mere two lines simply by citing Cicero with no further comment: 'What an historie is. Tullie calleth an historie the witnesse of times, the light of vertue, the life of memorie, maistres of life.'[44]

Like history, 'antiquities,' the remnants of the past, can be grouped easily into two broad classes. The written accounts of the more remote past – chronicles, histories, and records – touched on antiquities in the sense of 'matters pertaining to the distant past' (ie, to antiquity). Since the political facts of the distant past were often very sparse, narrative accounts often dealt in passing with antiquities in this sense, such as the religion of the ancient Britons, or the laws of the Saxon kings. Brian Melbancke referred to 'auncient antiquities' in this sense in 1583. Richard White of Basingstoke could include, in his Latin *Historiarum Britanniae libri,* notes and comments on *antiquitates,* meaning things that occurred in antiquity, without ever considering himself an antiquary in the alternative sense of a student of topography, monuments, and philological problems. As we shall see in the next chapter, John Speed's *History* refers to antiquities in the former sense, and its earlier chapters are devoted partly to a description of the cultures, religions, and institutions of the Britons, Romans, Saxons, and Danes, largely because of what Speed regarded (despite the readily available, if unverifiable, sources such as Tacitus and Bede) as the uncertainty and paucity of historical facts in this period. For him, such an antiquarian digression could only be a filler, and from the Norman Conquest on, his book is a straightforward narrative of events.[45]

In a different but closely related sense, 'antiquities' could also mean, more tangibly, the actual physical remains of the past. By the end of the sixteenth century these were turning up in growing quantities. Old coins, charters, manuscript chronicles, bones, fossils, funeral urns, and a wide variety of legal records were the 'antiquities' which the 'antiquary' studied so that he could make some sense out of 'antiquity,' the obscure past. But the written form in which he expressed his views generally did not take the form of a narrative, and he did not call his work a history. The surviving essays of the Elizabethan Society of Antiquaries provide a good example. These exploit a wide range of legal records, muniments, and non-literary evidence such as coins and seals in order to deal with a variety of topics which would now be deemed historical: the origins of knights or of the earl marshal's office, the beginning of land measurement, the early Christian church, and the division of England into shires. Yet not one of these brief tracts is called a history, nor is there any hint among them that their authors considered them to be so.

This seems to be not only because these discourses were non-narrative (for in a crude sense, they were, since they generally followed the development of institutions and customs chronologically) but for a number of other reasons: because they dealt with things rather than men, with customs or institutions rather than with events; because they were devoid of moral or exemplary content; and because their authors were almost entirely unconcerned with the rhetorical conventions of form which applied to true history-writing.[46] In other words, contemporaries had few doubts that whatever history was, it did not include antiquarian writings. There were points of contact between the two – the past was still the past, no matter how it was studied – but we do well not to underestimate the importance of formal distinctions to minds which placed a high premium on eloquence and order.

The distinction between history and antiquities was a consequence of late Elizabethan over-exposure to the rays of continental rhetoric. It

was not the indigenous inheritance of an unbroken medieval convention, and earlier in the century it seems to have mattered a good deal
less. John Leland, the first great Tudor antiquary, did not recognize such
a distinction. Leland's projected *magnum opus* was to be called 'De
Antiquitate Britannica, or els civilis historia,' of which the first part
(fifty books) would deal, in a narrative form, with 'the beginninges,
encreaces and memorable actes of the chief tounes and castelles of the
province allotid to hit.' A second section would chronicle the kings,
queens, and nobles from British times to his own day. We all know what
happened to Leland, and it is worth remembering that his Elizabethan
disciples knew it, too: the problem of putting his vast store of data into
a rhetorically satisfactory form drove him insane. All that remains of
his grand design is its data base, the manuscript collections now known
as the *Itinerary* and the *Collectanea*. Useful as these have proven to
later scholars, the only section of either which is cast in anything like
a narrative is part vii of the *Itinerary*, a brief travelogue written in the
first person. Leland was the Marley's ghost of Tudor historical writing,
and one of the consequences of his failure was that he was the first and
last sixteenth-century antiquary to attempt a general history from non-
narrative sources.[47]

Nevertheless, there is little sign of a firm distinction before the reign
of Elizabeth. It appears to have arisen amid the sharp increase in the
publication of antiquarian and topographical treatises which began in
the 1570s and continued through the last two decades of the century.
Sheer volume soon demanded some sort of *modus vivendi* between new
and old forms of writing about the past, particularly since acceptance
of the Ciceronian rhetorical conception of *historia* and the rules of
discourse which governed it also reached a high watermark at about the
same time. Even so, it was still possible for Sidney, as late as the 1580s,
to confuse the two types of writers about the past in his witty but rather
unfair caricature of the historian:

The historian scarcely giveth leisure to the moralist to say so much,
but that he, loaden with old mouse-eaten records, authorising
himself (for the most part) upon other histories, whose greatest
authorities are built upon the notable foundations of hearsay;
having much ado to accord differing writers and to pick truth out
of partiality; better acquainted with a thousand years ago than
with the present age, and yet better knowing how this world goeth
than how his own wit runneth; curious for antiquities and inquisitive of novelties; a wonder to young folks and a tyrant in table talk,

denieth, in a great chafe, that any man for teaching of virtue, and virtuous actions is comparable to him. 'I am *testis temporum, lux veritatis, magistra vitae, nuncia vetustatis.*"[48]

There is an obvious internal contradiction in this caricature which Sidney either did not see or chose to ignore: his historian was both obsessed with old records like the new-fangled antiquary *and* at the same time reliant 'for the most part ... upon other histories' like the old-fashioned chronicler. Such a confusion of terms was useful, of course, to his argument that poetry, the act of imagining or *making* the past, was superior to any form of writing that sought to record the merely factual and, as far as Sidney was concerned, the unknowable.[49]

With this sword of Damocles suspended over their heads, it is hardly surprising that the antiquaries sought to distance themselves from the narrative historians and chroniclers. Thus it was the antiquaries themselves, first and foremost, who persistently proclaimed their independence of the aims and rules of history-writing, abdicating the title of historian at the same time. It is undeniable that there are occasional hints of the view that erudite studies might be of use in the improvement of history. As early as 1591 in his *Archion*, which remained in manuscript until 1635, William Lambarde refers to 'some records of history' that he had seen concerning the earl marshal's court: clearly an antiquarian topic.[50] But in his *Perambulation of Kent* (1576), the first of the county chorographies, Lambarde highlights the principal rhetorical problem facing the topographer: how to describe the past without writing a history. Having listed the Anglo-Saxon kings of Kent, he immediately apologizes for having lapsed into history:

> Now, although it might heere seeme convenient, before I passed any further, to disclose such memorable things, as have chanced during the reignes of all these forenamed kings: yet ... my purpose specially is to write a topographie, or description of places, and no chronographie, or storie of times (although I must now and then use both, since one can not fully bee performed without enterlacing the other) and ... I shall have just occasion heereafter in the particulars of this shyre, to disclose many of the same ...[51]

The tensions between *descriptio* and *narratio*, between disposition along spatial or along temporal axes, leap out of this passage. History and antiquarian chorography were distinct genres, but how could one keep them apart? The trick was to reconcile content with form, the presentation of truth embodied in factual detail with the requirement that the presentation itself be both orderly and aesthetic.[52] The rambling, shapeless, and often dull prose of this and many other topographical works shows that the solution was not close at hand.

Remarks such as Lambarde's are rare, and are drowned out by the more numerous protestations by scholars that they were not engaging in history-writing. If Camden's *Britannia*, which was unquestionably the most widely read and influential book of topographical antiquities, makes one thing clear, it is that its author believed that he was not a historian. This old acquaintance of Sidney derived his title of chorographer from geography rather than history. Not only did Camden persistently disclaim any intention of writing a history, 'remembring my selfe to be a chorographer,' he went out of his way to abort any unconscious slips into a narrative of men and deeds. At one point, his discussion of the razing of Reading Castle by Henry II leads him briefly into a paean on that king's great deeds. The brakes are applied almost instantly. 'But these are things without our element,' he apologizes. 'Let us returne againe from persons to places.' Elsewhere, he aborts an account of the successive invaders of the Isle of Thanet, 'which I leave to historians ... least I might seeme to digresse extraordinarily.' The description of Barclay Castle, Gloucestershire, occasions a mention of the murder of Edward II, a subject which Camden 'had rather you should seeke in *Historians*, than looke for at my hands.' At another point he begs 'leave for a while to play the part of an historiographer, which I will speedily give over againe as not well able to act it.'[53] These remarks illustrate both the strength and the flexibility of categories like 'historian' and 'antiquary,' for, paradoxically, Camden was obliged to state the distinction only at those points where he was, in effect, ignoring it.

It was not that Camden thought he was better or worse than a recounter of names and dates. On the contrary, his disclaimers were a sign that he did not wish to be judged by the rhetorical standards which applied to historians. With his classical training, he knew perfectly well that the *Britannia* lacked both the form and the function of a history.[54] It is true that Camden and many other Elizabethan topographers achieved an order *of some sort* by dividing their works by counties, and by following a pre-existing spatial pattern (following rivers imaginatively in their prose, from town to town, as they had followed them literally on their travels). A few others, like John Norden, used different systems, such as the alphabet, to organize their materials.[55] But they all eschewed chronology, the *sine qua non* of history. Moreover, the antiquaries subscribed to the widespread notion that historians should properly be men of state, diplomats, or military leaders. Most of the greats, Thucydides, Polybius, Josephus, and Tacitus, had been politicians or generals themselves, and this sort of man had the personal experience and social stature necessary to the re-teller of remote events and indispensable to the historian of recent times. The student of antiquities needed linguistic agility, an enthusiasm for the past, and a large capacity for tedium: he did not have to be Julius Caesar.

There is thus a certain irony, of which Camden himself was painfully aware, in the criticisms of his *Britannia* by Ralph Brooke, the obnoxious York herald who would plague him and the College of Arms for several decades. Brooke accused Camden – quite erroneously – of pretending to the title of historian, since the *Britannia* dealt with the pedigrees of great families, and incidentally with their great deeds, often (this much was true) inaccurately. Brooke's argument was simply that scholars were not historians and never could be, because of their lack of political experience: 'And doubtles for a meere scholler to be an historian, that must take up all by hearesay, and uncertaine rumors, not being acquainted with the secretes and occurrences of state matters, I take it (as many others affirme with me) verie unfit, and dangerous.'[56]

Camden could not have agreed more; he confessed in his last revision of *Britannia* that he had once contemplated writing the history of England in Latin, 'being but young, not well advised nor of sufficiencie to undergoe so great a burden.'[57] The *Britannia* was not that work, and as far as we can tell, he believed to the end of his days that it was not a history at all. Even when, late in life and doubtless with Brooke's stinging attack still in mind, Camden finally did write a narrative history, the *Annales,* he found it heavy going. He complained to his friend, Jacques-Auguste de Thou, that he found history-writing a tiresome, odious task, enforced on him against his will by royal command. The man who wrote one of the greatest works of chorography and perhaps the most meticulously researched political history of the age, the scholar whose interests were as wide as his intellectual circle, did not recognize the essential similarity of his two masterpieces.[58]

John Stow, Camden's older friend and disciple, also believed that he was writing something quite different in kind from the many *Chronicles* and *Annales* he had produced over the years when he published his *Survay of London* in 1598. At no point did he call this work a history of London and, like Camden, Stow avoided slipping into narrative. The only 'history' in the book is a brief prefatory account of the ancient Britons and Romans. William Claxton, one of Stow's correspondents, shared his friend's recognition of the distinction. He praised Stow for 'proceding to the publishing of such grave histories and antiquities of worthy memorie,' by which he meant the chronicles and other sources, both documentary and architectural, that Stow had 'published' insofar as he had used them as evidence in his work. Claxton suggested that Stow augment the book, 'because never any hath taken the like matter of antiquitie in hand.'[59] Even those, like Thomas Martin, who actually wrote history from archival sources, rather than from chronicles, could not make the conceptual link between their pursuit and that of the antiquaries. Martin's Latin biography of William of Wickham exploits a wide range of manuscript material. When he came to list the most famous writers on Wickham, however, he termed Leland 'antiquitatis cum primis studiosus,' and Camden the author of a *descriptio* of Britain. Of all his sources, only two merited the title of *historiographus:* the fifteenth-century chronicler, Thomas of Walsingham, and the early sixteenth-century Italian emigré, Polydore Vergil.[60]

If the historians and antiquaries could agree so readily to an amicable divorce, how can one expect their lay readers to have attempted a reconciliation? Casual comments illustrate how the dichotomy had become axiomatic by the beginning of the seventeenth century. The anonymous author of a Jacobean manual for aspiring courtiers recommended that a courtier be both 'an excellent antiquary, and well red Historian.' Henry Peacham, who took a similar view, treated history and antiquities in different chapters of *The Complete Gentleman.* Richard Brathwait had more respect for the 'laborious and judicious antiquaries' of his day than for historians, but he asserted that historians who did venture to dabble in erudition benefited none but themselves, since they 'hardly can communicate the best of their knowledge unto others' – a fairly clear statement of the unsuitability of narrative as a medium for the communication of scholarly detail.[61] When Fulke Greville sought to erect a history lectureship in 1615, a plan which did not reach fruition for another twelve years, Sir John Coke warned him to choose his man carefully. The ideal candidate for the job would be a historian learned in matters of theology and church history, perhaps even a divine, 'able to joyne church and comonwealth together w[hi]ch to seperate is to betray.' If Greville elected such a historian, his endowment would be productive, 'wheras if you plant but a critical antiquarie instead of an historian, nothing can bee more unthriftie nor vaine.' Since Coke's letter goes on to reveal that he himself had acquired a good deal of knowledge about epitaphs and funeral laws, his distinction suggests not that he found the pursuits of the antiquaries dull or unimportant, but that he felt they did not belong in a university history lectureship.[62]

Politics, History, and the 'Common-Law Mind'

So far it has been argued that the distinction between history on the one hand and antiquities, erudition, or scholarship on the other, tended, particularly towards the end of Elizabeth's reign and early in her successor's, to be maintained with a degree of rigidity which has not been recognized. Yet despite this, it remained a theoretical tendency rather than an inviolable practical rule. Michael McKeon has recently noted the degree to which the early seventeenth century marks a period of 'destabilization' of generic categories, and what he says about fictional compositions may be applied to their historical counterparts.[63] Exceptions did occur: because the concept of history, for all Cicero's influence, was still in a state of ferment; because the same writers often did in fact write both sorts of work; and, most importantly, because whatever the rhetorical necessity of a formal distinction, there was a countervailing tendency in the Renaissance mind which allowed it to apply insights borrowed from one sphere of knowledge to problems presented by another, all for the sake of that elusive goddess, Truth.

Geography had already proven useful to students of the past; now, as lawyers joined heralds in this pursuit, the legal humanists' love of philology began to exercise an even more potent influence, as it had done earlier in France.[64] Furthermore, as the comments by Peacham, Brathwait, and other courtly writers make clear, the study of antiquities was fast acquiring a social acceptability which it lacked before the later sixteenth century. By 1600, the traditional civic humanist conception of the historian as an orator of his country's greatness had for some time been giving way to a newer ideal of the complete gentleman and scholar, an ideal which encouraged a certain amount of erudite learning. As the courtier-soldier of the sixteenth century gradually evolved into the virtuoso of the seventeenth, legal scholars such as Sir Edward Coke, Sir John Davies, and Francis Tate, together with collectors such as Sir Robert Cotton, became involved in the affairs of the kingdom to a far greater degree than most of their Tudor predecessors: in this, they were following the lead of such earlier Elizabethan scholars as Lambarde, who had combined his antiquarian and linguistic studies with a successful career as a lawyer and MP.

The political debates of the early Stuart era ensured that the politicization of erudition, especially legal erudition, would continue to develop, aided by such accidents of history as the succession in 1603 of a monarch who held peaceful study and literary pursuits in higher regard than military adventurism. It was also the consequence of changes in the educational program followed by the ordinary gentleman or peer in Elizabeth's and then James's reign, in particular of the increasing value placed on time spent at the universities, in the inns of court, and on travels abroad. Learning of various kinds had, by 1600, become a legitimate tool for the service of the commonwealth as well as an important part of the 'compleat gentleman's' public image, and even the erudite, bookish learning of the scholar was coming to have its place in the new intellectual armoury of the later Renaissance gentry. This redefinition of the social function of erudite learning, which made it almost as acceptable a pursuit as traditional history, was bound to contribute to a fruitful interchange between the two, albeit initially a slow one.

At the same time, there was a growing awareness among *fin-de-siècle* Englishmen that they lived in an unstable world. The crises of the last years of Elizabeth's reign and the controversies of James's forced men to turn to the past for solace and reassurance: it was no longer sufficient to analyse vicissitude simply in terms of the rise and fall of Fortune's wheel. What some of them found was that time could change not only dynasties but societies, not only individuals but institutions. As the confessional controversies that had dominated sixteenth-century political discourse faded – for the time being – into the background, the attention of the politically conscious was directed with a new intensity toward the common law.

Insofar as it affected legal studies, this heightened awareness of time and mutability was a two-edged blade. On the one hand it could lead some, such as Sir Edward Coke, to avoid the spectre of change altogether by denying it or minimizing its importance: the 'common-law mind' and the myth which it spawned of an 'immemorial' ancient constitution, unaltered by the Norman Conquest, indicate a conscious attempt to push the origins of the law so far back in time that they lay, in effect, beyond history. On the other hand, though, close examination of legal institutions through the documents which they had generated over the centuries could lead to consciousness not only of change, but of *development*. Closely linked to this was a nascent sense of relativism, an understanding that the phenomena of the past had to be understood on their own terms as the products of specific times and locations. It was this sort of historical *verstehen* which led Sir Henry Spelman, the greatest legal mind among the antiquaries, to the realization that Norman England, with its 'feudal' system, differed fundamentally both from Anglo-Saxon England and from the society of his own time.[65]

The ideas of Coke and Spelman have been dealt with thoroughly by

Professor Pocock and need not detain us long. The concepts of a 'common-law mind,' of an insular set of assumptions brought to the study of the past, and of a constitution unchanged in its essentials over the centuries have proven remarkably useful to scholars of the past generation as explanatory tools; they are helpful in analysing the discourse of lawyers, judges, and MPs throughout the seventeenth century. There has been a general tendency, however, to forget that both concepts are historiographical abstractions, not contemporary realities. A particularly unfortunate (and unintended) implication of Pocock's work, exacerbated by its very persuasiveness, has been the frequently expressed view that somehow the writings of Spelman, which recognized the impact of the Conquest, are 'historical' while those of Coke, because they are 'insular' and argue that the law dated from time immemorial, are 'fantastic.'[66]

Such language is not very helpful in coming to terms with the historical thought of earlier periods. An analysis of other interpretations of the Norman Conquest shows that few writers – even among the common lawyers – shared Coke's extreme view of that event; as J.P. Sommerville has recently pointed out, 'the idea that the common law had not been altered since prehistoric times was neither dominant nor, indeed, very important.'[67] Hans S. Pawlisch's recent study of Davies has filled out our understanding of his works, while Paul Christianson has demonstrated the highly sophisticated understanding of the historical transformation of law to be found in the thought of John Selden.[68] I shall later show that prose historians operating from outside the language of the common law (for example Sir John Hayward and Samuel Daniel) could have widely diverging interpretations both of the character of an event like the Norman Conquest and of its long-term implications, and that the issue was not one of great controversy in the early decades of the seventeenth century.

Nor should we make the mistake of regarding Coke's construction of the ancient constitution as historically without merit. There is no doubt that he lacked the critical linguistic skills which had been developed by French scholars and put into use by some of his own countrymen; he was frequently guilty of citing documents with inadequate attention (even by contemporary standards) to their origin and date. And although he was familiar with the writings of civil lawyers and with the works of continental scholars such as Hotman, it is quite correct to say that Coke's devotion to the common law obliged him to project it back into the remotest periods of prehistoric antiquity.

Yet to have the wrong view of history is not the same as to be antihistorical: from Coke's perspective, and that of many like-minded contemporaries, there was ample evidence to support the notion that institutions such as parliaments, sheriffs, and hereditary tenures had existed from murky antiquity, and good reason to suspect the veracity of sources which denied this. Late medieval documents such as the *Modus tenendi parliamentum* and the *Mirror of Justices* which purported to describe the laws as they had been handed down since Anglo-Saxon or even British times fooled more critical and better-trained scholars than Coke;[69] one such work, the fifteenth-century pseudo-Ingulph of Croyland, was not exposed until the nineteenth century. Coke cited these texts at length because they seemed to demonstrate convincingly that particular laws and institutions, such as parliament, predated the Conquest. Logic took over where evidence left off: since boroughs sent burgesses to parliament, and since there was no evidence that they had acquired this right since the Conquest, then logically they must have been returning members long before.

'And let it be granted, that William the Conqueror changed the name of this court, and first called it by the name of a parliament, yet manifest it is by that which hath beene said, that he changed not the frame or jurisdiction of this court in any point.'[70] Coke's opinions may not now be judged correct, but neither were they utterly fabulous – certainly not to an era in which many readers of history took seriously the notion that the island had first been discovered by Trojans and or had been populated by giants, and in which just about everyone believed the world itself to be only a few thousand years old, an 'ahistorical' myth towards which we have tended to be much more forgiving. Coke was perfectly capable of looking at the past historically and of examining sources such as the *Mirror*; if he lacked the ability to criticize them properly he at least knew to consult those more learned than he: thus he cited and praised his friend, the antiquary Joseph Holland, in the preface to his *Third Reports*; so, too, did he rely (in this case, with unfortunate results) on the apocryphal *Laga Eadwardi* and the laws of William I and Henry I as reproduced in Lambarde's *Archaionomia* (1568).[71]

Whatever his faith in the scholarship of antiquaries such as Lambarde and Holland, Coke held a much less charitable view of the state of history-writing proper at the start of the seventeenth century, commenting that 'Englishmens actions have beene renowned in the care of the world, but farre better done than they have been told, for want of a good hystorie.'[72] In particular, Coke lashed out at those authors who cited medieval chroniclers as authorities for the law – a point Selden himself would later take up in a different context. 'I pray thee beware of chronicle law reported in our annales, for that will undoubtedly lead thee to error,' Coke enjoined his reader, correctly attacking the notion, derived from the chronicles, that William I had introduced both sheriffs and justices of the peace: learned men all know, said Coke, that the former predated the conquest, and the latter did not appear till the fourteenth century.[73]

From Coke's point of view, the writing of history ought not to be confused with the interpretation of the law. Just as he advised the civilian and canonist not to involve themselves in discussion of the common law 'which they professe not,' so he recommended that the writers of history 'meddle not with any point or secreat of any art or science, especially with the lawes of this realme, *before they conferre with some learned in that profession.*'[74] The final saving phrase in this remark indicates, however, that he did not see the activities of the lawyer and the historian as entirely at odds: the writer of history could and should seek the advice of the learned lawyer if he was accurately to describe such matters as the legislative contributions of past monarchs. For his part, the common law provided its own best defence without 'the aide of any historian,' though Coke was perfectly willing to quote 'out of the consent of storie' evidence from such chroniclers as Matthew Paris and the pseudo-Ingulph of Croyland, who appeared to support the case for the common law's antiquity.[75]

In the present context, Coke is most famous for his argument, derived from earlier writers such as Sir John Fortescue, and put most succinctly in the prefaces to his eleven *Reports,* that 'the comon law of England had been time out of minde of man before the Conquest, and was not altered or changed by the Conquerour.'[76] William I had added only a few Norman customs to the laws of the Anglo-Saxons, and these in any case had been entirely abandoned within half a century by his son, Henry I, who had 'abolished such custome of Normandie as his father added to our common lawes,' thereby restoring the constitution as it had existed in the reign of Edward the Confessor.[77] The greatness and the clarity of the common law were demonstrable *ipso facto* by its having survived several successive foreign incursions, of which Coke considered the most threatening to have been not the Norman Conquest but the much earlier Roman invasion: 'If the auncient lawes of this noble island had not excelled all others, it could not be but some of the severall conquerors, and governors thereof; that is to say, the Romanes, Saxons, Danes, or Normans, and specially the Romanes, who (as they justly may) doe boast of their civill lawes, would (as every of them might) have altered or changed the same.'[78]

It is well known that Sir Henry Spelman, Coke's fellow common lawyer, came to a very different assessment of the impact of the Conquest. In Spelman's view, there was little evidence that could support the existence of hereditary tenures before William I; he successfully traced the origins of feudal obligations such as wardship and marriage to the Conqueror, and showed that parliament in its seventeenth-century form – including the house of commons – did not exist before the thirteenth century.[79] Yet in many ways Spelman was as much a prisoner of his own categories as Coke was of his: as we shall see in chapter 7, he found it necessary to repudiate the Conquest when arguing for the antiquity of an institution such as tithes, which he saw as a kind of feudal service owed to God; and he severely underrated the extent of continuity between royal offices under the late Saxon kings and those of the Anglo-Norman era.[80]

There are two lessons to be drawn from this brief discussion of historical attitudes toward the common law and the Conquest. The first is that one must resist the temptation, when discussing the historical vocabulary of an earlier era, to judge the works of a given writer exclusively in terms of his apparent 'correctness,' that is, according to his conformity with modern views – these, after all, can change, as the vicissitudes of historical interpretation in recent decades demonstrate. It is both fair and reasonable to note that Spelman or Selden may have brought superior philological training and a less closed set of categories to the analysis of the past; it is not legitimate, however, to judge them as the 'winners' and as the objective champions of modern scholarship, in contrast to the biased insularity of someone like Coke. The second point, which will become clearer as we proceed, is that there was no common voice either on the Norman Conquest or even on the historicity of the laws. Both were much discussed, but without much sense of urgency throughout most of our period, and individual positions on these issues were often determined incidentally by intellectual and ideological positions that had little to do with the niceties of law. And despite a wide spectrum of opinion on the antiquity of the law and its relationship to the successive conquests not just of the Normans, but of Romans, Anglo-Saxons, and Danes, neither proved to be the occasion of an early Stuart historical controversy, either among prose historians or lawyers.

Disagreement, Opinion, and Controversy

Coke puts us in mind of another peculiar fact about historical interpretation in early Stuart England: that despite the existence of differing views on issues such as the antiquity of the common law, to dwell on such differences, much less to argue about the past in polemical terms, was held neither desirable nor in good taste. He himself complained in 1605 that 'now a dayes those that write of such matters doe for the most part by their bitter and uncharitable invectives, transported with passion and fury, either beget new controversies, or do as much as in them lye to make the former immortal.'[81]

The distaste of a born fighter and debater such as Coke for open argument, in an age which valued consensus over conflict, concord over controversy, applies even more strongly to the formal historical writing of the era. Because sixteenth- and early seventeenth-century historians were not particularly interested in advancing historical knowledge to greater levels of accuracy and sophistication, for the benefit of their remote successors, they did not very often quarrel over their subject. There was little dialectical clash of ideas in Tudor historiography on a regular basis, and there were very few major historical controversies. This is a point which, perhaps more than any other, separates the modern structure of historiography from theirs, and it requires some emphasis.[82]

On most issues, at most times, late Tudor and early Stuart historians simply saw no need to pursue historical debate for its own sake.[83] By this I do not mean that every historian and antiquary agreed on every point, which was manifestly not the case, particularly where the thin data of 'antiquity,' the distant past, were concerned. Nor can it be argued that vigorous debate over the past did not occur in other forums than historical writing proper – among common lawyers and MPs for instance. Arthur Ferguson, who has pointed to the restrictions imposed by *formal* historical narrative on the range of interpretations and explanations of the past, is surely correct in arguing that ideological (religious or political) disputes provoked a conflict of views of the past among non-historians.[84] Nevertheless, it remains true that there was fundamental agreement on the main points of English and classical history: that England had always been or had had a tendency toward monarchical government; that certain kings and other historical personalities were good or bad; that evil deeds had a 'boomerang' effect; and that certain types of human activity had generally proven beneficial, and others disastrous.

Individual historical figures had gradually become associated with particular vices or virtues in interludes, plays, and didactic poems (such as *The Mirror for Magistrates*) from the end of the fifteenth century till the reign of Elizabeth; some were known for famous accomplishments or for notorious failures, and were adjudged good or bad on this basis.

For certain English kings the jury spoke with unanimity. Henry vii was uniformly (and necessarily, under the Tudors) considered a good king, Richard iii the archetypal tyrant. Edward i and Henry v were successful, Edward ii a failure. On most there was a somewhat wider range of opinion. Richard ii was generally seen as a bad, or at least badly misled king; but hindsight showed that Henry iv's usurpation had more dire consequences in the long run, as Polydore Vergil and Edward Hall had revealed.

Once a number of influential histories had been produced in the early Tudor decades, and reproduced by the medium of print, it was far easier, and more natural, to imitate than to challenge them; by the end of the sixteenth century a nebula of stereotyped opinions and *topoi* about the character of past kings and nobles, about the causes and consequences of great events and about the whole course of history from the Creation to the present, had hardened into a rigid orthodoxy. And while one might take issue with a particular opinion or detail – whether Richard ii was stabbed or smothered, the number of men killed at the Battle of Hastings, or the motives of Queen Isabel in helping to dethrone Edward ii – no one ever questioned the fundamental 'facts' of history, nor sought to reshape them into an innovative interpretation.[85] Thus there was often a kind of 'second-order' refinement and rejection of facts (though historians usually resented doing even this) within a wider framework, but almost never did there occur 'first-order' disagreements, paradigmatic shifts away from one set of beliefs or assumptions to another. Historians all agreed on essentials, and they wrote from an ideologically unified perspective, that of the Tudor and Stuart monarchy. They also agreed on other historical axioms, such as that evil had always been repaid with evil: the standard account of English history after Edward ii, for instance, was built around the metahistorical pattern whereby every successive dynasty was destroyed in the third generation. Edward iii's grandson was deposed by Henry iv, as was the latter's grandson, Henry vi; Edward iv's third successor, Richard iii, was also deposed.[86] Similarly, William i's spoliation of the New Forest in Hampshire had been properly requited when two of his sons perished there.

These historical patterns depended on the assumption that events periodically recurred. So did types of personality, as Plutarch's parallel lives, translated by Sir Thomas North in 1579, so clearly demonstrated. Comparisons of contemporaries with great figures of the past was one of the most common forms of praise, though it could cut two ways: Elizabeth i seems to have grown particularly sensitive to comparisons between herself and Richard ii. Henry vii was compared with Lycurgus, the Spartan lawgiver, by Charles Aleyn in 1638.[87] William Harbert's *A Prophesie of Cadwallader* (1604) and Robert Fletcher's *The Nine English Worthies* (1606) consisted entirely of Plutarchan comparisons between great English worthies and their classical 'types.' James I was constantly flattered by comparisons with Solomon, Augustus, and Henry VII.[88] Early Stuart panegyrists and historians would make much of James's double descent from Henry VII, and would describe his projected union of the kingdoms as the logical, and inevitable, consequence of the union of the Roses.

In other words, there existed by 1600 an identifiable 'corridor' or safe zone of correct opinion about the past, which was flexible enough to allow for some deviation and nuance, a corridor policed partly by external authorities such as church and crown but mainly by historians themselves, through a process which looks very much like a collective version of that self-censorship ascribed by Annabel Patterson to poets and dramatists. In a wide-ranging and thoughtful discussion of the mental and political structures governing the reading and writing of literature in the sixteenth and seventeenth centuries, Patterson has concluded that early modern authors were able to protect themselves, at the same time that they presented gentle criticisms of the regimes within which they wrote, by hiding political and moral messages between the lines of their texts, forcing the reader to tease out the meaning for himself. She has further suggested that within limits generally accepted both by authors and by authority (which could, however, expand or shrink in response to events), a certain amount of criticism and dissent could be tolerated without invoking punishment. Indeed, it could be positively encouraged by politicians vying for the rulers' ear. Such patrons regularly supported the writing of poems, and the performance of plays, which presented opinions on current topics in fictional guise.[89]

Over the first four decades of the seventeenth century, as more histories came to be written, and as the newer antiquarian scholarship began gradually to influence the writing of narratives, the interpretive corridor began to expand: cracks even appeared in the walls. Such were the complex political issues of the period that the very same historians who generally kept themselves within the bounds of acceptable opinion sometimes found themselves offering comments on contemporary matters carefully (and sometimes obscurely) disguised as reflections on the past. In his classic study of the *Crisis of the Early Italian Renaissance*, Hans Baron alerted scholars to the clues which shifting perspectives on the past can provide for the understanding of political attitudes and behaviour; we should no more expect the historians of the period to have agreed on every aspect of the past, or its contemporary significance, than we should expect every Member of Parliament to concur on a given political or religious issue. But moderate dissent and subtle shadings in various historians' personal pictures of the past do not amount to the existence, still less the acceptance, of widespread historical debate. It would take civil war and the suspension of censorship in the 1640s to bring about a framework of historical discussion that was truly dialectical, even confrontational, rather than consensual in character. Changes in the structure of seventeenth-century historical writing shadow developments in the modes of political and religious debate.

One very important reason for the continued dominance of a consensual structure in historical writing was the complete absence of anything like a theory of 'historical interpretation.' It is not exaggerating to say that, from his own perspective, the sixteenth- and early seventeenth-century historian did not construct 'interpretations' at all; nor did he very often criticize contemporary historians (sources were another matter) and revise his own views, because he simply did not know that 'interpretations' existed. The term is never used in the sense in which we intend, that is, a coherent explanation of a related and sequential series of historical facts. The word 'opinion,' by contrast, was used quite commonly to describe an individual's view of a particular problematic aspect of the past. Thus the Elizabethan antiquary and future secretary of state, Thomas Lake, spoke of 'three common opinions' in his sources on the origins of sterling money.[90] In his and the writings of other Elizabethan antiquaries, one does find evidence of different opinions; the antiquaries recognized the conflicting testimony of their sources, though they did not debate among themselves, nor resolve any of the issues they discussed.[91]

On occasion, a writer might criticize another's factual inaccuracy, as Ralph Brooke attacked William Camden for genealogical slips in the *Britannia* or as John Stow quarrelled with Richard Grafton over the latter's failure to list his sources.[92] The best-known Tudor instance of this is the attack on Polydore Vergil by English and Welsh writers over his debunking of the British history of Geoffrey of Monmouth and the legends of Brutus the Trojan and King Arthur.[93] The indignation of Geoffrey's defenders, from John Leland in the 1530s to George Saltern in the 1600s, reveals that anyone who challenged existing beliefs was, *prima facie*, not seen as daring and original – just wrong.

Originality in historical thought was no more a virtue than innovative religious opinion. The Renaissance concept of a single, unitary truth did not allow a subjective element, at least in theory. Insofar as human knowledge could grasp it, a fact was a fact. Coke, as we have seen, openly deplored invective employed in defence of truth; those arguing a case should allow the truth to demonstrate itself and persuade the ignorant gently, without force or insult – an ideal somewhat belied by the sarcasm in some of his later parliamentary speeches. Coke's statement presumed the existence of a self-evidently correct position on any issue: truth was to him 'of that constitution and constancie, as she cannot at any time or in any part or poynt bee disagreeable to her selfe.' The man who perversely impugned a 'knowne truth' must be doing so 'eyther in respect of himselfe or of others; of himselfe, in that he hath within him a discontented heart; of others, whom for certaine worldly respects he seeketh to please.'[94] In sixteenth-century religious debates one could similarly either doubt an opponent's sincerity and moral probity or his evidence; there was no question of allowing each man his opinion on an issue, of 'agreeing to differ.' There was only one truth in religion, absolute and immutable, and the enemies of that truth were the enemies of religious unity. As Bishop Jewel put it, 'the bond of unity is simple verity.'[95]

So in history. Scholars of the Italian and French Renaissance deplored the deficiencies of chronicles and histories, which disagreed in their accounts of the same event, and they sought to rewrite those events to *remove* such conflicts. The task facing the Elizabethan author was likewise not the discovery of new facts, nor the reweaving of the old into new cloth, but the harmonizing of conflicting accounts. As the Elizabethan martyr and historian of Ireland, Edmund Campion, observed in 1571, when most of his sources agreed on a particular issue, 'they are in effect one writer, seeing the latest ever borrowed of the former, and they all of [Giraldus] Cambrensis.'[96] William Camden, writing to Justus Lipsius in 1604, confronted the problem of Constantine the Great's birth in Britain. 'All histories,' he observed, 'in one voice assert that he was born in Britain, except the two Greeks, Cedrenus and Nicephoras.' He believed that reliable, if not absolute and perfect, historical truth was obtainable, refusing to take a pyrrhonist stand. One simply had to use common sense and choose one's sources judiciously. 'The truth of history, and its reliability, is supported since most historians agree in their accounts.'[97]

One reason why the questioning of accepted historical opinions continued to cause discomfort was that it seemed to play into the hands of sceptics like the anti-intellectual Cornelius Agrippa and his English reader, Sidney, who, though he saw some value in the political lessons of history, denied the possibility of accurate historical knowledge. If Sidney was correct, then the historians merely wasted their time by sorting through earlier chronicles and histories and records which were themselves based on hearsay and which often disagreed.[98] Sidney's biographer, Fulke Greville, shared both his friend's scepticism about the capacity of human wisdom, and his distaste for pedantry. Greville particularly deplored the use of learning to challenge received wisdom:

> Againe, the use of Knowledge is not strife,
> To contradict, and criticall become,
> As well in bookes, as practise of our life.[99]

If any two opinions were equally plausible, how could one know the truth? In the controversy which most disrupted the stability of early Stuart historical writing, discussed below in chapter 7, the clergyman Richard Montagu would fling this charge at the philologist John Selden in 1618 over the latter's *Historie of Tithes*. In 1611, the minor poet Robert Chester's *Anuals of Great Brittaine*, an Arthurian romance, complained that 'there yet remaines in this doubtfull age of opinions a controversie of that esteemed Prince of Brittaine.' Richard Brathwait, however, remarked approvingly on 'the generall union of historians, about the time, place, and occasion, so concordantly jumping, as if all ... had beene set downe by one penne.' He added that most modern historians agreed on most things with their predecessors. 'The like harmony of historians in their relations, though writ in severall ages, may be gathered from the annals both of antient and our more moderne authors.' Brathwait suggested that the conflicting facts in some histories could be harmonized by 'a judicious collation or comparing of histories one with another.' He clearly believed that one historical truth existed objectively, just waiting to be seized upon and set down. He urged the reconciliation of diverse opinions, for 'opinion is a maine opponent to judgement.' Brathwait could not conceal his disgust that 'the very chiefest historians have opposed themselves one against another' on some points of fact.[100]

Ideology and Dissent: The Case of the Catholics

What was lacking in Tudor and early Stuart historiography was a reason for divergent points of view: historical narrative had yet to be firmly tied to the wagon of ideological and political conflict. The most notable, and earliest, exception to this occurred in the arena of ecclesiastical history.

In Valois France, for instance, the wars of religion had resulted in a flood of historical writing and in bitter clashes among historians and scholars. Elsewhere in Europe, Catholic authors like Cardinal Baronius found their scholarship assaulted by protestant critics like Isaac Casaubon. The Venetian priest Paolo Sarpi would undermine the official Roman interpretation of the Counter-Reformation from within in his celebrated *History of the Council of Trent*.[101] Such debates were rarely objective and cool-headed; they frequently involved some form of violent *ad hominem* argument: there is nothing in Elizabethan or early Stuart secular historiography – even in the tithes controversy of 1618–21 – which quite compares with the Huguenot François Hotman's denunciation of his Catholic opponent, Papire Masson, as 'a renegade Jesuit and hired sycophant, who should be taken to the asylum of Saint Mathurin in Paris, where maniacs are cared for, and put to death by whipping.'[102] Selden, among other early seventeenth-century commentators, recognized the overtly partisan character of ecclesiastical history-writing; he recommended that the student interested in the subject read both Baronius and the protestant *Magdeburg Centuries* and 'bee his owne judge, the one being extreamly for the papists, the other extreamly for the protestants.'[103]

I have suggested that where there was no clash of ideology, political or religious, there was unlikely to be a clash of historical interpretations. English Catholics writing history in the late Elizabethan and early Stuart period reveal the converse – the immense potential for historical disagreement and controversy when the past was turned to for polemical rather than didactic purposes. They also demonstrate how erudition of the type employed by the antiquaries *could* be brought to bear on the past within the context of debates over theology and ecclesiology. As I hope to show further on, the politicization of antiquarian learning in the early seventeenth century would owe at least as much, if not more, to the long tradition of erudite theological debate as it did to the antiquaries' more obvious roots in the study of the common law and in disputes over its place in the English constitution; this would be especially true of the critical work which best marks the juncture of history, erudition, and ideological dispute during James's reign, John Selden's *Historie of Tithes* (1618), to which we will turn in chapter 7. For the moment, it is worthwhile to look at the reactions of a group of historical writers, each looking at England's past from the outside (both literally and figuratively), and each to varying degrees drawing both his learning and his historical perspective from the ecclesiastical controversies of the late sixteenth and early seventeenth centuries.

The Reformation had initiated an historical controversy all across Europe over the development of the 'true' church from Apostolic times to the present. Countless polemicists turned to historical arguments to justify the Catholic or Lutheran position. Many set down their arguments in the form of narrative histories. Carion's chronicle, edited by Melanchthon, revived the concept of the four monarchies of the world which Bodin was to take such pains to refute. The idea was further elaborated by Johannes Sleidan in his *De quatuor summis imperiis.*[104] The most ponderous polemic of all was the compilation generally known as the *Magdeburg Centuries* (1539–46). Into this work Matthias Flacius Illyricus and his helpers stuffed every historical fact which supported their thesis that the doctrine of the Roman church had wandered further and further away from apostolic and patristic teaching, which, they claimed, was represented by the reformers. The formal reply of the Counter-Reformation to the *Centuries* was the even larger *Annales ecclesiasticae* by the Neapolitan Cardinal Baronius, who was Vatican librarian from 1597 to 1607. His work traced the history of the church from its beginnings to the end of the twelfth century, arguing that the Catholic church had developed naturally and continuously from its origins to the present.[105]

Englishmen participated in these historical debates as early as the reign of Henry VIII, when the reformer Robert Barnes's *Vitae Romanorum pontificum* depicted the rule of Rome as an unmitigated disaster of several centuries' duration.[106] More famous is the work of John Foxe, perhaps the most influential book ever printed in Elizabethan England in terms of its general influence on public perceptions of the nation's religious history. The *Acts and Monuments* began as an account of 'protestant' martyrs from Wyclif to the reign of Mary Tudor, but Foxe soon expanded it into a general history of the church, in which the Roman forces of darkness contended with those of Christ through the ages.[107] Other authors followed suit: the more sophisticated Bishop John Jewel did not write history as such, but he made extensive use of historical arguments to defend the Anglican church from Catholic assailants.[108] Foxe's account itself soon hardened into a framework of interpretation within which future historians were to work, though considerable scope still remained for filling in the details of the account and calculating the apocalyptic schedule which would lead to the completion of the Reformation and the eventual return of Christ. By the end of the sixteenth century, the English church and its doctrine had stabilized sufficiently to render further elaborations of protestant ecclesiastical history less urgent: sectaries, precisians, and recusants were more effectively dealt with in polemical discourses such as those by Archbishop John Whitgift and his successor, Richard Bancroft. The most able scholars of the reign of Elizabeth, Camden, Stow, and Lambarde, instead poured their energies into works of antiquarian erudition or into secular chronicles and histories. Lambarde's *Archaionomia* and *Perambulation of Kent*, Camden's *Britannia*, and Stow's *Survay of London* are devoid of any attempt to plead the case of the Anglican church, except incidentally. Camden integrated an account of Elizabeth's ecclesiastical policies into his *Annales*, though he 'touched them but with a light and chary hand.'[109] When James I established Chelsea College as a centre for Anglican polemic, he appointed Camden and Sir John Hayward as historiographers. They did little or nothing in these positions, and the college itself was soon moribund as much from lack of interest as anything else.[110] Though it would be revived as a consequence of the religious issues of the Civil War, protestant sacred history, except where integrated into secular histories such as those by Camden and John Speed, was a rare bird. When it did appear it was usually in the form of examples cited by pamphleteers seeking to make a point, as in William Prynne's 1632 denunciation of stage plays, *Histriomastix*.[111]

From a different perspective, however, a number of Englishmen, all Roman Catholics, continued to write historical narratives that were to varying degrees polemical. Nicholas Sanders, a former fellow of New College, Oxford, died in 1581 having spent his final years in Ireland provoking Catholic rebellion. His posthumously published *Rise and Growth of the Anglican Schism* (1585), a scurrilous attack on English reformers and kings since Henry VIII, earned him the name 'Dr Slanders.' It was difficult to take seriously a book which accused Henry VIII, 'a most impious and sacrilegious tyrant' of being the father of his own promiscuous queen, Anne Boleyn.[112]

Much more formidable was the work of Robert Parsons, Jesuit missionary and controversialist. Among his many polemics was a response, which he published anonymously and abroad in 1606, to Coke's *Fifth Reports*. In this work, Parsons challenged Coke's argument that the common law could be used to defend both the Reformation and the persecution of Catholics. In Parsons' view, no law was valid unless it conformed to Christian law; and that derived ultimately from the Catholic church. All English law issued 'from our very first Christian kings & queenes, which must nedes be the origen, and beginning of all Christian common lawes in England.' To use the law to attack Catholicism was therefore to turn it on itself: Parsons likened this to using Aristotle against himself on behalf of Ramists, or citing Galen's own teachings against him for the furtherance of new-fangled medical writers such as Paracelsus.[113] Much of Coke's own criticism of the use of chronicles as a source for the common law can be understood as a response to their citation by Catholic writers such as Parsons, on behalf of the supremacy of the Roman church. In a reign-by-reign analysis of the attitudes of English kings, both before and after the Conquest, to the church and to ecclesiastical law, Parsons freely cited chroniclers from Matthew Paris and Roger Hoveden to Polydore Vergil.

Yet despite their radically different ideological bents, and their very different purposes in reviewing the antiquity of the laws, there was one issue on which Coke and Parsons were virtually agreed: the Conquest marked no significant break in the English legal tradition. Parsons traced such institutions as Peter's pence back to the Anglo-Saxon king Ina who, according to 'historiographers full of piety,' had been among the first Christian monarchs to make his realm 'tributary to the Bishop of Rome.'[114] William the Conqueror proved a loyal servant of Rome, to whom he owed his crown, and 1066 marked less a conquest than the completion of a just war against a usurper, Harold II, who had broken faith with his master. Because Parsons wished to stress the conformity of English kings and their laws to the law of the church over a period of centuries, he was no more inclined than Coke to see the Conquest as a constitutional watershed. Thus he describes how William I, on the advice of his barons and of a jury of twelve men from each shire, 'did review the auncient lawes both of the English and Danes, approving those that were thought expedient, and adding others of his owne; beginning with those that appertained to the liberty & exaltation of the church.'[115] Any additions to the law were valid less because they conformed to existing Anglo-Saxon laws than because these all conformed to the law of Christ as administered by Rome.

In Parsons' skilful use of medieval chronicles, which slides silently over such issues as the medieval conflict of church and crown, every successive monarch up to the sixteenth century could be shown to have legislated only in conformity with the laws of God and the interests of the church. Henry VIII and his offspring marked the real break with the past, since post-Reformation laws could not by definition conform to Christianity. By extension, the persecution of faithful Catholics could not therefore be defended at law; speaking at the conclusion of his work, in which he accuses Coke of having used invective, Parsons denies the attorney-general's claim that Elizabethan martyrs such as Edmund Campion had been legally tried and executed according to the most ancient laws of the kingdom: 'And as for the auncient common laws of England, wherby M. Attorney saith they were condemned, wee have shewed now often before, that this is but a word of course with him, & that there bee no such common-laws extant, not [sic] ever were, or could bee under catholicke princes against priests, before the breach of King Henry the 8.'[116]

Parsons' devaluing of the Conquest as a break in legal traditions differed little from Coke's in substance; it provides one example of something which recurs again and again in the formal historical writing of the early Stuart period, namely that differences in opinion over what actually happened in the past were of less consequence than the conclusions drawn therefrom, and the conflicting points of view brought to such issues. Parsons was far closer to Coke on the issue of Norman impact on the laws than Coke himself was to his fellow protestant and legal colleague, Spelman.

Ultimately, Parsons' attempt to assign the common law popish origins proved of much less concern to English readers than had an earlier treatise which challenged the received interpretation of a much more recent era, that of the fifteenth-century civil wars. Parsons' *A Conference about the Next Succession to the Crowne of Ingland*, written with the assistance of a number of other Catholic exiles, had been published abroad in 1594 under the pseudonym Doleman.[117] In it Parsons attempted to show that the heir to the childless Elizabeth ought not to be the Calvinist James VI of Scotland, but one of a number of Catholic princes, of whom he favoured the Spanish infanta, daughter of Philip II, his former master. Parsons fooled no one with his claim that he was 'neutral' on the issue and was merely conjecturing as to who the heir would be: the *Conference* was plainly a direct attack on the legitimacy of the Tudor (and by implication the Stuart) dynasty. Since the days of Polydore Vergil and Thomas More it had been accepted as little short of gospel that God had raised Henry Tudor to destroy Richard III and restore unity to the warring kingdom. Henry's accession marked an epoch for Tudor historians, a kind of secular Incarnation. No one had since disputed the teleology of such accounts, for to do so would have been to convict Henry (and his successors) of rebellion and usurpation.

An unabashed opponent of any protestant succession, Parsons naturally had few such reservations. Consequently, he aimed his erudite guns below the water-line of the Tudor interpretation of history, noting that all historians since Polydore 'do take al right from the house of Lancaster.' He knew that they agreed that the Yorkist claim had been superior, and that Henry VII's claim was based more upon his marriage to Edward IV's daughter Elizabeth than upon his distant descent from Edward III via his mother Margaret Beaufort. Parsons therefore rejected the Tudor claim by rejecting the Yorkist. Richard II's deposition became a divinely and popularly approved act, while thirteen years of successful rule, sustained against numerous ill-fated rebellions, made Henry IV perfectly legitimate; the peaceful succession of his son and Henry V's glorious reign sealed the authority of the house of Lancaster. The Lancastrians also proved to be better kings and kinder people than the bloodthirsty Yorkists who seized their throne. Edward IV was a usurper: so was his son-in-law Henry Tudor, and, Parsons implied, so would be Henry's descendant, James VI.[118]

The historical and genealogical sleight of hand which Parsons performed to prove his point is only a small part of a work which was neither written as historical narrative nor even conceived as a 'history.' Parsons was above all else a divine and a casuist, skilled in the rhetoric of ecclesiastical polemic and the tricks of scholastic discourse; his not inconsiderable learning thus derived from a tradition quite outside Blundeville or Brathwait's requirements that the historian be a well-read gentleman and that he relate the past without prejudice. Yet even if it fell outside the boundaries of historical writing, Parsons' tract could hardly be ignored; it amounted to a subversion of the anticipated future as much as of the accepted picture of the past, and English scholars accordingly went to considerable lengths to refute it.[119]

Less well known than Parsons, though more able as a historian, was his slightly older contemporary, Richard White of Basingstoke, or Vitus Basinstochius (1539–1611). A fellow of New College from 1557 to 1564, where he may have encountered Nicholas Sanders, White left England for good early in Elizabeth's reign and enjoyed an illustrious continental career as professor of civil and of canon law in the English college at Douai. After the death of his second wife he was ordained a priest by papal dispensation.[120]

A competent classicist and jurist who wrote a commentary on the Roman laws of the Twelve Tables, White's principal interest lay in British history, and he spent his last few years compiling a series of eleven books on the history of Britain from the Flood to the Norman Conquest. The *Historiarum Britannicae libri XI* appeared in parts between 1597 and 1607. Published abroad and in Latin, it was not widely read in England, though John Selden made considerable use of it.[121] White's main purpose seems to have been the writing of a textbook for the college and an introduction to early English history, or 'antiquity,' for a Catholic audience. His most well-known supporter was no less a figure than Baronius himself, with whom he had corresponded.[122]

Despite his connections with the Counter-Reformation, White managed to maintain a scholarly objectivity of sorts. His work is neither a polemic like Parsons' or Sanders', nor strictly an ecclesiastical history, though White's heroes are all pious Catholics, who invoke Mary and the saints.[123] It was more an attempt to bring Polydore Vergil up to date, and only for the earliest part of British history. Unlike Parsons, White had little stomach for controversy, and on most points he could agree with (and cite) the statements of English protestant authors. He readily quoted Camden to prove 'that Britain received the Christian religion in the beginning of the church.'

White was, nevertheless, skilful in reinterpreting accepted stories to suit his perspective. It was, for example, a commonplace that the first Christian king in Britain was Lucius, a legendary figure of the second century who appears in Bede, and was accepted by John Foxe and John Jewel.[124] It was also widely held that Lucius was the first great lawgiver of British history, and that he had borrowed from Eleutherius, the bishop of Rome, divine and Christian precepts for the foundation of common law. Protestants had no difficulty in accepting this legend, since an alleged letter from Eleutherius to Lucius survived.[125] Moreover, since the Roman church of the second century had not yet become corrupt, the legend established Britain as a Christian kingdom, independent of Rome, before the conversion of St Augustine of Canterbury in the late sixth century, at which later date the rot had set in. White accepted the legend, but twisted it to support a tie between Britain and a papacy which was already acknowledged as the apostolic see, not just as another bishopric. St Peter had already established papal authority by preaching in Britain before his martyrdom. White skirts the issue of Lucius' temporal laws, dwelling instead on his conversion by Eleutherius' ambassadors, and his acts of piety: 'Lucius, king of the Britons, forthrightly sent letters to Eleutherius by Elvanus and Medwinus, two holy men; in which letters he craved that he and his people be received into the number of Christians.'[126]

White appended extensive *notae* or appendixes to each book. These were often longer than the text itself, and reveal him as an extremely well-read antiquary. His work had a number of idiosyncracies: he rarely gave dates for events, merely reporting them in order; and he ignored much of the critical scholarship of the preceding fifty years, though the *notae* show that he had read it. He continued to rely on discredited documents like the pseudo-Berosus and the Galfridian legends of ancient Britain, myths which even at the end of the sixteenth century were no longer accepted, except with the greatest caution, by most English antiquaries.[127]

Much more candidly polemical were the ecclesiastical histories of another Douai seminarian, Richard Broughton. Born near the end of Mary's reign, he left England in the 1580s for the English college and was ordained in 1593. Shortly after, he was sent to England to proselytize. It seems unlikely that he was the same Mr Broughton who was a member of the Elizabethan Society of Antiquaries, though his works suggest he had some contact with its members.[128] An able Greek and Hebrew scholar, he served as vicar-general to Thomas Smith, bishop of Chalcedon in England from 1625 to 1631. He seems to have had powerful patrons, including the duchess of Buckingham, and in 1626 he was living undisturbed in Oxford.[129]

Broughton was much less interested than White in adducing philological evidence and, like Parsons, more intent on arguing a case. His *An Ecclesiasticall Protestant Historie* (1624) set out to prove that the pope had always exercised 'fatherly chardge and care' over the church in Britain, from St Peter to St Augustine. The topic was nothing new: Parsons himself had tackled it in his massive, three-volume *Treatise of the Three Conversions of England*, an undisguised polemic against Foxe, John Bale, and the Magdeburg Centuriators. Parsons' argument, based largely on Baronius, had rested on the proposition that the Roman Church of St Augustine's day was exactly the same in doctrine and liturgy as that imported earlier, first by Joseph of Arimathaea and then by Lucius.

Broughton was more conciliatory: he deliberately relied on the writings of 'the best learned protestant antiquaries.'[130] Matthew Parker (chronicler of the archbishops of Canterbury who had preceded him), Camden, Holinshed, Stow, and Selden all furnished him, unintentionally, with material which was ingeniously reshaped into an argument 'proving' the historicity of Rome's claim to spiritual jurisdiction in Britain. He made particular use of 'the Theater writers,' by which he meant the 1611 compilation published by John Speed. Pushing White's arguments for the antiquity of the modern Catholic church much further than White himself, Broughton established that the first founder of a hierarchical order of the church was St Aristobulus, a disciple of St Peter. He turned Joseph of Arimathaea (traditionally the first Christian in Britain) and his son, a bishop, into the subordinates of 'Archbishop' St Aristobulus, and hence of St Peter and Rome. Correctly pointing out that the protestants had admitted the legitimacy and holiness of all bishops of Rome up to and including Eleutherius, he asked how they could deny the legitimacy of the church since Eleutherius' day.[131] Like White, Broughton made of Lucius the obedient pious son of the church, using the famous letter from Eleutherius to good effect. The pope 'by his [Lucius'] suite and petition interposed himselfe in the ordeyninge, altering, or correctinge and settlinge, *the very temporal lawes themselves* in this kingedome, to governe and rule and direct it, even in civill and meerely humane thinges.' He made explicit what White had only implied, that Eleutherius was the first Christian lawmaker, and Lucius but the 'vicar, or vicegerent in his kingdome.'[132]

Broughton filled out his account in the much lengthier *The Ecclesiasticall Historie of Great Britaine* (1633), which he dedicated to the duchess of Buckingham and her mother, the countess of Rutland. The work was organized like its predecessor, in centuries, and extended to AD 600.[133] Broughton's catalogue of sources numbered over five hundred works, several in manuscript. Again, his strategy was to play upon weaknesses and inconsistencies in the protestant view of English church history and turn them to his advantage. He reiterated his assertion that Lucius had asked the pope 'for civill and temporall lawes, also to be allowed by him to rule heare in temporall affaires.'[134]

Broughton's clever work left his protestant opponents with little room to manoeuvre. They could not refute his fundamental thesis that English episcopal hierarchy was of apostolic origins without allowing the arguments of antiprelatical writers that episcopacy was not an historically established form of government. In a way, Broughton almost succeeded in reconciling Catholic and protestant positions on the history of the English church at precisely the time that Laud's Arminian hierarchy was attempting to find a *modus vivendi* with Rome. But no historian could be bothered to take issue with him. By then the 'best protestant antiquaries and historians' had other things to talk about.

CHAPTER TWO

Early Jacobean Historiography

The Historian as Satirist

There is perhaps no better place to begin a study of early Stuart historical writing than with Sir Walter Ralegh's *History of the World*, the product of a decade's imprisonment in the Tower under sentence of death.[1] In the English context, it remains an anomaly, the only work of its scope produced during the period (though similar European and medieval histories were plentiful); yet in it we find represented most of the currents of sixteenth-century historical thought. Ralegh was familiar with a wide selection of continental authors, including some of the foremost French *érudits*; he cited some seven hundred ancient, medieval, and modern writers. Though only four years separate his universal history from John Selden's *Historie of Tithes* (which we will encounter further on), the two are worlds apart.[2]

The frontispiece to the first edition of the *History*, supposedly designed by Ralegh himself and executed by the engraver Reinold Elstracke, is a complex image in the tradition of the Renaissance emblem; the brief text accompanying it (written by Ben Jonson, who prepared the *History* for publication), entitled 'the minde of the front,' scarcely does it justice. At the centre of the frontispiece stands the disrobed female figure of the *magistra vitae*, History herself, bearing aloft a globe representing the world. Her head radiates a nimbus of light, flames from which lick out, up towards the globe, and down to either side. The globe itself depicts the known world, including the continents of America and Asia; various biblical and historical events are represented on the globe, from the fall of man and the settling of Noah's ark to the English battle against the Spanish Armada. The globe is flanked on either side by two winged angels with trumpets, *Fama bona*, again radiating heat and light, and *Fama mala*, covered over with spots and enshrouded in cloud. These two figures stand on an entablature which is actually the fore-edge of a book, across which runs the title of the work, thereby suggesting the close tie between history and the authority of writing (and, in particular, of the Scriptures). The book/platform is supported by four columns. At the far left, the column labelled 'testis temporum,' displays what amounts to a library, including a table, arranged vertically. To its right stands a column called 'nuncia vetustatis,' the herald of antiquity, which displays hieroglyphics. To the right of the *Magistra* are two further columns, respectively the 'lux veritatis' and 'vita memoriae,' the former a Solomonic column representing wisdom, the latter entwined in vines. Between these columns stand the figures of *Experientia* and *Veritas*, an old and a young woman respectively. The former holds a staff and a plumb; the latter, Truth – significantly devoid of even the *Magistra's* minimal garb – bears her right hand aloft into a flaming, illuminating sun which itself radiates into and out of the nimbus which surrounds the central figure of the *Magistra vitae*. The *Magistra* herself stands on top of a skeleton (*Mors*) and a figure of everyman (*Oblivio*). And high up amid the clouds, at the top of the illustration, the reader can easily miss the hidden eye of providence which oversees all in this fusion of classical and biblical traditions.

The *History* begins with Creation and ends, five books and fifteen hundred pages later, with the Roman subjection of Macedonia in 130 BC. It is neither sacred nor profane history, but both: a division between the two simply does not apply to Ralegh's conception of history.[3] Such universal histories were not new. The first had been written in the fourth century by Eusebius, who had also compiled the first chronology to chart synchronously the events of all the great empires of the world. Borrowing mainly from the more recent chronologies of Beroaldus and Scaliger, Ralegh appended one of his own, enabling the reader to establish at a glance the date of an individual biblical or historical event and the events taking place elsewhere at the same time.[4]

Ralegh's dabblings in scepticism and his own contribution to the literature had left him with a dim view of the reliability of ancient histories.[5] However, instead of denying the possibility of historical knowledge outright, he sought shelter in bibliolatry. Though Ralegh knew no Hebrew and had to call on the assistance of his more learned friends, the Old Testament remained for him *the* unimpeachable source, a true story which relegated all profane histories to supportive positions; as he put it, 'all histories must yeeld to Moses' (I.viii.2: 130).

Only when the Hebrew account of the world ends should one turn to pagan histories:

> And if any prophane authour may receive allowance herein, the same must bee with this caution, that they take their beginning where the Scriptures end. For so farre as the storie of nations is therein handled, wee must know that both the truth and antiquitie of the bookes of God finde no companions equall, either in age or authoritie. All record, memorie, and testimonie of antiquitie whatso-ever, which hath come to the knowledge of men, the same hath beene borrowed thence, and therefore later then it, as all careful observers of time have noted: among which thus writeth Eusebius in the prooeme of his Chronologie. (Ibid)

Profane writers contend endlessly on the antiquity of nations. It is impossible to discern who is right. Where Jean Bodin postulated general rules against which specific claims could be judged, Ralegh, fifty years later, falls back on the Scriptures and their commentators, and on chronologers (I.viii.2).[6] He does not deny the possibility of human historical knowledge, but it is difficult to attain, so much of the record having been forever wiped clean by the ages. In the place of truth one finds only her bastard sister, 'Opinion, that can travaile the world without a passeport' (sig A1v).

There are two reasons for studying history says Ralegh, echoing Aconcio. The first is to reveal 'God's judgements upon the greater and the greatest'; the second is that history is instructive. 'In a word, wee may gather out of history a policy no lesse wise than eternall, by the comparison and application of other mens fore-passed miseries with our owne like errours and ill-deservings' (sig A2v). Typically, history lies in the realm of the definite and preordained, for God's judgments, though they *operate* in time, *exist* outside it. 'The judgements of God are for ever unchangeable; neither is he wearied by the long process of time' (sig A3r).

Not only are all events preordained; God's judgments are also consistent. The central theme of the book is that 'ill doing hath alwaies beene attended with ill successe' (sig A3r). A brief prefatory essay on English history since the Norman Conquest recounts the by now painfully familiar saga of the misdeeds of English kings and barons. God destroys the children of Henry I for their father's use of 'force, craft, and crueltie' against his older brother Robert. Edward III is criticized for putting his uncle Kent to death. This sin is visited on his grandson, Richard II, by

Henry IV, whose own grandson, Henry VI, is deposed, and so on. The familiar gloomy tale ends with Henry VII: 'a politicke prince hee was if ever there were any.' Henry was '(no doubt) the immediate instrument of Gods justice' in destroying the evil Richard III. Cleverly Machiavellian, Henry succeeds in casting blame for his unpopular acts on to his ministers. Yet this politic behaviour still draws the vengeance of God (sig B1r–v), and his grandchildren die heirless. Ralegh's ambivalence to the *realpolitik* of Tacitus and Machiavelli represents a conflict in early Stuart historiography between the duty to recommend effective worldly policy and the desire to advocate moral behaviour, a conflict which Ralegh (who was not alone) never resolved.[7]

The *History* is full of examples of the rise and fall of individuals and entire nations. Adhering closely to the universal histories of the Reformation,[8] Ralegh had no difficulty at all in reconciling the political life-cycle of growth, stasis, and decay with his belief that all history is a downward progression. The waning of every realm merely foreshadows the end of the world itself. Thus he reflected on the beginning of Carthage's decline in the first Punic war: 'So as this glorious citie, ranne the same fortune, which many other great ones have done, both before and since. The ruine of the goodliest peeces of the world, foreshewes the dissolution of the whole' (v.i.2: 314).[9]

Ralegh devoted several sections of his first chapter to an unexceptionable discussion of the relationship between fortune, providence and foresight. 'God foreknew all things before he had created them' (I.i.13: 18). His solution to the problem of free will was thoroughly traditional and was little more than a paraphrase of Boethius. Prescience does not cause things, though it knows them; providence, on the other hand, both foreknows and causes them: 'Now providence (which the Greekes call *pronoia*) is an intellectuall knowledge, both fore-seeing, caring for, and ordering all things, and doth not only behold all past, all present, and all to come, but is the cause of their so being, which prescience (simply taken) is not.' Predestination represents a 'special case' of providence confined to men and their salvation (I.i.13–14: 18–19).[10] Ralegh makes crystal clear the subordination of intermediate causal agents to God in a lengthy section 'Of Fortune.' Fortune herself he rejects as 'a power imaginary,' constructed out of ignorance, 'as if there were no cause of those things.' Men often use words such as fate or necessity to explain the inexplicable, 'because of many effects there appear unto us no certain causes' (I.i.15: 19–22).[11] Ralegh recognized fortune for what it was, a useful means of accounting for apparently random events, but not as an ultimate arbiter of those events. Thus he could continue to use the device himself, just as he could accept the influence of the stars and of fate as 'an obedience of second causes to the first' (sig D2r; I.i.11: 14; v.i.8: 356).

Where his biblical compass failed him, Ralegh was forced to rely on profane histories. Conscious of the spuriousness of some documents, such as Annius of Viterbo's pseudo-Berosus, a fifteenth-century forgery purporting to be the work of an ancient Chaldaean sage, he nevertheless used such material freely to fill in the holes left by more reliable works: 'where other histories are silent, or speake not enough' (II.xxiii.4: 570).[12] It was far worse to leave a gap in universal history than to use dubious sources. The loss of many profane sources had rendered absolute certainty impossible; Ralegh compared the historian with a geographer mapping territories 'whereof as yet there is made no true discoverie.' It would be harmful for a geographer to map territories he does not know, since he might drive ships on to rocks, and risk ridicule by future explorers. The historian, however, can do no such physical harm, and he can fill in gaps in ancient accounts by using conjectures arrived at by common sense, since *there is no chance that he will be challenged or supplanted by later historians' discoveries* (II.xxiii.4: 573–4): there is certainly no notion here of historical knowledge as a cumulative process.

Stephen Greenblatt has correctly observed that the *History* is 'riddled with uncertainties, ambiguities, and outright contradictions.'[13] Despite his apparently pragmatic attitude toward the historians' art, Ralegh ultimately remained a sceptic toward the past. Though it shares a common vocabulary with other histories, there is a dark element in the *History* which sets it apart from most contemporary works. Ralegh could not resist cutting historical legends down to size. One traditionally great figure of history was Regulus, the noble Roman who was released by Carthaginian captors only to recommend that the Senate not return its own Carthaginian prisoners, and who then kept his word by returning to Carthage to meet a horrible death. Ralegh pokes a critical finger at the legend, accusing Regulus of ostentation and (more perceptively) indicating that the historians who praised him all lived under Roman rule. 'Philinus, the Carthaginian, perhaps did censure it otherwise' (v.i.8: 356).[14]

Henry VIII received especially critical treatment. The hero of Hall's *Union* and the initiator of the Reformation posed a problem. How could one reconcile his many bloody deeds with their pious consequences? Most historians had ignored this problem, of necessity in the reign of Henry's daughter: Ralegh gave Henry his first real historiographical drubbing. His crimes, in addition to the decimation of the nobility, included an unwarranted attack on his peaceable nephew James v of Scotland, a deed which God repaid by ensuring that the Tudors should be superseded by the Stuarts. As with all his 'divine judgements,' Ralegh was hopelessly obscure as to their relation to the overall design of history. Would the Tudors have continued to rule if Henry viii had been a pleasant man? In a sense, the question was irrelevant, because Henry's evil deeds, like those of Richard iii, were pre-programmed (sig B1v).[15] Ralegh's villains are never the masters of their own fate. But neither was any other person in history. How one was supposed to learn valuable lessons from the past when the future was already mapped out is a tension in the didactic view of historiography that did not resolve itself in Ralegh's day, nor in the rest of this period; indeed, its resolution required an abandoning of strict predestinarianism that would only come slowly, in the course of the century.

The *History of the World* is in many ways the mirror image of that other English attempt at universal history, John Foxe's *Acts and Monuments*. Whereas the 'Book of Martyrs' bore witness again and again to the ability of God's human instruments to triumph over adversity, Ralegh's history shows the vulnerability of the human spirit to its material environment and to its own will to death.

There are few heroes in the *History of the World*, and a host of idols with feet of clay. The empires of the past have dissipated into nothingness: 'their very roots and ruines doe hardly remaine' (sig A3r). Any action will almost certainly issue in a peripeteia, bringing the vengeance of man or God upon the agent (eg, ii.xvii.7: 445; v.iii.17: 547–9; v.iv.1: 585), and if one finds a connecting theme at all it is that of revenge, both human and divine – it is significant that the *History* was written in the same decade as *The Revenger's Tragedy* and *The White Devil*. The work is almost an extended sermon on *Ecclesiastes*, a literary *danse macabre* with dissolution, mutability, and madness everywhere. There is no discernible *telos* to the chaos of historical events which the *History* depicts, not even the providential goal of man's salvation. Providence itself figures not as a benevolent guide of the collective human destiny, only as an unseen, incomprehensible and generally hostile force. This aimlessness is best illustrated by the *History*'s total lack of closure: it does not so much conclude as simply stop, in a famous apostrophe to death (v.vi.12: 776) which, for Ralegh, signified not the soul's reunion with the godhead but a 'long and darke night' (sig C3v) which entailed the annihilation of individual conscious-

ness. Life, like history, is for Ralegh in the end like Macbeth's tale – ·
told by a madman, full of sound and fury, signifying nothing.

This bitter attitude, not surprising in a disillusioned man who wrote,
like Boethius, with the axe dangling above his neck, extended to Ralegh's
views on the possibility of knowing the truth of the past. The popular
tale that its author burned the second part of the *History* upon concluding that it could not possibly be truthful may well be apocryphal, but it
invites thought. Ralegh *did* believe that the past held lessons for the
present; but it was the inability of the present to grasp these that most
fascinated him. To borrow a phrase from Stephen Greenblatt, Ralegh
fashioned himself not in the traditional historian's garb of tragedian,
helping the reader to profit morally or politically from the spectacle of
error and defeat, but as a satirist of human weakness and stupidity –
or, as he put it, as a 'fool in print' (sig E4v).[16] His abilities, he declared,
were not up to the task before him; even the 'disjointed and scattered
frame of our English affairs' would be less challenging than the history
of the world. Only the persuasion of friends had forced him to 'make
my thoughts legible, and myself the subject of every opinion, wise or
weak' (sig A1r).

The past itself, with all its men and empires, is dead and gone. It has
no existence in the present, for 'what-so-ever is cast behind us is just
nothing' (sig D1v). The writing and reading of history, then, is a worthwhile pursuit not because it is either rational or true, but only because
through it man can, using his intuition, 'live in the very time' that the
world was created (sig A2v): in Ralegh's world, the present has no greater
claim to sanity than the past. The reader, in short, must not be an idle
spectator; he must enter into each historical scene as it is played in the
text. Ralegh's vivid descriptions of places, and the strong sense of 'scene'
that they evoke for the reader, are not intended to achieve geographical
accuracy but only 'to make the storie the more perceivable' (II.iii.2:
249): their function is entirely aesthetic and has little to do with the
conveyance of truth. His colourful character portraits of Semiramis,
Alexander, Pyrrhus, and others emphasize, in a similar way, both the
wilfulness and the utter impotence of the individual before an unpredictable, almost capricious deity; they are examples to be pitied, not imitated. History is less something made by men and women than
something done to them.

There is no discernible process informing events except a wrathful
and unpredictable deity. There are few 'laws' except the ironic law that
whatsoever rises will soon come down with a crash: 'a day, an houre,

a moment, is enough,' muses Ralegh, paraphrasing Isaac Casaubon, 'to overturne the things that seemed to have been founded and rooted in adamant' (sig A4r). There is only the succession of historical moments, endless episodes from the past in which he invites the reader to participate: 'But what of all this? and to what end doe we lay before the eies of the living, the fal and fortunes of the dead: seeing the world is the same that it hath bin ... ? It is in the present time that all the wits of the world are exercised' (sig C2r).

The gloomy preface to the *History* spells out the sceptical, fideistic tenets by which the author intends to proceed. It sets the tone for the work as a whole, thereby allowing Ralegh to maintain his ironic attitude without having to interrupt his narrative with incessant reminders; it permits him to subvert his own account of the past before he has written it. No sooner does he make what *appears*, at a glance, to be a positive statement, than the reader is abruptly reminded of the lack of conviction behind it. When Ralegh remarks of Queen Semiramis that 'there never lived any prince or princesse more worthy of fame ... both for the workes she did at Babylon and elsewhere, and for the warres she made with glorious successe' (I.xii.4: 215), he is also telling us both that no subsequent monarch has come up to the mark and that even Semiramis' great works are now dust. And if the reader is ever, for a moment, convinced by the descriptive detail of the narrative, by the tidy precision of the genealogical charts, or by the lengthy considerations of such problems as the resting place of Noah's ark or the longevity of the Patriarchs, he or she is soon reminded that none of this is necessarily accurate – except, of course, where it derives directly from the Scriptures. The only truth is that it is 'God's will by which all things are ordered,' a truth that provides small comfort when the nature of that order as it exits on earth defies human reason. As for the secondary causes of events, they can never really be known. Where there is no scriptural authority, the best one can do is to offer inspired guesses or 'conjectures':

True it is that the concurrence of second causes with their effects, is in these bookes nothing largely described, nor perhaps exactly in any of those histories that are in these points most copious. For it was well noted by that worthie gentleman Sir Philip Sidnie, that historians doe borrow of poets, not onely much of their ornament, but somewhat of their substance. Informations are often false, records not alwaies true, and notorious actions commonly insufficient to discover the passions, which did set them first on foote.

The 'heart of man is unsearchable' and the historian must be excused · when 'finding apparent cause enough of things done' he forbears to search further (II.xxi.6: 536).

With respect to the venerable notion that history is philosophy teaching by example, Ralegh abandoned the practice of his earlier works, *The Maxims of State* and *Cabinet-Council*. These were the reflections of an active citizen, not a condemned prisoner who for ten years had been legally dead. Inspired by Machiavelli, they elicited historical laws from the similarities that existed between episodes in the past.[17] But in the *History*, Ralegh sounds less like the author of *The Prince* than like that other sixteenth-century Florentine, Guicciardini, who objected to Machiavelli's generalizations on the grounds that no two historical events are ever exactly alike. No matter what the apparent similarities between two phenomena, 'diversitie of circumstance may alter the case' (II.xxii.9: 554); in any event, has foolish man ever really profited from his past errors? 'Against the same stone whereat Xerxes, and before him (as I take it) Evilmerodach, had stumbled, Pyrrhus the Epirote hath dasht his foot' (v.iv.1: 585). The sole lesson of history is that we learn nothing from history.

In Ralegh's world, sudden change and innovation are the norm, tradition and stability the exception. 'All great alterations are storme-like, suddaine, and violent' (IV.i.1: 158). The only predictable phenomenon is the inevitable destruction of men, institutions, and empires at the hands of providence, operating through that irrational force which men have called fortune. Ralegh delights in considering the ways in which providence uses man to wreak its vengeance on man, and this leads him into an interesting explanation of the appearance on the historical stage of the occasional giant like Alexander the Great:

For so much hath the spirit of some one man excelled, as it hath undertaken and effected the alteration of the greatest states and common-weales, the erection of monarchies, the conquest of king-domes and empires, guided handfuls of men against multitudes of equall bodily strength, contrived victories beyond all hope and discourse of reason, converted the fearefull passions of his owne followers into magnanimitie, and the valour of his enemies into cowardize; such spirits have been stirred up in sundrie ages of the world, and in divers parts thereof, to erect and cast down againe, to establish and to destroy, and to bring all things, persons and states, to the same certaine ends, which the infinite spirit of the universall, piercing, moving, and governing all thinges hath ordained. (IV.ii.3: 174)

History is an interminable stage play from which even the reader cannot escape. In religion, men are all 'comedians' (sig C2v); in the conduct of their lives, they are ambitious fools, figures of farce grasping at straws. Even the 'heroes' of history are mere role-players; trapped on the stage of experience, they struggle against the inevitable, with predictable results. 'They shew an obstinate and giant-like valour, against the terrible judgments of the all-powerful God,' Ralegh reflects. 'Yea they shew themselves gods against God, and slaves towards men; towards men whose bodies and consciences are alike rotten' (sig D1r). When the final chapters conclude in a consideration of death, which alone 'can suddenly make man to know himselfe' (v.vi.12: 776), we have, in essence, the message of history as understood by Ralegh: in the long run, we are all dead.

The *History of the World* proved immensely popular; it held the same appeal as other examples of the late medieval and Renaissance fascination with death, decay, impiety, and folly, such as Sebastian Brant's *Narrenschiff*. It supposedly aroused the wrath of James I because it was 'too saucy in censuring princes.' It was one thing to criticize 'established' bad monarchs for tyranny, but quite another to issue the blanket condemnation of monarchs (though never of monarchy) which appears in the *History*. Yet the crown did little in response, save removing the author's name from the first edition;[18] this could not prevent it running into another edition in 1614, four more by 1630, and an abridgment entitled *Tubus historicus*, highlighting the history's apocalyptic scheme, in 1636. It was popular largely because it was the only book available in elegantly written English to reduce all history into a single, relatively coherent narrative. The public could ignore the ironic tone of the work to take pleasure in its great learning, could rely on Ralegh's maps and chronologies while paying little heed to his warnings about unseen shores. Perhaps most important, the *History* fulfilled the expectations of a reader who wished to have an instructive study of the past in which every event could be shown to have an underlying significance. To the Renaissance mind, entranced by notions of cosmic harmony, a history that put everything in its proper place was more than welcome.[19] But despite its mouthing of many of the platitudes of medieval and Renaissance historical theory, Ralegh's *History* is one of a kind. It reveals a deep pessimism about the capacity of human nature to understand or profit from the past, and that sets it apart from the vast majority of Elizabethan and early Stuart historical narratives.

The Union of the Kingdoms

In April 1605, Francis Bacon wrote a letter to Lord Chancellor Ellesmere on the subject of recent English history. It was miraculous, said Bacon, that the nation had survived the reign of a child, a near-usurpation by Lady Jane Grey, and the reigns of two women, one wed to a foreign prince, the other unmarried and heirless. That England had endured intact and avoided renewed civil war over the succession was a sure sign that England was under the 'providence of God.'[20] Bacon went on to suggest that since the two realms of England and Scotland were now 'joined in monarchy for the ages to come' as Great Britain, it would be an honour to the king if they 'were joined in history for the times past.' Bacon wanted 'one just and complete history ... compiled of both nations'; what he really meant was that he wanted Ellesmere's support in rewriting English history in order to incorporate its evident 'end,' the union of the monarchies.[21]

Bacon's plan hints at what would become a prominent theme of Jacobean historiography: that the union of the kingdoms was the end result of a divine plan, a fulfilment of the union of the Roses in 1485. The topic of union was, of course, not confined to historians. It was one of the most important political issues in the first five years of James's reign. Between 1603 and 1608 the king proposed a number of different plans which would bring about a 'perfect union' between the kingdoms. James wanted the island renamed the kingdom of Great Britain and he envisaged a single realm, ruled from London, under one law and practising one religion. Studies by Bruce Galloway and Brian P. Levack have added greatly to our knowledge of the union project, but little attention has thus far been paid to its importance in early Jacobean historical writing.[22]

The union ultimately foundered not so much because people were opposed to the idea in principle (everyone could agree that unity was better than division); but because no formula satisfactory to the king and the parliaments of both realms could be worked out. It had, how-ever, received a great deal of support. Bacon argued the case in the Commons, while in the Lords it was advanced by Ellesmere and Robert Cecil. Wider support came from outside Parliament. Bishop John Thornborough pointed to the metaphysical superiority of unity and argued for the 'necessity' of a union of the two realms under one name. Sir Henry Savile, the foremost classical scholar of his day, and an editor of medieval chronicles, wrote a tract on the union which demonstrated the historical advantages that had accrued to united realms such as Spain. The antiquaries Sir John Dodderidge and Sir Henry Spelman advanced similar arguments, while the civil lawyer John Hayward, having recently attacked Robert Parsons' assault on the inevitability of a Stuart succession, also lent his pen to the cause of the union. Hayward asserted that the far-sighted Henry vii had envisaged the joining of the kingdoms when he had married his daughter Margaret to James iv of Scotland. Sir William Cornwallis pointed out that the two nations 'differ not in language'; this was 'a signe that God ever meant to have us one kingdome.'[23]

The first historian to lend support for the union was John Clapham, a minor royal official. Born in 1566, Clapham had been a clerk to Lord Burghley since about 1590, in which position he would likely have encountered Burghley's ward, Francis Bacon, his elder by five years. It may have been Bacon who helped Clapham gain admission to Gray's Inn in 1602. The following year, Clapham was appointed one of the six clerks of chancery, a position he held until December 1618, a few months before his death.[24] Clapham kept the good graces of the Cecils even after Burghley's death in 1598. The old man left him £6 13s 4d a year for life, and in 1605 Robert Cecil helped him with the revisions for his *Certain Observations Concerning the Life and Reign of Queen Elizabeth*, which he had begun in 1603, and which is largely a biography of Burghley. Clapham also knew Sir Thomas Bodley, refounder of the Oxford library, and in 1606 he donated to the library five pounds, which were used to buy several books, including his own *Historie of Great Britannie* (1606). Clapham also contributed Latin verses to the memorial volume on Bodley's death in 1613.[25]

In 1590 Clapham had published a translation of part of Plutarch's *Moralia*, from the French version by Amyot; a year later he followed it with a Latin poem, based on Ovid. In 1602 he produced a *Historie of England* from Julius Caesar's invasion to the recall of the Roman legions in the fifth century AD. In 1606, when union fever was at its height, he reprinted the first section of this *Historie*, expanding it up to the reign of Egbert, who was the first Saxon king to rule over a united England following the age of the 'heptarchy';[26] with a new preface, this was his retitled *Historie of Great Britannie*.

Clapham had access to the public records, but he based his survey of Romano-British and Anglo-Saxon history, the period before such records began, on a small number of printed sources. These included Caesar and Dio Cassius, Tacitus' *Annales, Histories,* and *Agricola,* and a few English works: Bede, William of Malmesbury, William of Newburgh, and the St Alban's Chronicle, supplemented by the chronicles of Stow, Holinshed, and Grafton, and by Camden's *Britannia.* Clapham's original purpose was to compose a brief history of England free of the 'barbarous' language of the chronicles. He believed that though translations of Roman, French, and Italian histories were both available and delightful, 'yet is not the knowledge of them altogether so pertinent, and proper to us,' as knowledge of English history.

Not wishing to engage in controversy, Clapham kept an open if uneasy mind on the issue of Brutus and the other mythical kings. He accepted Arthur's historicity, but not the wholesale reliability of Geoffrey of Monmouth. Yet he was no antiquary poring over evidence. He took his role to be only that of an architect constructing a house from the raw materials of chronicles: a 'continued History' as he called it. His definition of historical truth was faith to his sources, not their criticism. He delivered things 'as I receved them from others.'[27]

By way of justifying the change of title from the *Historie of England* to *The Historie of Great Britannie,* Clapham confessed that his work had been occasioned by the union of the two kingdoms, a theme he had already heralded elsewhere as the culmination of English history:

> The Roman oft assayed, but in vain,
> To make a perfect Conquest of this Isle;
> The warlike Saxon and the sturdy Dane
> Pursued the same in tempering force with Guile;
> The Norman race, as forward as the best
> Made proof but sped no better than the rest ...
> Success of time hath made two kingdoms one,
> Now link'd in league, never to be divorced ...
>
> No wit, or power of Man, but God alone
> Hath wrought this work, for He Himself is one.

The history begins with the establishment of 'civill kinds of government' by the Romans. This had previously been unknown in the island, whose many princes ruled a variety of regions.[28] Under the Romans, these different kingdoms were maintained as 'a kind of absolute government in several.' The course of Clapham's narrative runs through all the stock events of British history, including the reign of Lucius. Clapham explained him as a kind of princeling, governing 'by permission of the Roman lieutenant,' yet accepted him as the legislator of a code which was superior to imperial law. Due attention is paid to the familiar tale of Constantine the Great's British birth and conversion, and the first part concludes with the Roman forces' evacuation of Britain (108, 136–9).

The second part consists of a potted narrative of the succession of British and Saxon kings to Egbert's accession in the ninth century. Clapham's choice of a *terminus ad quem* is significant. In summarizing the achievements of Egbert's reign in a brief epilogue, he commented that Egbert had 'ordained that the inhabitants (who had been a long time distinguished by divers names), should be made an entire nation, and being governed by one prince, should bear jointly one name.' He noted that this was a significant turning point in English history, the first foundation of an 'absolute government,' though Clapham knew that Egbert had really been only *primus inter pares* ruler of the heptarchy. 'The greatest part of the ile [was] made, in a maner, one monarchie, which forme of government it seemed in some sort to retaine, even during the continuance of the seven-fold regiment of the English Saxons, amongst whom some one prince was alwaies of greater power then other, & had a right of superioritie above the rest' (295–6).

There is little doubt that Clapham, whether or not he wrote at Cecil's behest, saw in Egbert's reign an analogue of James's union, establishing both a single realm and an 'absolute' rule. Significantly, he stressed that Egbert's monarchy was beneficial and that it had preserved the inherited constitutions of the different kingdoms. Indeed, it was not the consolidating Egbert but the earlier West Saxon tyrant, Sigebert, who had attempted to change 'the antient lawes and customes' (278, 293–6). More importantly, Clapham's book shows that support for the idea of union in no way depended on either a belief in Brutus or even an admiration of the ancient Britons, whom Clapham regarded as barbarians.

A more sustained and detailed effort to justify the union historically was published in 1607 by Edward Ayscu. Several men of the same name have been confused but there seems little doubt that the author of *A Historie Contayning the Warres, Treaties, Marriages, and Other Occurrents betweene England and Scotland, from King William the Conqueror, Untill the Happy Union of Them Both in Our Gratious King James* was the Edward Ayscu or Ayscough who lived between 1550 and

1616 in Cotham, Lincolnshire, a county in which several branches of the Ayscough family were prominent.[29]

As the title of his book suggests, Ayscu read his history backwards from the great consummation of 1603. In the dedication of the work to Prince Henry, Ayscu spoke of the union as an act of God designed to strengthen British protestantism against the papal antichrist. He wished to rewrite Anglo-Scottish history, he said, to harmonize the conflicting and hostile accounts of English and Scottish historians.[30] Unlike Clapham, who merely used the reign of Egbert as a suggestive analogy, Ayscu actually fulfilled Bacon's wish that the two kingdoms be united in history. An introductory chapter on the first inhabitants of the island asserts a common parentage for Scots and English; all were descended from ancient barbarian tribes such as the Goths, as the Britons descended from the Gauls and their father, Gomer, grandson of Noah (12–20). The whole work is permeated by the belief that union was inevitable and preordained in the fullness of time. Like Clapham, Ayscu did not accept Brutus as the first king of all Britain, and he followed Camden in deriving the name 'Britain' from the barbarous way in which the ancient people, the Britons, had painted themselves. The true founder of Britain was Gomer, whose name had underlying significance: when translated into English via Latin, Gomer meant 'ending': 'And herein the providence of God is also to be observed, who by the signification of the name of our first parent in this part of the world, foreshewed his purpose therein.' Ayscu, too, believed the Britons to be a barbarous lot, 'nurtured and framed to a more civile carriage of themselves' by Roman and Christian influence. His first chapter summarized events up to the Norman Conquest, which constituted a complete break with Saxon government: William abrogated all laws in order to establish his own, and the island, for the first time, fell under the sway of 'two absolute kings' (4–6, 11, 45–7).

Ayscu then narrowed the scope of the narrative to Anglo-Scottish relations. Quoting from a charter he found in the thirteenth-century chronicle of Roger Hoveden, he established that King William of Scotland had done homage to Henry II of England in 1175, thereby supporting one of the arguments of the unionists and reassuring the reader that England had remained the dominant state (68).[31] Ensuing wars between the two realms are treated by Ayscu as a breaking of fealty: thus Alexander II's invasions of England in 1215 and 1217 were duly requited with his death in 1249: 'the heavie hand of the Lord ceassed not here' (78, 89). Edward I, that archetypal good king, conceived 'how exceeding beneficial it would be to both nations, if by any good meanes they might bee united and made one monarchie,' and began the subjugation of 'the rebellious Scots' (90, 123). Ayscu was capable of showing respect for Scottish heroes like William Wallace, but he had no doubt that God intended England to rule Scotland. This absolute subjugation might have been accomplished by Edward III, but the time was not ripe. Edward frittered away his efforts in France, though Scotland was 'a more convenient and fit member of the crowne of England, then the one halfe of France' (177). The two kingdoms had much more in common with each other than either had with France, sharing the same climate and being 'so like in there language, lawes, manners, customes, complexion, constitution of bodie and disposition of minde' (275). In advancing his case for the similarity of the two nations, and by repudiating the Anglo-French connection, Ayscu thus virtually ignored the fact that the ruling aristocracy of England had remained part of a predominantly franco-phone, continental-oriented culture until the fifteenth century.

The union was brought one step closer by Henry VII's union of the two houses and by the marriage of his daughter to James IV. The latter, after making the initial mistake of assisting the pretender Perkin Warbeck, soon foresaw that the kingdoms would one day be united and that this would be advantageous to Scotland. Ayscu unconsciously undermined his own case here, for many anti-unionists were afraid that the benefits of union would all accrue to Scotland, which could offer little in return (242, 247–8).[32]

The union nearly took place once again when a marriage between Mary Queen of Scots and Edward VI was temporarily considered, but again the hand of providence restrained the wills of men (321). The rest of the sixteenth century brought the two realms closer together under the great princes Elizabeth and James. Ayscu discreetly ignored the 'auld alliance' between France and Scotland, though his fear of 'that man of Rome and his agents,' evident throughout, is demonstrated by his attribution of the death of Mary Stuart to Spanish and papal plotting and by his explicit attack on Robert Parsons' view of the succession issue (388, 393–4).

Ayscu's work was more sophisticated than Clapham's, because he used a larger body of sources and frequently printed charters and treaties to support a point and because he also managed to write an *explanatory* history of the union, a thematic narrative which traced it from its origins to its consummation, rather than merely justifying it by an analogy with an earlier reign. Like Hall's chronicle sixty years earlier, but much more concisely, Ayscu's history describes a movement from division to unity. He was putting new wine in an old bottle: reapplying the metahistorical framework of Hall in order to make the union of the *kingdoms* (he does not merely say *crowns*) appear inevitable. For him and others, the union – which in 1608 was not quite dead – was a providential goal through which the events of English history could be interpreted in a meaningful pattern. Accordingly, he judged the people and events of the past by their contribution to the present. Ayscu's historiography is thus whiggery in its nascent form, a middle ground between the apocalyptic teleology of biblical, medieval, and Reformation sacred history, and the secular, constitutional teleology of the later English whig tradition.

As events turned out, the union of the kingdoms did not occur for another century. James abandoned his plans in 1608, though he continued to style himself 'King of Great Britain.'[33] As a historical theme, it dominated the first decade of the century, and echoes of it would be heard even after that. Rubens would depict Britannia's union of England and Scotland among the scenes of his famous Banqueting House ceiling in the 1620s, while poetic panegyrists needed little encouragement to return to the subject as occasions such as Queen Anne's funeral permitted:

O happy union! labour'd long in vain,
Reserved by God to James his joyfull raigne,
And Annes; O blessed couple so esteemed,
By all fore-knowing Jove, that He them deem'd
Worthie each other, and to wear that Jemme
Blest Britaines now united diademe.[34]

The union cut across all types of historical writing, from extended narratives like Ayscu's, to panegyric and drama, and to legal scholarship. In 1605 George Saltern, a Bristol lawyer and member of the Middle Temple, presented the king with a manuscript of his treatise *Of the Antient Lawes of Great Britaine.* 'Some learned and grave gentleman' had asked Saltern 'to put in writing what I could touching your godly intention of the union.'[35] The *Antient Lawes*, which appeared in print later that year, was a follow-up to the lost first tract and argued that through all the invasions by Saxons, Danes and Normans, the ancient constitution, established by Lucius, had survived intact. As with Clapham, the point was to reassure those who, like Sir Edwin Sandys, feared that the union would subvert the ancient laws.[36]

Saltern is an example of the 'common-law mind' at its most insular, stressing the imperviousness of the laws to foreign influence and their resilience in times of great change. But quite unlike such legal spokesmen as Coke, he saw no need to insist on the 'immemorial' nature of the constitution. To push it back to a specific time, however remote, and to suggest the priority of a royal legislator was to have one's cake and eat it; it was a clever way of reconciling the authority of the crown with the antiquity of the laws, and it entailed no discussion of the influence upon those laws of the much later Norman Conquest. Thus was James I's union advocated at nearly the same time by one writer, Saltern, who thought the laws had not changed at all, and by another, Ayscu, who believed that the conquest had abrogated the ancient constitution entirely.[37]

Unlike the more subtle Ayscu, Saltern tied his case to Brutus' coattails: his arguments depended in large measure upon placing absolute trust in the already much-doubted legends of that mythical Trojan founder and of his latter-day successor, Lucius. The same can be said of John Lewis, whose *History of Great Britain* remained unpublished till 1729. A former barrister, Lewis had inherited from earlier Welsh authors like Humphrey Llwyd and David Powell a reluctance to part with any aspect of British mythology. Some time after the succession he sent the king a proposal for a ten-book history, asking for his 'incoragement or discoragement.' The reaction must have been favourable, for Lewis sent six books of the work to James some time between 1605 and 1612.[38]

Lewis' purpose was to write a complete history of Britain leading from the founding of a unified kingdom by Brutus (who, he reluctantly conceded, was probably not a Trojan) to the reunion under James. He got only as far as Cadwallader, the last king of the Britons, whose prophecy that the British would rise again was recorded by Monmouth and had already served the Tudors quite well. Lewis' book was clearly modelled on Richard White of Basingstoke's, which he cites, but reveals an even less critical attitude to the ancient legends. Paradoxically, his is one of the most determined attempts to deflate the arguments of the detractors of Brutus and Arthur, from Polydore to Camden. Lewis rounds on these sceptics for dismissing Geoffrey of Monmouth's British history: 'a history ought not to be rejected for some fables in it.' Lewis' response was to accept almost everything: King Arthur appears in all his glory, complete with extended speeches.[39]

Cadwallader had already popped up as a prophet not only of the return of the Britons, but of their rule over the entire island, in a verse *Prophesie of Cadwallader* by the precocious William Harbert, who in 1604 was a twenty-one-year-old undergraduate at Christ Church, Oxford. Another Welshman, Harbert was probably distantly related to the Herberts of the earldom of Pembroke, and he dedicated his poem to Sir Philip Herbert, later the fourth earl. Assuming the persona of Cadwallader, the last British king, he eschewed a narrative to write Plutarchan parallel lives of English and Roman worthies up to and including James I, 'our second Brute.' Taken together, these provided a 'prophecy' of the way in which Cadwallader's dream of the return of the Britons would be fulfilled in the new king of 'Britain.'[40] Harbert's poem was neither a work of antiquarian research nor a narrative history, and it is unfair to judge such works by the same standards that apply to prose historians such as Clapham and Lewis, much less by those of modern scholarship. It is worth observing, however, that the poem seemed sufficiently historical to attract the attention of Fulke Greville, a poet and patron much interested in the lessons to be drawn from the past. Greville briefly considered Harbert for his chair of history at Cambridge, but rejected him as too young.[41]

Like the makers of popular verse, would-be royal genealogists were also busy in the first years of the new reign, tracing the ancestry of James VI and I, and applying Hall's vision of history to the greater union of the kingdoms; again, Henry VII's reign served as a kind of prototype of James's. George Owen Harry, a parson whose *Genealogy of the High and Mighty Monarch, James ... King of Great Brittayne* was used by John Lewis, put the case more explicitly than most: 'By uniting and knitting together all the scattered members of the Brittish monarchy under the government of him, as one sent of God, to fulfill his divine predestinate will, revealed to Kadwallader, as our ancient histories doe testify, fifteene hundred yeeres past that the time should come, that the heires descended of his loynes, should bee restored agayne to the kingdome of Brittayne, which was partly performed in King Henry the seventh; but now wholly fulfilled in his Majesties owne person.'[42] Future melted into present and past as history confirmed the workings of prophecy.

In 1608, the year that the plans for union fell apart, another genealogy arguing the same case appeared, this time by Morgan Colman. Like John Clapham, Colman had once been a servant to Lord Burghley, and had tutored his son Thomas in 1588.[43] By 1596, he had become steward to Thomas Egerton, later Lord Ellesmere, James's Lord Chancellor; like Clapham, he may have drawn the inspiration for his contribution to the union propaganda of 1608 from this government connection. A brief poetic account of the succession of kings ends with the predestined union:

> Henry the seventh doth union first procure
> And in his bloud brings backe the Britaines raigne,
> Drawing in Scotland (of brave Albions Maine
> A famous moitie) by sweete Hymens hand ...
> All rights conjoind in Stewarts four-fold crowne
> Whose mystical high name the heavens decree
> Shall of their giftes the sole dispenser bee.[44]

Colman and Harry were no historians, but such prophetical panegyrics further illustrate the belief that a divine plan had been consummated, a sense which would provide the theme for Samuel Daniel's *Collection of the Historie of England*, the most sophisticated full-length narrative of medieval English history. It also figured, though much less prominently, in the longest account of English history published in the period, John Speed's *History of Great Britaine*.

John Speed and the Labyrinth of Ambiguity

John Lewis had referred to the ancient times depicted in Geoffrey of Monmouth's *British History* as a 'labyrinth.'[45] The further back in time the historian looked, the thinner was the source material and the rarer were the verifiable facts. The dearth of evidence in the period before the Norman Conquest meant that the course of English history was *ambiguous:* the more remote the period under examination, the more ambiguous it became.

This meant that there was much wider room for conjecture, invention, and outright disagreement about remote antiquity than about more recent periods. No one had any trouble agreeing on the course of later medieval history, as we have already seen. This held less true of ancient times: George Saltern and Edward Ayscu, with radically different opinions of the effects of great events such as the Norman Conquest on English law, could both argue in favour of the union of the kingdoms. Beyond the relatively sure ground marked off by the Norman Conquest, however, the sea was extremely rough. Although a number of legends had been seriously doubted or at least cleansed of the patently fabulous, most writers were reluctant to make a definitive statement. It was far safer to repeat a story wholesale, to present the varying 'opinions' to the reader and let him decide, or to skirt the issue entirely and refer the reader elsewhere.[46] A great deal of ink had been spilled over seventy-five years in defending or prosecuting such legend-makers as Geoffrey of Monmouth and Annius of Viterbo, but no one had as yet dared to synthesize even these limited debates – to utter even a tenuous 'last word.' Perhaps because of its cobwebs, distant antiquity attracted not only narrative historians, but antiquaries; in the study of the old English past (the classical past, we shall see, presented fewer problems) the approaches and interests of the antiquary and the historian overlapped. Ayscu, Lewis, and White all leaned as heavily on the *Britannia* and *Remaines* of Camden as on classical histories and medieval chronicles. For most historians of the early seventeenth century, a recent authority such as Camden carried as much weight as an old chronicle.

Many late Elizabethan and early Stuart historical writers agreed that the history of England needed to be rewritten in the form of a continuous narrative rather than a chronicle. The case against chronicles was three-fold. Sir Henry Savile was pained by the corrupt Latin of the medieval chronicles, a point with which Edmund Bolton would concur two decades later.[47] Others objected that chronicles and annals (the skeletal lists of a year's events) related nothing but the event itself, with no reference either to prior or motivating causes, and no attempt to piece the events together into a picture of a whole reign or series of reigns. Bacon, for one, wished above all that 'events be coupled with their causes.' Finally, it was objected that the biased opinions of popish monks were not to be credited, though no one questioned the value of medieval chronicles as source material – they were still better than nothing at all.[48]

It is in the context of such turn-of-the-century hostility to the chronicle as a literary form that the writing of John Speed's *History of Great Britaine* must be understood: such objections could only be answered by a narrative history of Britain which aspired to the comprehensiveness of the best chronicles while avoiding their pitfalls. The Merchant Taylors' company had already produced a superb antiquary and reliable chronicler in John Stow, who had died very old in 1605. It was fitting that Speed, another tailor, should try to outdo him. As early as 1598, Speed had been patronized by Fulke Greville, who secured him a waiter's room in the customs house and the lease of a prebendal estate held of the chapter of St Paul's Cathedral by the Merchant Taylors' Company.[49] This freed the fifty year-old Speed from his former occupation and allowed him to concentrate fully on two projects: a complete geographical description of the realm in the form of detailed maps, and a comprehensive history of England from antiquity to his own time.

Though warned of the difficulties facing him by several 'judicious' friends,[50] Speed was undeterred. He made good use of his connections with the best antiquaries of the decade, especially Sir Robert Cotton, whose library was already the single biggest private repository of medieval manuscripts and charters in the kingdom. The first four books, the geographical section published as the *Theatre of the Empire of Great Britaine*, incorporated maps by Christopher Saxton, John Norden, and others (sig 6P3r), as well as a few by Speed himself. The history itself presented a bigger challenge and ultimately proved too much for an individual. Having suffered for years from the stone, Speed found it necessary to ask Cotton for help assembling materials. Cotton first found him an assistant, Edmund Bolton, a London recusant then in his mid-thirties, who in 1610 had published a treatise on the theory of heraldry, *The Elements of Armories*.[51] Later, Cotton provided Speed with a rough narrative of the reign of Henry VIII which took account of the foreign perspective offered by Guicciardini, and he drew up from the *Valor ecclesiasticus* and the charters in his library a list of the monasteries and abbeys in England prior to the dissolution (786–802).[52] John Barkham or Barcham, a prebendary of St Paul's and the chaplain to Archbishop Bancroft, provided his knowledge of numismatics and wrote the reign of King John for the *History*. Barkham may also have written the reign of Henry II, though this was initially assigned to Bolton.[53] Francis Bacon provided a fragmentary account of Henry VII, and John Davies of Hereford lent Speed a manuscript pertaining to Lambert Simnel's rebellion. John Clapham provided copies of the rolls of parliament, and Sir Henry Spelman helped Speed with the section of the *Theatre* on Norfolk. George Lord Carew, who had made large collections of Irish history in the course of several years there, may have helped Speed with Irish affairs, though these receive comparatively little attention in the *History*; Carew, a former envoy to France, also wrote the life of Henry V. The herald William Smith assisted Speed with his genealogies. The final product, published in 1611, was written by Speed from the collections, sketches, and lives provided by Bolton, Cotton, and the others, though it is impossible to tell with how much revision on Speed's part. Cotton acted as a kind of associate editor, checking the proofs for Speed before printing.[54]

The principal difference between Speed and the chroniclers he tried to surpass was that the *History* was – or tried to be – a continuous narrative, in which one paragraph led to the next. It was based loosely on two humanist models, the *Anglica historia* of Polydore Vergil and the recent history of France by Bernard Girard du Haillan, and it played upon Bacon's distinction between 'perfect history' and chronicles.[55] Instead of merely repeating what his sources told him, Speed took a critical look at them. He had read Bodin's *Methodus* and knew that the further back one went in time, the more elusive became the truth. 'The records of Great Britaine are eaten up with times teeth,' he lamented (153). Nevertheless, many of them had survived – enough, he thought, to glean from them a reliable, true history.

Histories were the record of the past, commemorating the accomplishments and fates of the most famous peoples and places, and saving them from oblivion. 'For when as empires and kingdomes, common weales and cities, do end and perish, yet the histories thereof do remaine and live.' True to his humanist aspirations, he believed that history also served as the educating mistress of life, the light of truth (sig 6P2r; 152). Like Bodin, he felt that the history of an entire people was as instructive as a relation of the deeds of great men, but mainly because a whole country provided a bigger target to hit at a distance than did individuals.

The biggest problem facing an historian, observed Speed, was that histories before the Flood are 'uncertaine' and from then till the first Olympiad, 'fabulous.' Men had not always kept a record of events. The Greeks before Herodotus and the early Romans had been primitive and unlettered. In Britain the Druids, who had ruled Britain before the Romans, were 'merely barbarous, [and] never troubled themselves with care to transmit their originals to posteritie.' The stories that had survived had become contaminated with the fables of poets. Antiquity was 'a labyrinth of ambiguitie,' and it was impossible to tell with any certainty what had been done when, and by whom. Even the names of the first inhabitants of Britain are: 'things so farre cast into the mistie darknesse of obscuritie and oblivion, that there is no hope left us, so lately born, to discover them' (153, 157–8). Therefore, it was safer to sketch the *verifiable*, the manners and customs of a people as a whole, and draw moral lessons from its rise and fall.

Speed had absorbed this sceptical attitude to the details of the earliest history both from his antiquarian friends and from foreign commentators such as 'learned Bodine.' This was no Raleghesque statement on the impossibility of achieving historical truth; it was simply a pragmatic recognition that one could only go so far back before the signposts disappeared. Speed believed that where reliable histories were available (the Romans were the best) the truth would emerge. But he never felt very happy dealing with uncertain antiquity, even in the Saxon period, and he could scarcely conceal his relief when his narrative arrived at the Norman Conquest. 'I am lastly approached to these times of more light, and unto affaires of more certaine truth' (153–4, 411).

Paradoxically, it was precisely when dealing with the distant past that Speed was at his best, and the early part of his *History*, which he liked least, is of much more interest to a modern reader than the later sections. Speed was the first English historian to incorporate non-literary evidence into a historical narrative for more than its curiosity value, and he was forced to do so by the contradictions and *lacunae* in the written record. Having obtained Roman, British, and Saxon coins from Cotton, he had them engraved for inclusion in his book. (The engraver, he complained to Cotton, was an unreliable man, and many of the spaces set aside for coins had to be left blank.) Cotton also allowed Speed to see and print the inscriptions on a number of ancient altar-pieces, and Speed was able to use the inscriptions to establish with greater certainty the names of several ancient British kings (173, 175, 219, 228, 239).[56] Since the data on individuals were so sparse, Speed focused on the collective history of the groups which had populated the island. He included chapters on the 'customs' and 'manners' of the Britons and Saxons, examining their pagan religious rituals, which he despised as 'diabolicall superstition,' their 'inhumane sacrifices,' and their rudimentary and minimal clothing.

The use of such evidence was in itself unoriginal, though rare in narrative histories prior to this time. Speed had read as much in Camden, Clapham, and Richard Verstegan. The discovery of the savages of the New World in the previous century had given historians an idea that civilizations develop from a primitive stage, though their truncated view of the expanse of time did not allow for any kind of 'evolutionary' theory. It would no longer suffice to depict a Briton or a Roman in the garb of an Elizabethan soldier (167–8, 286).[57] A growing familiarity with external descriptions of ancient Britain by classical writers drummed this point in, but it could not inculcate an appreciation of the worthiness of individual cultures, nor any sort of romantic approval of the noble savage. Speed offers a perfect example: drawing on Tacitus and Caesar, 'the best recorders of kingdoms affairs,' he described the early Britons as a savage painted race, naked except for chains worn about the neck, who knew no proper manners until the invading Romans made them 'more civill.' Life for them was truly nasty, brutish, and short, even if they did have civil government of a sort. Ignorant of the benefits of monarchy, they were 'governed rather after the manner of an aristocratie, that is, by certaine great nobles and potent men, then under the command of any one as an absolute monarch' (170).[58] On the other hand, argued Speed, Britain was an aristocracy with a difference. It was really a collection of little monarchies, for whereas in a classical aristocracy 'the rulers are all peeres of one common wealth,' in ancient Britain the nobles were sovereign rulers, 'as many princes' over several autonomous 'publike weales' (ibid).[59]

The description of civilization and customs as opposed to the straight-forward relation of politics proved too difficult for Speed to sustain as he moved on in time, and as his narrative sources proliferated, after the Danish invasions, he too became essentially a narrator of events. The inscriptions and coins previously used as evidence now became unex-plained decorations to his chapter headings, simply showing the image of the king whose reign was about to be recounted. By modern standards, the earliest parts of the *History* are the most exciting, for nowhere had history and antiquarianism ever been blended so well. But it is import-ant to remember that contemporaries would not have seen Speed's book in this light, and Speed himself regarded this as a deficiency, forced on him by the dearth of facts. One *had* to discuss the more general aspects of history, not because they were intrinsically more important, but because it was impossible to be precise as to dates and deeds. While rejecting Brutus, the Trojan descent, and much of the British history quite explicitly, Speed accepted a pruned version of the Arthurian leg-ends, though he was frustrated by the lack of firm dates for Arthur's successors, as all his sources gave them differently. 'Such extremes are wee driven unto,' he sighed, 'that have our relations onelie from them' (316–17, 319, 385–6).

Speed followed the blueprint for reading ancient historians laid out in Bodin's *Methodus*, though he could never achieve Bodin's philosophic vision of the past. Bodin himself had not seen the reconstruction of the origins and cultures of ancient peoples as an end in itself: for him it served as a prolegomenon to the understanding of politics for 'history for the most part deals with the state and with the changes taking place within it.' Like Bodin, Speed also believed that 'divine vengeance' was a ruling force in the subjugation of one people to another (281–3, 385).[60] Bodin's own chapter on the origins of peoples had been designed to discover general rules against which the truth or likelihood of assertions could be judged; Speed adopted his criterion of a common language to explain the British and Gaulish joint descent from the ancient Cimbri (883ff). Speed regarded his investigations into the distant past not as an exciting exercise in historical anthropology, but merely as a necessary and difficult clearance of foliage before his proper business as a historian could begin.

Once he became sure of his sources, Speed found it much easier to turn them into a series of regnal narratives; the *History* becomes what most histories of the period were – one damned king after another. Points previously buttressed in marginal notes by half a dozen citations now got one. We can see this process at work in his recently discovered notebook on the Yorkist kings. For Edward v and Richard iii, Speed largely reprinted More's history verbatim, though he attempted to supplement it with notes from Commynes, Hall, Grafton, and Stow.[61] He cut out transcripts from these histories, assembled them together on a page and added his own reflections on the meaning of the events described – literally 'scissors-and-paste' historiography!

It therefore comes as no surprise that Speed's assessment of individual reigns and of the course of English history towards the union of the kingdoms is entirely derivative. It is clear from his notebook that he actually believed the union to be the final stage of an intricate divine plan – there was no need to write an insincere panegyric in an unpublished manuscript. Elizabeth of York should have married the king of France, 'but better destiny attending her, she was reserved to ... marie with the only heir of Lancaster which was Henry of Richmond, afterward king of England,' from which marriage sprang 'James our great soveraign and great Britanes monarch.' Yet in no sense is the union either a crucial motif, as it had been for Clapham and Lewis, or the central organizing theme, as it was for Ayscu. Although there are remarks aplenty to hint at the benefits to be gained for two kingdoms under a single ruler, these do not figure prominently in the organization of the book.[62]

A devout protestant, Speed was as interested in sacred genealogy and history as in profane, and he enjoyed a ten-year licence to provide such genealogies for the Authorized Version of the Bible. Some time between 1616 and 1618 he presented James Montagu, bishop of Winchester, with a life of Christ in which Speed sought to prove that Jesus was an earthly king, descended from David. The tract shows a protestant, perhaps even a puritan, piety which also pervades the *History*.[63] Although sceptical of the prodigies, omens, and natural signs recorded by pagan historians, he did not balk at attributing great historical events directly to God's intervening hand, without reference to earthly agents.[64] The affinity with Ralegh is striking, though the two were very different writers. Whereas Ralegh generally raised God to the position of supreme cause, working through suprahuman but subdivine agents such as fortune – the 'concatenation of means' – Speed often referred to God alone.

Moreover, Speed did not blend his pious judgments with the political observations made by Ralegh. If he lacked Ralegh's bitter acumen and wit, he also lacked his political cynicism – one looks in vain for any kind of Machiavellianism in Speed's *History* (670).[65] Though he could criticize Henry III as 'a prince whose devotion was greater than his discretion,' he blamed the unrest of Henry's reign on 'papall oversway-ings,' noting that 'God almighty did strangelie deliver him.' Edward I's subordination of Wales is not hailed as a good idea, but simply as the timely execution of God's will: the Welsh were going the way of the Romans, British, Saxons, and Danes before them, for 'the ruin of a nation is by God decreed.' The four nations, like the four world empires, each came to an end on schedule, 'fulfilling their times by heavens assignement' (sig 6P2v, pp 321, 385, 539, 544).

Speed's verdicts on individual kings were a function of his religious convictions, which manifested themselves in a preference for biblical rather than classical similes and parallels.[66] In general, he cast his characters in moulds built decades earlier by the great martyrologist, Foxe. This holds true even in the reigns for which he had considerable assistance. King John, as furnished by Barkham, is a good prince, the noble victim of papal incursions and monkish poisoners. Speed even doubted John's murder of his nephew, Arthur of Brittany, which he dismissed as the fabrication of hostile chroniclers: 'But not to trouble our selves with refuting a gooses gagling against Foxes true relation; easie it is to observe the hatred of monks against that king, both in thus procuring his death then, and his dishonour (a second death) in their slanderous inventions ever since' (506). Similarly, Henry VIII is 'a most magnanimous and heroical prince.' His minion, Cromwell, rises not through fortune but through God as a 'pillar for the gospels defence.' Speed even accepts the German historian Johannes Sleidan's statement that Anne Boleyn was a full-fledged Lutheran, while dismissing Nicholas Sanders' account of Henry VIII's unfortunate second queen along the way. The quarrel of the two Seymour brothers in Edward VI's reign is laid not at the door of the duke of Northumberland, but ascribed directly to the devil, 'so subtle is the old serpent' (574, 621, 753, 770, 779, 809). Speed had comparatively little to say about Elizabeth, since he knew that Camden, a 'farre more noble pen,' was then writing her life, but he consistently described her as Deborah leading God's people to victory over the pope and Spain. For Speed, if a king was both active and religious, he had a sure recipe for success. Not prudence but piety was 'the soveraigne ornament and safety of soveraigne princes'; the best thing Speed could say about a ruler was not that he was a shrewd or 'politic' prince but that, like Henry v, he showed 'how divine a beautie Christian goodnes hath' (839, 841).[67] The use of material derived from Cotton, Bacon, Guicciardini, and Machiavelli made little impact on what was didactic narrative of the moral and religious, not political kind.[68]

For all its failings, which were evident to many readers even at the time, Speed had provided a convenient summary of English history. His work was reprinted and revised several times and thoroughly eclipsed the chroniclers as a standard work of reference with a good index. It was regrettable, though hardly surprising, that he abandoned his ambitious antiquarian approach for a straightforward political and religious narrative. But it is worth remembering that compendia, even today, remain difficult to write: the tension between wit and information, between an elegant style and fullness of substance, has proven a thorny problem for historians at all times.

Sad Stories of the Deaths of Kings

The virtues of Speed's book appear more clearly when compared with those in the work of his immediate successor, William Martyn, who was born in Exeter in 1562. Martyn was admitted to the Middle Temple on 1 May 1582 and called to the bar in 1589, having first been educated at Broadgates Hall (Pembroke College) Oxford. He returned to Exeter, where his family was prominent, and served as its Recorder from 1607 until his death in 1617. Martyn likely knew both George Saltern and Sir George Buck, master of the revels (on whom more below), who were his contemporaries at the Temple, and perhaps also John Barkham, who also came from Exeter. But aside from these connections, he was removed from the centre of historiographical activity, in London, and to some extent insulated from its influence. A certain provincialism, with a discernible hostility towards centralizing forces, may explain why his history has nothing to say on the union of the kingdoms, though this admittedly had been a dead issue for six years by the time Martyn wrote.[69]

Youth's Instruction, Martyn's first work, was a Polonian exercise offering his son, Nicholas, advice on living virtuously and avoiding sin. He had nothing to say about the uses of history here, though he mixed a few historical examples, plucked mainly from Richard Grafton, with classical and biblical ones.[70] Then, in 1615, he published *The Historie, and Lives, of the Kings of England* to the death of Henry viii. Unlike Speed, Martyn had nothing against chronicles as such, and he used the words 'chronicle' and 'history' interchangeably. He did complain that the 'histories of this kingdome are frequently interrupted by too too [*sic*] many intervening occurrences, and by a multitude of extravagant observations' – a vague criticism which could apply equally to the chronicles' digressions or to the moralizing of Speed. If his objections were to excessive didacticism, then Martyn broke his own rules, for his is one of the most sententious histories of the period.[71]

Perhaps following the lead of Samuel Daniel, whose *First Part of the Historie of England* had been published two years earlier, Martyn avoided peering back beyond the Norman Conquest. He began with the end of the Saxon period and the victory of William, the rightful king, who unfortunately turned out to be a great dissembler and tyrant, ruling England 'as a conqueror, with more policie than by profitable laws' (*Historie*, p 2). Besides making frequent pessimistic Tacitean observations on human behaviour, Martyn occasionally indulged in outright invective against his story's villains. He turned the observation of Holinshed that Richard III could never rest securely in his tyranny into a curious, scathing lecture directed at Richard himself rather than the reader: 'But wicked and bloudy tyrant, let such as hate thy vices, demand of thee some questions; and then thou shalt plainly see, and be thine own judge, whether this land did ever breed a more ungodly monster than thy selfe ... Could not the gastly examples of Gods severe judgements, wrathfully poured downe upon such murderers, make thee affraid to kill thine owne kinsmen?' (247)[72]

Martyn was perplexed by the problem of the illegitimate king or usurper, and how such a prince could nevertheless prove to be an effective ruler. Stephen, for example, was a clear usurper, having ridden rough-shod over the title of Maud, Henry I's daughter and heir. But, argued Martyn, this was simply human nature, and 'if a kingdome may be obtained (though with the breach of a most solemne oath) no scruple is then made' (25ff). Yet Stephen proved a beneficent monarch. So did Henry I, who had usurped the throne from his brother Robert. John, though he finally gave in to papal pressure, was personally 'very wise, politike and wonderfull valiant' (49–50), and even Richard III, monster that he was, made some good laws. For all his moral outrage at sin, Martyn the Exeter gentleman was more capable than Speed the pious merchant of judging a reign for its political consequences and of discerning the human motives behind events.

This never led him, however, to Ralegh's stark division of the political and religious spheres. If Martyn was lukewarm on King John, he was vitriolic in the condemnation of Edward II's many crimes. Edward's 'adulterous consortship of wanton curtizans, and shamelesse whores' led Martyn to offer perhaps the most scathing denunciation of that king before 1640. Like Ralegh a year earlier, Martyn ventured here onto thin ice (74).[73] Perhaps aware of this, he apologized for his description by pointing to the utility of the study of wicked princes. Just as good kings 'are crowned with many blessings from above,' so evil ones and their people 'are severely punished by God, before whom princes must fall as well as the common subjects' (77). Martyn protected himself partially with an unequivocal condemnation of any kind of rebellion, but he had no hesitation about calling a ruler a villain. It is clear enough, despite his half-hearted conclusion that Henry VIII was 'a famous, a worthie and a most noble king,' that he really thought the second Tudor an odious tyrant, 'busily imployed in cutting off his subjects heads' (321, 331). Unlike Speed, he had no illusions about Henry's motives for dissolving the monasteries. Sheer greed and personal spite against the pope were the immediate causes of the Reformation, whatever the godly consequences.

Martyn may have gradually grown bored with his history, for his account of the reign of Henry VIII amounts to little more than a rewriting of Stow and Holinshed, in something much like their chronicle format. He concluded with the wish that someone else 'will (with more sufficiencie) write the rest' (331). His book surpassed Speed's in realistic depiction of characters and analysis of politics, but fell short of it in another respect. In his own way, Speed had at least seen a pattern to history, and one reign led naturally to the next. Martyn contented himself with a series of unrelated biographies.

Ironically, despite his best efforts not to cause offence in his own assessment of evil kings, Martyn may have been too saucy in censuring Scottish princes. Instead of the noble and far-sighted James IV whom we saw in Ayscu, and who would turn up again twenty years later in John Ford's play *Perkin Warbeck*, Martyn's Stuart kings are blatant liars and political cynics. James IV committed a 'wilfull breach of his promise, and of the peace' by invading England in 1513; his son also practised 'crafty dissimulation' (285, 324).[74] Many years later, Thomas Fuller wrote that he had been 'credibly informed' that either these or other passages had angered King James. On 25 February 1615, little over a month after Martyn had dated his preface, John Pultar, a messenger of the king's chamber, was ordered to arrest the historian and bring him before the council. Martyn appeared on 14 March, but no one could decide what to do with him, and he was left in Pultar's hands. By 3 April the attorney-general – Francis Bacon – had prepared a case and charged Martyn with having 'written a history of England, wherin were many passages so inaptly inserted, as might justly have drawne some heavy and seveare sensure up on him for the same.' Bacon did not specify the offending passages, but it is likely that either Martyn's anti-tyrannical tirades or his observations on the Scottish kings caused his troubles. Fuller's statement that the king's anger eventually cooled seems correct, for the reissue of 1615 deletes nothing. Martyn acknowledged his fault in writing, and was soon released, but the shock proved too much for him, and he 'never recovered his former cheerfulnesse,' dying two years later.[75]

In Exeter, Martyn had enjoyed no access to manuscript sources of the type kept by Cotton, and his biographies were derived entirely from Stow's and Holinshed's chronicles. He included a number of documents, such as the articles of the deposition of Richard II, and a table listing by name all the dukes, earls, and other peers since the conquest, taken from Speed and Camden's *Britannia*. Nevertheless, his book proved popular, and was reprinted in 1638 with a continuation to the death of Elizabeth I by 'B.R., master of arts.' This sequel did not live up even to the modest ambitions of its progenitor. B.R. lifted his accounts almost verbatim from Camden's *Annales* of Elizabeth and Francis Godwin's *Annales* of Edward VI and Mary.[76] Speed, at least, had been honest about it.

With the exception of Ralegh's idiosyncratic book, the histories of the first half of James I's reign represent the early Stuart vision of history at its flattest and least complex. Although they differ on detail, and although several of them were occasioned by contemporary issues (in particular, the union), they broadly reflect a single outlook on the past, an outlook shared with the Tudor chronicles from which they drew much of their matter and from which, ironically, their authors were attempting to emancipate themselves – with only limited success. The works of Ayscu, Clapham, and the others clearly make ideological assumptions and political (as well as moral) judgments on the events and personages which they describe; because of the topicality of the union, they have a point to make, however much their authors lay claim to the historian's impartiality; consequently, they are more tightly argued and clearly organized than a late Elizabethan chronicle such as by Holinshed or Stow. The more general works of Speed and Martyn, less fixed on the inevitability of union, hang together less well, doubling back into the realm of the chronicle. Though both Speed and especially Martyn were capable of probing into the great political changes of the past, both lacked a real theme, a necklace on which to string their reigns; this is often a weakness of general histories, of whatever age. For Clapham and, still more, Ayscu, that cord was provided by the teleology of the union; for Ralegh, it was provided in quite a different way, by a severely pessimistic providentialism which made of history not a road with an obvious end, but a maze filled with divine judgments and quirks of fate.

It was still possible to write a general history, even after the heady expectations of James's early years had passed; there were ample models available among the ancients, and still others could be found in Renaissance historians such as Guicciardini. For the best example of such a history, a highly sophisticated and closely argued account of the evolution of England and her institutions into their current state, we must turn back to the court, and to the poetic vision of Samuel Daniel.

CHAPTER THREE

Samuel Daniel and the Emergence of the English State

History and Poetry

The frontier between history and poetry, between memory and imagination, provided a focus for much of the discussion of poetics in Elizabethan and early Stuart England. Despite the hard lines drawn between them by theorists from Aristotle through Sidney, many poets and playwrights picked history as their subject matter. Some even went so far as to try to combine the two, since the poetic and dramatic forms offered the writer ready-made subjects without binding him to relate the literal truth in the manner of a chronicler. Thus Ben Jonson would gloss his Roman play, *Sejanus his Fall,* with learned notes from his classical sources, though without ever pretending to follow them with complete accuracy: for him 'truth of argument' rather than literal truth was of greatest importance. Michael Drayton, influenced by the antiquarian researches of his contemporaries, versified *Britannia* and other chorographies as *Poly-Olbion,* adding some research of his own and inviting the promising young lawyer and philologist, John Selden, to provide notes and 'illustrations' for it.[1] Drayton's friend Dr William Slatyer (1587–1647) believed that 'Poesie should shadow historie,' since both drew lessons from the past. He tried to imitate Drayton in a narrative rather than a topographical poem. The result, his *Palae-Albion* (1621), was a kind of versified Speed, a regnal history from earliest times to his own, and though Slatyer, like Drayton, refused to be over-scrupulous in dealing with the myths of ancient Britain, he documented his tales with extensive marginalia – sufficiently so that Camden was impressed by the breadth of his 'historicall learning.'[2]

In practice history could provide the poet with an almost limitless stock of increasingly familiar material; yet there was no easy agreement on the correct mixture of two rival modes of discourse one of which, by consensus, dealt with the realities of the past insofar as they could be known, and the other of which painted timeless pictures of imaginary or idealized human behaviour. The criticism of history by poets such as Sidney is well known, as is the rejection as poetic fancy of certain medieval works – most notably Geoffrey of Monmouth – by some historians and antiquaries. Yet perhaps the harshest criticism of historical poesy came from those who knew it best. Drayton and Jonson, aware of the much greater freedom of expression that the poetic form offered the historical imagination, were nevertheless ill at ease with their own experiments in historical verse and drama. Drayton rewrote his account of the reign of Edward II, *Piers Gaveston*, several times, and was displeased by the reception of *Poly-Olbion*; and he and Jonson each in turn criticized Samuel Daniel, their older contemporary, who tried harder than any to effect a synthesis of poetry and history, verse and prose. Drayton thought Daniel 'too much historian in verse' because of his attention to detail. Jonson was even harder: 'Daniel wrott civil wars & yett hath not a battle in all his Book,' he sneered, adding that he was 'a good honest man but no Poet.'[3] From Jonson's point of view, Daniel had overlooked the nuances of style and expression that separate the narrative historian or chronicler from the more reflective mood of the poet. Many critics would agree that Jonson correctly identified Daniel's tendency to write prose in verse form, but he seriously misjudged the latter's ability to apply his poetic mind to an extended narrative of the past.

Subsequent generations have been kinder to Daniel, but at the cost of treating him as two men rather than one: the first being the poet and dramatist, the author of *Musophilus* and *Philotas*; the second being the prose historian and the author of *The Collection of the Historie of England*, with his lengthy verse epic, *The Civil Wars*, marking an uneasy transition between the two. On the whole, more attention has been paid to Daniel the poet than to Daniel the historian. Several students of Tudor and early Stuart historiography have praised his *Collection* for its intelligent and scrupulous use of sources.[4] More recently, Arthur B. Ferguson and Clark Hulse have illustrated Daniel's highly developed sense of literary and cultural change.[5] We still lack a detailed study of the ways in which Daniel's historical writing reflects both the general tenor of his thought and his critical response to the changes he perceived in the world around him, changes which were legal, political, and technological as well as cultural. It is possible, however, without neglecting the differences between verse and prose, to see Daniel's later views on political history as an outgrowth and development of his earlier essays on language and cultural evolution. Of the issues that compelled Daniel's attention throughout his literary career, the most important turned on his concepts of community, state, and law.[6]

Communion and Community

Although the idea of a 'community,' of a social collectivity bound together by common interests and a shared past, pervades his writings, Daniel rarely uses the term: he prefers the word 'communion,' which carries with it the religious overtones that Daniel saw in the political as much as in the ecclesiastical community. An Aristotelian concept which had been further developed by medieval scholasticism (of which, we shall see, Daniel was an admirer), *communitas* entails not only a concept of common *present* interests (political, economic, religious) but also one of shared identity, an identity best expressed in a people's attitude to its history. Yet the outlines of Daniel's vision of the past were wide enough to encompass more than English history alone; they stretch out and back to the beginning of Christendom, which for Daniel constituted a meta-community, a grand society within which all nations must exist in harmonious relation with the whole.

Any discussion of Daniel's historical thought must begin with his famous poem *Musophilus* (1599), a dialogue between two men, Musophilus and Philocosmus, on the virtues of learning and literature. Here not one but two competing notions of the world as a community abut on each other. The optimistic Musophilus, the defender of learning, views knowledge as the 'soule of the world,' as the medium through which ages past, present, and future are united:

> O blessed letters that combine in one
> All ages past, and make one live with all,
> By you we do confer with who are gone,
> And the dead living into councell call:
> By you th'unborne shall have *communion*
> Of what we feele, and what doth us befall.
>
> (lines 189–95, emphasis mine)

Letters allow us to hear the voice of those ancient nations who were wise enough to prize eloquence, that 'Powre above powres,' as highly as action, nations which 'Did with no lesse glory speake then do' (939, 988).

Musophilus, then, regards mankind as a diachronic community, transcending time through art and literature, which are more durable than the hardest tombstone (120–40). Philocosmus, his worldly friend, has a more pessimistic outlook. He does not dismiss learning altogether; he merely ignores all but its practical applications in the day-to-day world. Philocosmus has his own sense of mankind as a community, but in his case the community is that of the moment, of mundane commerce and politics. Discourse for him is communication with his contemporary fellow man, rather than with his ancestors or descendants. Philocosmus is attuned to an oral world which Daniel well knew had gone forever, a world in which the most fundamental human actions – love and hate, for instance – take place in face-to-face discourse. As one of Daniel's dramatic characters observes, written, and even spoken, language is unnecessary to an act that takes place solely in the present:

> Ah 'tis the silent rhetoricke of a looke,
> That works the league betwixt the states of hearts;
> Not words I see, nor knowledge of the booke,
> Nor incantations made by hidden artes.
>
> (*The Queenes Arcadia* 2159–62)

It should be emphasized that *Musophilus* is a colloquy, not a debate. It raises questions rather than resolving them, and the title character must not be taken as the authorial voice, closing off further thought as the poem winds down.[7] If anything, we will see in Daniel's later thought the triumph of Philocosmus the pessimist. Particularly significant are the attitudes of the two speakers to one of the bright beacons of the modern age, the then relatively new device of printing. For the optimistic Musophilus, the most effective medium of language is not prose but poetry. With an almost mystical fervour, he argues that the 'speech of heaven,' the divine 'numbers' that move earth and sky, demonstrate that 'Weaknes speaks in prose, but powre in verse' (980), verse which through the amplifier of the press can bestow immortality. Paradoxically, it is Philocosmus, the apparently vulgar, worldly man, who distrusts print precisely because it vulgarizes knowledge and removes it from the realm of immediate, oral communication. Though Musophilus urges him not to declaim against 'the swelling tide' and 'streame of words that now doth rise so hie' (928), Philocosmus is unswayable; he shudders with scorn and fear amid a hailstorm of libels, tracts, and pamphlets:

These strange confused tumults of the minde,
Are growne to be the sicknes of these times,
The great disease inflicted on mankinde. (447–9)

This is typical of Daniel: to stand in awe of the fame bestowed by writing and yet lament the instrument by which writing disseminates itself. In one of his earliest works, the sonnet-cycle *Delia* (1592), the poet inveighed against the book-pirates who had forced him to publish in order to preserve his verse from corrupt editions (*Poems*, p 9). In his poetic epistle, 'To the Reader,' he expressed the hope that he would be read 'So long as men speake English'; yet he feared that the press would immortalize his errors,

Which I do hope to live yet to retract
And crave that England never wil take note
That it was mine. Ile disavow mine act,
And wish it may for ever be forgot ... (lines 91–4, *Poems* p 5)

Happier the man who is forgotten completely rather than remembered, like the unfortunate Rosamond, in notoriety: Fame, she reminds us, is 'Of truth and falsehood both an equal teller' (*Complaint of Rosamond*, line 571). When, in the *Queenes Arcadia*, Amarillis warns Cloris that her betrayal of Amyntas may have driven the unfortunate swain to suicide, she threatens Cloris with a guilty conscience that will resemble a *printed* record of her crime: 'This deed instampt in bloody Characters / Within the blacke records of thine owne thoughts' (1824–5; cf 1827–9).

The printed book violates nature; it enforces slavish conformity to outdated customs and artificial rules; it enshrines error. 'It is not in bookes,' Daniel remarks elsewhere, 'but onely that great booke of the world, and the overspreading grace of heaven that makes men truely judiciall' (*Poems* p 139). The deed itself is what matters, not what men may write about it. Urging Prince Henry not to pattern his future reign after such would-be conquerors as Charles v and Francis i, but to rule in peace, Daniel recommends that the heir to the throne

learne to know your owne,
Which is a science wch doth more contayne
Then all the books, that ever yet were knowne.

Great acts spring naturally from a great soul, and 'Few letters serve for great heroicq mynds' ('To Prince Henrie' lines 230–6). Can we really believe that this is still the voice of Musophilus?

In *The Civil Wars*, much of which was written at about the same time as *Musophilus*, Daniel protests that print has broken down the boundaries between sacred and profane, and caused the dissolution of medieval Christendom into the disjointed, schismatic Europe of his own day. It is in this minor epic that we see the development of Philocosmus' line of thought most fully, particularly in the famous 'Nemesis' passage of Book VI. Nemesis is a kind of super-Fortune, the 'sword-bearer of th'eternall Providence,' who dictates the fall of states which are enjoying too much prosperity (*Civil Wars*, VI, 30).[8] She uses two weapons to work her will: artillery, which allows men to kill coldly from a distance, and printing, which nurtures heresy and schism (VI, 37):

And better to effect a speedy end
Let there be found two fatall instruments,
The one to publish, th'other to defend
Impious Contention, and proud Discontents:
Make, that instamped characters may send
Abroad to thousands, thousand mens intents;
And in a moment may dispatch much more,
Then could a world of Pennes performe before.

(VI, 37; cf *Musophilus*, 725)

Both devices involve the deferral, even the *cancellation*, of face-to-face interaction, but print had proven the more insidious. Daniel contrasts the piety and devotion of medieval Christendom, visible in those 'monuments of zeale' (VI, 33), the great churches and religious houses of the period, with the unbelief of his own day, when Christendom has ceased to exist, and universal belief has given way to a quest for certain knowledge and its inevitable byproducts: scepticism and dissent.

The effect of this is to 'loose the linkes of that soule-binding chaine' (VI, 35), universal Christian faith, which has united the nations of Europe as a family since the fall of the Roman empire. The Christian community dissolves in a conflagration of 'reform' and heresy of which England's civil wars of the fifteenth century provide a foreshadowing. Old Christendom, as Daniel points out in a marginal gloss, consisted of a great many small realms, none of which was either capable or desirous of destroying another. The Europe of print, artillery, and Reformation had become a continent of superpowers: Spain, France, and other previously decentralized kingdoms were now powerful enough to swallow their smaller neighbours through mechanized violence (VI, 28 and gloss).

But even if the community-in-time has been disrupted, the contemplative intellect can still find solace in the community-over-time, which exists in the remembrance of the past through letters. Here, Daniel is letting the voice of Musophilus speak again, albeit in muted tones: as in the earlier poem, this implied community carries with it a sense of duty, of pious communion between men and their ancestors. In the episode of *The Civil Wars* depicting the heroic deaths of the Talbots in France, the elder Talbot tells his son that they shall be remembered for all time; the son in response avows his desire to enter the 'rowle of Immortalitie' (VI, 83, 87). The poet's gloss to this holds that the blood of the Talbots, 'th'eternall evidence of what we were,' remains to unite 'our fathers, wee, and who succeed' (VI, 98). Similarly, in the *Queenes Arcadia*, Meliboeus – a Jacobean ancestor of Edmund Burke – advises his fellow citizens of their duty to leave to posterity,

The *Arcadia* that we found continued thus
By our fore-fathers care who left it us. (2215–17)

In a world where there has ceased to exist any community of humankind above the nation, it is more important than ever that man commune with the past and future through art and learning.

Law and State

Yet, as Philocosmus knows, we must learn to live in this world, in our own time, amid the distractions and pains of daily existence. The individual, and by extension learning and the arts, can flourish only within a stable political environment. Confronted with the fact that in his day there was no longer any sense of a collectivity of Christian peoples, Daniel set himself to examine a different but related problem: the emergence of that *national* community which he saw rising in the fifteenth and sixteenth centuries. It is this kind of community which he consistently calls the 'state,' and it is the English state in particular which attracted his attention.

Letters, faith, and piety may suffice to hold together a decentralized community such as medieval Christendom, but they cannot hold a modern state together; they cannot integrate its disparate elements into an organic whole. The 'state,' the political focus, as we shall see, of Daniel's later writings, and especially of his prose historical works, might be defined as a special case of community, one formally constituted by laws and possessing that absolute autonomy expressed in the famous preamble to the 1533 Act of Appeals: 'this realm of England is an empire, and so hath been accepted in the world, governed by one supreme head and king ... unto whom a body politic, compact of all sorts and degrees of people divided in terms and by names of spiritualty and temporalty, be bounden and owe to bear next to God a natural and humble obedience.'[9]

The ties which bind England are her laws, which together with religion are 'the main supporters of humane societie' (*Collection*, p 107). Daniel gives us some idea of the importance of law in his verse epistle to the great common lawyer, Sir Thomas Egerton, Baron Ellesmere, James I's lord chancellor:

> Now when we see the most combining band,
> The strongest fastning of societie
> Law, whereon all this frame of men doth stand.
>
> ('To Sir Thomas Egerton,' lines 13–15)

This is not the law of codes or even of 'written lines,' but of equity and custom. The law exists in the hearts and mouths of men, and though it leaves written traces, it derives ultimately from unwritten use, practice, and prescription – what the common lawyers of Daniel's day considered 'artificial reason.'[10] Daniel's formulation bears a striking resemblance to a somewhat later definition of the common law, expressed in an epistle to Ellesmere by Sir John Davies, as an unwritten *jus commune:*

> Therefore as the lawe of nature, which the schoolmen call *jus commune*, and which is also *jus non scriptum*, being written onely in the heart of man, is better then all the written lawes in the world to make men honest and happy in this life, if they would observe the rules thereof. So the customary law of England, which we doe likewise call *jus commune*, as comming neerest to the lawe of nature, which is the root and touchstone of all good lawes, and which is also *jus non scriptum*, and written onely in the memory of man (for every custome though it tooke beginning

beyond the memory of any living man, yet it is continued and preserved in the memory of men living) doeth far excell our written lawes, namely our statutes or acts of parliament.

Daniel would have had no difficulty agreeing with Davies that a law engraved on the soul is preferable to one contained in books, or in concurring that 'our native common lawe is farre more apt and agreeable, than the civill or canon lawe, or any other written lawe in the world besides.'[11] The English legal system had escaped the stupefying complexity of European laws, worsened by 'These great Italian Bartolists,' as Daniel terms the continental civilians ('Egerton' line 102). English law has been generated in a number of case-by-case decisions, by judges exercising a 'spirit of right' over the centuries, and by parliamentary statues ratifying and clarifying custom; it was not the work of disinterested scholars compiling and glossing an abstract code (126–30). Moreover, whereas in some nations rulers and ruled resort to different legal codes – Daniel probably had in mind the tensions between civil law and local customary laws in realms like France – English law unites rulers and ruled: 'And this is that great blessing of this land, / That both the Prince and people use one Barre' (193–4). The common-law courts of Common Pleas and King's Bench, and the local justices and circuit judges who administer that law in the provinces, provide points of contact between king, nobility and people; Daniel's 'one barre' is apparently broad enough to include courts technically outside the common law proper, such as that of chancery.

Much of Daniel's legalism has its origins in the writings of Lord Ellesmere, which show that same historical awareness for which Daniel has become famous.[12] In his speech on the case of the *post-nati*, the chancellor argued that all laws are historically created, time-bound customs, not eternal principles (divine law and the law of nature excepted); from this derived the ability of the modern legislature to amend and add to custom by statute. Conversely, the ancient *dicta* of the Greek lawgivers, Solon and Lycurgus, so praised by contemporaries, had to be understood within their temporal context. The Greeks were historical – that is to say, flawed – beings who lived in 'popular states' and were enemies to monarchy; they were intolerant of other political systems and 'accompted all the world barbarous, but their owne countrey of Greece.' Their laws thus had limited application to a polity such as monarchical England.[13]

Daniel's *Defence of Ryme* echoes Ellesmere's antihellenism and expands it into a general revaluation of the contribution of Greece to modern civilization. This short essay, often seen as the pinnacle of Daniel's historical achievement, contains in skeleton that view of history as an organic process which Daniel would flesh out in the *Collection*. The *Defence* is most notable for its sympathetic view of the Middle Ages. Daniel seems to have read the writings of Loys (or Louis) Le Roy and adopted his belief that cultural history was progressive; nations rose and fell in a natural cycle, but each new society could achieve new heights in the arts, rising beyond its predecessors. Thus the Greeks merited credit in their own day, and the Romans in theirs, but not at the expense of medieval Englishmen.[14] Daniel has no patience with the view that the Middle Ages was nothing more than a millennium of superstition, bloodshed, and barbarism; echoing Ellesmere, he warns us not to succumb to the hubris of the Greeks, who 'held all nations barbarous but themselves.' One might scorn the Goths, Vandals, and Lombards who had 'overwhelmed, as they say, al the glory of learning in Europe,' yet these same rude tribesmen 'have yet left us still their lawes and customes, as the originalls of most of the provinciall constitutions of Christendome.' If nothing else, this should 'cleere them from this imputation of ignorance' (*Poems* 140).

How could one condemn an age that had produced the Venerable Bede, Walter Map, Roger Bacon, and William of Ockham? These were but a few of 'an infinite catalogue of excellent men, most of them living about foure hundred yeares since,' whose monuments of learning survived in the present. How could one not but admire an age which produced the great Gothic churches? 'Let us go no further,' he enjoins us, 'but looke upon the wonderfull architecture of this state of *England* and see whether they were deformed times, that could give it such a forme' (*Poems* 143). Daniel needed the comfort of myth, the glitter of a golden age, but he found this in the thirteenth and fourteenth centuries, not in classical antiquity or, *a fortiori*, in its artificial sixteenth-century revival. If anything, his own time marked a cultural decline from an earlier peak, and in his verses for Prince Henry Daniel expressed the belief that England's 'ymmoderate humors' might some day make her 'prey unto some Gothicq barbarous hand' ('To Prince Henrie' lines 86–7).

If it is 'law' that constitutes a national community, then the abuse of law, excessive litigation, can destabilize it. The Elizabethan and early Stuart decades were a period of rapid legal change, visible in the reports of Dyer, Plowden, Coke, and other judges. Much of this change was occasioned by a litigiousness which to us suggests wide respect for the legal system, but which Daniel detested. Here again, his fixation on the later Middle Ages proves critical: he distinguishes clearly between the great jurists of the past, on the one hand – Bracton, Thorpe, Fortescue, and worthy modern heirs such as Ellesmere (*Civil Wars* VII, 77) – and, on the other, the hundreds of pettifogging parasites who foment and then feed on the disputes of others. In the *Queenes Arcadia* (1606), Daniel presented his vision of the perfect community. Surrounded by mountains, the Arcadians have dwelt for generations free of the infection of outsiders:

> They live as if still in the golden age,
> When as the world was in his pupillage. (1027; 1031–2)

One of the villains of this drama is the scoundrel lawyer, Lincus, who aspires to introduce endless litigation among the placid Arcadians. Lincus observes that there is no legal system in Arcadia, no 'frame composed, whereby / Contention may proceed in a practicke forme.' Nor do the Arcadians have any occasion to go to law, since they have no property:

> But having here no matter whereupon
> To furnish reall actions, as else where;
> No tenures, but a customary hold
> Of what they have from their progenitors
> Common, without individuitie;
> No purchasings, no contracts, no comerse,
> No politique commands, no services,
> No generall assemblies, but to feast,
> And to delight themselves with fresh pastimes.
> (*Queenes Arcadia* 981–9)

Lincus will starve in Arcadia; he must either leave, or endeavor to teach the citizens about property,

> ... by drawing them
> To appr'hend of these proprieties
> Of *mine and thine,* and teach them to incroch
> And get them states apart, and private shares. (1000–3)

An ideal society, yes – but as imaginary as More's Utopia. Daniel knew full well that real, historical men understood *meum et tuum* and that they required laws to protect it. When Lincus's friend Alcon asks if it is possible that a society 'Can with so little noyse, and sweat subsist,' Lincus replies that it may, as long as its citizens have yet to transform 'their state of nature' into one of social degree and possession. But such conditions pertain nowhere in the real world, where flesh-and-blood Lincuses daily ply their trade, and do very well for themselves.

Daniel had travelled in France and Italy, and he seems to have been passingly familiar with the works of Jean Bodin, though he never explicitly cites them.[15] He subscribes to Bodin's innovative currency-surfeit theory of the sixteenth-century price rise (*Collection* p 204). When he criticizes Richard II for misuse of the state's treasure, 'Whereof he being the simple usager / But for the State (not in proprietie)' (*Civil Wars* I, 85–9 and gloss), he comes close to expressing Bodin's doctrine that the most absolute of princes must use public moneys for the benefit of the people, its legitimate owners.[16] Other examples of Daniel's debt to Bodin can be found throughout the poet's works. One of the most striking occurs in the *Queenes Arcadia*. As this play opens, two old citizens, Meliboeus and Ergastus, lament the decay in their ideal commonwealth. Meliboeus comments that he has never known, 'So universall a distemperature / In all parts of the body of our state' (14–15).

His comrade replies that he believes the 'very aire is chang'd,' that the 'wholesome climate grows more maladive' (25–6). These two ancient pessimists are clearly caricatures of those old men, pilloried in Bodin's *Methodus*, who pass their dotage lamenting the good old days; Ergastus even spouts Bodin's celebrated version of the medieval theory of the influence of climate upon society.[17]

But the most important and consistent borrowing of Daniel from Bodin occurs in his adoption of the latter's modern usage of the word 'state' (*estat*), rather than more conventional terms such as the 'common weal,' or *res publica*, or the realm, to denote the national political community.[18] When Daniel uses the word 'state,' he does not mean it in any traditional sense of 'estate' or 'status'; he uses it as a shorthand for the sovereign association of prince and people under the law. Though the notion of England as an autonomous, sovereign realm had grown relatively commonplace since the 1530s, Daniel's version of national sovereignty differs from many earlier Tudor formulations in its emphasis on the supremacy of the law rather than the independence and freedom of the monarch. The interests of the state must take precedence over those of all men, even kings, because it has a corporate existence which transcends the brief frame of time allotted to the individual. As Henry VI exclaims, surveying the carnage of Towton: 'Stay, Edward, stay. They must a People bee, / When we shall not be Kings' (*Civil Wars*

VIII, 23). A king without a people is nothing, and Henry realizes, albeit too late, that 'What chayre so-ever Monarch sate / Upon, on Earth, the People was the State' (VIII, 31). However great he may be, the individual is but a part of a more important organic entity – a microcosm within the political and social macrocosm. To venture beyond one's proper place is to erode this relationship, to the harm both of part and whole. Daniel's subscription to the microcosm/macrocosm theory appears quite explicitly in the final stanzas of the *Civil Wars*, where the earl of Warwick's stoic confessor reminds him that the man who remains detached from events and content with his lot is himself a king:

> Heere have you state inough to be a cort
> Unto your selfe; here, where the world attends
> On you, not you on it, observed sole:
> You, elsewhere but a part, are heere the whole.
>
> (*Civil Wars* VIII, 96)[19]

Occasional uses of 'state' occur throughout Daniel's poems, and in a manuscript draft of his *Panegyrike Congratulatory* to James I in 1603, he consciously changed the line, 'Shake hands with union, O thou mighty Isle' to 'Shake hands with Union, O thou mighty State.'[20] It is in the prose *Collection*, however, that one finds this concept of the state as an entity in its most articulate form. The *Collection* is indeed a history of England's development from a collection of primitive tribal regimes into the strong centralized monarchy of Daniel's own day. His decision to write such a work, announced in the preface to the 1609 edition of the unfinished *Civil Wars*, represents a shift in focus from the community of the world as a whole to its microcosm, the single state of England. The *Civil Wars* had been undertaken in the dark, waning days of Elizabeth's reign, 'a time which was not so well-secur'd of the future, as God be blessed now it is' in order to demonstrate the horrors of civil dissension (*Civil Wars* p 67); Essex's fatal rebellion, with its resemblances to medieval aristocratic conspiracies, undoubtedly reinforced his sense of foreboding.

Daniel's Scepticism

Though the unexpectedly peaceful succession of James I in 1603 engendered in Daniel a more optimistic perspective on history, he could never rule out the possibility of future civil discord. The ongoing discussion during James's first decade of the relationship between royal prerogative, parliament, and common law suggested that even a 'full-grown' state could come to grief. With his respect for the common law, he could not but be alarmed by such legal conflicts as Bate's Case (1606), in which the royal right of imposing was held up above a customary freedom from new non-parliamentary taxes. Daniel's anxiety sprang from no fear that James would prove a tyrannical absolutist, but from an intense dislike of *any* judicial conflict between prince and people which might disturb the balance between law and monarchical power that had been settled over the centuries. If one no longer needed to fear a recurrence of the merely political, dynastic struggles of the fifteenth century, it was still possible to fret over an unnecessary repetition of the constitutional conflicts of the thirteenth and fourteenth centuries.

In this regard, the past could serve the present. In 1609 it seemed to Daniel that the lessons of England's constitutional history needed retelling, but this disciple of Sidney had lost his conviction that such lessons could be taught in verse. It was precisely because *Philotas* had, intentionally or not, pointed to parallels between the downfall of its hero and that of the earl of Essex that Daniel had found himself in disgrace in 1605.[21] That experience had taught him a number of things: that it was more discreet to deal with the greater issues of English history than to dwell on personalities and risk offending modern readers; and, sadly, that any historical utterance written in poetic or dramatic form was open to misinterpretation. The poor reception of *The Civil Wars* had hammered the point home: Daniel concluded that he would be heard more clearly if he spoke in prose, the 'common tongue of the world' (*Civil Wars* p 69). Yet he could not speak to all: he carried Philocosmus' distrust of print into the production of his own history, the *First Part* of which was issued in 1612 as an edition limited only to the author's friends. Even in subsequent reprintings of the *First Part* (1613) and its longer, final version, *The Collection of the Historie of England* (1618), unlicensed printing of the history was prohibited by order of the king – a royal favour to a man who had suffered much at the hands of unscrupulous publishers.[22] The *Collection* is a humanist lesson book in the tradition stretching from Machiavelli to Bacon, but it is aimed at select readers in positions of influence, not at the wide audience catered to by recent chroniclers and historians such as Holinshed and Speed. Daniel wrote not as Thucydides, for future ages, nor even for the reading public of his own day, but for the select few he deemed fit to share his thoughts.[23]

In this respect, he emulated another French writer whose similarly contemplative temperament and critical mind had affected him even more strongly than Bodin. Michel de Montaigne's influence on Daniel was so profound that it demands fuller treatment than can be afforded here. Daniel's brother-in-law, John Florio, had translated Montaigne's *Essays,* and Daniel contributed a commendatory verse to this, extolling the virtues of the essayist as much as those of the translator. Not surprisingly, this commences with yet another spasm of chronic bibliophobia:

> Books, like superfluous humors bred with ease
> So stuffe the world, as it becomes opprest
> With taking more than it can well digest;
> And now are turn'd to be a great disease.[24]

It is the great virtue of Florio's translation that it frees Montaigne's pen from vassalage to one monarchy and allows him to dwell among 'the better world of men, / Whose spirits all are of one *communitie*' (lines 65–6, my emphasis).

Lines of affinity between Montaigne and Daniel are easy to find. The controversial *Philotas* may have been inspired by Montaigne's essay 'Of Conscience,' in which the luckless lieutenant of Alexander is cited as an example of an innocent man tortured into a false confession. Similarly, Daniel's epistle to Egerton is in part a versification of Montaigne's essay, 'Of Experience.' But the similarities are most pronounced in the attitudes of the two men toward history. For Montaigne – a real-life Musophilus – history provided a forum for dialogue with the past. The humblest schoolboy could 'associate, by means of histories, with those great souls of the best ages.' The purpose of such an exercise was not the memorizing of trivial details, dates, and numbers of those killed in battle – these were in any case obscure and often unknowable – but the judgment and evaluation of historical events:

> But let my guide remember the object of his task, and let him not impress on his pupil so much the date of the destruction of Carthage as the characters of Hannibal and Scipio, nor so much where Marcellus died as why his death there showed him unworthy of his duty. Let him be taught not so much the histories as how to judge them.[25]

Daniel adopted precisely this pragmatic attitude to the past. The historian's task, to be sure, was to depict the truth as accurately as possible: even in the *Civil Wars,* Daniel claimed to 'versifie the troth, not poetize,' while in the history he made repeated reference to an appendix of source material which he had assembled but never published.[26] But the *what* of history was of less interest than the *why*. Daniel confessed himself to be 'more an honorer than searcher of antiquities' (*First Part* p 240); as he would write in the *Collection*, it was the lesson of an event and its significance in the overall design of history that was important. 'The 10. of July, and the 6. of August, with a yeare over or under, makes not a man the wiser in the businesse then done, which is only that hee desires' (*Collection* sig A4r). The past had a shape, and it was the historian's task to reveal this, by searching for the patterns that give discrete occurrences or individuals a long-term significance. Daniel would have concurred with Montaigne's statement that 'all things hold together by some similarity ... As no event and no shape is entirely like another, so none is entirely different from another.'[27] The solution to the riddle of the historical record lay in finding that quality which connected the particular with the general, the momentary historical event with the past as a whole. If this is scepticism, it is at least of a much milder variety than Ralegh's.

Like Montaigne, Daniel held to what would now be called a relativist's view of history. Throughout his works we find him opposed, like Montaigne, to the 'mightie tyrant,' custom, which restrains nature,

> And so inchaines our judgements and discourse
> Unto the present usances, that we
> Must all our senses thereunto refer.
> ('To Florio' line 48; *Queenes Arcadia* 2567–9)

Enslavement to the customs of the past was not the same as reverence of the past; when we elevate any era, including our own, above others, we commit an affront to history, for in the grand scheme of things every period, every people has contributed to man's present condition. Montaigne knew that the judgment passed by one age upon another was a matter of perspective:

> Things may be considered in various lights and from various viewpoints: it is principally from this that diversity of opinions arises. One nation looks at one side of a thing and stops there; another at another.[28]

Daniel, too, warned against judging earlier epochs by the standards of the present. Making dwarves of the men of the past was as bad as making them into giants:

> it is but the clowds gathered about our owne judgement that makes us thinke all other ages wrapt up in mists, and the great distance betwixt us, that causes us to imagine men so farre off, to be so little in respect of our selves. We must not looke upon the immense course of times past, as men over-looke spacious and wide countries, from off high Mountaines and are never the neere to judge of the true Nature of the soyle, or the particular syte and face of those territories they see. (*Poems* p 143)

Breaking the narrative of the *Collection* at one point to engage in a brief apostrophe to Antiquity, he begs that she pardon the present for misjudging her 'according to the vogue, and sway of times.' Men deal with the past but as posterity, 'which ever thinkes it selfe the wiser,' will deal with them (*Collection* 101). Meliboeus repeats this admonition against believing that there is no other truth 'then the nations of the times, / And place wherein we live,' against thinking that 'all lookes ill, that doth not looke like us' (*Queenes Arcadia* 2571–2, 2575). Even the record of written history distorted the past. It was 'but a mappe of men,' vague and colourless, which could no more present the 'true substance of circumstances' – what we might call the 'past-in-itself' – than a mariner's map could accurately chart the bays and coves of an unseen coastline (*Poems* p 143).

Daniel's relativism was limited and counterbalanced, however, by his belief in the uniformity of human nature, as Arthur Ferguson has demonstrated. In the dedication to *Philotas*, Daniel points out that

> These ancient representments of times past
> Tell us that men have, doe, and always runne
> The self same line of action, and doe cast
> Their course alike, and nothing can be done,
> Whilst they, their ends, and nature are the same:
> But will be wrought upon the selfe same frame.
>
> (*Philotas*, 'The Epistle' lines 26–31)

This is perhaps Daniel's clearest comment on that essential humanness that makes us like our ancestors: by nature neither better nor worse, and psychologically likely to respond to similar circumstances in similar ways. Without such a belief the entire humanist theory of history would have collapsed. Yet the tension between relativism and uniformity, between custom and nature, is less crucial than it might at first appear: a humanist such as Daniel could believe in the consistency of human behaviour without having to affirm that the environment within which acts and utterances are created itself remained changeless. It is not men, but language, law, religion, and technology that have evolved. Mankind, like a 'frame' repaired piecemeal over the centuries, can be subtly modified by persistent change without losing its essential characteristics; the very fact that a practice or custom has continued long in use shows that 'nature hath thus ratified' it (Poems p 134).

The Shape of English History

Most of Daniel's history is devoted to the period after the Norman Conquest: Daniel was sceptical as to the possibility of recovering the remote past. Nevertheless, the few pages he devotes to the British, Romano-British, and Anglo-Saxon periods provide ample evidence of his views on the main currents of English history. Following another French model, the Histoire de France of Bernard Girard, sieur du Haillan, Daniel traced the development of a 'state' unified by law.[29] The Collection was to be divided into three parts: the First Part, from primitive beginnings to King Stephen; part two from Henry II, the first Plantagenet, to Richard III, the last of that line; and part three from Henry VII to Daniel's own day. Daniel did not get past Edward III (the point at which his Civil Wars begins) and the last part remained entirely unwritten; all we know of his thoughts on the Tudor period derives from his brief, incidental statement that it was: 'a time not of that virilitie as the former, but more subtile, and let out into wider notions, and bolder discoveries of what lay hidden before. A time wherein began a greater improvement of the soveraigntie, and more came to be affected by wit then the sword' (First Part sig A3r, my emphasis). This surface endorsement of the century just ended is at best half-hearted. Reiterating the concerns of Musophilus, Daniel continued to view his own age with a sense of loss, as an era of print communication, commerce, diplomacy, and bribery. The vast treasures of the New World had 'strangely altered the manner of this' by increasing prices and opening 'a wider way to corruption.' This is the world of Philocosmus, where even religion has been made 'an actor in the greatest designes of ambition and faction' (First Part sig A3r).

His own distaste for the Tudor ethos likely discouraged Daniel from writing about the period in greater detail. But there is another reason for the truncation of the *Collection* in 1377: most of the crucial historical developments, to Daniel's mind, had come earlier. There was thus no need to repeat the dismal tale of the *Civil Wars*, because what concerned him now was the constitutional and legal settlement of the thirteenth and fourteenth centuries, not the later dynastic struggle for the crown, a resumption of which he had envisaged a decade earlier. In comparison with grave matters of law and state-building, more ordinary political events now seemed trivial, even epiphenomenal.

In contrast to the fully developed state of his own day, the Britain of ancient times was a land divided among warrior chieftains. The ancient Britons, like their close relatives the Gauls, may have called their war leaders kings, but early Britain 'was no monarchie' (*Collection* p 2). As so often, Daniel was here putting into narrative form the thoughts of his patron Ellesmere, who had himself wondered 'whether in the beginning there were one or severall kingdomes in great Britaine.'[30] Daniel's familiarity with contemporary accounts of American savages suggested to him that civil government developed only when stimulated by external threat or internal anarchy. When it did develop, it was not always as a monarchy, and he accused those who thought that it had always been ruled by kings of failing to note 'the progresses in the affaires of mankind.' Daniel felt justified in dismissing Monmouth's 'line of absolute kings,' pointing out that since the ancient Britons were unlettered, the record of their rulers from Brute to Cassivellaunus must be the invention of a later age. Unlike Speed and Clapham, who regarded the ancient Britons as savage heathens, desperately in need of Roman and Christian civilization, Daniel assessed them on their own terms. A simple people, they were 'more just and honest' than later men (*Collection* 2, 6, 7). This Tacitean appreciation of the 'noble savage' by itself sets Daniel apart from his predecessors.

Not that Daniel thought monarchy a bad thing – on the contrary, it was the Britons' lack of it which allowed the Romans and then the Saxons to conquer them, at the same time that other barbarian tribes were dismembering the carcass of the Roman empire, a period at which 'there was no one countrey, or province but changed bounds, inhabitants, customes, language, and in a manner, all their names' (8–9).[31] Amid the 'generall dissolution,' the history of *England* began, 'with a new bodie of people, with a new state, and government of this Land, which retained nothing of the former' (9). Under the Saxons, England's evolution into a 'state' consisting of a single king, nobles and people, truly began. One by one, the Anglo-Saxon 'heptarchs' swallowed one another up: Egbert was first to rule the whole kingdom, though Danish raids prevented him from 'enjoying such a fulnesse of power, as that we may account him the absolute monarch of the kingdome' (10). Alfred continued his work, bringing in learned men – a point Daniel emphasizes rather more than Alfred's military victories – and erecting public schools. Finally, in the tenth century, King Edgar became 'the first, and most absolute monarch of this land' (12–13), primarily because of his willingness to take counsel from his bishops, 'who in that time of zeale held especially the raines on the hearts, and affections of men': as always, Daniel continues to take the measure of an age according to the criteria of learning and piety as much as those of politics.

But even this was only a temporary achievement, soon vitiated by Danish incursions and by the weakness of Edgar's successors. The really permanent developments began with the Norman Conquest, where the history proper begins. From William I and his sons, who were successively 'elected by the state' to rule after the death of the last English king, Harold II (30, 44, 51, 58), a new phase in English history commenced.

The Conquest and After

The Norman Conquest was a direct consequence of a collapse of English morals under Cnut and Edward the Confessor, during which time, as William of Malmesbury informed Daniel, the clergy had grown licentious, the nobility gluttonous, and the commons persistently drunken and lethargic (22). Nevertheless, the Anglo-Saxons' social institutions, and the progress they had made toward the integration of a single state, provided the foundations upon which the conquerors could build. Indeed, William's victory came so easily precisely because of the unique structure of Anglo-Saxon society. The system of frank-pledge, which Daniel calls the 'borough-law,' grouped householders into tithings, the members of which were responsible for one another's good conduct: 'These lincks thus intermutually fastened, made so strong a chaine to hold the whole frame of the State together in peace and order, as, all the most pollitique regiments upon earth, all the interleagued societies of men, cannot shew us a streighter forme of combination.' The borough-law was like a citadel built for defence: once captured, it could be used against its builders, making the state 'batter her selfe with her owne weapon' (38–9).

The Conquest thus proved nearly as complete and thorough as the earlier defeat of the Britons; it illustrated the point, first made in the *Defence*, that a 'barbarian race' might overcome a civilized society beset by what he elsewhere called 'Asiatique weaknes' ('To Prince Henrie' line 84). Like earlier invasions, the coming of the Normans contributed to the evolution of the English language, which though it 'remained in the Saxon, yet it came so altered in the habit of the French tongue, as now we hardly know it, in the auntient forme it had' (*Collection* 23). Daniel the cultural historian is again at work, describing the process of linguistic change as he had in the *Defence*; he pays similar attention to alterations in fashion, architecture, and lifestyle introduced by the invaders.

The most critical changes, however, lay in the field of law. Daniel stresses that Norman laws constituted a complete break with the past, whatever the Conqueror's pretence that he observed the laws of Edward the Confessor. Although the Conqueror maintained a few Anglo-Saxon laws for show, his most significant contribution to English history was the introduction of Norman customs. Prior to this there had been, Daniel believed, 'no universall law of the kingdome.' Every province of England had been governed according to her own peculiar customs, sharing nothing save religion and certain universal principals such as the law of property ('the universalitie of *meum & tuum*') and the *ius innatum*, 'the common-law of all the world, which we see to be as universall, as are the cohabitations, and societies of men' (37). William I had brought 'New termes, new constitutions, new formes of pleas, new offices, and courts.' He had even attempted to make French the language of governance, but with limited success; only that curious fossil, legal French remained, for the conquerors were soon to be swallowed up by the conquered through intermarriage, 'as rivers to the Ocean, that changed not it, but were changed into it' (ibid). The settlement of a national legal system had at least one unfortunate side-effect: it excited that litigious spirit, thitherto alien to the English, which Daniel so despised.

In company with the most perceptive antiquaries of the day, Daniel recognized that the law of his age was a Norman tree with a few scattered roots in the Anglo-Saxon, Danish, and British earth.[32] Or, to use his metaphor, 'though there might bee some veynes issuing from former originals, yet the maine streame, of our Common-law, with the practise thereof, flowed out of Normandie, notwithstanding all objections can bee made to the contrary.' Those who imagined an immemorial constitution dating back into the pre-Norman, even pre-Saxon past, would search in 'an uncertaine vastnesse, beyond our discerning' (36–7). This six-hundred-year pedigree did not make the common law any less vener-able in Daniel's view than it had in the opinion of so learned an authority as Ellesmere, who also believed that only 'some remenants and patches' of the pre-Conquest law remained, and who dated the English constitu-tion from William I's introduction of feudal tenures (37).[33] Daniel thereby mediates between James I's views, according to which the kings of Scotland derived their power over the laws from the conquest of their distant ancestor, Fergus,[34] and those of MPS such as Thomas Hedley. Hedley had stated in the Commons on 28 June 1610, during the debate on impositions, that the law predated the Norman invasion and was both immutable and immemorial. His speech, one of the most concise statements of the nature of the common law to be uttered in the early years of James I's reign, merits some attention because it casts Daniel's views into sharper relief.

Hedley defined the law as primarily an unwritten set of practices, dependent 'wholly upon reason and custom,' though he also believed that every principle or maxim of English law was contained somewhere in the country's law books. Though it derived from time immemorial, it was forever growing to serve the interests of the commonwealth: 'The common law is a reasonable usage, throughout the whole realm, approved time out of mind in the king's courts of record which have jurisdiction over the whole kingdom.' Thus Hedley's view was in some ways quite similar to that of Daniel. Both acknowledged that law was a changing body of conventions and customs; both believed that the strength of the law lay in its predominantly unwritten, uncodified char-acter. Yet Hedley still stuck firmly to the belief that, whatever its gradual modifications, the law as a whole, and the institutions which put it into practice, dated from before the Conquest. Thus Magna Carta, which Daniel would regard as an essentially new measure, Hedley saw as simply a charter for the restoration of liberties 'obscured' by the Conquest.[35]

Daniel would prove unimpeachably orthodox in condemning the deposition of legitimate kings such as Edward II, but how a king got to the throne was another matter entirely. The Conqueror bequeathed his crown to his eldest son Robert, duke of Normandy, but the *state*, whose representatives (the nobility) were tempted by offers of money for the Normans and 'liberties' for the English, chose William Rufus instead. 'For, the succession in right of primogeniture, being none of his, and the elder brother living: howsoever his fathers will was, he must now be put, and held in possession of the crowne of England, *by the will of the kingdome. (Collection* 44). Again, the word "usurper" is never used, and Daniel thinks that Rufus could have been a great king, 'absolute in state,' a sovereign acting within the now-established laws, had he not tried to be 'absolute in power,' governing tyrannically. Daniel never defines what he means by 'absolute'; he seems to intend not arbitrary power but an unchallenged supremacy of the king governing with the consent of the state.

After Rufus' death, which providence justly brings about in the same New Forest which his father had depopulated, the state again chose his successor, once more passing over Robert of Normandy for another younger brother, Henry I. A good king, Henry governed well, 'for the good and quiet of the state.' He invented royal progresses so that he could venture abroad to 'see how the state was ordered'; he rescinded many of his father's draconian laws, reformed manners, and replaced severe punishments with fines 'by the consent of the state'; and he left behind him many 'stately structures' which, Daniel lamented, 'lye now deformed heapes of rubble' (56–7). Nevertheless, the collective misdeeds of his family caused the extinction of most of his children: whatever Daniel's beliefs about the consensual nature of the early Anglo-Norman regime, he had as much faith as any man in the unforgiving hand of providence.

Henry I's most important deed was his summoning of the 'first parliament' at Salisbury in 1116. Never very clear as to exactly by what means the 'state' had been choosing and advising its kings, Daniel is even more ambiguous on the issue of the origins of parliament, which he defined as simply an 'assembly of the state.' Uneasy with the question of parliament's antiquity, which had been debated by many of the Elizabethan and Jacobean antiquaries, he describes the 1116 assembly as the *first* parliament in a gloss to the *First Part*. By 1618, however, Daniel had experienced a change of heart, and the gloss was altered slightly but significantly to read 'the first parliament, *after the conquest*' (*First Part* 194; *Collection* 56, 78).[36] Did he simply discover more persuasive information about Anglo-Saxon assemblies in the writings of antiquaries like Selden? Or have we a hint here that he now thought this institution, unsummoned for four years, in jeopardy, and with it the balance between king and subject?

The *First Part* ends with the anarchic reign of the unfortunate Stephen, but in the 1618 *Collection* Daniel continued the tale to the death of Edward III, coming 'to a state full built, to a government reared up with all those mayne couplements of forme and order, as have held it together ever since' (222), though as he would go on to show, individual medieval kings would not be so secure as their sixteenth- and seventeenth-century successors. Perhaps the most striking feature of his account of the Plantagenet kings is his freedom from the stereotypes to be found in other historians. Daniel judged each king on the evidence, rather than fitting the facts to a preconceived portrait. This led him to some interesting and unusual reappraisals. Richard I, for instance, is demoted from the pious crusader Daniel himself had briefly described in the *Civil Wars*, to a self-centred absentee. Daniel's obituary of Coeur-de-Lion pulls no punches: 'This was the end of this lyon-like king, when he had raigned nine yeares, and 9 monthes, wherein hee exacted, and consumed more of this kingdome, then all his predecessors from the Norman had done before him, and yet lesse deserved then any, having neither lived here, neither left behinde him monument of piety, or of any other publique worke, or ever shewed love or care to this common-wealth, but onely to get what hee could from it' (*Collection* 107; *Civil Wars* I, 14).[37] Harsh words indeed! The one good effect of Richard's reign was that his excessive taxes, levied in the name of the crusades, caused restraints to be put on future kings: 'their boundlessnes came to bee broght within some limits.' They learned 'to provide for themselves.' John proved an even worse despot and tax-taker, until 'the Great Charter [was] made to keepe the beame right betwixt soveraingtie [sic] and subjection' (*Collection* 107, 111); for Daniel, unlike the common lawyers, Magna Carta was no restorer and codifier of ancient Anglo-Saxon freedoms, but an essentially new measure designed to correct the imbalance that had developed between monarchs and their subjects over the previous century and a half.

Even Edward I, though he passed a great number of statutes, which Daniel summarizes, could be as ruthless and untrustworthy as his father and grandfather. And what king ever shed so much blood? Edward's Welsh invasion was a good idea, though it proceeded from 'a desire more martiall than Christian.' In explaining an event such as this, Daniel generally looked less to the psychology of its agents than to its eventual consequences, good or ill:

For in such acquisitions as these, the sword is not to give an account to justice; the publique benefit makes amends. Those miserable mischiefes that afflicted both nations come hereby extinguished. The devision and pluralitie of states in this isle, having ever made it the stage of bloud, and confusion: as if nature that had ordained it but one peece, would have it to bee *governed but by one prince, and one law*, as the most absolute glory and strength thereof, which otherwise it could never enjoy. (159)

And so inevitability raises her head yet again. The time had come to subdue the Welsh, though not the Scots. Daniel had a strong sense of *kairos,* of everything in its appointed time, and for all his attention to personal motives he believed that ultimately God, rather than men, ruled great constitutional changes as much as the less important battles and conspiracies of rival peers and princes. As with the Conquest, so with the union of the two kingdoms: Edward I, his nobles, and all the armies in England could not achieve this by force before the intended time.

> Although the intention of this great and marshall king for reducing this whole isle under one government, was noble, and according to the nature of powre, and greatnesse, that ever seekes to extend it selfe as farre as it can: yet as all such actions hath much of iniquity, so had this, and we see it was not force or the sword could effect it. God had fore-decreed to make it his owne worke by a cleaner way, and ordained it for an unstained hand to set it together in peace, that it might take the more sure, and lasting hold, which otherwise it could never have done. Violence may joyne territories, but never affections together; which onely must grow voluntarily, and bee the worke of it selfe. (162)

The union, as achieved in Daniel's own time by James I, is the *telos* of English history, the end intended by God. Again one hears the voice of Ellesmere at Daniel's shoulder: 'Shall there bee a dis-union for ever?' the chancellor had asked during the case of the *post-nati.*[38] What Daniel sought to do was to show that the union of the kingdoms existed in fact if not in statute, and to endow that union with historical significance by making it the outcome of a centuries-long process. In doing so, Daniel did what virtually no other secular historian had managed: he found a meaningful pattern of progress in the English past. The lesson for Jacobean readers was that law, like language, had developed into something worth preserving, and that Meliboeus' injunction to the Arcadians, to respect their heritage, should govern contemporary relations between king and parliament. It was a point that would be repeated many times in the decade following Daniel's death in 1619.

Another significant feature of the later chapters of the *Collection* is Daniel's attention to the origins of customs such as duelling or the regulation of food and clothing through sumptuary laws, and to the beginnings of political habits or tendencies. Because he saw the whole course of English history as a unified, integrated picture, he was able to point out that evil deeds recur in time not simply because of divine justice, but because of their psychological effect – they set bad examples. Piers Gaveston, Edward II's minion, was 'the first privado of this kinde ever noted in our history.' Edward's reign also set two other bad precedents: Thomas of Lancaster's execution, the first of a nobleman since William I's time, 'opened veines for more to follow, and procured a most hideous revenge, which shortly after insued'; and Edward's own deposition proved to be the first but not the last example of the 'execrable doctrine' that allowed subjects to rise against their anointed prince (*Collection* 174–5, 180, 184). Daniel was applying here the same approach employed by the Elizabethan antiquaries: in order to study an historical phenomenon, first find its 'originall' – its first occurrence in the written record – and then trace it forward in time.

Above all else, Daniel was a careful plot-crafter, a fact that stands out in comparison with the rambling episodes of Ralegh or the subservience of Speed to the regnal period. More than any other early Stuart historian, he consistently subordinated the 'what' and 'how' of events – precise knowledge of which was ultimately unattainable – to the 'why' which could be directly apprehended by the historian with the advantage of hindsight. But if his close attention to plot development is little more than a strategy for convincing the reader that events really did point in a particular direction, it is captivating all the same. This is much less true of his minimal efforts at historical characterization. Throughout the *Civil Wars* and subsequently in the *Collection*, he refused to explain events in terms of simple cause and effect, agent and act, or motive and behaviour. Daniel does not perceive the world, present or past, as a set of mechanical relationships between entities who interact in a thoroughly predictable manner. In this sense his historical style lies closer to the scepticism of Ralegh than to the writers of politic history, and especially Francis Bacon, who would place great store in the connection between inner psychology and outward consequence.

The virtues and failings of historical individuals were, for Daniel, both too unclear and, in God's grand scheme, too trivial, for the historian to place much stock in them. Why, for example, blame the Wars of the Roses on one event such as the adultery of Queen Margaret with Suffolk? The causes of that conflict were far too unclear to permit making one person, or even one side, into a scapegoat.

Muse, what may we imagine was the Cause
That Furie workes thus universally?
What horror, what affection, is it, drawes

Sides, of such powre, to this Nobilitie?
Was it their Conscience to redresse the Lawes;
Or malice, to a wrong-plac't Sov'raigntie
That caus'd them (more then wealth or life) desire
Destruction, ruine, bloud-shed, sword and fire? (*Civil Wars* VII, 54)

Unlike Ralegh, Daniel never lingers on the physical setting of events, and throughout the *Collection*, even more than in the *Civil Wars*, he fails utterly to interest the reader in his kings and nobles; this remains true in spite of the biographical structure of the prose history. His characters remain paper cut-outs with neither the pious courage of Foxe's martyrs nor the grand pathos of Ralegh's victims. What Daniel says with reference to King Stephen is true of most of his other characters in the *Collection:* each is 'so continually in motion, as we cannot take his dimension' (*Collection* 67). This provides a measure of how far Daniel had come since the beginning of his career, for he had revealed in earlier lyrical and dramatic texts – *The Complaint of Rosamond* and *Philotas* in particular – that he in fact had the poetic ability to evoke sympathy by concentrating on personality rather than event.

There was much in Daniel's eclectic political thought to raise eyebrows. Like the Bodin of the *République*, he saw the absolute, undivided sovereignty of the monarch as essential, but unlike Bodin he fettered his post-Conquest monarchs within 'those bounds wherein by the law of the state they are placed.'[39] He was thus able to reconcile the abrogation of the old law with the binding quality of the new. If any history deserved to be censored by a tyrannical monarch, nervous of the past, Daniel's Janus-faced book was a good candidate. Subsequent writers ignored his first face, that of the panegyrist of absolute sovereignty, and seized upon the recorder of elective monarchies. John Lilburne and the Levellers cited Daniel in support of their argument that English law since the Conquest was little more than a 'Norman yoke.' Marchamont Nedham, the republican propagandist, inserted excerpts from Daniel's section on the British warleader or *dux bellorum* in his *Case of the Commonwealth Stated* (1650). During the troubles of the 1680s, William Petyt took down extracts from the *Collection* on the Conqueror's token obedience to existing Anglo-Saxon law, blithely ignoring Daniel's plain statement that the Conquest had, in fact, abrogated the English constitution. Daniel's depiction of the power of the state to choose its head, from Cassivellaunus to Edward III, ensured his popularity after 1688. The latter-day election of William III to the throne vacated by James II bore an interesting resemblance to the estates' submission to William I and the nobles' election of the Conqueror as described by Daniel. Later still, the whig bishop White Kennett included Daniel's history with the republican Milton's history of Britain and the parliamentarian Arthur Wilson's anti-Stuart history of James I; there was more than a stylistic similarity between Daniel's Tacitean verdicts on certain monarchs and Wilson's own depiction of James as a weak, dissembling Tiberius. Through Kennett's widely read collection, Daniel's history lived on into the eighteenth century.[40]

Daniel's historical prose was in large measure devoted to the working-out of problems raised earlier in his poetry. Although his position on a number of issues changed with time, and though there is a shift of emphasis away from problems of poetics and culture toward the consideration of issues of law and sovereignty, Daniel remained preoccupied with essentially the same questions, and used much the same vocabulary to address them, from *Musophilus* to the *Collection*. He was always fascinated by the strings that tied men together, whether in Musophilus' literary dialogue of ancients and moderns, or in the realm of action. Daniel knew that he wished to present English history as a national drama: the only problem lay in his lack of moral certainty as to whether to cast that drama as comedy or tragedy. We are left with both, and neither. On the one hand there is his regret for the passing of the Middle Ages and the dissolution of Christendom into the large national states, divided by religion and infused with the vulgar impiety occasioned by the advent of print; on the other hand, this collapse had been offset by the internal integration of England into a coherent community within itself, a 'state' whose conflicting elements were reconciled, synthesized, and bound together by the laws which had evolved over the centuries.

Daniel was the first to write a history of England which incorporated an idea of *gradual*, step-by-step, constitutional progress. In comparison with the *Collection*, Edward Ayscu's single-minded account of the events leading up to the union seems flat and unsophisticated. Daniel shared certain beliefs with the majority of his contemporaries, such as the conviction that the union of the kingdoms marked the culmination of a long-term providential plan, but his analysis of this and other developments was much more subtle, and his sense of their social and cultural context unrivalled. By wedding a politically acute mind to an appreciation of cultural change within a historical narrative, by persistently applying his poetic imagination to the realm of memory, this contemplative soul became, quite unintentionally, the distant progenitor of English constitutional history.

CHAPTER FOUR

Politic Biographers and the Stuart Court

James I and the Politics of History

It has been said of King James that he disliked and feared history because he knew that his own performance would appear poor by comparison with past monarchs such as Elizabeth, or because he knew that the lawyers and antiquaries, researching into ancient laws and precedents, were busily forging chains to bind his prerogative. But every early modern monarch was sensitive to the past, and there seems no reason to find in James an unusual degree of paranoia. His 'mislike' of the attempt to revive the Society of Antiquaries in 1614, as recalled by Spelman, has been cited too often, since it is by no means clear exactly why the king objected to the society. He may simply have disliked the antiquaries' independence, for when Speed's erstwhile associate, Edmund Bolton, proposed an 'academ roial' to produce a complete history of England, barely three years later, the plan received serious consideration at the court.[1]

On the whole, the charge that James was a modern Tiberius, silencing the Cremutii Cordi of his day, will not stand up. William Martyn was left to his own devices, without a word in his book being altered, while Ralegh's history was left untouched, except for the removal of the author's name. James's record here is thus no worse than Elizabeth's. It was not he, but his late predecessor, who had forced excisions from Holinshed's chronicle and who had candidly admitted that she feared comparisons with Richard II.

There is no room here for an extended consideration of James's intellectual and political merits, though it is fair to say that recent scholarship has dealt with him sympathetically. It is sufficient to note that his reign witnessed the writing of some of the most original pieces of historical scholarship yet conceived in England, such as Spelman's *Archaeologus* and Selden's *Historie of Tithes*. When objections were made to Selden's book, the king called Selden in to discuss the subject with him on three occasions, and then put him to work supporting the royal claim to sovereignty of the neighbouring seas: Elizabeth would probably have had the book burnt. As he had already proven in Scotland, the new king was a great lover of *belles lettres*;[2] he simply preferred that scholarship be carried out under the royal aegis, under the sponsorship of either himself or a trusted councillor.

Under James I, and, to a much smaller degree, under his successor, the humanist tradition of political history in England reached its peak in five historians who, unlike Samuel Daniel, chose to write about shorter spans of time. Each of these 'politic biographers,' Sir John Hayward, William Camden, Bishop Francis Godwin, Sir George Buck, and, somewhat later, Edward, Lord Herbert of Cherbury, focused on a particular reign and its events. All enjoyed the patronage of the king or of an influential patron at the court, and all knew and used Cotton's library. Each was also, though to varying degrees, influenced by classical models of historical writing and by categories of political analysis which they derived either from Renaissance commentators such as Machiavelli or, equally often, directly from such seminal Greek and Latin authors as Polybius and Tacitus.[3]

Sovereignty, Civil Law, and History

Tacitus, as much as Machiavelli, provided the inspiration for Sir John Hayward (c 1564–1627), one of a group of 'Taciteans' associated with the earl of Essex in the 1590s. The qualities of Hayward's historical writing have never been fully appreciated, partly because the most interesting two-thirds of his notorious history of Henry IV has never been published, and partly because he has been overshadowed by the enormous erudition of Camden and Selden.[4] Born at Felixstowe, Suffolk, and educated at Pembroke College, Cambridge, Hayward was among the few dozen Englishmen who practised the civil law. After receiving his LL D in 1591 he enjoyed a steady, if unspectacular, career in the court of arches and the high court of admiralty, earning the patronage of Sir Julius Caesar and of Thomas Howard, earl of Arundel, who commissioned him to write a history of the Howard family.[5] In 1616 Hayward attained the lucrative post of a master in chancery, and this was followed in 1619 by a knighthood and honorary admission to Gray's Inn.

Hayward was no narrow lawyer. Like many of the best members of his profession, he had outside interests, and dabbled in religious and devotional writing as well as history – so much so that he was accounted 'better read in theological authors than in those belonging to his own profession.' His legal knowledge may well have fallen short of the spectacular erudition of his older contemporaries, Alberico Gentili and John Cowell, and of his junior, Arthur Duck, but it constantly informs his historical writings.[6]

Hayward's conception of the purpose and scope of histories, outlined in his preface to Sir Roger Williams' *Actions of the Lowe Countries* (1618), is straightforward enough. He praised Williams' 'compleate Historie' because it related 'sieges, assaults, surprizes, ambushes, skirmishes, battailes, lively described.' Hayward was pleased that the book contained 'great varietie both of persons and of actions; much mutabilitie of fortune, many changes in affaires; admirable advices, unexpected events, ponderous judgements.' It avoided 'senseless fictions' of ancient British kings (an easy compliment, since it was about sixteenth-century Holland!).[7] There can be no doubt from these remarks that Hayward accepted all the Ciceronian commonplaces about the purpose and scope of history. Yet within this conventional humanist framework Hayward brought his knowledge of the civil law, and his familiarity with the written legal codes of other nations, to bear on the national past.

Hayward achieved his greatest notoriety over his earliest work, *The First Part of the Life and Raigne of King Henrie the IIII* (1599). Because he was a follower of Essex, and his history seemed to condone the deposition of Richard II, he was twice examined by the council and imprisoned, only narrowly escaping his patron's fate.[8] Especially alarming to the government was the history's prefatory letter from 'A.P. to the Reader' and the dedication to Essex: 'A.P.' was widely reputed to be the earl himself. The suggestion that histories taught 'not onely precepts, but lively patterns, both for private directions and for affayres of state,' though a humanist topos, was tactless in the context, and it is scarcely surprising that it offended the queen.[9]

Yet too much has been made of this affair. Despite the suggestive preface, the published *Henrie IIII*, which covers only the first year of the king's reign, is quite innocuous. Hayward began with a conventional depiction of Richard II as a bad king, less because he was inherently evil than because he failed to govern prudently. Richard coddled unworthy favourites, exacted large sums from his subjects (including a fictitious 'benevolence' invented by Hayward for dramatic effect), and invaded traditional liberties. His banishment of Henry Bolingbroke was 'against the custome of the realme.' Hayward knew his Machiavelli and realized that when Richard lost 'both the feare and love of his subjects' his days as king were numbered. Using the set speech for more than rhetorical effect, Hayward put his own knowledge of English history and of the laws of other realms into the mouths of his characters: Archbishop Arundel persuades the exiled Bolingbroke to invade England by citing examples of the deposition of tyrants in Sweden, Denmark, Germany, and ancient Britain, knowledge the original Arundel would certainly have lacked.[10]

The arguments for deposition would alarm Queen Elizabeth, but to Hayward the act of rebellion was anathema. Bolingbroke himself wished only to set the king right, but he realized that half-measures would be impossible, observing that 'He that aymeth at a kingdome, hath no middle course betwene the life of a prince, & the death of a traytor.' Sure enough, once back in England the returned exile was driven to depose his monarch and mount the throne. Hayward's own point of view is that of the bishop of Carlisle, 'a man learned and wise,' whom he gives an exceptionally long speech warning of the consequences of the rebellion. Like Archbishop Arundel, the bishop is *extremely* learned: so much so that he quotes from books written in the sixteenth century![11] To the traditional argument that deposition will bring divine vengeance, Hayward adds a lawyer's case: rebellion is bad because it violates human as well as divine law.[12] Giving examples from classical and biblical writers, from France, Spain, Muscovy, Turkey, Ethiopia, and Persia, the bishop points out that nowhere, including England, is there 'any custome, that the people at pleasure should elect theyre king.'[13] Hayward himself would show how right the bishop's prognostications were to prove.

Politically, Hayward was unimpeachably orthodox; the most he was guilty of was opportunism. If he offered general advice to his monarch and commended virtuous men like his patron, then he also offered a warning to Essex himself, who would have done well to listen. Although Hayward's troubles deterred him from finishing his history, he did continue it up to the fourth year of Henry's reign. This still-unpublished sequel, apparently written about the same time as the *Henrie IIII*, was found among Hayward's papers at his death. It is more than twice the length of the printed work, and in many ways more interesting.[14] The continuation, like *Henrie IIII*, part one, mixes religious and legal elements, but it gives us a clearer picture of Hayward's politico-historical ideas. Noting with some regret the growth of Lollardy, Hayward places Henry IV's reign in a European context, lamenting the decay of religion all across fifteenth-century Europe – a position which, we have already seen, was at the same time being staked out by Daniel. 'Cheifely by reason of a great disunion in the church,' he complains, describing the Great Schism, 'the common cause of christianitie was generally neglected.' Hayward believed that this 'miserable schisme' had allowed the growth of heresy and caused 'distruction in everie christian countrie and common wealth.' Again one can see that religion more than any other issue could split the historical consensus. For Hayward, quite unlike John Foxe, Lollards were not early protestants but progenitors of Elizabethan Brownists, violators of the Reformation principle *cuius regio, eius religio.* Hayward was no advocate of religious toleration, but he did have an irenic, conciliatory and 'politique' view of the church, and it was probably this which appealed to James I, leading to the king's choice of Hayward to share, with Camden, the post of historiographer at the newly established Chelsea College in 1610.[15]

The manuscript demonstrates even more clearly than the published *Henrie IIII* the consequences of 1399. Once one king had been deposed, rebellion came easily, again and again, and Henry had his hands full with Welsh and Scottish incursions and the Percy uprisings. Despite his capable, if 'unsettled and unjust' government, Henry committed some blunders which had dangerous consequences. Hayward's religiosity expressed itself throughout his works in a sympathy with clericalism, and he deplored Henry's treatment of the church and of churchmen such as the executed Archbishop Scrope. Henry's was 'the first invasion which I find ... by any king of this land upon religious possessions.' This precedent would proceed 'further by degrees' and inspire Henry VIII's dissolution of the monasteries.[16] Yet though his piety told Hayward that such incursions were bad, he remained capable of seeing their consequences as an historical development rather than merely criticizing them as blasphemy.

Hayward's Henry continues to be the textbook new prince. Confronting Hotspur's army, he tries to avoid a fight, and then holds back some of his forces, worrying that 'fortune might change upon him, having good experience of her mutabilitie by such things as shee had taken from others and cast upon him; *hee held it a manifest defect in judgement to putt the whole body of his state upon adventure of battaile.*' Henry survives only because he is shrewder than his opponents, and more ruthless.[17]

Most interestingly, Hayward dwells on Henry's use of parliament to legitimize his rule. In a long passage giving details of the debates, he describes how the parliament of 1402 finally struck a bargain with the king. In exchange for a subsidy, he revived three statutes of Edward III, providing for the liberty of the subject from certain kinds of military service: 'And thus both the king and the people held themselves now contented; the king being furnished for the time with money and the people in hope of after ease, willingly submitting themselves to the present burden.' In this interesting episode, Hayward had come close to postulating a new relationship between king and parliament, dating from Henry's reign; in a way, he anticipates William Stubbs's famous theory of the 'Lancastrian experiment.'[18]

The accession of James I saw Hayward, only recently released from the Tower, return to historical writing as a means of winning the new king's favour. Early in 1603 he attacked Parsons' *Conference* in order to defend the Stuart succession. Fighting on Parsons' own ground, he restated the traditional view that the Lancastrians were usurpers and the Yorkists (and hence the Tudors and the Stuarts) the true Plantagenet heirs. He stressed the sanctity of unbroken succession by primogeniture, while pointing to the 'pure anarchie' of democratic or elective principalities.[19] Once again his familiarity with the practices of other realms gave him a continental perspective, allowing him to stand on precisely that comparative ground occupied by his Catholic opponents.

Striking while the iron was hot, Hayward wrote to the king recommending the uses of history and historians, including Sallust and himself.[20] Then, whether voluntarily or by command, he turned his pen to the case for the union of the realms. History, he argued, shows that momentous changes such as the union were often necessary. To the sort of teleological view held by Ayscu and Clapham he added a new dimension, asserting not simply the natural inevitability but also the political urgency of the union: in remote times the Saxons and Danes had been able to invade Britain only because the inhabitants were at odds, and only a united Britain would be safe from foreign threats, by which he clearly intended the forces of international Catholicism, headed by Spain. None of this political practicality was to deny the historical inevitability of a union, which Henry VII had 'aimed at ... when he married his eldest daughter Margaret into Scotland.'[21]

As a civilian, aware of the contrasts but also the structural similarities between national legal systems, Hayward knew that the politic union must extend beyond a joining of crowns, or even kingdoms: a perfect union of laws was required. Against the arguments being advanced by many common lawyers of the incompatibility of English and Scots law, Hayward pointed out that such great changes in English law were not without precedent. He denied the cherished continuity of the common law, as a fact 'not commonly received.' His civilian mind was geared toward codes and statutes rather than custom – toward lawgivers rather than the slow growth of precedent – and he even believed that 'sometimes entire alteration of government is necessarie.' Had not the Romans profitably exchanged an anarchic republic for the benefits of monarchy under Augustus? Hayward tended – like James I himself – to assume the priority and superiority of the person of the ruler to particular laws and even to the very system of government itself.[22]

Few would have questioned Hayward's assertion that changes in government were natural; it was part of the character of commonwealths that they decayed. But Hayward saw in the transition of governments the opportunity to achieve wide-ranging, fundamental reforms of the law. Aware of the radical character of this position in common lawyers' eyes, he even played down the profundity of prospective legal alterations by distinguishing between the substance of a government – its absolutely sovereign character, its *power* – and its 'accidentall' form: 'The Romane empire did alwaies remaine, although the government thereof was sometimes regal, sometimes popular, and sometimes mixt: although the soveraigntie was transferred, from kings to consuls, and from consuls to emperors.'[23] The empire always existed as a sovereign body; only the office in which sovereignty reposed had changed. What matter that the sovereignty had shifted from one form of government to another, as long as it was absolute and *unbroken*? The same commitment to continuity of authority, demonstrated in the *Henrie IIII*, emerges again, but it sits uneasily with Hayward's readiness to admit a break in the constitution.

Taking his cue from Bodin, Hayward rejected any kind of mixed sovereignty. While addressing the issue of secular control over the church elsewhere, he defined sovereignty as 'an absolute and perpetual power' which exists above and outside of mutable human laws.[24] The union would preserve and enhance sovereignty, no matter what it did to the form of government and laws of the realms. Sovereignty for Hayward meant not arbitrary rule, but autonomy and supremacy: precisely what James I had termed 'Free Monarchy.' The king could make laws and could occasionally use his prerogative to override them; though he should do so only in great matters on which the safety of the people depended, and in the kingdom's interest, his power to do so must not be shared or diminished by other authorities, nor restrained by custom.[25]

Evidently, the exchange of one form of government for another and the modernization and codification of law did less harm in Hayward's eyes than the replacement of one king by another through rebellion, the sheer breaking of law and defiance of authority. Hayward had forced himself into this position simply because he had to avoid providing inadvertent support for the arguments of Parsons. Like Daniel, he too had progressed from preoccupation with dynastic questions in the 1590s to issues of sovereignty and law a decade later; but his and Daniel's respective interpretations of the relationship between power and legality could not be more different.

Hayward's appeal for the union fell on deaf ears, but ensured his favour with the king. He enjoyed the patronage of Prince Henry and at his request wrote his most complex work, *The Lives of the III. Normans, Kings of England*. Henry had expressed the wish to 'know the actions of his auncestors,' and had complained to Hayward of the poor quality of other histories of England, asking him to write a new one. The prince died shortly thereafter, but Hayward published the work in 1613, with a dedication to Prince Charles.[26]

The source material of *The III. Normans* was available in the medieval chronicles edited by Savile, Camden, and others.[27] Hayward was no antiquary – he did no research in original manuscripts, and in this respect he differs from the other four historians discussed in the present chapter. He did, however, apply his knowledge of classical and legal texts to the analysis of William I's conquest and its significance, playing down the 'Conquest' itself by stressing William's proprietary right to the throne and the need for a preservation of strong rule. Prior English and ancient history showed that foreigners and even bastards could legitimately inherit crowns. Edgar Aetheling's right to Edward the Confessor's crown was the best, but he was too weak to defend it, and 'not gracious to the English.' Harold, by contrast, had power but no right, and William thus presented a compromise between a weak heir and a strong usurper (43–5, 50, 122).[28]

Although William's 'entrance was not by way of conquest, but with pretence of title to the crowne,' the new king made great changes. He paid only lip service to existing laws, as codified by the Confessor, of which 'hee changed the greatest part, and brought in the customes of Normandie in their stead.' A wary new prince, he carried out his legal changes 'by degrees' to avoid rebellion. He was tacitly supported by the

English themselves, 'who have alwaies been inclinable to accommodate themselves to the fashions of France' (96, 122–4). Hayward admired William both for his swift and ruthless victory, and for his prudent government. He was also pious, generally beneficent to the clergy, and impeccably moral – the perfect model for a future king of Britain (108, 116).

Hayward adopts Sir Thomas Smith's definition of sovereignty, or 'rule,' as the power to 'controwle, correct, and direct all other members of the common wealth.'[29] Hayward's recurring theme that great changes in government are legitimate as long as sovereignty remains perpetual appears in his account of William II's succession. Though Robert was William's elder son, the king was entitled to leave his crown, and hence the realm, to whomever he liked, an assertion that Hayward supports with reference to 'the best approved interpreters of the canon and civill law.' This was not quite the argument for arbitrary disposal of land at the royal whim which it seems: Hayward conceded that in ordinary circumstances a king has no such right to alter succession by proximity of blood. But in a new state such as Norman England – or, by extension, the united Stuart realm of Great Britain – the right of succession depends on the king's will, since earlier customs are abrogated and new ones have not yet developed. The king may inscribe his will upon a clean slate, in the manner of the ancient Scottish conqueror, Fergus, referred to by James I in *The Trew Law of Free Monarchies*.[30] And because Hayward, unlike Samuel Daniel, would not go so far as to admit that Rufus had in any sense been 'elected' by either nobility or people, the sovereignty could still be said to have passed unbroken (143–6).[31]

Henry I's succession was also defended by Hayward with reference to civil and canon law, and to the lack of a legitimate common-law custom. Henry was the monarch who in Hayward's admiring words had 'first instituted the forme of the high court of Parliament, as now it is in use.' Hayward's knowledge of old English history was thin, but had it been deeper he would likely not have changed his perspective on the origins of parliament. He carefully avoided any comparative discussion of the 'new,' royal-controlled parliament with the Anglo–Saxon *witenagemot*, merely asserting that earlier assemblies had consisted only of certain nobles and prelates, summoned at the king's will, and without the commons (228, 283). Like his father, Henry was a dissembler. He promised to restore Edward's laws only in order to make his subjects more obedient: 'And albeit in trueth they were never either reviewed or corrected, yet the onely hope thereof did worke in the people a favourable inclination to his part.' (242) Again, policy is balanced by piety, wisdom, and courage. Henry I had a few vices, but these were 'farre exceeded by his vertues' (312).

Despite its great learning, *The III. Normans* was marred by a civilian's lack of appreciation of the common law and of the importance of custom, as well as by Hayward's relative lack of familiarity with or interest in the Anglo-Saxon background. Like John Speed – and quite unlike Samuel Daniel – he had little instinctive sympathy for the Middle Ages and tended to regard any departure from classical models as a decline. As far as Hayward was concerned, if the Normans had come close to introducing a neat, Roman-style legal code to England in place of barbarous custom, it could only be an improvement.[32]

As a narrative, the history suffers, too, from Hayward's failure to integrate his material into one continuous story-line. He relegated the interesting events of each reign to a series of annals, following the life of each king. His need to provide a princely model who was both pious and prudent forced him into making the awkward argument that despite their political acumen, the few misdeeds of the Norman kings neverthe-less ensured their extinction after three reigns. Politic governance ought not to include vice and sacrilege; as Hayward had said in 1606, religion provides the cohesive element in any kind of government, and the king must be personally worthy of the trust placed in him as supreme head of the church and state (297).[33] This emphasis on the place of religion, on the king as godly proprietor, provided Hayward with a safety valve, a way of conceding the needs of royal power without condoning all the uses to which it might be put.

Despite his ill-treatment at her hands, Hayward's model head of the ecclesiastical polity was Elizabeth. As a supplement to *The III. Normans* he drew up *Annals* of her reign, on the model of his *Henrie IIII*. Like that book, this project did not get past the fourth year, since in Hay-ward's circles it was by now well known that his colleague Camden had embarked with the crown's support on a full-scale history of Elizabeth's reign. Based on printed sources where Camden would turn piles of documents upside down, and, as usual, including carefully crafted set speeches, Hayward's *Annals* were a summation of the events of 1558–62, seeded with Tacitean political lessons derived from these events and supported by similar examples from other times. The *Annals* extol Elizabeth as an ideal ruler of church and state. Hayward tried to integrate prodigies, omens, peripheral events, and interesting digres-sions, such as a short account of the history of St Paul's Cathedral from Saxon times to the present,[34] but the result is a disjointed history which borders on chronicle, reminiscent of the later books of Speed.

In his last historical work, *The Life, and Raigne of King Edward the Sixt*, published posthumously in 1630, but written before 1625,[35] Hayward used the manuscript journal and literary remains of Edward VI, preserved in the Cottonian library, to supplement Holinshed, Stow, Grafton, Sanders' *Anglican Schism*, and Foxe.[36] The chronicles rather than the manuscripts remained his guide, and the source of the statutes and letters that he printed. Where the chroniclers report more than thirty-five hundred of Kett's rebels slain at the battle of Dussindale in 1549, and the king's journal only two thousand, he chooses to follow the chronicles. He studied the reign thematically, apologizing 'for not alwaies observing the just order of time, but sometime coherence or propinquity of matter.' As in the *Annals*, he tried to integrate the function of story-teller and compiler of facts, with even less success. The fundamental problem was that the child Edward was himself not interesting enough to lend unity to a badly organized work; his life could not provide a narrative thread in the way a Henry IV or William the Conqueror could do. After the execution of the Duke of Somerset, 'few matters of high nature or observable note happened in England during King Edward's life,' a limp dismissal of the two and one half years of the duke of Northumberland's supremacy, during which such events had occurred as the issuance of the second Book of Common Prayer.[37]

The *Annals* and *Edward VI* were disappointing after Hayward's high achievement in his earlier works. It is true that he marked a departure in the realistic depiction of men and events, the first really Tacitean, perhaps even Machiavellian 'politic' historian in England, but it must again be emphasized that his version of *realpolitik* was one softened by religion and played out in a world where Christian providence has as great a hand in events as fickle fortune; Hayward's attitude to politics remained the one summed up by his motto, 'Fly from evil, do good.' The most interesting aspect of his historical writing lies not in its depiction of politics but rather in his use of medieval and civilian legal erudition as an aid in analysing events, and in his perceptive, if brief, description of the impact of the Norman Conquest on English law and royal sovereignty.

The Two Hats of William Camden

It has been suggested above that a strong theoretical distinction existed between 'history' as a form of narrative literature and the kind of antiquarian and philological scholarship which in practice was beginning to influence history-writing. This theoretical gap is nowhere better demonstrated than in a very great representative of both forms, William Camden (1551–1623).[38] Successively a schoolmaster, antiquary, herald, and historian, Camden fell heir to two traditions. The first was that of topographical or 'chorographical' research, originating with Varro and Strabo, continued in Renaissance Italy by Flavio Biondo, and founded in England by John Leland and William Lambarde.[39] The second tradition was that of the humanist historian of his own life and times: this stretched back to Polybius, via Jacques-Auguste de Thou, Francesco Guicciardini, and Leonardo Bruni. In the mind of William Camden, these two modes of studying the past enjoyed an amicable co-existence, but not a marriage.

While still a young man, Camden began to correspond with foreign scholars. The Dutch geographer Abraham Ortelius, who visited Britain in 1577, suggested that Camden compile a complete description of the island and her Roman antiquities.[40] Camden had already made some preliminary investigations of his own, and Ortelius' prodding sent him to work again. His love of the remnants of the past, particularly old coins and epitaphs bearing inscriptions, emerges from his writings and his correspondence; he would study epitaphs briefly in a short discourse for the Society of Antiquaries in 1600, and he published a detailed study of the tombs in Westminster Abbey later that year.[41] He undoubtedly stimulated the interest in Roman inscriptions of Janus Gruter, the Dutch scholar who had spent his youth in England from 1567 to some time after 1577, and whose debts to Camden serve as a reminder that the communication lines between English and continental scholars ran in more than one direction.[42]

The *Britannia* (1586), which Camden dedicated to Lord Burghley, was the result of his detailed investigation of the ancient geography, place-names, and artifacts of Roman Britain.[43] Unlike Leland, who had attempted to visit every place of interest himself, Camden relied on second-hand sources, including Leland's own collections, for much of his material.[44] Still, this was an enormous challenge for a man of thirty-five, without great means and with a school in his charge. In subsequent editions (1587, 1590, 1594, 1600, 1607), Camden added much genealogical material and gradually expanded the scope of the book to include the Saxon and Danish past as well as the Romano-British. Not surprisingly, the *Britannia* contained a number of errors. In replying to the criticisms made of the 1594 edition by Ralph Brooke, Camden revealed himself as a shy man, hypersensitive to criticism, who wished only to study the past, not engage in controversy.[45]

The *Britannia* exerted an enormous influence over subsequent antiquarian scholarship, yet Camden had no pretensions to authority. It is true that he confronted the pantheon of British history – Brutus, Samothes, Albion, and the other ancient kings and giants, and found them dubious. He admitted the facts of so distant a past were obscure and defended conjecture as a means of filling in the gaps. But he had no stomach for polemic, and he steadfastly refused to commit himself on the veracity of Geoffrey of Monmouth's account of ancient Britain; that would be 'to strive with the streame and current of time, and to struggle against an opinion commonly and long since received.' Nevertheless, Camden's attitude was so clearly, if subtly, sceptical that the *Britannia*, through sheer weight of learning, all but put the lid on Brutus' coffin as far as most antiquaries were concerned; and Camden, at least, did not lie open to the charge made against Polydore Vergil of being an ignorant foreigner. Henceforward other, less erudite, men, both historians and antiquaries, could take the Galfridian legends with a grain of salt and appeal to Camden's growing authority.[46]

The virtues and failings of the *Britannia* have been well studied elsewhere. Of more immediate concern is Camden's *Annales* of Elizabeth's reign, begun at royal command in 1608 and published in 1615 in a Latin edition extending to 1588. The circumstances surrounding the writing and publication of this work, the only contemporary history of the period, are almost as interesting as the book itself.[47]

James I was unhappy with the portrait of his mother, Mary Stuart, as a murderess and adulteress by his ex-tutor George Buchanan, a dislike accentuated by Buchanan's dangerous quasi-republican beliefs. James had always regarded Buchanan as a principal architect of the rebellion of 1566 against Mary – to which, of course, he owed his own early succession. He had tried to persuade Jacques-Auguste de Thou, the Gallican Catholic, to incorporate a more favourable sketch of Mary in his *Historiae sui temporis*.[48] As the *politique* heir of Bodin, with no love of the kind of rampant clericalism which had destroyed Mary, de Thou seemed a good choice. Anxious to please, the Frenchman had sought the aid of Camden on the subject of recent British and Irish history, but had finally endorsed Buchanan's view – much to the annoyance of the king of England. James complained of de Thou's book, the first part of which appeared in 1606, to his librarian, Patrick Young, who had a suggestion: why not set the record straight with a complete history? 'It is not my purpose to repel or requite such a libel with more libels,' Young wrote the king some time in 1606 or 1607. 'I merely wish to show your serene Majesty a man, certainly not of the lowest sort, who from archives and ambassadors' papers (on this and the other side) from witnesses of each kingdom and from the original letters of those queens, which he saved from the flames, might be able to compile a complete history of the two queens, Mary and Elizabeth.'[49]

Camden was hitherto little known to the king, but he was, as Young implied, no stranger to the sources surviving for the late queen's reign. A decade earlier he had been given a collection of Elizabethan state papers by Lord Burghley, patron of the *Britannia*, who had suggested to Camden that he write a life of Queen Elizabeth: these presumably are the papers to which Young refers. On Burghley's death in 1598, Camden abandoned the project: as he later told de Thou, he found the writing of history an annoyance.[50] He preferred to edit his chronicles, to revise the *Britannia* (putting it, in 1607, into a style modelled on de Thou's history), and to issue the *Remaines* of his researches, an important little book to which we shall return.[51] But he still had the papers, and was an obvious choice to salvage Mary Stuart's historical reputation. Young's suggestion, supported by George Carew, de Thou's friend and James's ambassador in Paris, proved persuasive, and the king soon acted.[52]

At first, the plan was simple: Camden would draw up his *Annales* in abbreviated form and present them to de Thou, on the assumption that the Frenchman would, if provided with better information, change his mind about Mary Stuart and alter subsequent editions of his work. Because he was always sensitive to controversy and wished to avoid offending either the king or de Thou, Camden communicated with both through intermediaries. Cotton played courier between the king and Camden, while from 1610 the visiting Huguenot scholar, Isaac Casaubon, communicated with de Thou on behalf of the king.

Sorting out the question of who knew what can be tricky, even when the game of diplomacy is played by scholars instead of statesmen. But the letters of de Thou and Casaubon do reveal that the former believed Cotton to be the author of these materials, and Camden, the Latin master, merely the translator. The confusion was compounded by Cotton's likely authorship of a set of memoirs on Elizabeth which had also been sent to de Thou at James's command. Francis Bacon, who contributed corrections to the manuscript of the published *Annales*, also believed Cotton to be the author.[53] They may not, in fact, have been far off the truth. It is likely that Cotton, a younger man who boasted a Scottish ancestry, had a greater share than has hitherto been acknowledged in the writing of the published *Annales*, especially the sections on Scotland. Camden was now elderly, and by his own admission he knew little about Scottish history. Even in 1612, when Camden finally admitted his authorship to de Thou, he refused to take all the credit.[54]

The publication of the *Annales* became necessary when de Thou, having received a copy of the manuscript ending with the year 1572, refused to alter what he had written about Scottish matters. James ordered Camden and Cotton to publish the first part of the *Annales* in 1615 – much to Camden's surprise and discomfort, as he told his Dutch friend, Jan de Laet. Printing began on 13 March and by 8 June Camden could write in his journal, 'Annales prodierunt.'[55] Because the second part, from 1588 to 1603, was only published in 1625, at Leiden, it has been assumed that the king had no interest in continuing the saga, that he dreaded Elizabeth's name, and that he 'opposed publication.'[56] Camden himself certainly opposed their publication in English before his death, having already received much criticism for his handling of Scottish affairs. To ensure that the work would some day be published, he sent a copy to Pierre Dupuy, de Thou's literary executor; this became the source of the Leiden edition.[57]

But the Clarenceux king-of-arms had again underestimated King James's interest. In early 1624, only a few months after Camden's death the previous November, the king began to show a renewed interest in the corrections to the first three books and in the unprinted fourth book. James ordered Cotton to interpolate the corrections, and he commissioned an English translation of the first part by the Frenchman Abraham Darcie.[58] The translation appeared in 1625, and the Latin fourth book may only have been held up till 1627 because the complete Leiden edition made it unnecessary. Far from quaking at the sacred name of Elizabeth, James went out of his way to ensure that the second part of the *Annales* would eventually be printed, though he, too, was dead by the time it appeared. Why was he so interested? For this we must turn to the work itself.

Camden modelled himself on the two most admired classical historians of his day. He aspired to the level of truth and impartiality achieved by Polybius, and also to that historian's understanding of the causes and consequences of political events in the long and short terms (sig B2r [1615, sig A4r]). He had received a copy of Polybius from Casaubon, the Greek's most recent editor.[59] Camden's friendship with Sir Henry Savile and his acquaintance with Sir John Hayward may also have taught him the virtues of Tacitus, from whom he learned 'that weighty and remarkable occurrences are to be digested by way of annals'; it was in imitation of the Roman that he organized his material into a year by year account (sig B3r [1615, sig A4v]).[60] His annals were not simply lists of events, a mere record of the facts of each year; they were continuous narratives which, strung together, formed a complete history. The problem with the annalistic form was that it restricted the writer's freedom to place individual events in a sequence of cause and effect longer than a year. Camden, like de Thou in France, skilfully overcame this by the use of foreshadowing and recall, always giving the necessary background to an event and hinting at the outcome he would later describe in full.[61] The subthemes of the book – Scotland, Ireland, rebels, papists, and puritans – ran together in a historical fugue in which the annal itself merely provided the measure on the scoresheet.

Anticipating criticism of his own views, Camden resolved to rely on the opinions of his sources and of surviving witnesses, rather than recording his own perceptions, for 'it is a question whether an historian may lawfully doe it.' He eschewed fictional speeches, though the majority of his contemporaries employed them. He may have feared lest they be challenged by eye-witnesses. In 1615 a great many men who had grown up under and served Elizabeth in her later years were still alive, with memories of their own: Camden knew he could not possibly please everybody. This as much as natural inclination forced him to rely, like de Thou, on an enormous range of manuscript sources in the form of state papers, charters, letters, statutes, parliamentary diaries, and council records.[62] He had many of these from Burghley and Cotton supplied others. Camden would repay his younger associate handsomely by leaving him his own collections, thereby making the Cottonian library one of the richest sources of sixteenth-century political history. From these documents, Camden constructed the first English narrative history founded almost entirely on what we would now call 'primary' sources.

Troubles in Scotland, the reign and fall of Mary Stuart, and its subsidiary events – the murders of David Riccio and Henry Darnley – Mary's complicity in French and papal plots, and her final doom figure prominently in the first three books of the *Annales*. Rather than praise Mary uncritically and unpersuasively, in reaction to Buchanan, Camden steered a middle course and described a worthy, virtuous, but unfortunate princess. 'Thrust forward into dangerous designes,' she was merely the pawn, not the willing accomplice, of the Guises, the Spanish, Ridolfi, Babington, and the pope (III, 113 [1615, 458]). Her deposition was the product of greed and self-interest on the part of her supporters and enemies alike; her eventual death was a painful, tragic necessity, from which Camden exonerates Elizabeth (III, 115–22 [1615, 460–9]), while suggesting rather elliptically that much of Elizabeth's grief and her victimization of secretary William Davison was laid on for the benefit of James. Only once, in his eulogy of Sir Francis Walsingham, the puritan secretary whose spies provided the evidence at her trial, did Camden feel he might have gone too far, but even this passage was left untouched (IV, 20–1 [1627, 25–6]).[63] Throughout his account, Camden adduced evidence in the form of letters and state papers, printed *in extenso*.

Camden deftly wove the drama of Mary into other themes in Elizabeth's reign, such as the threats of Rome, of Spain, and of domestic rebels such as the northern earls, and to the equally tragic tale of the executed duke of Norfolk (II, 40 [1615, 217–18]).[64] But the full picture was even more panoramic, and at its centre stood Elizabeth herself, the embodiment of England, who symbolized for Camden the *via media* in all things. This included the church, for though Camden did not wish to meddle with ecclesiastical history, he was forced, like de Thou, to integrate it into his account, because in actuality it had been inseparable from politics. Throughout, he usually treated religion as a secular issue and radical dissent as a political offence rather than as heresy.[65] Camden never distinguished between the reformed religion of Edward VI's reign, of which he elsewhere spoke favourably, and that of Elizabeth, for to do so would be to imply that the Elizabethan church, and its Jacobean successor, was perhaps not as reformed as it might be. His point was precisely the opposite: once Elizabeth had 'by authority of Parliament,' re-established protestantism, no further change was desirable. 'The protestant religion being now by authority of parliament established, Queen Elizabeths first and chiefest care was for the most constant defence thereof, against all the practises of all men amidst the enemies in that behalfe; neither indeed did she ever suffer the least innovation therein' (I, 31 [1615, 40]).[66]

Because he saw the church through the eyes of his former patron, Burghley, Camden gave short shrift to religious dissenters from either side. The *politique* in him, the admirer of de Thou and Bodin, had no patience for puritans, 'breathing nothing but the purity of the Gospell' who 'calumniated the ecclesiastical policy (as corrupted with Romish dregs)' (I, 16, 107; II, 55 [1615, 23, 132–3, 233]). On the other side, the schemes of the papacy, the Spanish and the League presented a constant menace. Elizabeth was always careful to balance protestantism with prudence by cunningly playing off her Catholic opponents against each other and never deliberately picking a fight. Camden himself, who had several recusant friends, is careful to distinguish between the ordinary

English Catholic, who obeyed his queen and ignored the 1570 papal bull of excommunication, and the insidious Jesuits (especially Robert Parsons), whom every protestant prince had to fear (I, 134; III, 10–11 [1615, 166, 326–7]).

The queen ruled as astutely in politics as in religion. Coupling open neutrality with underhand involvement, she persistently supported the underdog in any dispute, aiding the Dutch rebels against the Spanish, and Henry IV against his ultramontane opponents (II, 54 [1615, 232]; IV, 12–13 [1627, 12–13]). In handling domestic affairs, Elizabeth heeded the advice of her councillors and the grievances of parliaments, though she generally knew best herself. Her refusal to name a successor, irksome to parliament, was designed to prevent an early transference of loyalty. Camden notes that many turned to James VI anyway 'in a false beliefe that the disprayse of the predecessor is a most pleasing delight to the successors' (IV, 222 [1627, 284]). Elizabeth favoured and protected worthy councillors such as Burghley, but she did have an unfortunate weak spot for men of less worth and more ambition, such as the earl of Leicester and his stepson, Essex. Leicester in particular Camden painted as an unscrupulous self-seeker (I, 72, 75; III, 64–5, 145 [1615, 91, 94, 391–2, 496]); this was the follower of Burghley talking again, here falling short of his own ideal of Polybian impartiality.

All things considered, Elizabeth handled her parliaments with velvet gloves, presided over the crushing of English and Irish rebellions, and ruled a prosperous island kingdom, feared and respected by all foreign powers. 'Thus sate she as an heroicall princesse and umpier betwixt the Spaniards, the French, and the Estates.' France and Spain lay in the scales; the balance was precariously maintained by England's queen (II, 86 [1615, 271]). It was this image of Elizabeth which appealed to James I as much as Camden's portrait of Mary Stuart, because most of what he praised in Elizabeth was still Jacobean practice, at least as far as the king was concerned. Like Elizabeth, James was the supreme governor of a balanced, reformed church. Like Elizabeth, 'who had alwaies made peace the summe of her cogitations,' he was a peacemaker. In the 1570s Elizabeth had promised to support Spain or the Dutch states, depending on which side tried harder to make a peace; even in the 1580s, when conflict with Spain appeared unavoidable, she had avoided a war until it became absolutely necessary.

James himself ended the Spanish war in 1605 and consistently held to a policy of directing foreign affairs from above the fray. From 1618, he attempted to halt the burgeoning Thirty Years' War through diplomacy, without involving England in an expensive conflict (II, 89 [1615, 274–5];

IV, 16 [1627, 20]).[67] His predecessor had also put up with no nonsense from firebrand puritans or ill-mannered MPs. This was music to James's ears; he once scolded his councillors for failing to silence outspoken members in the way Elizabeth had dealt with Peter Wentworth.[68] Camden not only described Elizabeth as the architect of the policies currently practised by James; even better, he also depicted the historical James VI, the future 'monarch of Britaine,' as her godson, admirer, protégé, and hand-picked successor. James learned the arts of kingship from his godmother, brought his own factious kingdom to heel, and proved himself worthy to unite the two realms. Again choosing discreetly to ignore some of the evidence, Camden exonerated James from any involvement in Essex's rebellion, and he glossed over the sparks that occasionally flew between the two princes (I, 83; III, 120–1, 132 [1615, 103, 466, 481]; IV, 69 [1627, 88]).[69]

In the early 1620s, James's Fabian tactics towards the Spanish and the Empire came under attack from puritan polemicists like Thomas Scott, who appealed to the age of Elizabeth by using the ghosts of the queen and some of her worthies to speak for him. Scott saw Elizabeth as Foxe's and Speed's new Deborah, leading a holy crusade against Spain and Rome, culminating in the apocalyptic defeat of the Armada. In John Reynolds' tract *Vox coeli*, which shares Scott's perspective, the queen attends a heavenly conference at which war with Spain is the main topic. Through his spirits, the author of this tract urged the king to take immediate steps to defend the realm and regain the Palatinate by attacking Spain, as Elizabeth would have done.[70]

The king greeted such publications with hostility, not because he disliked being compared with Elizabeth but because he himself did not envisage her as a warrior queen. It is likely for the same reasons that James's leading councillor Salisbury, perhaps at the king's instigation, had several years earlier denied Fulke Greville access to the state papers for his own projected life of Elizabeth. Salisbury had remarked that the king would have to approve anything that Greville wrote, and the latter had given up the project since it 'would necessarily require sheet after sheet to be viewed, which I had no confidence in my own powers to abide the hazard of.'[71] Elizabeth's image was not to be suppressed; but it was to be controlled, shaped, and manipulated to the benefit of the Jacobean regime.

By the 1620s, however, it was no longer possible to prevent unpalatable versions of the late queen from appearing. At this stage, the best way to counteract the growing image of Elizabeth the protestant crusader was simply to present a convincing alternative. It is not stretching a point to suggest that the king's sudden interest in the publication of the remainder of the *Annales* and in the translation was in large part due to his and his advisers' wish that he be perceived as the champion of an Elizabethan foreign policy, a prudent peacemaker rather than either a belligerent warlord or a quivering coward.

As a work of narrative political history, the *Annales* is unrivalled in its grasp of the complexity of causes behind effects, of wheels within wheels, and of the domino effect linking one event to another years and miles away, though Camden deliberately avoided reading between the lines. His attitude to fortune remains ambiguous. Like Ralegh, he employed it as a rhetorical device rather than dismissing it. Following Bodin's *Methodus*, he discounted astrological influences as the cause of the earl of Essex's downfall, 'though fortune many times failed him' (IV, 189 [1627, 241]).[72] The victory of the English over Irish rebels in 1579 is blamed on fortune, but while Camden knew that rebellion was an offence against God, he stopped short of ascribing anything directly to divine intervention. He felt obliged to report (though he placed little stock in them) omens such as the earthquake of 1580 which preceded the renewed hounding of the English Catholics (II, 69, 106 [1615, 251, 297]). On the whole, he appealed to the superhuman much less than other historians of Elizabeth, such as Foxe and Speed.

It seems fair to say that Camden's understanding of the web of interlocking events he was describing (most of which were within his memory), complemented by the abundance of his evidence and by his close imitation of Polybius and de Thou, brought him the closest of all his contemporaries toward an appreciation of the contingent in history. As he tells it, England had been saved from Spanish invasion in 1578 by the sudden death of King Sebastian of Portugal: Spanish forces had to be sent there instead. Whether or not Camden believed this to be the will of God, as all things were assumed to be, he explained it in thoroughly secular terms as a confluence of happy circumstances (II, 93–4 [1615, 280–1]). Partly because the short time-scale of a single reign did not allow it, there is also less sign of the teleological approach which permeates other histories. Although he had Elizabeth groom James VI for the succession from an early age, Camden read the evidence of his documents forward, not backward. He would make reference to the distant outcome of an event, but he never described that outcome as inevitable, since a congeries of factors contributed in his account to the occurrence of another event in the future. Like the memorialists before him, Polybius, Guicciardini, and de Thou, he was part of the events he described, and could see them from two positions, as much the observer as the historian.

Unlike many of his less talented contemporaries, Camden left no methodological tract, beyond the short preface to the *Annales*; he was a practitioner rather than a theorist. We do not know how he would have handled the problem of long-term political development, though the close friend of Samuel Daniel had no doubt given the matter some thought. Not gifted with an especially original mind, he depended as much as any writer on models, whether Ortelius, de Thou, or Polybius. His most interesting insights into more remote periods of the English past were captured in his short *Remaines*, which was not a history.[73] The *Annales* was a superb and fascinating account of the recent past, elegantly written, and glowing with a brilliant understanding of the events of his own lifetime, yet it remains bound by the limits which humanist eloquence had imposed upon the historian. Though matters of the economy, of foreign exploration, of architecture, and of art are given their place in the *Annales*, Camden remained confident that 'matters of warre, and matters of policy, are things most proper to history' (sig B2v [1615, sig A4r]).

Francis Godwin and the Early Tudors

Camden's adaptation of the annalistic form to the purposes of humanist historiography proved successful, and it soon evoked imitators. Among Camden's many friends and admirers was Francis Godwin (1562–1633), successively bishop of Llandaff and Hereford. Godwin accompanied Camden on an antiquarian excursion into Wales, and the schoolmaster was godfather to Thomas, one of Godwin's sons. Godwin sent Camden transcripts of an old English charter in 1608 and offered to have several others copied for him. In 1620, when Godwin was fifty-eight and Camden nearly seventy, Godwin lamented that they might never meet again. On this occasion, he urged Camden to publish the second part of the *Annales*, which had been finished since 1618, adding his voice to the continental chorus crying out for a book which Camden himself gladly never saw in print.[74]

In 1601, at the age of thirty-nine, Godwin published a *Catalogue of the Bishops of England*, which is still consulted today by ecclesiastical historians. For this labour he was rewarded by Queen Elizabeth with the see of Llandaff. In 1615 he expanded the work, adding a short essay on the conversion of England to Christianity, which would later provide one of Richard Broughton's targets. Again, reward followed, and Godwin was translated in 1616 to the wealthier see of Hereford.[75]

Despite the publication of Speed's *History of Great Britaine* in 1611, Godwin was unhappy with the state of historical writing in England. The best account, he contended, remained that by Polydore Vergil, a work praised only because it was the most recent attempt at a general history of England, and because it was perhaps the most eloquent or 'polite.' The lack of a history of the eventful sixteenth century particularly distressed him. Hayward had yet to begin his *Edward VI*, so Godwin, inspired by Camden's study of Elizabeth, turned his hand to a Latin account of political events under Henry VIII, Edward VI, and Mary. His *Rerum anglicarum ... annales* enjoyed royal support, and was published by John Bill, the king's printer. In 1630 another of the bishop's sons, Morgan, translated the book and added corrections under his father's supervision.[76]

The bishop prefaced his book with a complaint: why, he asked, was there no history being written to replace that by Polydore Vergil? Historians, he claimed, were wasting their time by pasting bits and pieces on to the Italian's account of English history, which now looked inadequate and erratic. Instead, someone ought to 'compile a history of our nation worthy of the British name.' (Godwin makes no reference to Richard White or John Lewis, though he would probably have known at least the work of the former.) A man 'versed in our antiquities' should do for history what 'master Camden hath already done for the description of the island ... Our antiquaries may justly be taxed of sloth' (sig A2r).

From this last remark it is evident that Godwin perceived that there could be a fruitful relationship between antiquarian erudition and history, but it is also clear that he restricted that relationship to the traditional subjects of history: he wanted a didactic narrative of great men, 'examples of most eminent vertues,' rather than a general history which covered social, religious and cultural change. Nevertheless, his call for a history by the *eruditi* devoted to truth rather than style shows that he had a higher regard for the capacity of the scholar to write history than did most of his contemporaries.

Unhappily, Godwin's *Annales* fall short of his own mark, and are a dim shadow of Camden's own *Elizabeth*, which he used as a model. Perhaps because the chances of an eyewitness challenging him about Mary Tudor's reign were, by 1616, rather remote, Godwin did not put anything like the effort of Camden into his research. His principal sources were Guicciardini, de Thou, du Bellay, Sleidan, Stow, and a number of unnamed Scottish writers. He used George Cavendish's then unpublished *Life of Wolsey* extensively for Henry VIII's reign; his son's translation would lift speeches and scenes almost word for word from this source. He used a few of the state papers which were in the Tower or in Cotton's hands (141), but in no sense was his account founded primarily on these records as Camden's had been.[77]

Godwin's history presents no striking insights that were not to be found in his sources, though his use of Cavendish – and, naturally, his episcopal point of view – led him to a more favourable assessment of Wolsey than usual, an appraisal which contains within it an implicit criticism of the relatively small political influence wielded by the Jacobean episcopacy. Certainly, Godwin conceded, the cardinal's ambitions were harmful to himself and others in the short term; but, he asked admiringly, what prelate has ever before or since displayed such magnificence and wielded such power? Wolsey was a good counsellor, entirely responsible for the successes of Henry's early years. Using the analogy of Tacitus' Nero, Godwin describes Henry as an incipient tyrant, restrained only by the leash of his own Seneca, the cardinal. Even Wolsey's greed had a valuable end: 'It made way for that great alteration which afterward happened in the estate of the Church. Blessed be that almighty power, that converts the wicked designes of men to the good of his Church, and his owne glory' (58, 97, 207).

Sharing his sources' attitude to the motives behind political activities, Godwin was as scathing about Henry VIII's reasons for breaking with Rome as Ralegh had been two years earlier. 'Hee tooke this course more to satisfie his lust then his conscience' (86). Like Ralegh, but at much greater length, Godwin managed to combine a celebration of the Reformation with a distaste for the personality of the king himself, again departing from Foxe's more heroic interpretation.

The assumption, as always, is that God allows evil to transpire with some future good in mind, and Godwin certainly found providence a useful explanatory tool. Francis I's many tactical blunders, for example, led to his defeat at Pavia, but these themselves were the direct work of God. 'The divine power having decreed to chastise him,' Godwin observed, it 'permitted him through impatience to run headlong into these errours.' Luckily, 'Gods speciall favour' ensured that this was but a temporary setback for the French king, not the disaster it might have been. Providence allowed the death of Thomas Howard, fiancé of Henry VIII's niece, Margaret, so the maiden could marry the earl of Lennox and produce Henry Darnley, 'the father of King James ... the most happy unitor of divided Britaine' (63, 159). God prevented a massacre of the pilgrims of grace by causing a 'chance' flood. Unlike Camden, Godwin's analysis of the sudden political changes under Henry and, much more briefly and flatly, under Edward and Mary, was nailed firmly to 'fortunes wheele,' which raised and destroyed Wolsey and Cromwell in rapid succession. Instead of the detailed narrative and evidence offered by Camden, the reader is presented with the easy aphorism, rather in the fashion of Speed: 'the Court of England' is a stage, 'whereon are represented the vicissitudes of ever various fortune' (143, 149, 174).

It is inappropriate to evaluate seventeenth-century authors by the standards of the present, to pronounce one work bad and another brilliant. Yet Godwin's history *is* unimpressive by contemporary standards: one has only to set it against Camden's work to see that Godwin was neither as diligent a researcher as Camden, nor as sharp an analyst of the complexities of politics. Camden may have had models, but he possessed – perhaps more through the accident of Elizabeth's recency than through his own preference – a freedom from the influence of 'secondary' accounts that Godwin could not begin to imitate. Godwin had spotted the need for antiquaries to engage in the writing of history proper, but he himself remained a reteller of tales to which he had little to add.

The Rehabilitation of Richard III

The courtly poet Samuel Daniel had managed to break away from received opinions on the character of certain kings by judging their records for himself rather than through the eyes of his sources. Another courtier, who as master of the revels from 1607 to 1621 was responsible for the censorship of Jacobean drama, carried out a full-scale revision of the reputation of Richard III, the archetypal tyrant and usurper. Sir George Buck had a score to settle. His great-grandfather had been executed for fighting on Richard's side at Bosworth, and the fortunes of his ancient family had remained poor ever since. By vindicating Richard he could clear his own family name.[78]

Whatever Buck's motives, the *History of King Richard the Third* rates as one of the most original pieces of historical writing in the early seventeenth century. Through careful research, faultless documentation, and a skilful, lawyer-like erosion of the credibility of the architects of the Ricardian myth (especially Thomas More), Buck single-handedly carried out the first full-scale reappraisal of a king's reign in the history of English historiography.[79]

Not surprisingly, he did not publish it. The Ricardian myth was one of the most firmly held in the Tudor tradition. A favourite of poets and dramatists, it had been restated as recently as 1614 by Christopher Brooke, a friend of Sir Robert Cotton,[80] and it is likely that Buck's elaborate arguments would have been unfavourably received by all but the most open-minded readers – not a great number. Popular historical conceptions, no less than scientific theories, do not die, but fade away, and to suggest that Richard had in fact been a good king would to the Jacobean mind be rather like suggesting that man had descended from the ape. After he went mad and died in 1622, Buck's manuscript, which he was still busy revising, was 'edited' by his opportunistic great-nephew, also named George; the original manuscript gathered dust through the centuries, until Arthur Noel Kincaid edited it in 1979.[81]

Buck's acquaintances and interests were wide. He was one of the few historians or antiquaries with anything good to say about the herald Ralph Brooke, Camden's ill-tempered critic. Buck was friendly with John Stow till his death in 1605, and then with Cotton and Camden. He was servant to Lord Admiral Charles Howard in the Spanish war and subsequently the friend and client of the earls of Northampton and Arundel. He incorporated in his *History* a brief history of the Howard family, which like his had been very nearly ruined at Bosworth.[82] In a poem called Δαφνις Πολυστεφανος, written in 1602 but first published in 1605, he contributed to the 'union' literature by tracing James's descent back to Henry II and presenting him as the uniter of the realms.[83] A very different work, the 'Commentary upon the ... liber Domus Dei' was a weighty and learned manuscript of nearly five hundred folios. Assembled from charters, rolls, private and public archives, 'private evidences, histories and other monuments authentick,' the book gave the origins of all the noble families 'whose ancestors have bene at the least simple barons' and traced their descents; it included an especially detailed investigation of the Buck and Howard families.[84]

The 'Commentary' was finished by 1619, at which time Buck was already hard at work on the *History of King Richard the Third*. The heated reception a year earlier of an even greater work of historical revisionism, Selden's *Historie of Tithes*, may have deterred Buck from finishing his own *History*, though it is impossible to guess what he might have done with the manuscript had he not gone mad. Buck also worried that his work would be taken for a 'paradox,' a skilful but insincere defence of an indefensible subject for the sake of rhetorical display. He had seen the amusing encomium of Richard III by Sir William Cornwallis, which had circulated widely in manuscript before being printed in 1616.[85] Unlike Cornwallis, the master of the revels was entirely in earnest in arguing Richard's case. As Buck confessed in the preface, 'My scope was to write this unhappy king's story faithfully and at large and to plead his cause, and to answer and refell the many accusations and calumniations brought against him' (3, 8).

Buck proved even less sensitive to the conventions regarding the use of antiquarian research in narrative history than had Godwin or Camden. Mustering a large array of English and French sources, printed and unprinted, and drawing on the works of both 'good historians and learned antiquaries,' he built up a dossier for the defence. His antiquarian interests constantly overlapped with his historical ones, and the study included an investigation of the historical origins of the name 'Plantagenet,' carried out 'according to the methods I have held for the searching of the originals of the most ancient noble families in England, of their surnames, in my *Commentary*' (11, 16–17).

He organized the *History* into five books. The first two give a chrono-logical overview of Richard's life and reign, along with a digression on 'the nobility and greatness of the house of Howard' (67). The remaining books are topically arranged. In Book III, Buck attacks the veracity of Thomas More, whom he believed was only the lackey and copyist of the sinister John Morton, bishop of Ely, who figures here as the real villain. Buck tries to clear Richard of the murder of the little princes by suggesting that Perkin Warbeck really *was* the Duke of York and that Edward V, his brother, had simply succumbed to infirmity (138–42, 169, 172). Book IV returns to Richard's own title, argues the bastardy of Edward IV's children, again attacks More, and obliquely accuses Henry VII of treason against his lawful king (198). The final book eulogizes Richard's character, his good laws, and his charitable works.

Rather than simply asserting that Richard was innocent of the many charges against him, Buck engaged in a multi-pronged strategy. He revealed the Protector Richard as a subject loyal and kind to his neph-ews, who only took the crown when forced to do so by the 'election' of the barons, who recognized the superiority of his title (25, 29, 127).[86] Buck points out that Lord Hastings was not as innocent a victim of Richard as he seemed, and that his execution, Richard's bloodiest deed, is partially excusable 'in reason of state and policy.' Despite his use of this phrase, Buck was no Machiavellian, and the 'excellent politicians' of his work are not the fair-minded Richard but the nefarious Morton and his inscrutable master, Henry VII. Buck 'abhorred' such 'artes impe-rii' but, he asked, why should Richard alone stand condemned for what Edward IV and Henry VII did much more often with apparent impunity (28–9)?

Richard might have remained safely on the throne had not 'Fortune, that inconstant and unfaithful dame,' deserted him. Buck balanced on a tightrope here, between a conviction that fortune was largely responsible for Richard's eventual fall, and the politically necessary belief that Henry's accession was preordained by God. 'It may haply be thought that I neglect the will of God in ascribing so much to fortune,' he apologizes. 'But yet I pray you to think that I know not that punishment which is not the will of God and by his divine privilege.' Providence laid the plans, but Richmond's invasions were 'the formal and efficient and final cause of all the mischiefs and calamity' which befell England in 1485 (68).

Buck points out that all the chroniclers who have slandered Richard 'would have highly extolled him and his virtues' if he had won at Bosworth. Yet, despite this interesting 'if ... then' speculation, he himself could not envisage a scenario in which Richard had actually triumphed. It did not help that Buck was among those Englishmen who took seriously the idea that Henry's reign had been foretold in prophecy. Richmond was destined to be king, and if he forced a showdown with Richard, he would have to win. This did not, however, prohibit Buck from speculating that Henry could have succeeded by more peaceful means had he but waited until Richard died to make his claim:

I do not mislike his having of the crown and his possession of the kingdom, as I have said before that it was foretold by a divine prophet that the earl of Richmond should be a king. And I hold also that he was ordained from above to be the sovereign of this land. But ... I utterly mislike that he would not tarry the Lord's leisure and receive a kingdom in His time; and that would have been time enough. (38, 128, 213)

Buck had painted himself into a corner. Having asserted that God intended Henry to rule, he crossed himself by suggesting that the *occasion* of the earl's accession, if not the fact, was dependent on Henry's being in a hurry. 'The Lord's leisure' would have preferred him to wait. Buck's whole position was illogical insofar as it tried to make contingent an event which must logically – to early seventeenth-century eyes – have been under God's control. Buck's own providential convictions would not let him take the final step of acknowledging that Henry could actually have been defeated and killed and the course of subsequent history substantially changed.

Like the advocate that he was by training, Buck on occasion went to extremes in Richard's defence, naively contrasting Richard's generosity and sincerity with the machinations of Morton, giver of 'Machiavellian advice,' and with Henry himself, who 'overreached Perkin [Warbeck] with his arts and his policy,' and used his cunning to exterminate virtually all his Yorkist rivals. Richard chivalrously offered to fight Henry in single combat, but he had 'made choice of a man which loved no combats' (37–8, 102, 149, 159). Still, Buck would admit some flaws in his hero. Richard was as determined to destroy Henry (practically the only evil thought he had) as Henry was to defeat him, to the point of being wilful and obstinate. Prodigies and omens warned his advisers that a confrontation with Henry would lead to his destruction, but Richard ignored all counsel and met his doom at Bosworth (98–101).

Buck had overstated his case in reaction against an accepted view, and even a century later, the editor of his nephew's diluted version could not fathom why anyone would *want* to defend Richard III.[87] In 1619, Buck probably would not have convinced more than a handful of his friends. Unknown except in the pirated version, which makes a much weaker case, the *History* had little influence on later historians, but it is something of a milestone in seventeenth-century historiography nonetheless. Buck had assumed a radically innovative perspective on an important episode in English history, and from that position reordered and reshaped the evidence until it revealed an entirely different picture, while unravelling the arguments of his predecessors; furthermore, he had searched beyond the official narrative sources to examine all the evidence related to his case.

The Probable Past

Edward Herbert, the first Baron Herbert of Cherbury, was a poet, politician, autobiographer, historian, and philosopher. He was also the first Englishman to give direct attention to the principal epistemological problem facing historians in the seventeenth century: how one could know, and to what extent one could be certain of, the events of the past.[88]

Unlike the French historical theorists of the preceding century, especially Bodin, no Englishman had by 1620 directly met the sceptical attack on the validity of historical knowledge. In part this was simply because the English sceptical tradition was less well developed than the European. While Sidney's brief remarks on history had questioned the possibility of knowing the past, his was a lonely voice. This was not due to any lack of familiarity with scepticism: Agrippa had been translated into English; so had the more thoughtful 'pyrrhonist' works of

Montaigne and Pierre Charron.[89] Yet historians steadfastly refused to provide an answer to scepticism. They were well aware of the problems of recovering knowledge of the past, and by 1600 many had developed healthy doubts about omens, Trojan ancestors, and saints' miracles.

Ralegh and many others – Camden's nominee for his chair in history at Oxford, Degory Whear, for instance – shared Sidney's opinion that profane historical sources were incomplete and contradictory; but the Bible remained unimpeachable, and history was still worth studying because of the lessons it taught about God and about human behaviour. Samuel Daniel, the servant of Sidney's sister the countess of Pembroke, was a pragmatist, as we have seen. The 'historian in verse' had developed a deep scepticism toward the literal truth of the past while preserving faith in its moral and political value; like Montaigne (and unlike Sidney), he did not go so far as to say that history was inferior to poetry, though his early preference for verse over prose has been noted.

Herbert, whose many friends included the philosopher Pierre Gassendi and the philologist John Selden, began his early diplomatic career as a client of the duke of Buckingham, who secured him the post of ambassador to Paris. Herbert's years on the continent both as diplomat and private traveller made him many important contacts, and he often carried letters between European and English scholars.[90] While in Holland in the 1610s, he had met the great Dutch philologists Gerard Vossius and Hugo Grotius, two of his later correspondents. In Paris he encountered Pierre Dupuy and Isaac Casaubon, the latter then at work editing Polybius. It was there, too, that he met Gassendi and Marin Mersenne. The last two were natural philosophers who would attempt in their many writings to diminish the scepticism of Montaigne and his disciples. Gassendi and Mersenne believed that there were aspects of knowledge which could be classified as certain – at least sufficiently so to make worthwhile deductions; although Herbert and Gassendi would later argue over the former's *De veritate*, Herbert was clearly influenced by the philosophical issues addressed by French epistemology.[91]

It was in Paris, among such company, that Herbert published *De veritate* in 1624, shortly before he returned to England. This treatise attempted to establish that the human mind could enjoy secure knowledge in some form through certain 'common notions' innate in the mind. The philosophical nuances of the argument cannot be explored here. Herbert's French friends regarded *De veritate* as a valiant failure, and Locke demolished it at the end of the century with his radically empirical epistemology, but the work had some influence, most notably on Descartes and on the Cambridge Platonists.[92] For our purposes, its principal importance is that Herbert included a section on the character of knowledge of the past.

Herbert has often been described as the father of deism. It is certain that he did not believe that the differences which divided Christianity were irreconcilable, for who could be certain that his opinion was right? Herbert was, however, a confirmed Christian and though the Augustan deist Charles Blount claimed him as master, the link between Herbert and later deism is tenuous. It is safer to describe him as an irenical sceptic.[93] He never made of his God an impersonal force, the supreme being or 'divine clockmaker' of the Enlightenment; he simply denied that one church, let alone a single branch of one church, held a monopoly of religious truth.

Religious knowledge rested for Herbert not on the historical revelations in the Bible, soon to be more profoundly challenged by French scriptural critics such as Richard Simon, but on the 'common notions,' such as that God exists, that He ought to be worshipped, and that there is an afterlife. The true 'catholic' church rests on these notions, which are innate in every man, not simply the Christian (De veritate 83ff, 291, 303–7). As Herbert put it, though he had great respect for the writers of both sacred and profane history, his belief in God was 'not derived from history, but from the teaching of the common notions.' Written history simply recorded the mechanical details, showing how God acted in time (314–15).

God controls the world through 'general providence' (nature) and 'special providence' or grace, which affects only man. The same laws which govern nature also operate in the rise and fall of states. 'I have often observed,' Herbert comments, 'that the universal providence which governs empires does not fail to operate in matters of necessity' (312, 315). But although God will never annul the workings of nature before the end of the world, nor diminish grace, He is a totally free being; and man, created in His image, shares His freedom to act according to will. Thus, says Herbert, although we can make reasonable predictions about the future by studying the causes of natural events such as eclipses, earthquakes, and tides, the future itself is ultimately not predetermined, but merely possible (323–31). God, being free, can act in a number of ways. He has established contrary principles on earth such as fire and water, earth and air, man and woman, which act and react on each other; under the direction of providence, mediated in man's case by the common notions, they combine without destroying each other. God is capable either of allowing events to take their natural course, or of intervening directly through miracles – Herbert himself was convinced that God had given him a sign that he should publish *De veritate* (117–20, 135–6).[94] The future is therefore not simply uncertain from man's point of view: it has not yet been determined. The Boethian *nunc-stans*, so fundamental to medieval and Renaissance conceptions of time, has here been abandoned.

In a short essay first published in 1645, *De religione laici*, Herbert developed this view into a curt dismissal of fortune as a valid explanation of causation. When a thing appears to occur fortuitously, he says, it is because 'its causes are not yet investigated.' Such events, resulting from causes unknown, are 'generally attributed to fortune.' But fortune is neither a goddess nor an irrational force: she is 'nothing but causes, or several results of causes.' What we mortals deem 'contingent on fortune' is invariably the consequence of an unknown cause. So far, this is a perfectly commonplace view. Nevertheless, Herbert continues, we must not infer from this that causes and effects are either entirely necessary or, on the contrary, entirely irrational. Since God is free, since the contraries in nature can react in different ways, and since man, within the limits of special and general providence, and of the possession of physical capacity, is also free, *anything* can happen in the future.[95]

The implications of this outlook on the future for the study of the past are not difficult to see. If God can intervene directly, then one cannot dismiss, *prima facie*, the miracles and omens reported in chronicles; they are and must remain 'open questions.' All one can do is to rely on common sense. Only a miracle which seems unlikely insofar as it seems to contradict general or special providence, or one which relies on an untrustworthy authority, can be dismissed, and even then we can never be really certain (312, 317).

If the future can be known merely as possibility, then knowledge of the past can never be more than 'probable,' since the reader of histories must rely not on his own sense perception but on that of others: 'All tradition and history, every thing in short that concerns the past, whether it be true or false, good or evil, possesses for us only probability, since it depends on the authority of the narrator.' In the early modern sense of the word, used here by Herbert, the word 'probable' does not mean 'statistically more likely to be true than not.' Rather, it means 'likely because *proven* or *testified to* by authority.' As Ian Hacking has pointed out, the 'probable' fact in the Renaissance and for some time thereafter was that fact which had the 'approbation' or support of witnesses; a probable fact about the past would be a fact 'supported by testimony and the writ of authority.'[96]

Any history which does not rest on such probability is 'futile' (*De veritate,* 314). Let us take the Bible: though many events in it seem strange, we need not question it since it has long been accepted and since there is no way to prove it is not the word of God. This applies to profane history, too. If successive ages have accepted an historical event, we should not dismiss it, unless we know that the tradition originated with a 'primitive or ignorant period or country' (308–13, 317). For Herbert, the purpose of history remained much the same as it had been for Samuel Daniel: 'History presents us with the varying fortunes of events and consequently it affords us striking examples of God's general and particular providence.' When we read of the deeds of virtuous men, we are 'stirred to respond' (315, 317). But we can draw no valid conclusions from history unless the facts are first established to the highest level of probability.

Probability itself, however, is no absolute principle; it too admits of degrees where the past is concerned. Knowledge of the ancient world, by which Herbert seems to have intended both prehistoric and classical antiquity, 'rests upon conjecture' and is therefore uncertain in the extreme. Its writers may have been deceived themselves, and they may have wished to deceive their readers. One can make deductions from history, but only when reasonably certain of the facts. 'When the historical facts themselves are misleading, the historians destroy both truth and certainty.' Recent history is only slightly more probable, and the reader who is not himself an historian cannot *know* the truth of the matter, however likely it seems. He must use his judgment. He must evaluate the authority of the writer, distinguish between the facts reported and the conclusions the writer draws, and recognize that the narrative he is reading is the subjective product of a writer who may assume various roles – historian, preacher, statesman, philosopher, theologian, 'or possibly jester' (321–2).

In itself, this was not a very reassuring answer. One could never, merely by reading a history, know for certain if the events reported were fact or fiction. There was one way out, however – personal research. He who investigates history for himself can arrive at a level of probability which approximates certainty. This could never provide *absolute* knowledge, which God alone possesses; it is not even as certain as the knowledge that the sun will rise tomorrow; but it is as highly probable as anything not immediately available to our senses. Through research, Herbert assures us, we can come close to apprehending the past. 'As for the past, particular events which were formerly experienced by a few persons, and are current now in the form of narratives, can pass as true solely for those persons who have attained an understanding of such matters or events, whether they actually exist now or in the past, after a thorough investigation.' The historian working among the surviving material of the past can intuit the likelihood of an event. Unfortunately, this offers little solace for the reader, who cannot apprehend the facts in the same way, even by reading the scholarly historian's work, since he cannot know for certain if any historian, past or present, has actually 'undertaken such an investigation.' Historical knowledge must always remain less certain for the reader than the writer (321).

Herbert's theory, despite its manifest loopholes and weaknesses, represents an important development in English historical consciousness. Herbert had reconciled himself to the lack of complete certainty in history; at the same time, he had shown that although the subjective interpretation of facts prevented such certainty, one could approach that unobtainable ideal through firsthand investigation. In other words, history could never be perfect, but it could become more or less probable.[97]

Herbert reached his views in the wake of detailed antiquarian investigations of the ancient past by such scholars as John Selden and Gerard Vossius, the significance of which will be discussed below.[98] His *De religione gentilium (Of the Ancient Religion of the Gentiles)* was clearly indebted to Selden's *De dis Syris* both at first hand and indirectly, via Vossius' *De theologia gentili*, which was itself influenced by Selden's book.[99] But, as with Sir George Buck nearly two decades earlier, we can see Herbert's marriage of the antiquarian methodology and a considered epistemology of history most clearly in his *The Life and Raigne of King Henry the Eighth*. Herbert began this work in 1632, a few years after his recall from France. The king provided him with access to the Cottonian library, closed by royal command since 1629, and to the public records. Herbert was given an office in Whitehall and assistants to copy documents (thereby partly breaking his own rules, for how could he know that their transcripts were accurate?).[100] Apparently this proved inadequate, for the work was not finished until the mid-1640s and only published in 1649, a year after the author's death.

The *Henry VIII* is a significant historical work for a number of reasons.[101] Modern historians still consult it because Herbert transcribed sixteenth-century documents which no longer exist, or made statements drawn upon such vanished sources.[102] Eugene D. Hill has recently placed the work within the context of Herbert's broader attitude to the past, according to which history could be described as an ongoing 'conspiracy of the priests against the laity.'[103] While the *Henry VIII* certainly does reflect Herbert's religious beliefs, it is perhaps more interesting to us as the first work of English historiography after Camden's *Annales* to study a single reign from all the available evidence. Herbert used documents in much the same way that Camden had, including original treaties, letters and diaries, such as the journal kept by John Taylor, master of the rolls, of Henry's French campaign in 1513–14.[104] But Herbert did not simply transcribe these *verbatim* and take them at face value. He also criticized them, something Camden, deliberately refusing to read between the lines, had never done. Herbert knew from personal experience that what was written in formal diplomatic papers and what was thought and spoken privately were often quite different. He made good use of French, Spanish, and Italian histories and of source-books such as the archivist Jean du Tillet's guide to Anglo-French treaties.[105] The result was not really a life of Henry VIII at all but a history of England's interactions with Europe in the first half of the sixteenth century. Luther, the popes, Francis I and Charles V, the Reformation and the Council of Trent are not merely mentioned in passing: they are the subject of the history as much as the domestic affairs and enigmatic character of Henry himself.

Herbert was driven to put Henry's reign in its European context by a desire to rehabilitate the king's reputation, which had declined rapidly since the death of Elizabeth. There was little reason, under James I, to praise the king whose will had specifically excluded the Stuart line from the succession, and Henry's own character seemed unattractive at a century's remove; as early as 1610, the earl of Salisbury had commented in Parliament that he disliked citing Henry VIII as a precedent, 'for he was the child of lust and man of iniquity.'[106] As we have seen, Ralegh and Godwin had condemned Henry while Martyn and Speed had been at best lukewarm. Herbert was unconvinced, and believed that Henry's actions had to be understood as proceeding sometimes from normal human vices but often from 'reason of state' (*Henry VIII*, sigs B1v, B2r). Henry's contemporaries, Francis I and Charles V, acted on precisely the same principles. Herbert vowed 'not to describe him otherwise, either good or bad, but as he really was,' letting the documents, from which he transcribed and quoted, speak for themselves. Herbert insisted on giving the benefit of the doubt to the king where the facts were uncertain, but was prepared to abandon a favourable 'interpretation' (he actually uses this word) 'where arguments to the contrary convince me' (sig A2v).

The scope of the *Henry VIII* is wide, including the agrarian and commercial legislation of the reign, the value of English and European currency and the disastrous effects of the Henrician debasement of the coinage. The acts of each parliament are listed from the original records and letters; events are described in detail 'that I might correct the error of some of our historians' (sigs D2r, Y8r, 3Y4r–v). If the documents contradicted a chronicler (usually Hall or Polydore), Herbert left the question open, but inclined to believe the original source. Yet he frequently suspected documents of being bogus: he could not decide if the letter from the condemned Anne Boleyn to Henry was genuine or had been written 'by any else heretofore' (sig 3B4v).[107]

Despite a lengthy digression on the character of general providence and on the common notions (sigs 2O3r–4v),[108] the supernatural is even less to be seen than in Camden's *Annales*. Fortune is never cited as a specific cause, though a character might be 'fortunate.' The sudden falls of Wolsey and Cromwell, of Anne Boleyn and Katherine Howard, Herbert ascribed entirely to the particular circumstances behind them (sigs 2K4v–2L1r; 2Q1v, 3B3r–3C2r; 3N4r–3O1v). The storm which interrupted the Pilgrimage of Grace, attributed by Francis Godwin to God's direct intervention, was to Herbert simply an act of nature (sigs 3F3v, 3H3v). Except for a brief reference to 'God's will' in not granting Henry a male heir by his first queen, providence stays in the background, though Herbert kept an open mind to the unusual or miraculous, repeating, for example, John Stow's tale of a potter who slept for two weeks continuously (sig 4A2v).[109]

The last of the early Stuart politic biographers, Herbert was perhaps the most profound in terms of his insights into the past, though he had not the scholarly equipment of a Buck or Camden. He also lacked Camden's ability to weave his evidence into a smooth narrative; as a writer, Herbert was never quite able to digest his material and much of the history is disjointed, almost turning into a chronicle at several points. Like almost all historians, he was happy to construct imaginative speeches for his characters.[110] On the whole, the book is quite dull and its six hundred pages demand some stamina. But Herbert's application of some of his earlier ideas to practical historiography outweighs the book's literary shortcomings, while its store of material has kept it in that select number of early modern histories which remain alive and informative over three and a half centuries later.

To writers dissatisfied with the traditional mode of chronicling the past, and eager to highlight the role of personality in the determination of political events, the biographical form clearly provided an attractive medium. This was as true for authors such as Fulke Greville, whose own life of his friend Sir Philip Sidney is as much a retrospective on the

Elizabethan age (and a backhanded commentary on later times), as it was for those historians tackling larger subjects through the lives of monarchs. Judith H. Anderson's sensitive study of a number of life-writers in the sixteenth and seventeenth centuries clearly demonstrates the variety of narrative strategies and stylistic techniques that biographers could employ to bring to life their subjects, and the times in which they lived.[111] This chapter has focused less on the purely biographical aspects of 'politic biography' than on the place of princely life-writing in the historical corpus of the early Stuart period.

I have argued that the works of Hayward, Camden, and the others form a subgenre which is distinctive enough from the sort of extended work written by, say, Daniel, to be considered separately. This is not to say that these words differ radically from a history like the *Collection of the Historie of England,* or even from Speed's *History,* in terms of content and vocabulary; nor is it to say that each of these works may not have more points in common with histories of different sorts than they may with other biographies. Hayward's treatment of legal issues, especially the relationship between royal power, conquest, and law, shows some points of contact with Daniel's work even if Daniel lacked Hayward's civilian perspective, and Hayward Daniel's sympathetic imagination. Godwin's *Annales,* though cast in a form very similar to Camden's *Elizabeth,* lies closer to the providential, religious point of view taken by a godly layman such as Speed. Herbert's *Henry VIII* again resembles Camden in design, but conceals an epistemological attitude to the past considerably more complex and critical. Buck's *Richard III* is perhaps the strangest and least characteristic work of all. Unlike Herbert, Buck had no deep philosophical or theological theories about the truth of the past, only a lawyer's ability to ask awkward questions of a witness, be it man or manuscript. The scholarship behind his defence of Richard, as much as the cast of mind that conceived of it, attests to the viability of the biographical form in the hands of an antiquary; at the same time it shows that all historical 'truths,' no matter how widely held, may be subject to revision.

CHAPTER FIVE

The Historian as Counsellor

The final end of a courtier, wher to al his good condicions and honest qualities tende, is to beecome an instructor and teacher of his prince or lorde, inclininge him to vertuous practises: and to be francke and free with him, after he is once in favour in matters touching his honour and estimation, always putting him in minde to folow vertue and to flee vice, opening unto him the commodities of the one and inconveniences of the other ...[1]

Sir Thomas Hoby

The Problem of Counsel

Herbert's reappraisal of the character of Henry VIII provides a good example of the ways in which the spectrum of acceptable historical opinion was widening in the second and third decades of the seventeenth century. Even so, because historians and readers alike felt an ambivalence toward Henry VIII that they did not to other historical personages, such as Richard III, it does not represent so great a departure from a stereotype as did Buck's Richard. Such wholesale revisions as Buck's, on a subject of which strong opinions were held, are rare in early Stuart historiography. What was needed, before such a clash of interpretations became more widespread, was a conflict of ideologies on a much larger scale. That this did not occur before the civil war was a function both of the resilience of Tudor views of the past, and of the lack of an explicit link between narrative history and any ideology opposed to the conservative doctrine of obedience and loyalty to the crown which had been inculcated into subjects for a century. It was also a consequence of the fact that many historians saw the primary purpose of the politic biography not as arguing a case, or as providing information, but as a means of offering political advice.

Throughout the sixteenth century, Europeans had looked to history for instruction. In his *History of Florence,* as much as his *Discourses* and the notorious *Prince,* Machiavelli dredged up the past to serve as the statesman's guide, subordinating history to political philosophy. He was neither the first nor the last to do so.[2] Many medieval historical works were composed for the express purpose of instructing the powerful; a parallel tradition existed of non-historical advice books, from John of Salisbury's *Policraticus* through the *specula* or 'mirrors of princes' of the late Middle Ages to Erasmus' *Education of a Christian Prince* and More's *Utopia* at the beginning of the sixteenth century.

In the late sixteenth century, Giovanni Botero had attacked Machiavelli in his *Della ragione di stato;* but because Botero also viewed politics in Machiavelli's pragmatic fashion, he succeeded only in spreading many of the ideas he had planned to refute, and in creating for them a popular tag: reason of state.[3] Works such as Botero's, combined with the increasing popularity of the two most 'politic' of ancient historians, Tacitus and Polybius, helped spread a 'Machiavellian' attitude to politics and thus, incidentally, his attitude to history as the guidebook of political life. Among the most praised of recent historians by the beginning of the seventeenth century were a Frenchman, Commynes, and another Florentine, Guicciardini. Both were popular, like Tacitus and Polybius, because they wrote of the causes and consequences of human behaviour in realistic terms.

It has sometimes been said that later sixteenth-century historians 'reacted' against the 'rhetorical' histories of Livy and of the early Italian humanists. In France, writes George Huppert, history was 'rescued from rhetoric and allied with erudition' by Bodin, Pasquier, La Popelinière, and other *savants.*[4] This is quite true in the sense that history gradually evolved into a discipline distinct from the orator's, an activity which demanded allegiance to truth, whether of the moral or factual sort. But 'truth' by no means precluded rhetoric. It was the use of golden words to support the patently fabulous which became unpopular, not the use of rhetoric *per se.* As one Jacobean scholar put it, there was nothing wrong with the Roman historian Velleius Paterculus' flowing prose except the apparent lack of substance which it concealed.[5] No early Stuart historian complained of another writer's good style, though many, as we have already seen, abhorred the so-called crudities of medieval chronicles. Rhetoric maintained a strong position at the universities and inns of court, while manuals on speech and oratory, such as Thomas Farnaby's *Index rhetoricus,* ran through multiple editions throughout the seventeenth century.[6]

If Tudor and early Stuart historians aspired to little else, they certainly aimed to teach, and they could not afford to neglect rhetoric if they wished to persuade readers to emulate the good and godly. Figures of speech such as amplification, metaphor, hyperbole, and parable did not have to support the fabulous; they could also be used to drive home the point of the factual. In no sense did historians wish to purge history of rhetoric, and a persuasive, eloquent style is evident in varying degrees from More's larger-than-life depiction of Richard III's villainy to Camden's more low-key celebration of the virtues of Queen Elizabeth. As long as history was linked to any belief that the present could learn from the past it might remain distinct from rhetoric, but never very distant.

While most historians filled their works with generalizations of either the political or moral variety (and usually both, since they were uniformly loath to admit the difference), a few went even further. Instead of looking to the past for general guides to behaviour, they followed Machiavelli to look for parallels which could be imitated in specific situations. It is no coincidence that a number of English historians who had absorbed Machiavelli's approach to politics and his method of writing history produced princely advice books, in historical form, wherein a specific king was studied in order to teach one in the present how better to run his kingdom. This subgenre was closely related to the politic biography treated in the previous chapter, but it differed from its parent genre in a number of subtle ways. Most obviously, the historical advice book, unlike the politic biography, was a *pièce d'occasion,* conceived, researched, and written in a brief period of time, and most often inspired by a particular set of political circumstances. It was not a work of careful, prolonged research, and therefore cannot be read with expectations of the scrupulous scholarship one finds in Camden, or of the mature historical sensibility demonstrated by Samuel Daniel.

These are differences of emphasis and degree, not rigid distinctions. All history, and especially political narrative, aimed at giving advice, however subtly and obliquely; but it seems clear that the short works by Francis Bacon, Sir Robert Cotton, and William Habington, unlike those by Hayward, Godwin, or Herbert, were more exclusively devoted to providing advice of a specific character – often on subjects of great topicality, and always of a political nature – than they were to recounting an accurate, morally didactic account of a given reign. Like politic history in general, the clearest antecedents of the history written as a political advice lay in Florentine historiography, and in the Tacitean revival of the late sixteenth century. It is therefore not surprising to discover in these works that Machiavelli's view of the past as a guide to making tough political and military decisions tends to drown out the older, Ciceronian tradition of history as a general source of wisdom and moral behaviour. Thus, while they differ little in some respects from the histories of Camden, Hayward, and Buck, they have a harder edge; though they continue the tradition of ambivalence to *raison d'état* and machiavellian statecraft, each shows a greater willingness to accept the harsher requirements of princely rule than one finds in Camden or even Hayward.

Each of the authors in this chapter dared to do what Ralegh was supposedly punished for: that is, to censure, albeit mildly, monarchs long dead. Each hoped that his gentle criticism of a past prince might occasion a shift in the behaviour of the present ruler, without causing offence. But it would be a serious error to infer from such texts the existence of an 'opposition' tradition of historical writing in the period before the civil war. If anything, the existence of such works further demonstrates the elasticity of the Tudor and early Stuart picture of the past. Two of the historians in question, Bacon and Habington, found their advice unheeded, but paid no personal price to a hypersensitive monarch; in Cotton's case the threat of punishment would loom but never materialize, since he denied all responsibility for the publication of his tract.

Although each author had reasons to be critical of the political direction being taken by his prince, none can by any stretch of the imagination be considered an opponent of the court. 'Criticism and satire are not necessarily expressions of opposition,' R. Malcolm Smuts has recently remarked. 'They can be offered in a loyal spirit, to counteract flattery and to encourage reform.'[7] To chastise is not the same as to oppose. Each of the three writers would certainly have been familiar with Castiglione's *Courtier,* which in the translation of Bacon's uncle, Sir Thomas Hoby, recommends that the courtier use dissimulation, whereby 'a man speaketh one thinge and privilie meaneth another' in order to guide his lord without letting on that he is so doing.[8] The immediate stimulus of the works studied here was not a desire to subvert the government, or even to bring about the ruin of any individual minister; these historical advice books were occasioned, at different times and in response to different situations, by that general phenomenon of early Stuart politics which has come to be called the crisis of counsel, the belief among a segment of the political élite that the king was not getting the right advice from the right people.

Francis Bacon: History, Theory, and the Art of Persuasion

Bacon's ideas on history and his practical efforts at writing it have received more attention than those of any other Renaissance Englishman. Bacon was a more prolific writer than most and, since the publication of the Spedding edition of his works over a century ago, he has been among the most studied.[9] He was also among the most articulate of historical writers with regard to his own presuppositions as to history's scope and purpose. Whereas one must reconstruct most other authors' attitudes to historiography from prefaces to their works and scattered comments in their letters, Bacon left behind, in the *Advancement of Learning* and other writings, a concise, eloquent, and systematic presentation of his beliefs. Moreover, Bacon's historical ideas were only part of a broader vision of the potential of human inquiry.[10] Before we turn to his study of the reign of Henry VII, therefore, it is worth looking more generally at his attitude to the past, and to his conception of history as a mode of discourse.

Human consciousness has passed, in Bacon's view of historic time, through a variety of stages which are differentiated by consciousness's changing perception of the connections between the particular and the general, between the concrete and the abstract, and between words and things. In the *Novum organum* and elsewhere, Bacon defines each stage, negatively rather than positively, in terms of the 'idols' that distract the mind along the way. These idols are fourfold: those of the tribe, the cave, the market-place, and the theatre. They correspond to what Vico, with a more sympathetic understanding of their historical value, would a century later call the ages of gods, heroes, men, and 'second barbarism.'[11] The idols of the tribe (which is the tribe of man in his natural state and implies no sense of communal identity) are the shared characteristic of man as a species, and they consist in an inability to perceive *difference*: the difference between god and man, between subject and object, between cause and effect (IV, 54, 58). The salient quality of the primitive mind is its insistence on metaphorical thought in the form of fable and myth: 'we see therefore in the infancy of learning, and in rude times ... that the world was full of parables and similitudes' (IV, 452). Thus, the prominence of myth in primitive discourse, though Bacon allowed that even in his own day men with new ideas were 'obliged to have recourse to similitudes and metaphors to convey their meaning' (ibid).

The idols of the cave originate at that moment when individual consciousness departs from the tribe in search of 'a cave of its own.' These idols arise from the 'peculiar constitution, mental or bodily, of each individual.' At this stage, some minds continue to mark the resemblance of things and leap to ill-considered abstractions; others – he specifies Democritus and the atomists – go too far in the opposite direction and become obsessed with the particular and the unique, with difference rather than connection (iv, 54, 59). Civilization at this stage is unable to balance these two modes of experiential knowledge.

But the most troublesome idols of all are those of the third stage, the market-place. This stage results from the social interaction of individual minds in spoken language, 'for it is by discourse that men associate' (iv, 55). It is this human urge to commune, which necessitates language, the social convention that systematically allies *verbum* to *res*. There lies a problem, however, in the tendency of words to develop 'out of phase' with the things they denote. Words evolve for things which do not exist, such as 'fortune, the prime mover, planetary orbits, elements of fire, and like fictions' (iv, 61); conversely, the same word can be used to denote a number of different things, creating confusion. Because society is itself a desirable state, to which language is essential, the idols of the market-place are the most difficult to avoid. To men afflicted by them, the universe becomes a labyrinth – one recalls Speed's opinion of antiquity – full of 'ambiguities of way' which are no more than 'deceitful resemblances of objects and signs' (iv, 18). Bacon himself attempted to solve the problem, not by abandoning similitude altogether but by electing often to make his comparisons explicit through the use of simile rather than metaphor.[12]

In comparison, the idols of the theatre are easily avoided. The result of unbridled speculation and destructive criticism, they are not innate like the idols of tribe and cave, nor insidiously 'adventitious' like those of the market-place; rather, they are clearly and openly bequeathed to the mind by false philosophical systems, which are 'so many stage plays, representing worlds of their own creation after an unreal and scenic fashion' (iv, 55). Aristotle's *Natural History* began as a sound attempt at classifying experience; but when Aristotle departed from this valuable project to concentrate upon the syllogism, he created a false philosophy which elevated logic above experience, 'fashioning the world out of categories' (iv, 64). Though Bacon in general inveighed with more vehemence against medieval scholasticism than against Aristotle, he was obliged to concede that in this case the schoolmen were less culpable: because they abandoned experience altogether for their esoteric word-games, they at least did not *confuse* language and being. The worst offenders of all are the 'superstitious' philosophers – Plato, Pythagoras, and their modern disciples – who wrongly attribute reality to the ideal rather than the material (IV, 66). Bacon acknowledged that mankind owed a debt to Greek science, but primarily to the pre-Socratics, Empedocles, Anaxagoras, and Leucippus, rather than to the sophists or to Plato. Where the pre-Socratics had conducted research in the world of experience to wrest new truths from nature, the successors of Socrates had simply opened schools for the interminable contemplation and criticism of old ones (IV, 72). With few exceptions (such as his own namesake, Roger Bacon), the medieval scholars who followed them had too much leisure and too little to read (III, 285); they lingered forever on a corpus of received texts rather than pushing ahead to new conquests of the natural world. Collectively, the false philosophies had done little other than to engender 'despair, which has been one of the most powerful causes of delay and hindrance to the progress of knowledge' (IV, 103). Bacon's own age would dispel the gloom. By returning to the methods and goals of the pre-Socratics, his contemporaries could escape the sceptical frame of mind that had been the bane of learning since the foundation of the Academy two millennia earlier.

The four types of idol were not mutually exclusive. The same mind could be misled by more than one of these sirens, and Aristotle himself is taken to exemplify most of them. Nevertheless, because Bacon characterizes various ages in terms of their susceptibility to one idol over the others, it is clear that he perceived them not as mere afflictions of mind in the present, but as historical stages in the advancement of learning. As a framework for understanding the rise of learning, the categories carried over into his perception of 'history' which, as the record of experience in time and nature, was the highest form of human discourse: indeed, Bacon at one point explicitly equates history with 'experience' (IV, 293).

This equation has important implications for the history of scientific empiricism. Arno Seifert has argued persuasively that Bacon's thought is the culmination of a Renaissance tendency to reduce all empirical knowledge (*cognitio*) to various types of 'history.' In fact, this tendency can be seen at work decades before Bacon, in Bodin's use of the term *historia naturalis* and in other *artes historicae*. According to Seifert, 'history' becomes in Bacon a paradigm for all empirical inquiry, thereby reviving the classical Aristotelian sense of the word. The popularity of the term 'natural history' in ensuing centuries supports this line of argument, even if the originality and importance of Bacon's contribution to empirical theory must remain for now an open question.[13]

'All history,' Bacon tells James I, 'walks upon the earth, and performs the office rather of a guide than of a light.' In this aspect, history can claim superiority over poetry, which is 'as a dream of learning' (IV, 336). The poverty of ancient philosophy can be ascribed directly to its lack of a proper sense of the past, which implies a consciousness of chronological and spatial order (III, 285; IV, 73). Natural history and civil history thus walk hand in hand.

Natural history should consist of a step-by-step procedure from individual to individual. As the guide in this procedure, Bacon pledged himself to strict attention to 'the particulars themselves, and their series and order' (IV, 53). But more important than the study of any single thing-in-itself is the comprehension of the place of that thing in the web of relationships that connect it to other things. Nature is a plenum which can best be represented as a matrix of connections, not unlike a modern periodic table, in which the whole will appear once every part is in place. 'In laying out the divisions of the sciences,' Bacon informed his reader, 'I take into account not only things already invented and known, but likewise things omitted which ought to be there' (IV, 22–3). The instauration of knowledge can only lead to man's mastery of nature if it proceeds in an orderly fashion, 'as if by machinery' (IV, 40).

The *Advancement of Learning* and its Latin successor, the *De augmentis scientiarum*, contain between them an *ars historica* which is unrivalled in complexity by any other English work; the similar works of Peter Heylyn, Degory Whear, and Edmund Bolton, addressed in the next chapter, hold some interest but lack Bacon's breadth of vision, his easy ability to place history within a broader intellectual picture which encompassed all forms of human knowledge. As in his scientific works, Bacon's forte was not personal originality, but a knack of digesting and reshaping for an English audience the ideas he had picked up from others. His ideas on historiography can all be traced to earlier classical, French, and Italian writers. Fussner believes that Bacon's theory marked a 'radical break' with tradition, stressing his reduction of ecclesiastical history to a mere subcategory of 'civil' history. This change, first made in the *Descriptio globi intellectualis*, was an obvious departure both from the first version of the *Advancement* and from Jean Bodin's tripartite division of history into natural, divine, and human. But too much can be made of this, and Bacon would likely have been surprised at the suggestion that he was 'reducing' anything. He simply regrouped the various branches of human history, ecclesiastical, literary, and civil (proper) under the larger portmanteau category of civil history: the study of man, including matters relating to his soul, as distinct from the study of nature (III, 329–30; IV, 293–4; V, 505–7). This was less a brilliant flash of insight than a response to the work of de Thou and Camden, who had both written 'civil' history but included much ecclesiastical matter in their narratives. In the interim, Bacon may also have read the historical commentaries of Bartholomew Keckermann, who asserted unequivocally that the church could not be studied autonomously.[14]

Bacon's ideas of a systematic 'history' of the intellectual world, and of 'perfect' civil history suggest a debt to La Popelinière's 1599 work, *L'Idée de l'histoire accomplie*, parts of which Bacon had read by 1605. Both men wanted the historian to cover all aspects of human accomplishment, but there are some important differences between their uses of the term 'perfect' history. Bacon, ever the politician, restricted that term to one subgenre of civil history proper – what we would now see as political history – whereas La Popelinière's *histoire accomplie* referred not to a specific literary branch of conventional history-writing, but to a new and radically different general history of all aspects of a nation's past.[15] Showing something like La Popelinière's distaste for 'ruminated' histories (*histoires rompues et particulières*), Bacon nevertheless used 'perfect' history in a very different way to mean not a *general* history of a nation but simply a complete, unbroken narrative.[16] The simplest way to explain the difference between them may be to say that La Popelinière wanted a single general history which covered all aspects of France's past, whereas Bacon's scheme called for a large number of 'perfect histories' (that is, narratives) on a variety of different subjects – with the emphasis on political events. Thus, for example, he desired 'a perfect course of history for Graecia from Theseus to Philopoemon ... and for Rome from Romulus to Justinianus,' with the single reservation that the earliest period, antiquity, is 'muffled from our sight' (III, 335). Bacon's mind was obsessed with order and symmetry, and a series of 'perfect' histories would simply remove the untidiness of existing narratives, providing a definitive record of the past as a prolegomenon for the development of experiential knowledge of the present; in this respect his attempt to systematize history into a 'science of man' show an equally strong debt to Bodin. Like Bodin and La Popelinière, Bacon was no advocate of 'history for its own sake'; he was as concerned as any of his contemporaries with what the past had to teach the present.[17]

Bacon by no means eschewed rhetorical techniques, except when used to disguise a lack of truth. Rhetoric, he conceded, was essential in the communication of knowledge to the learned and the vulgar. 'The duty and office of rhetoric is to apply reason to imagination for the better moving of the will.' Bacon had read his Cicero, and he paid attention in the *Advancement* to the ways in which a writer should use style, the third of Cicero's five divisions of rhetoric, to present the material that he had found and organized. Bacon's other works are peppered with parables, analogies, and fables designed to explain and to persuade (eg III, 409–13);[18] and rhetoric could be applied to the realm of memory as much as to that of imagination, as Bacon's own practice suggests.

In comparison with his deployment of history as a master-method for discovery and as the truest mode of representing reality, what Bacon says about the nature and function of historical narrative seems in many ways quite conventional. 'Civil' history, the description of the human world, he conceives of as dealing especially with the past. It has several divisions, represented here in figure 1: sacred or ecclesiastical history; the history of learning and the arts; and civil history proper, the actions of men (IV, 300, 304).[19] This last, too, has several subdivisions. Bacon struggled to slot every conceivable variety of history into an exhaustive plan and the result was a good deal of ambiguity. 'Annals' for instance, might be two different things: either bare lists of events (a subcategory of 'memorials' or 'history unfinished'); or, following Tacitus, one of several kinds of 'perfect history,' a continuous narrative of events, their causes and their consequences.

Although he found space for them in his scheme, Bacon did not equate philological scholarship or antiquarianism with history. His inclusion of 'antiquities,' remnants of the past which have escaped the 'shipwreck' of time, suggests an awareness of the potential of non-literary evidence of the kind being used by antiquaries, but he regarded the collector of antiquities as merely a research assistant; the real historian was to be a statesman, not a scholar. Ever an opponent of any study that dwelt on words and signs rather than on material objects, Bacon exhibits little sympathy for the kind of advanced grammatical and philological study associated with the French Renaissance. 'Away with antiquities, and citations or testimonies of authors,' he urged; 'also with disputes and controversies and differing opinions; everything in short which is philological' (III, 334; IV, 254, 301, 303–4).[20]

Bacon was, as this last quotation suggests, as disdainful of the idea of historical disagreement as most of his contemporaries. His aim was to eliminate all doubts and arguments as to what happened in the past, by purging historical writing of the fabulous and the obscure. Historical

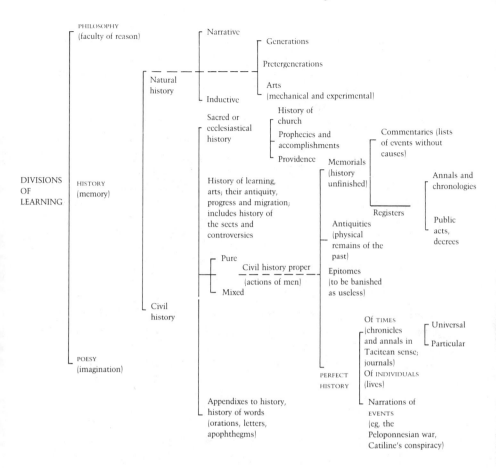

Figure 1   Francis Bacon's Divisions of History and Learning (abstracted from *De augmentis scientiarum*, in *Works*, vol IV)

certainty was obtainable by careful observation of the past, and definitive histories could be written once the fantastic had been excised.[21] Once again we sense the Renaissance conviction that the last word on any historical subject – within the limits of surviving sources – could and would eventually be uttered. Civil history does not differ from natural history in this respect, except that whereas the latter displays what we would now call a synchronic system of relationships, civil history represents a diachronic one: the diachronic counterpart of the lists and registers of natural history is provided by narrative.

All civil history, argues Bacon, should take the form of narrative, for it is only in narrative that the past can be represented realistically. 'Certainly when I read in Tacitus of the actions of Nero or Claudius, invested with all the circumstances of times, persons, and occasions, I see nothing in them very improbable; but when I read the same in Suetonius Tranquillus, gathered unto titles and common places, and not presented in order of time, they seem something prodigious and quite incredible' (IV, 359). The virtue of narrative history is that it presents events and men in an order of time and place that mirrors reality.[22] Event is tied to event, act to agent, location to time and character to plot; history is thereby superior to a mere description of personality. The 'character so worked into the narrative gives a better idea of the man than any formal criticism and review can' (V, 21). In comparison with an extended account such as that by Tacitus, other forms of history – chronicles, commentaries, memorials, antiquities – lack 'the perfect continuance or contexture of the thread of the narration' (IV, 303).[23]

For all his attention to the study of individual examples, Bacon had too subtle a mind to believe that the key to understanding either nature or the past lay in a simple cataloguing and arrangement of experience. 'No man can rightly and successfully investigate the nature of anything in the thing itself' (IV, 17). Any object points beyond itself to other objects, even in the past, and 'the affairs of men are not so far separated by the divisions of empires or countries, but they have a connexion in many things' (IV, 308). One can legitimately proceed from the arrangement of phenomena to speculative generalizations about the nature of their relationships, once these have been determined: in this way sound natural *history* can provide the basis for a more sophisticated natural *philosophy* (IV, 94). Similarly, the best sort of civil history would go beyond knowledge of the past to construct a praxis for future action.

For Bacon, even more than for Daniel, the pattern of English history seemed both meaningful and clear; and there is none of the pessimism and doubt that suffuses Ralegh's vision of the past. 'I had rather believe all the fables in the Legend, and the Talmud, and the Alcoran,' wrote Bacon, perhaps with Ralegh in mind, 'than that this universal frame is without a mind' (VI, 413). History was an ongoing chain of acts and consequences, the ultimate outcome of which, the conquest of nature, lay ahead: not in the past or the present, and perhaps not even in the near future, but certainly in this world. To be sure, history contained sudden change, horror, and misfortune in abundance. But one should profit from these rather than become mesmerized by them. 'It is not good to look too long upon these turning wheels of vicissitude, lest we become giddy' (VI, 517). The reader can learn from history, but he need not be trapped within it.

Bacon's ambitious collection of histories – civil, natural, and literary – was never realized. The project remained, like the *Great Instauration*, a magnificent blueprint. When he returned to civil history in 1621, following his impeachment and disgrace, he promised the king a complete history of the period from 1485 to 1603. As early as 1605, in his letter to Lord Ellesmere, he had suggested 'one just and complete history' of the two nations of England and Scotland: like Samuel Daniel before, and like the republican James Harrington three decades after, Bacon recognized the Tudor era as a distinct and historically meaningful period, during which the very character of English kingship had changed (III, 336; IV, 306).[24] Bacon's interests in 1621 were more practical than scholarly, as they had been in 1605 before his rise to power. He wished to be restored to influence, if not to office, and when the first part of the planned history, the *Henry VII*, failed to accomplish this, he abandoned the project, despite the interest of Prince Charles.

The shape of Bacon's *History of the Reign of King Henry the Seventh*, and the pragmatic view of history which it embodies, are the literary outgrowth of his vision of the way the world, past and present, ought to be represented. Like Samuel Daniel, Bacon was interested in the lessons of the past; but unlike Daniel, he found such lessons in the meticulous study of efficient causes, 'for where the cause is not known, the effect cannot be' (IV, 47). As the denizens of his New Atlantis put it, 'the end of our foundation is the knowledge of causes, and secret motions of things; and the enlarging of the bounds of human empire, to the effecting of all things possible' (III, 156). Where Daniel refused to engage in psychological speculation on the motives of historical figures, Bacon positively revelled in the detection and explanation of the connection between agent and act.

The statesman was in a better position to link causes with effects than the naive monkish chroniclers who had observed but never understood the political events they recounted.[25] Though Tacitus, not Polybius, was his favourite ancient historian, Bacon approved of Polybius' modern successors, especially Machiavelli and Guicciardini. He was certainly influenced by the histories of Guicciardini and Commynes, and though his *Henry VII* was not, like theirs, a memorial of recent and contemporary events, their penetrating analyses of human nature appealed to him.[26]

Bacon's debt to Machiavelli is more obvious, though at the same time more problematic. He refers to the Florentine many times throughout his works, often (but not always) favourably. He was thoroughly familiar with the ideas 'which the Italians call *ragioni di stato*' from Botero and other post-Machiavellians, and he praised 'politiques' such as Caesar and even Sulla (generally excoriated in the Renaissance as a vicious tyrant) for their political acumen.[27] When he came to describe the character of Henry VII, he invested him with the qualities, positive and negative, discussed by Machiavelli. Like the latter, Bacon turned to the past as crude ore from which he might extract evidence for his political maxims. The *Advancement* defined the ground over which the historian should hunt, the methods to be used to ensure a reliable sample, and the categories for the presentation of material. But the purpose and method of the *Henry VII* is quite different. It is a practical attempt not to learn from the past but to *teach* from it, for Bacon knew what he wanted to say about Henry before he opened his first book. Though it does not achieve even Bacon's own ideal of 'perfect' history – histories of single reigns were supposed to be only preliminary ingredients – it is nevertheless at least reconcilable with the utilitarian tenor of his general scheme of knowledge.

The parallel between Bacon's own situation in 1621 and that of the disgraced Machiavelli a century before is striking.[28] Like Machiavelli, Bacon used history to persuade his prince that he was worthy to give counsel. But, whereas Machiavelli chose to study history randomly in *Il Principe*, extracting events from their historical context in order to illustrate his ideas, Bacon chose instead to write a proper chronological narrative. In terms of his own categories, he opted for 'perfect' rather than 'ruminated' history, though limiting its chronological scope.

We have seen that Bacon favoured narrative over simple description as a means of depicting historical personages. In addition, a narrative offered many practical advantages over a collection of aphorisms and maxims. Unlike the Jacobean courtier and diplomat Sir Robert Dallington, whose *Aphorismes Civill and Militarie* (1613) were extracted out of Guicciardini for the education of Prince Henry, Bacon chose to write a narrative because it would be more readable. It would also be more popular, a fact which ought not be underrated in view of the desperate financial straits of the disgraced former chancellor in the summer of 1621. Impregnating a history with precepts was also a more subtle way of displaying his wisdom, and subtlety had always been among Bacon's virtues, except when proclaiming his own abilities; even in the history he lets his characters speak for him without the frequent interjection of Tacitean *sententiae* to which other authors were prone, a practice he himself had criticized in a perfect history.[29]

Bacon chose Henry VII as his subject for a number of reasons. He had already written a short sketch of the king's reign for Speed in 1611. Since he wished to confine himself to the Tudor dynasty, and since Camden had already done Elizabeth, Henry VII was the logical candidate. Bacon admired none of the middle three Tudors (who, again, had been dealt with by Godwin), nor could they be made easily into analogues or models. The cautious, deliberate Henry VII lacked the conspicuous daring and bravado of his son, but this made the first Tudor an example to be learned from rather than a spectacle to laugh at, unlike those bold men whose actions are 'seldom without some absurdity' and whose repeated disastrous failures make them 'fitter for a satire than for a serious observation' (VI, 402). Bacon's purpose required a flawed Solomon rather than either a saint or, on the other hand, the strutting, Raleghesque folly of an Agesilaus or a Xerxes – or, for that matter, a Henry VIII.[30]

Bacon was also attracted as much as any of James I's subjects by the notion of Henry VII's union of the Roses as a foreshadowing of James's union of the kingdoms, which he himself had unsuccessfully promoted. Despite that earlier failure, he returned to this theme as late as the *Henry VII*, commenting of Henry's truce with Scotland that 'the truce drew on the peace; the peace the marriage; and the marriage the union of the kingdoms.' Bacon ascribed Henry's success not only to the efficient cause, Henry's shrewdness, but to a final cause, the working out of God's plan for the reunion of the realms in Henry's descendant (*Henry VII* 65, 195). The same idea appears elsewhere, in the *Advancement* and in a short work revealingly called *The Beginning of the History of Great Britain.*[31]

But perhaps the greatest reason for selecting Henry was not his abilities but the weaknesses that periodically threatened to undermine his reign, and which made him something of a tragic figure – successful, but unloved and feared. No Xenophon, Bacon never intended to write a panegyric on the first Tudor, and he is often more critical of his subject than were his two main sources, Speed and Hall. Bacon's Henry owes less to Greek panegyric than to Greek tragedy; he is a flawed hero whose mistakes frequently cause disaster, though he has fortune on his side. Though gifted with a natural shrewdness, even he 'would be blinded (now and then) by human policy.' Generally, he administered justice well, 'save where the King was party.' He was generally merciful, though he could be ruthless when threatened, and was often unnecessarily suspicious. But above all – and here Bacon's own views have come to influence modern ones – the new king was excessively rapacious. This aspect of his character was initially tempered by wise 'counsellors of ancient authority with him' such as Sir Reginald Bray and Cardinal Morton. His later advisers, however, being more 'servile,' drove him to 'extremities, for which himself was touched with remorse at his death' (*Henry VII* 240–1).[32] In short, Henry VII presented no paragon, but an ordinary, if regal, man embodying a variety of contradictory attributes, and therefore a more persuasive model: Bacon wanted James and his heir not to imitate but to *excel* their ancestor.

Accordingly, Bacon makes the character of Henry and the 'plot' of the history virtually two sides of the same coin, through a kind of sustained metonymy of agent for act. Bacon's Henry is not so much an organic entity as a compound of many virtues and a few vices which are themselves the motive of much of the action in the history. Those of Henry's failures which cannot be attributed directly to the whims of fortune are blamed not on the king himself, but on various character deficiencies. Without these, all would have been well: 'Again, whether it were the shortness of his foresight, or the strength of his will, or the dazzling of his suspicions, or what it was; certain it is that the perpetual troubles of his fortunes (there being no more matter out of which they grew) could not have been without some great defects and main errors in his nature, customs, and proceedings, which he had enough to do to save and help with a thousand little industries and watches' (246).

As in any good tragedy, such flaws, especially Henry's avarice and tendency to suspicion, 'do best appear in the story itself' (221, 246). In endowing Henry with these failings, Bacon was embellishing on his chronicle sources, but with good reason. The whole point of the exercise was to present the spectacle of a man 'better than ourselves' but still imperfect, a figure from whose errors the future King Charles could profit.

Henry's fortune was the product of his nature and of providential decree: with the aid of 'the Divine Revenge' he seized the throne from a tyrant and then kept it, surviving a series of rebellions to die in his bed and leave behind a secure dynasty (67). His greatest virtue was his acceptance of wise counsel, and this facet of his character is stressed. 'The wisest princes,' he had long before written, 'need not think it any diminution to their greatness, or derogation to their sufficiency, to rely upon counsel.' Bacon consistently praised Solomon, the biblical king James liked to be compared with, for his pronouncement that 'in counsel is stability' (*Works* VI, 423).[33] Henry VII, though he never lost control over his servants, 'was served by the ablest men that were to be found' and was in turn loyal to them – in stark contrast to his son and heir. 'He never put down or discomposed councillor or near servant, save only Stanley the Lord Chamberlain.' His most capable counsellors were Bishop Foxe and Cardinal Morton. As Jonathan Marwil has shown, Bacon attributed many of his own ideas (which were in turn culled from Machiavelli) not just to Henry, but to these advisers; he assumed that all wise minds think alike (*Henry VII* 244).[34] Bacon's wholehearted employment of oratorical devices is evident in the set speeches he composes for characters such as Morton. The cardinal, speaking on behalf of Henry, persuades parliament to support the king in an alliance with Brittany against France. In fact, Morton's speech provides a perfect instance of an exercise in hortatory rhetoric, dividing a problem point by point in order to persuade the houses to Henry's side: good counsellors also had their uses in parliament, as Bacon knew from experience (107).[35]

Henry's career offered no easy solutions to the specific problems facing James I in 1621, and Bacon makes very few allusions to contemporary politics, though it is probably not stretching the text to read the acid portraits of Empson and Dudley, servile men who replace the king's older and more reliable ministers, as a poke at the new lord treasurer, Lionel Cranfield, who had hastened Bacon's impeachment in the Commons. Instead, Bacon presents a general set of rules which any monarch could follow, whether a model new prince like Henry, or a foreigner such as James, whose hereditary claim was less open to dispute, at least among his own subjects. Bacon was much less concerned with drawing specific analogies between the first Tudor and the first Stuart than with displaying his own general understanding of politics and his worthiness to give advice to James and his heir, Prince Charles, to whom the work was dedicated. For Bacon, the crisis of counsel could be observed most strikingly in the fact that he was not giving it.

As a history, the *Henry VII* has been dealt with unkindly by those who see it as the failure of the great progressive to carry his ambitious instauration of history into reality. It is true enough that Bacon broke many of his own rules. As Marwil points out, the *Henry VII* is really neither a 'life' nor a 'history of times.' It is far too broad in scope for a life; though Henry provides the unifying element, he is frequently in the wings. Bacon also felt he had to proceed annalistically, padding out the narrative of a year with details not proper in a life. Yet because the character of Henry dominates the plot, the work is not a 'history of times' either.[36] This inconsistency is less a fault of the history than of the strangling complexity and rigidity of the *Advancement*'s schema, and Bacon was no worse an offender than John Hayward had been in the *Lives of the III. Normans*. The genres of history were simply not as well defined as Bacon the theorist would have liked.

If one makes allowances for Bacon's limited time and resources, he did rather well. Contrary to current belief, he did consult original sources, despite his exile from London. John Selden served briefly as his research assistant, gathering material from the Tower and from Cotton's library and sending it to the banished ex-chancellor. This included royal proclamations, 'commissions touching state,' and a list of the men assigned to levy the benevolence of 1492.[37] Thus the statesman used the antiquary's research to write history. And this is exactly what he had always said should happen. Bacon himself looked first to Speed, filling out his account with material from Hall, Stow, and occasionally Bernard André. Given his scissors-and-paste method, he manipulated his material ingeniously and persuasively.

The immediate reception of the work is rather amazing. Fulke Greville praised it, as did the king. Selden (hardly a disinterested opinion) ranked it with Camden's *Annales*.[38] Though it failed to restore Bacon to the council, it was the most readable attempt to use narrative history as a vehicle for political advice. Its very didacticism makes it much less inconsistent with Bacon's general emphasis on the utility of history than has often been supposed. Though the *Henry VII* has long been dismissed, rightly, as a source for the first Tudor's reign, and though it contains many factual errors (such as the year of Henry's death!), its portrait has survived the centuries virtually intact. Bacon created the modern Henry VII in the same sense that More had moulded the definitive Richard III and Camden the textbook Elizabeth.

Sir Robert Cotton and the Crisis of Counsel

Like his older friend and mentor Camden, Sir Robert Cotton was an important figure in both historical writing and antiquarian scholarship.

He had the greatest single private collection of manuscripts then in existence in England, and he freely lent them to all who wished their use. His collection placed him at the centre of several overlapping circles of scholars, historians, and public figures, and most of the historians in the present study had at least some contact with him.

As neither historian nor antiquary, however, was Cotton himself especially outstanding. Though he had a greater command of the material in his own library than anyone else, he lacked the linguistic proficiency and broad philological erudition of a Camden, Selden, or Spelman. Despite some shrewd insight into the nature of the post-Conquest knight's fee, there is little evidence in either his occasional writings or his antiquarian discourses that he achieved Selden or Spelman's depth of understanding of feudal tenures.[39] Nevertheless, it is clear that he, like Camden, often broke one of the rules of the Society of Antiquaries by looking to French sources in his investigations.[40]

Most of Cotton's work consisted of antiquarian researches, performed either for the society or for one of his successive patrons.[41] Like Camden, he distinguished in theory between history and the study of antiquities, though by using the same sources in both pursuits and by encouraging others to do so he also contributed to the dissolution of this dichotomy. Without Cotton and his collections, Camden, Clapham, Daniel, Speed, and innumerable others would have been severely hampered in their researches; Selden's *Historie of Tithes* would have been inconceivable, and Selden did well to dedicate it to his friend. Cotton would have been, today, the ideal reference librarian – one of Bacon's industrious collectors of antiquities. He assisted many men in their writing as well as their research and at one point helped an anonymous friend compile a topographical study of Britain, a work which was not simply a revision of the *Britannia* but an attempt to place the island within a global context.[42] His authorship of the life of Henry VIII in Speed is suggested both by the contemporary testimony of Edmund Bolton, who was in a position to know, and by the frequent references in the life to Guicciardini's *History of Italy*, on which Cotton had taken extensive notes.[43]

The circumstances surrounding the composition of Cotton's *A Short View of the Long Life and Raigne of Henry the Third* remain unclear despite Kevin Sharpe's careful examination of the evidence. The tract was published in 1627 and, because much of it is critical of overmighty favourites, created trouble for Cotton and his publishers. He escaped punishment both by claiming that it had been published without his permission and by arguing that he had in fact written it fifteen years before, in 1611 or 1612.[44] Cotton's testimony is the only evidence for a date this early and it must, under the circumstances, be highly suspect.

Two other possible dates, 1614 and 1622, head manuscript copies of the tract, but both dates could very easily have been written in after 1627.[45] It seems safer to let the tract speak for itself. It is certainly a poke at overmighty favourites, and given that Cotton's patrons in 1612 and 1614 were the earls of Northampton and Somerset respectively, these dates, though not impossible, present many more problems than 1622 or 1627. Central to the work is a common Renaissance theme: the problem of the evil counsellor, the minion who gains near-sovereign control of the council and realm by taking advantage of an unsuspecting, well-intentioned master, only to turn against him. Accordingly, it is less likely, though by no means impossible, that Cotton wrote the tract between 1612 and 1614, since his patrons were then in positions of trust and – in his view if not in others' – no crisis of counsel yet existed.

Cotton, like Bacon, was concerned with the realities of political life, not with its moralities. His *Henry III* is nevertheless probably the work least influenced by Machiavelli of those studied in this chapter. Henry III was suited to the roles of neither tyrant nor new prince, and Cotton was in any case more concerned with the maintenance of legitimate, peaceful rule by king-in-council in an inherited kingdom than with the seizure and consolidation of power. If Cotton had wished to criticize Charles I and not his counsellors, he could have made a far more convincing analogy out of Edward II; but Henry, like Charles, was an inherently good prince, who simply needed good advice. Even so, there is a hint of Machiavellianism in Cotton's depiction of Montfort, exercising his 'vertue' at the king's expense, though the real model was probably Tacitus' Sejanus. In any case, the *Henry III* is full of the kind of precepts supported by example that Machiavelli had excelled at; in many ways, it is like an extended chapter of *Il Principe*.

The problems facing Henry III in the thirteenth century were, as far as Cotton could see, very similar to those facing Charles I in the late 1620s. What is a king to do, even an inherently good one, when he lacks worthy counsel? Human nature drives men to seek honour and preferment, says Cotton, echoing Bacon's essay 'Of Ambition'; rewards given the subject 'maketh the mind only capable of merit, nothing of duty.'[46] Henry's troubles began with the 'surfeit of peace' which had allowed abuses in government to arise, and young, ambitious men had replaced worthy old counsellors such as Pembroke, de Burgh, and Roger Bigod, second earl of Norfolk. The last name was an odd choice for Cotton; Norfolk had been one of the barons to confront King John at Runnymede and had died in 1221 having never, until a few months before his death, enjoyed Henry's favour (4, 6).[47]

The king made the initial mistake of employing Frenchmen such as Simon de Montfort in high office. This damaged his reputation with his subjects, 'for nothing is more against the nature of the English then to have strangers rule over them' (11).[48] Montfort rose rapidly, and he soon became the *de facto* ruler: 'hee draweth all publike affayres into his owne hands, all favours must passe from him, all preferments by him, all suites addressed to him, the king but as a cypher set to adde to this figure' (14). The magnates, predictably, began to grieve, while famine caused popular riots. Calling a parliament – an institution which Cotton assumes to have existed before the thirteenth century – did little good. Without trusty and respected advisers to manage his business, the king was unable to control the Commons, which gave him so little money that he became dependent on it, an improper state of affairs. 'Thus parliaments that before were ever a medicine to heale up any rupture in princes fortunes, are now growne worse then the mallady.' (25) From this ensued a dangerous deterioration of 'sole power into the rule of many.' (32)

The king's council, dominated by a trimvirate of Montfort, Gloucester, and Despenser, soon forced upon the king the Provisions of Oxford, thereby infringing his sovereignty still further. They also 'forst agayne the king to call a parliament' (19, 25, 29–34 [mispaginated as p 33]). When Henry finally saw the error of his ways and tried to restrain Montfort, it was almost too late. Fortunately, most of the kingdom remained loyal and the proud former minion, refusing to submit to the king's mercy, was vanquished and killed.

Montfort was to Cotton much more the Machiavellian citizen 'exercis[ing] his vertue' (42) than the king himself, who remains a passive figure throughout. But even a weak king can learn his lesson, and Henry realized that 'reward and reprehension justly layd doe ballance goverment [*sic*], and that it much importeth a prince the hand to bee equall that holdeth the scale.' The king reformed his household and court and put 'nobly borne' men into positions of influence. He himself sat with his council daily, taking advice, but ruling himself as a sovereign ought (45–6). In fact, this is a travesty of history; the weight of contemporary evidence, with which Cotton was quite familiar, strongly suggests that the real Henry remained much the same after 1265, a pious nonentity. And since it would have done little other than complicate his barebones narrative and confuse the central issues, Cotton all but ignored perhaps the most controversial aspect of the reign, papal influence over Henry's government.

Cotton believed that examples are more useful than 'generall rules,' which are not always applicable to specific situations (6), and the *Henry III* is really less a history than a single, extended example. Nor is it a work of 'scholarship,' even on the level of Bacon's *Henry VII*, despite Cotton's use of a larger number of manuscript sources, which were readily available in his own collections.[49] The characters are cardboard cutouts and the pictures of Montfort and Henry deliberately one-sided and inaccurate, even by contemporary standards. The tract is a rhetorical parable, designed solely to persuade its royal reader to a specific course of action, illustrated by analogy from the past. As such, it is perhaps the most extreme Jacobean example of the deliberate distortion and compression of historical fact for the sake of offering counsel – the furthest extent to which early Stuart politic history could be taken.

Cotton's own inclination to give advice, whether asked for it or not, reveals itself in many of his other works, including *The Danger Wherein the Kingdom Now Standeth and the Remedy*, published in 1628.[50] Again using history to illustrate his arguments, he urged the calling of a parliament to settle the kingdom's grievances and the king's finances, a change of perspective from the *Henry III*, which stressed the importance of the council rather than parliament. This may have been stimulated by the continued failure of the opponents of Buckingham, the earls of Pembroke and Arundel, to supplant the duke. In the *Henry III* either Cotton or (if we accept his denials) the pirate publisher who saw the tract's topicality was advising Charles I to displace an upstart like Buckingham and take the advice of a 'nobly born' counsellor such as Cotton's patron, Arundel. Like Bacon, but with a much less delicate touch, Cotton constructed his narrative around a set of precepts already drawn up.[51]

William Habington and the End of the Personal Rule

William Habington's *Historie of Edward the Fourth* is the last historical advice-book written before 1640, and is perhaps the one most concerned with finding an answer to the problems of the present in an earlier reign. As a work of historiography, it was thinly researched and was based upon even fewer sources than its model, Bacon's *Henry VII*. There may, however, be an explanation for this speedily composed history in the circumstances of the year in which it was written.

Born on 5 November 1605, the first anniversary of the Gunpowder Plot, William was the son of Thomas Habington (1560–1647), a recusant who had himself been in and out of prison in earlier life, and whose brother had been executed twenty years earlier for complicity in the

Babington plot. Thomas Habington was a capable antiquary. Permanently exiled to his Worcestershire manor of Hindlip, he had no direct access to the Cottonian or other London libraries, but he managed to write an impressive *Survey of Worcestershire* from the material he found in local church records. Thomas sent his son to be educated by Jesuits in France. William was pressed to join the order but, on his own son's testimony, 'by excuses got free and left them.'[52] The experience left William with a pronounced francophobia which is detectable in much of his writing. Afterwards, he returned home to be instructed by his father 'in matters of history,' but he soon found poetry more to his taste.

William's marriage in 1633 to Lucy Herbert, the daughter of William, first Baron Powys, placed him directly in the orbit of the powerful Herbert family. His father-in-law's first cousin was Philip Herbert, fourth earl of Pembroke; in 1636, Pembroke supported Habington for the position of ambassador to Rome, but the king chose Sir William Hamilton, a Scotsman nominated by the queen. Despite his Catholicism, it is scarcely surprising that Habington never became one of Henrietta Maria's circle of wits. Though he was, like his friends Davenant and Shirley, a 'son of Ben,' his poetry lacks the sensual and erotic imagery of much early Cavalier verse; always uneasy with the manners of court, he has been not unjustly dubbed a 'catholic puritan.'[53]

It was the Scottish rebellion of 1638 which finally turned Habington from love lyricist into historian, possibly at Pembroke's prodding. The lord chamberlain, who opposed the first 'Bishops' War,' as the rebellion became known in England, was one of the main architects of the shaky Treaty of Berwick which ended the conflict temporarily; he led a court faction which urged moderation in dealing with the Scots. Before long, he found himself at odds with the newly formed alliance of Henrietta Maria and Thomas Wentworth, now earl of Strafford, the former lord deputy in Ireland and, from September 1539, Charles's principal adviser. The hopes of the moderates to maintain an accord with the Covenanters began to fade from the moment Strafford arrived back in England.[54]

Habington had already written at the king's request a history of Henry v's reign, which has not survived. This may well have been a contribution to the cult of Charles i the warrior, a cult which expressed itself in a variety of ways in the 1630s, most notably in the portraits of Van Dyck and in the court masques which celebrated the power of the Stuart regime. Henry v would have appealed to Charles as an analogue, despite his failure to wage a successful war against France in the 1620s, in rather the same way that Henry vii, the peacemaker, had appealed to his father.[55] But Edward iv offered even louder echoes of the present, particularly to the beleaguered king of 1639, and it was to this reign that Habington turned in writing his most extensive historical work.

The *Historie of Edward the Fourth* is misunderstood if taken for a serious attempt at scholarship: it is, like Bacon's *Henry vii*, an exercise in political persuasion, and Habington spent little time in its research. His earlier writings explicitly cite Machiavelli's works with approval,[56] though in the history Habington maintains the ambivalence toward Machiavellian politics typical of the time. As had Bacon, Habington availed himself of Speed's marginal references. He never wandered much further afield, though he incorporated material directly from other sources such as Hall's chronicle; he also borrowed extensively from Commynes, his principal authority for Edward's relations with France, though Habington shared neither Bacon's approval of the great French diplomat nor Commynes' own pro-French bias.

The influence of Machiavelli on the *Edward iv* shows early as Habington commends Edward both for allowing the crowd to believe it has chosen him king (though Edward wisely never relies on a popular title), and for the ruthless execution of a grocer who had joked about making his own son king. 'The extraordinary punishment of such saucie language, was not then unnecessary to beget authority, and make men cautious to dispute the descent of princes' (*Edward iv* p 11).

But if Bacon had believed Henry vii over-suspicious, Habington took the opposite view of Edward, whose fears of the continued Lancastrian threat were justified. Indeed, Edward was not wary enough, for he carelessly ignored the continuing existence of Henry vi and Queen Margaret. As Machiavelli had shown, 'A prince cannot live securely in a principality whilst those are alive who have been despoiled of it.'[57] Edward's marriage to Elizabeth Woodville was a gross error which alienated both his own lieutenant, Warwick, and the king of France. Habington is uniformly hostile to the influence of women on their husbands and portrays both queens, Margaret and Elizabeth, equally unsympathetically. His own potential antipathy toward Henrietta Maria's party may have been shaped by Machiavelli's chapter in the *Discourses* on 'how women have caused the downfall of states.'[58]

Yet wariness and caution do not justify excessive, pointless violence, and Habington condemns Edward for a profitless combination of cruelty and dishonesty in the execution of Lord Wells (the father of the Lancastrian commander, Sir Robert Wells), to whom he had earlier given a safe-conduct. Though this was 'an act barbarous and unfaithfull,'

Habington's attitude toward it is not unequivocal, since Edward's perfidy had the good effect of provoking Lord Wells's vengeful son into a premature attack in which he was routed (55). This illustrates Habington's ambivalence toward Machiavellianism and reason of state, an ambivalence typical of the early Stuart reception of Machiavelli's texts: bad acts may be necessary, but they are still bad.[59] Edward's tendency to perjure himself for political gain was his greatest fault and was the crime 'which rendered him most odious to the societie of man' and to God, who visited his sins upon Edward's children. Similarly, Habington considered only to reject the Machiavellian doctrine that 'no faith was to be held with an enemy' though he recognized that Edward's enemies could actually outdo him in the art of deception (230).[60]

The second half of the history is principally concerned with Edward's diplomatic affairs. Habington denounced in scathing language the foreign rulers with whom Edward had to deal, especially the French. He described Louis XI's payment of an annuity to Edward as a 'tribute', differing with Commynes. 'There is much controversie among French and English writers about the name,' he observed. 'They call it a pension, we a tribute' (146). Habington's recognition that his sources did not agree merit the word 'controversie,' but as usual, one view (the English one) is regarded as unarguably, axiomatically, correct; the disparity is resolved simply by taking Commynes to task for 'an apparent defect in order and method' (134).[61]

King Edward grew increasingly susceptible to lust and expensive pastimes in his later years. In order to impress foreigners he 'began to addict himselfe to a profuse hospitality' (176). This and the endless demands of the queen and her horde of kinsmen cost money, which Edward raised by a variety of unpopular means such as executing penal laws purely for their revenue. He called a parliament in 1474 which reversed Henry VI's attainders and willingly granted the king a subsidy, but when forced later that year into a war with France he had to fall back on other measures. Hall had referred to Edward's extortion of a free gift from his wealthier subjects as a 'benevolence' and had simply commented that it was a cunning means of raising extra money. Habington pushed this argument further, asking why Edward did not call a parliament: 'The ordinary course for supply was by parlament, and that at this time was held difficult if not impossible: in regard the king but a little before had dissolved the assembly, having received for discharge of his debts a large contribution ...' (130). Despite these difficult circumstances, Edward should still have summoned parliament; and if he had done so he would likely have found it pliant, for 'the subject repents not the free gift of the kingdomes substance, when hee sees the returne of it in triumph; but repines if the least part of his contribution, bee the reward of parasites, or persons to whom fortune not merit gives a growth' (196).[62]

The final years of Edward's reign were dominated by the rise of the even more ruthless and cunning duke of Gloucester, who used the unwitting queen to ruin his brother, the duke of Clarence, while staying above the fray himself. Gloucester's reputation increased enormously through his military success in the pointless Scottish war of 1482, a conflict fomented by the French. Again, Habington deliberately departed from and expanded on his sources: neither Hall nor Speed had anything bad to say about Gloucester at this point in his career, nor did either even attempt to judge the consequences of the war. Habington was forced to admit that the successful invasion of Scotland and capture of Berwick redeemed Edward in the eyes of his people, who once again compared 'their felicity with the misery of their fathers, to blesse the present government' (200–3, 205–8).[63] Following his Baconian model to the end, Habington ended with a brief character of the king, praising Edward's generally just administration of the laws. He noted that the king's behaviour improved after the Scottish war and that his earlier severity and avarice were 'not imputed to the king: but to Tiptoft, earle of Worcester, and some under informers: or else to the queene and her necessitous kindred' (226). The reference to Tiptoft was perhaps inspired by Machiavelli's commendation of Cesare Borgia for executing his own governor, Remirro d'Orca, after making him the scapegoat for unpopular policies.[64]

Although most of the history deals, like Bacon's, with general rules of politics for princes, a number of clues suggest that Habington had more in mind than the production of simply another politic history. His discussion of the Scottish war and the power it gave an overmighty subject points straight at Strafford, Pembroke's nemesis in 1639–40. Habington had finished the work by 15 November 1639, five months after Strafford's return to England. Strafford had in the meantime effected an alliance with the queen; while Habington's recurring criticism of Edward's indulgence of his wife (an ironic repetition of the fatal flaw of his predecessor, Henry VI) are probably not directly aimed at Henrietta Maria – that would have exceeded the bounds of good taste and safety – they gently hint at the unpopularity and problems awaiting a uxorious prince. Habington's *Edward IV* thus provides further evidence for Annabel Patterson's argument that early Stuart authors could stray a certain distance from the polite or correct line without fearing reprisals; Habington was practising precisely that self-censorship which permitted him to offer advice through suggestive analogy and innuendo without making his purpose explicit.[65]

The prologue of the history (which is dedicated to Charles I) reveals the author's didactic purpose. 'Faction begot many tempests,' observed Habington, 'but soveraigntie found a happie calme in the destruction (since no gentler way had authoritie) of mighty opposers.' Expressing gratitude for the peace of the last decade he implored the king to be merciful to his enemies if possible. 'But if you shall be forc't to draw your sword, may your enemies submit and tast part of your mercy: if not, perish in your victories' (sig A2r–v).

As we have seen, the history also recommends the calling of parliament as the usual means of securing supply for a war. It is unknown whether Pembroke actually pressed the king to call a parliament in the spring of 1640, and by the autumn he lacked sufficient influence to do so; but Pembroke certainly saw a parliament as the best means of ridding himself and the king of Strafford, and both he and his client, Sir Henry Vane the elder, would contribute to the earl's ruin in 1641.[66] Habington's references to Edward's parliaments smack strongly of an attempt to persuade the king to take this road out of his financial troubles.

Any specific link between Pembroke and the *Historie of Edward the Fourth* must remain conjectural: we have none of the correspondence that may have passed between them – no 'smoking gun' to prove such a link definitively. Yet the internal and external evidence suggest both such a connection and a certain topicality for the history. Habington's book may therefore be read as an attempt not simply to imitate Baconian didactic narrative, but to carry the historian's function as counsellor to a level Bacon would not have contemplated: ironically, it seems to have had no greater impact upon the king than had Bacon's *Henry VII* years before on James I.

Habington left the court in 1641 and returned to Hindlip, probably frightened by the increasing anti-Catholic feeling in the city and the eclipse of his patron at court. It is possible that he had fallen out with Pembroke over the publication of his play *The Queene of Arragon;* his son told Anthony Wood that the work had been performed and published by the lord chamberlain against its author's will. Habington was also shocked by the popular disturbances which followed the dissolution of the Short Parliament, the subject of his only extant letter. He spent the next few years in financial hardship, relying on the charity of friends and family.[67]

Despite his troubles, Habington did not remain idle. In 1641 he published a set of *Observations upon Historie* modelled on Machiavelli's *Discorsi*. Habington claimed to have been compiling these observations for several years, and for once we may believe such a claim, for the work has no pattern or thread to suggest that it was written at one time. Habington abandoned his earlier attempt to harvest political lessons from an entire reign and turned to a more traditional method of extracting episodes from history and commenting upon them.[68] This appears to have been his last work. Presented for recusancy in April, 1642, Habington became an active royalist in the civil war and was among the garrison of Worcester at its surrender in July, 1646. He died on the last day of 1654. Wood claimed he was 'not unknown to Oliver the usurper,' though in what capacity, if any, it is unknown.[69]

Perhaps nothing emerges so clearly from these 'Machiavellian' historians as the tension between an ambivalence to the politics of statecraft and the urge to provide political counsel. Each historian eventually found himself caught between the general requirement that history be ethically correct, Christian and moral, and the topicality of their subjects, which demanded harder judgments on the efficacy of certain types of political behaviour. In offering subtle criticisms of past policies with a view to suggesting changes of course in the present, each also found himself straddling the fine line between a directness that might cause offence – it was difficult to miss the allusions in Cotton's short piece – and a more oblique approach which, as Bacon and Habington both discovered, preserved the prince's good temper at the cost of making him miss the point.

The 'history-as-advice-book' had a short life-span, though the various reissues of Cotton's little essay demonstrate that the usefulness of such works depended as much on the response of the reader, on his ability to draw connections with a current situation, as it did on the wit of the author. Yet the very topicality of these books creates a distance between the author and the reader that has expanded as we grow more remote from the events which inspired them. One can still read a work such as Hayward's or Godwin's, for all the moralizing, without having to strain to hear hidden messages issuing from underneath the text; the same is not true of the works of Cotton and Habington. Of the three would-be counsellors, only Bacon, partly because of his greater literary talent, but also because his advice remained for the most part at the level of generalities, managed to produce a history which can still be read with enjoyment by a wide audience.

Habington's book, the last of the genre, was reprinted in 1642, and again in 1648; it appeared a fourth time in 1659 as *Praeces Principum: or the President of Illustrious Princes.* By this time, the original occasion had long since been forgotten, though doubtless his Edward could have been read with profit by a Richard Cromwell or a John Lambert. But the moment for such works had passed. By the 1640s and 1650s, more pressing issues had emerged; the early Stuart crisis of counsel had by that time evolved into a crisis of rather a different sort, one in which the historian was quite out of his depth.

CHAPTER SIX

The Roman World

Roman History under the Early Stuarts

The late sixteenth and early seventeenth centuries saw much discussion of British history among English antiquaries and their European friends. Letters, books, and manuscripts flew back and forth across the channel. In Paris, André Duchesne wrote a history of the British Isles in French. Jacques-Auguste de Thou's interests have already been mentioned. Camden's friend Pierre Dupuy arranged the translation into French of Bacon's *Henry VII* and he used Francis Godwin's *Annales* in his own researches. Jean Hotman, son of François, had spent time in England as the earl of Leicester's secretary; he helped arrange the French translation of the first part of Camden's *Annales* in 1617. Nicolas Fabri de Peiresc, who visited Cotton in 1606, imported English histories and collected British and Saxon coins. In the Netherlands, Gerard Vossius contemplated writing the life of Mary Stuart, while Jan de Laet assisted Sir Henry Spelman and his Cambridge Anglo-Saxon lecturer, Abraham Wheloc, in the compilation of an old English dictionary.[1]

The main topic of correspondence within the republic of letters was not, however, Britain, but the ancient world. In the sixteenth century, the goal of humanist scholarship had remained to a great extent the study and restoration of Greek and Roman culture. In France, Guillaume Budé had edited the *Pandects* of the civil law and, building on earlier Italian achievements, developed the study of ancient coins.[2] Other lawyer-scholars, such as François Baudouin and François Hotman, also studied the law historically, while Jacques Cujas turned the study of legal philology into a systematic discipline. Near the end of the century, Cujas' Huguenot disciple, Joseph Scaliger, brought two centuries of humanist philology to bear on the problems of ancient chronology; through his brilliant editions of ancient authors, and his massive knowledge of oriental tongues, Scaliger came closest of all to reconstructing the life of the ancient world.[3]

The French religious wars ensured that by 1600 the centre of gravity had shifted to the low countries. When Scaliger, who moved to Leiden in 1593, declared that France would never produce another Budé, he was criticizing the state of French scholarship, not praising Budé.[4] Scaliger's great predecessor at Leiden, Justus Lipsius, and his followers Janus Gruter, Daniel Heinsius, and Gerard Vossius were all Dutchmen. Still, France was far from becoming an intellectual wasteland. The Pithou brothers, François and Pierre, were both lawyers who studied the ancient past. Isaac Casaubon edited Polybius before leaving for England in 1610. Co-operation in this republic of letters could transcend religious divisions: the Jesuit scholar Fronto de Duc, editing the Old Testament, borrowed a Greek text of the book of Genesis from Sir Robert Cotton.[5] For these and other scholars across Europe, the ancient world remained as fascinating as the Middle Ages.

With a few conspicuous exceptions, such as Sir Henry Savile, whose edition of St John Chrysostom was of great importance, the lawyer John Selden, and the divine Thomas Gataker, each of whose interests lay elsewhere than ancient Rome, England produced no outstanding classical philologist until Richard Bentley at the end of the seventeenth century.[6] Yet this was not for lack of enthusiasm: Camden used the *Antonine Itineraries* to piece together the ancient Roman road network in Britain, while Selden's own treatise *De dis Syris*, on the Syrian gods described in the Bible, put him on the European intellectual map, drawing high praise from foreign scholars.[7]

Most discussions of Rome had a much more pedestrian and practical purpose. In 1614, an Abingdon schoolmaster named Thomas Godwyn (apparently unrelated to the bishop) wrote an immensely popular textbook on Roman religion, laws, and customs. Godwyn sacrificed historical understanding for pedagogical convenience and insisted on explaining Roman institutions in English terms: a Roman lictor became a 'serjeant.' This was fine as long as the correspondence was seen to be only analogical, but in lesser minds it could be dangerous. One of Godwyn's readers made notes in which the *fiscus* became the 'king's exchequer' – in Republican Rome![8]

There was space in the English mind for two Romes, both the corrupt popish Babylon of Foxe's martyrology, a Jezebel to be feared rather than studied, and the great ancient city, whose mighty past and ruinous fall inspired awe.[9] As with the medieval past, the antiquaries and philologists were greatly outnumbered by those more interested in the lessons of antiquity – the poets, political and military writers, and dramatists. By 1640, at least fifty-seven Roman history plays had been produced in England, of which forty survive.[10] Translations flourished: Livy had been translated in various bits and pieces during the sixteenth century and Philemon Holland (later the translator of *Britannia*) published a complete English edition in 1600. Holland filled in the gaps left by Livy's missing books with Lucius Florus' so-called epitome of Livy, thereby stimulating a brief period of interest in that minor author.[11] Henry Savile and Richard Grenewey each translated Tacitus. A popular translation of Quintus Curtius' *Alexander* by John Brende went through thirteen editions between 1553 and 1614. Josephus' works were translated by the poet Thomas Lodge, whose play *The Wounds of Civill War* (1594), on the factions of the first century BC, created a nightmare of civil strife as vivid as Shakespeare's plays on fifteenth-century England. Caesar was translated by Arthur Golding in 1565 and again by Clement Edmonds in 1600 and 1604.[12]

Potted histories were in vogue: a sixteenth-century work by the Spaniard Pedro Mexia on the lives of the Roman emperors from Julius Caesar to the Holy Roman Empire of his own day was twice translated into English and continued to recent times in the early seventeenth century; a brief summary of Mexia by one Robert Basset appeared in 1636.[13] Rome had also long provided a suitable 'once-upon-a-time' setting for moralists. Such hangovers from the medieval educational tradition as *The Seven Wyse Maysters of Rome* and *A Record of Auncient Histories* had nothing whatsoever to do with Roman history, but wove tales with religious or ethical lessons around timeless, fictitious 'Roman' characters.[14]

Historical interest was political interest: as usual, the past held messages for the present. Rome provided an enormous gallery of archetypes. Although playwrights dramatized the folly of Tacitus' early emperors, especially Tiberius and Nero, the republic was a more popular topic. This was partly because less was known about the later Roman empire (the sources were not as full and fewer had been translated) and partly because the great stylists, Cicero, Livy, Sallust, Horace, and Virgil, all lived before the death of Augustus in AD 14. Most important, the troubles of a republic were of much more relevance than those of an empire to writers convinced of the virtues of monarchy. Rome offered a model of political change running the full course from monarchy through aristocracy and democracy and back to monarchy.

It was generally acknowledged that the disastrous civil wars of the first century BC had ultimately ruined the republic, but this collapse was perceived both as historically inevitable and as politically beneficial, since monarchy was naturally preferable to a republic. As early as 1576, John Barston had used Rome to show that 'no state is to be compared to the royall sceptre of a king, garded with good and holesome lawes.' The pretensions of the plebeians, who were allowed to intermarry with the patricians under the *lex Canuleia* of 445 BC, had led Rome the way of Athens, into 'that most pernicious state of democratia.' Richard Beacon or Becon, an attorney in Munster, turned to Athens itself in 1594 to show the weakness of democracy and to recommend harsh repressive measures in Ireland. An early exponent of political ideas derived from Machiavelli and Bodin, Becon believed commonwealths needed strong laws and decisive, ruthless leaders, and he drew on the same stories of ancient and Italian politics which had already served Machiavelli and Guicciardini.[15]

Under James I interest in Roman history continued to flourish in a variety of forms, perhaps most notably in a number of history plays from Matthew Gwinne's *Nero* in 1603 to an anonymous play on the same subject in 1624. David Fishel has noticed a shift of focus in these plays away from Rome herself to the periphery as dramatists wrote of Roman colonies and minor historical figures such as Shakespeare's *Cymbeline* (1609) and Fletcher's *Bonduca* (1613). This may be ascribed to interest in England's British and Roman past, which continued to flourish in the Jacobean period, and also to the cultivation by James I of what Jonathan Goldberg has called a 'Roman' style for his court and the government.[16]

Translations of classical histories continued to proliferate, though at a slower rate after 1600. In 1608 the poet Thomas Heywood translated Sallust with a preface extracted from Bodin's *Methodus*. Thomas May, the future parliamentarian historian, englished Lucan's *Pharsalia* in 1626 and wrote his own continuation of the poem four years later. Turning the difficult Greek of Thucydides into English taught Thomas Hobbes the flaws of democratic constitutions.[17] In 1619 Edmund Bolton translated Lucius Florus. Through his version, and several cheap Latin editions, the epitome became the most readily available synopsis of republican history. Sir Simonds d'Ewes recalled reading Florus as an undergraduate, and the Cambridge scholar Joseph Mede recorded that the epitome was selling for a shilling a copy in the 1630s. Florus was easier to read in Latin and briefer than Sallust, Livy, or Polybius, as Bolton told the duke of Buckingham in the dedication to his translation.[18] But more important, Florus' depiction of the triumph of Augustus amid the anarchy of civil war appealed to James I's projected image as a new Augustus, healing the rifts in England's political fabric.

The writings of Tacitus proved to be more open-ended. A wave of continental interest in that historian, led by the great Dutch scholar Justus Lipsius, soon carried across the channel, where Tacitus' pithy style and political acumen helped inspire much of the politic history of the 1590s and early 1600s. It was assisted by a parallel revival of interest in the later Roman stoics, especially Seneca, and in the rise of a 'neostoic' attitude to politics and religion, in which Lipsius himself played not a small part.[19] The principal English conduit for this Tacitism was the translation of the *Histories* by Sir Henry Savile, first published at Oxford in 1591 and reissued in 1598 together with Richard Grenewey's rendering of the *Annals*. Savile's own attempt to bridge the gap between these two works, in a piece entitled *The Ende of Nero and Beginning of Galba*, had also appeared in 1591, together with his version of the *Agricola*, and in many ways it marks the first attempt by an Englishman to imitate Tacitus' historical style.[20]

The principal trouble with Tacitus was that he could be used either as a guidebook for absolute monarchy or in praise of republicanism, and Stuart students of his works found themselves treading a fine line between acceptance of Tacitus' political lessons and endorsement of his antimonarchical sentiments. Fulke Greville tried unsuccessfully to get a rising star of Dutch scholarship, Gerard Vossius, for his chair in history at Cambridge. When Vossius declined, Greville appointed another Dutchman, Isaac Dorislaus. But when the new lecturer (who years later would later draw up the charges against Charles I, and suffer assassination for his pains) tactlessly elicited pro-republican lessons from passages in Tacitus' *Annales* in 1627, the resulting outcry brought the Brooke chair in history to a speedy end.[21] As always, William Camden chose more carefully. He had given a manuscript of Florus to the Bodleian Library in 1601, and in 1621 he prescribed the epitome as the principal text for his own professor of history. He also insisted that his incumbent concentrate on civil (political) history, 'not intermedling with the history of the church or controversies farther than shal give light into those times.'[22]

The growing popularity of Florus and Tacitus, combined with contemporary reverence for these and other ancient historians, may account for the lack of attempts to write narrative histories of ancient Rome until late in James I's reign. It is also true that the market for works drawing on Roman history was being cornered by continental authors such as Giovanni Botero, who wrote three sets of *Observations upon* the Lives of Alexander, Caesar, Scipio (translated anonymously in 1602) which praised Caesar as the caricature of a Machiavel; 'there was never anie treason or conspiracie in his time,' wrote Botero, 'wherin his hand was not deepely in.'[23] In 1628, the year of the duke of Buckingham's murder, two different translations appeared of Pierre Matthieu's The Powerfull Favorite, or the Life of Aelius Sejanus. Sir John Eliot had already compared Buckingham with Sejanus in the parliament of 1626; the Matthieu tract was translated as a not-too-oblique warning to Charles I about the dangers to himself and the kingdom of nurturing evil counsellors.[24] Buckingham soon fell to the assassin's knife, but in 1634 Sejanus remained alive and well in Sir Thomas Hawkins' translation of Giovanni Manzini's Politicall Observations upon the Fall of Sejanus. Overflowing with aphorisms, it was not so much a history as a latterday Book of the Courtier.[25]

In a similar vein, Henry Carey, Lord Leppington, translated two works by the Italian Virgilio Malvezzi, who had visited England as the ambassador of Philip IV of Spain. The result, Romulus and Tarquin, was dedicated to Charles I and juxtaposed the reign of a king, Romulus, and a tyrant, Tarquin. Charles I had ruled without parliament since 1629, so Malvezzi's comment that Romulus' only fault was 'indowing the Senate with so much power' only to bereave them of it may have met a receptive ear.[26] In another examination of tyranny, an English clergyman named Edward Leigh, who was a friend of the antiquary Sir Simonds D'Ewes, extracted Selected and Choice Observations Concerning the Twelve First Caesars. Leigh's book, drawn largely from Suetonius, was a cut above a mere translation, since he at least gave some attention to the problems of establishing ancient chronology and verifying conflicting reports; his citations provide a further instance of the growing influence of Bodin's Methodus in England.[27]

As the above discussion suggests, the principal motives for the writing of Roman history were political, whether the author had a specific message to put across or simply wished to write didactically for a general audience. The balance of this chapter will be taken up with the specific contributions to the writing of Roman history of five individuals: Fulke Greville, William Fulbecke, Peter Heylyn, Degory Whear, and Edmund Bolton.

Fulke Greville on the Roman Republic

We have already seen that Fulke Greville, though frustrated in his efforts to write Queen Elizabeth's life, turned nevertheless into a vigorous patron of historical writing. His own poetic treatise Of Monarchy discusses at length the mutations in the Roman commonwealth which was 'for all free states a glass.' For a poet as obsessed with mutability as was Greville, Rome offered a fount of examples to prove the dictum 'Worth must decay, and height of power declyne.'[28] Although *Of Monarchy* is no narrative history, it is nevertheless worth examining briefly since it contains many of the ideas about ancient Rome which appear in different forms throughout the early seventeenth century.

To Greville, government was necessitated by the Fall, and the best kind of government was a monarchy in which the prince ruled with the advice of his subjects. Kings need the counsel of aristocrats, but 'must wiselie bounde their owne nobilitie' (347). Assemblies of the people are 'true glasses' in great monarchies:

To shew mens greifes, excesses to abate;
Brave mowlds for lawes; a medium that in one
Joynes with content a people to a throne. (288)

Parliament was to Greville precisely what Sir Geoffrey Elton, in a now famous phrase, termed a 'point of contact' between crown and people, a space for productive encounters between kingly authority and the subject's liberties: Greville's intellectual resemblance to his friend Samuel Daniel is nowhere more marked than in this belief. But the example of Rome showed that a balance between liberty and chaos could be difficult to strike. Although Greville criticized the later emperors for their 'martiall mutinous election' (306, 634), he knew that the occupants and not the office were to blame. Even if all her later emperors had been good men, the empire was destined to fall when she reached the preordained end of her life, 'Which no republique can exceed' (627). In any case, he asks, what democracy has ever produced leaders as great as Augustus, Trajan, and Constantine? Imperial Rome, at least, managed to survive even with her weakling rulers until AD 1453, whereas in a mere five centuries as a republic, and despite all her great heroes, '... Rome corrupted her selfe so / As change she must, or suffer overthrowe' (629, 633–5).[29]

Greville is ambiguous on the issue when precisely corruption set in, but we may draw a clue from an incidental remark made in another of his verse treatises, *Of Humane Learning*. Despite his patronage of historians and poets, Greville was always deeply suspicious of book learning, and especially of sophistry; like the great Roman stoic, Cato the censor, he attributes much of Rome's decline to the advent of Greek philosophy and a consequent decay of moral values such as obedience and simplicity:

> Yea Rome it selfe, while there in her remain'd
> That antient, ingenuous austerity
> The Greeke professors from her wals restrain'd
> And with the Turks they still exilèd be.[30]

H.N. Maclean has pointed to a possible link between Greville and the sixteenth century authors of the French treatise on resistance, the *Vindiciae contra tyrannos,* Philippe du Plessis-Mornay and Hubert Languet, whom Greville's close friend Sir Philip Sidney knew well. It is tempting to see in Greville an apologist for the Polybian mixed state and an opponent of 'Stuart absolutism.'[31] Yet though he believed (again like Daniel) in the limitations placed on a king by positive law, *Of Monarchy* shows nothing more clearly than the historical failure of the mixed state. Greville takes the expulsion of the kings as a disaster, the consequence of the first Brutus having mistaken the sins of one tyrant, Tarquin, for the faults of a system. The record of the ensuing republic was poor, and Rome eventually came 'To such descent of Anarchie' through the pretensions of the tribunes that she finally succumbed to civil war and to the restoration of monarchy by Augustus:

> Her State alike beinge each way overthrowne;
> > Wherin yet he that brought back monarchie
> > Err'd less, then he who sett the people free. (591)

The European hegemony of the republic was deceptive and was certainly not the fruit of a democracy. He denied

> Either the Empires growth or consummation
> To be the worcke of Romes Democratie;
> Since between her first Caesars domination,
> > And Tarquine, her Soveraignitie was mixt
> > Of one, fewe, manie; wavinge, never fixt. (618)

Above all, it was only when the monarchical element in the state, the consuls or dictators, was predominant that Rome expanded. Internally, Rome eventually declined into 'manie-headed powre' (592) from which she was ultimately rescued by Augustus. Although motivated by ambition, the first emperor was no tyrant; men could continue to speak freely under his principate (247). Concluding with a series of comparisons between monarchy, aristocracy and democracy, Greville generalizes to ask

> Can mankinde under anie Soveraigne
> Hope to finde rest, but in the Monarch's raigne? (650)

In a section probably written after the accession of James, he goes even further in a verse with obvious contemporary implications:

> Lastlie where many states become united
> Under one throne, though not one governemente
> Civill dissentions easilie are invited ... (359)

Greville's affirmation that a mixed state could exist but was inherently unstable suggests that there is some validity to the theory put forward by some recent historians of political thought, that theories of mixed or limited monarchy fell into decline between Richard Hooker and the 1640s.[32] Historians came down with virtual unanimity on the side of a monarchy in which the king governed with the advice of his nobles and people but did not in any sense share sovereignty, except insofar as parliamentary statutes constituted law.

William Fulbecke and the Ages of Rome

The first serious attempt by an Englishman to write a prose narrative of Roman history was the work of William Fulbecke (d 1603). A civil lawyer who had also studied the common and canon laws, Fulbecke is best known for his introduction of neo-Bartolist legal scholarship into England.[33] This consisted in the search for general principles of justice in Roman and other legal systems through the application of a comparative perspective. Well-versed in the works of Bartolus, Machiavelli, Alciato, and Bodin, he adopted Bodin's systematizing method.

In a series of fictitious dialogues between a canonist, a civilian, and a common lawyer, which Fulbecke published in two parts as *A Parallele or Conference of the Civill Law, the Canon Law and the Common Law of England*, he set out to establish the similarities and connections of the three laws. In Fulbecke's view, all just laws agreed on fundamentals; differences of detail were the product of local custom. Modern English law was an amalgam of various elements, Anglo-Saxon and Norman.

Much of it had already been established at the Conquest in the law codes of 'our greatest law makers,' kings Ina, Alfred, Edmund, Edgar, Cnut, and Edward the Confessor; nevertheless, William I abandoned many of the existing laws and added some customs of Normandy 'whereof many for the resonablenes of them have to this day continued.' Fulbecke's formulation of the relationship between custom and natural justice thus approximated, on the surface, the Cokean interpretation of the common law as 'artificial reason.' Yet in a work published in the following year, *The Pandectes of the Law of Nations*, he went on to emphasize that William's less than total abrogation of the Confessor's laws was a matter of royal choice, not necessity, since the Norman's 'universal conquest' had made him absolute.[34]

The study of law led to the study of history. In the *Pandectes* Fulbecke would use historical examples to compare the stability of commonwealths.[35] But he had already applied his political ideas to historical narrative in *An Historicall Collection of the Continuall Factions, Tumults, and Massacres of the Romans and Italians during the Space of One Hundred and Twentie Yeares Next before the Peaceable Empire of Augustus Caesar* (1601). He intended this work as a summary to fill in the gap between the end of Livy and the beginning of Tacitus' *Annales*. Lucius Florus' epitome was one of his staple sources, though he cited some thirty others, several of which (such as Dio Cassius) were not yet in translation. Recognizing the 'great disagreement and contrariety of narration' in his sources, Fulbecke nevertheless believed he could 'single and sequester the undeniable truth of the historie from the drosse and falshood,' simply by accepting the most likely account of each event. The purpose, as usual, was didactic: 'the revealing of the mischiefes of discord and civill discention' – precisely that impulse which had inspired Daniel's historical poetry of the 1590s (sigs A1v–2r).

Largely completed by October 1600, but not published until the following year, after the earl of Essex's revolt, Fulbecke's book was a tale for the times. He claimed to have written it fourteen years earlier; if so, his decision to publish it then was even more interesting. He included a lengthy discussion of Catiline's conspiracy (the attempt, recounted by Sallust, of an impoverished nobleman to seize power in 63 BC) and dedicated the work to one of Essex's principal opponents, the Lord Treasurer Thomas Sackville, Lord Buckhurst. Coincidence or not, Fulbecke's book could not but have been read by contemporaries as an indictment of Essex in precisely the way Hayward's *Henry IIII* was believed to support the earl.[36]

Like Greville a year or two later, Fulbecke condemned the exile of the kings by Lucius Junius Brutus, a mistake repeated centuries later when Marcus Brutus slew Julius Caesar. Borrowing a stock recurrence image from Florus he found 'the two Bruti ... both fatall to the estate of the Romane common-weale' (170).[37] Fulbecke saw Roman history as a series of constitutional changes from monarchy down to the depths of democracy, the worst period of which began when the people, through their tribunes, acquired a share in government. This cyclical pattern is complicated by Fulbecke's adoption of an alternative metaphor of explanation: Rome was also a human body, growing from infancy to maturity and then declining into senescence. This organic image appears in Florus, who postulated four ages of Rome ending with decay under the early emperors and rejuvenation under Trajan in the second century. Fulbecke created his own variant of this model by superimposing the Florean scheme on the seven ages of St Augustine's 'Great Week' (6–13).[38] This allowed Fulbecke, instead of portraying the empire as a period of decline, to make it one of rejuvenation after the sixth, decrepit age of the republic. The result is an interesting synthesis of linear development and historical recurrence:

1st and 2nd ages	Infancy	To founding of Rome, 753 BC
3rd age	Adolescence	Rule of Kings (to c 509 BC)
4th age	Youth	Rome conquers Italy and some of Greece
MIXED STATE		
5th age	Maturity	Conquest of Carthage and Asia, to 146 BC
POPULAR STATE		
6th age	Senescence	Rome declines into civil war
	Rejuvenation	The principate of Augustus

Fulbecke explains the inconvenient fact that Rome had conquered the world without kings in much the same way as Greville: it was a mixed state whose successes derived from the predominant monarchical element of the consuls. Yet as a civilian he was drawn more to the importance of legal codes than was Greville; he was apt, therefore, to consider laws themselves rather than lawmakers as the crucial agents of historical change. This emerges especially in his treatment of the *lex Hortensia*, which in 287 BC had given the plebeians equal voice with the Senate and consuls. The result of this measure was the 'good and temperate constitution' commended by Polybius (4). But human nature can vitiate even the best laws, and while mixed states may be good in principle, they are unstable in practice; whenever the people or the Senate (*populares* and *optimates*) passed the bounds of 'aequall regiment' trouble followed. Once Rome had conquered Carthage it declined into vice (5). Demagogues like the Gracchi and ambitious nobles like Sulla between them led the republic into civil war, until a strongman emerged in Julius Caesar, whose own attempt to revive the monarchy was cut short by his assassination (9–23, 60ff, 168).

In an especially interesting passage which could have been written fifty years later by Hobbes, Fulbecke accused Caesar's assassin, Marcus Brutus, of regicide. It mattered not that Julius Caesar was initially a usurper; by the mere act of seizing power, he automatically became the *de facto* ruler of the republic, legally protected by the *lex Cornelia*. In stressing the right of Conquest, Fulbecke made little distinction among kings, tyrants or usurpers, 'for he which attaineth to an imperiall or regall soveraigntie, by warlike industrie and victorious exploit, is no lesse a monarke, then he which cometh to it by election, succession or descent' (172).

As Caesar's heir, Augustus too was legitimate, and by defeating Brutus, Antony, and his other rivals, he attained sovereignty as 'the sole governour and absolute emperour of Rome' (197–9). Fulbecke shared a standard contemporary interpretation of the Augustan principate as a beneficent despotism; in reality, the Roman emperors were *principes* (first citizens) not *domini* (lords) until the end of the first century AD. Like Greville, Fulbecke was content to show that absolute monarchy could succeed where the mixed state had failed, but – paradoxically in view of his legal training – he was even less interested than Greville in defining the precise relationship of the monarch to the laws.

Augustus Redivivus

Examples from Roman history had greater currency all across Europe than national ones. A Frenchman might not take the point of an allusion to the Wars of the Roses; a reference to the character of a minor Italian prince might be lost on an English reader; but every literate European knew about Tarquin, Tiberius, and Trajan. Before and after Bodin, most writers of *artes historicae* in Europe and in England had given pride of place to the ancient world and its histories ahead of national history.

Peter Heylyn's notorious royalist histories, written after 1640, await a thorough study, and will be addressed briefly in our final chapter. But Heylyn (1599–1662), whose son-in-law and biographer, John Barnard, described him as 'a man of an aiery and active spirit,' was an active purveyor of the past as early as 1621.[39] In that year he wrote an enormously popular little book called *Microcosmus*, which neatly summarized the historical and geographical facts about the most famous commonwealths, cities, and empires of the world. He included a short scheme of the divisions of history, which was influenced by Bodin and by Bacon's *Advancement of Learning*, but which drew much more from Johannes Freigius' *Historiae synopsis* (1580).[40] Heylyn elevated geography and astronomy ('history' in the Plinian sense) to great importance by making them together the first of the two major divisions, greater and lesser history (*historia maior et minor*). Lesser history, the history of man and his works (the microcosm of the title), he further subdivided into 'inner works' (religion and philosophy) and 'outer works'; these in turn he divided into (a) manners, customs, laws, and statesmen, and (b) actions or events. This last category, historical narrative proper, was further divided and redivided into its various forms with civil and ecclesiastical history becoming the two smallest subdivisions in the scheme. True history was a 'quintescence' of four elements: annals, commentaries, diaries, and chronologies. He represented the whole by means of a Ramist diagram (figure 2) taken directly from Freigius. His list of the 'best writers' of history from its beginning to the present, derived mainly from the tenth chapter of the *Methodus*, is unremarkable, except for its peculiarly strong praise of William Martyn's *The Historie and Lives of the Kings of England* as 'a worthy chronicle of our state.'[41]

From rationalizing the study of history, Heylyn turned to history itself. Having resolved 'not to bury his parts in a country parish,' he secured the patronage of the governor of Jersey and Guernsey, Henry Danvers, earl of Danby. The earl in turn brought him to court and introduced him to William Laud, then bishop of London. It was through Laud's recommendation that Heylyn became a chaplain to Charles I in 1630, a year after the stormy dismissal of parliament.[42] Though of course it was unknown how long Charles would rule exclusively through his council, there were those (including the king himself) who thought that parliament should never be called again. It is with this in mind that one must read Heylyn's *Augustus, or an Essay of Those Meanes and Counsells Whereby the Commonwealth of Rome Was Reduced unto a Monarchy* (1632).

Heylyn's *Augustus* revived the thirty-year-old analysis of Fulbecke, but stripped it of its Augustinian 'six ages,' and of Florus' body metaphor. His sources include Polybius, Livy, Florus, Tacitus, and especially

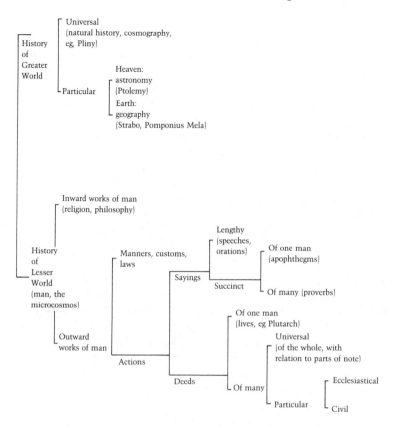

Figure 2   Peter Heylyn's 'General Praecognita of Historie' (from
Microcosmus (621). History is a 'quintescence' of four elements:
(1) Commentaries (events in chronological order, without causes or
motives); (2) Annals (bare events; not annals in the Tacitean sense);
(3) Diaries (record of daily actions); (4) Chronologies (eg, Scaliger).

Dio Cassius; he leavened these with historical parallels and observations from Machiavelli and Guicciardini.[43] Heylyn began with an exposition of the three pure and three perverse forms of government and of the natural tendency of one form to degenerate into another. His narrative would specifically follow the Polybian *anacyclosis*, as government turned successively from monarchy to tyranny, to aristocracy, to oligarchy, to a 'republicke,' to a democracy, and finally back to monarchy. His task, he declared (2–3), was to demonstrate that monarchy was the first and final point in a cycle which could be repeated at any place or time: Rome merely provided a case study. Thus from the very beginning Heylyn invited his reader to take what followed less as a history of Rome than as a description of political change applicable to any society.

Heylyn was much more explicit that Fulbecke on the chronology of the political cycle. Lucius Brutus expelled the kings after Tarquin had turned the monarchy into tyranny, but since he had 'taught the people, both the theorie and practise of rebellion,' Brutus could not himself become king; he instead established an aristocracy of Rome's 'fathers' (that is, the patricians). Rome flourished for a time, but the aristocracy soon degenerated into an oligarchy under the Decemvirate. The fall of that regime in turn gave 'the people' (plebeians) an excessively high view of their position, and they secured the right to intermarry with patricians under the *lex Canuleia*. This was 'the first step to the republique' (8–9, 14), which was fully established when the people were able to share civil honours with the nobles.[44]

Though in his introduction he called the pure popular form a 'republicke' (2), Heylyn was inconsistent with his terminology. He clearly intended 'republicke' as a *mixed* rather than a pure form, and he used it in this sense elsewhere in the text. The mixed state offered its citizens many benefits – for instance, it allowed individuals to rise by 'vertue' as much as by birth. Accordingly, one might expect this 'commonwealth,' he commented, 'being thus equally poysed had been immortall.' But a balance proved impossible to maintain. One 'element' eventually had to predominate, and the creation of tribunes of the people turned the mixed republic into a straightforward democracy:

And now were the Romans governed by that forme of rule, than which there is no lower. So that *as well by an inevitable necessity in nature, as the ordinary course of policies*, there must be a recession to the first, and monarchicall jurisdiction. (17–21 [my emphasis])

Though a new monarchy provided the obvious solution, the road back to kingship lay uphill. Successive sets of rivals, Marius and Sulla, then Caesar and Pompey, battled for control of the state. In a passage reminiscent of Ralegh's treatment of Alexander the Great, Heylyn acknowledged their personal ambitions, but gave them credit as agents of history; whatever their flaws and selfish aims, it was these men who 'first opened the passage to others, and first mooved the stone, which rowling along tumbled the people out of the government' (26).[45]

The remainder of the tract shows how Augustus established a stable and absolute monarchy. Heylyn drew an explicit parallel between Augustus' victory and Henry vii's. 'I cannot here omit the like effect springing from the like cause.' In both cases, only one heir to the throne was left when the dust cleared, 'so unsearchable are the judgements of God' (45–6). Heylyn depicted an Augustus even more ruthless and politic than in Fulbecke's version, and his book offers perhaps the most unadulterated commendation of Machiavellian ethics and absolute rule to be found anywhere in early Stuart historiography: there is none of Bacon's or Habington's ambivalence here. A master dissembler, Augustus kept up the appearance of respecting both Senate and people (here revealingly called the 'Lords' and 'Commons') only while it served his purpose (98, 106–9, 112). He cunningly rid himself of Antony by sending him away from Rome; in Heylyn's view, the best way for a prince to dispose of an enemy or unwanted servant was 'to remove that man out of the way, under pretence of some honourable charge' (54).

As he recounted Augustus' establishment of the new constitution, Heylyn slipped increasingly into contemporary commentary. He praised Lycurgus' Spartan constitution above those of Athens and of Plato's idealized republic. In Sparta, the nobles had 'convenient authority' and the people 'entire liberty,' but government belonged completely to the king, who had 'absolute majesty.' This is an outrageous misrepresentation of Book vi of Polybius, which describes the republic, not the principate – which Polybius never lived to see – as a copy of Sparta; so is Heylyn's stress on the power of the Spartan kings (which in fact was almost negligible) rather than the ephoral aristocracy. Clearly one did not have to be one of Zera Fink's classical republicans to perceive Sparta's constitution, however perversely, as a model of stable government, 'mixing the soveraignty of one, with the liberty of all' (122–3).[46] Augustus' powers amounted to a 'prerogative' unlimited by anything except the prudential need to keep the nobles and people happy and occupied. Without popular power, the monarchy grew so strong that the empire survived the 'monsters' who immediately followed Augustus as emperor (116–17, 141, 220ff).

It is difficult not to read Heylyn's *Augustus* as a conscious defence of the three-year-old personal rule, and a soothing reassurance from his chaplain to Charles I that the king's strategy was tried and true. Heylyn may even have received some encouragement in writing it from one of Charles's advisers, such as the attorney-general, William Noy, who was one of Heylyn's close friends and who shared his antiquarian and legal researches with him.[47] Heylyn clearly perceived upstart nobles, as much as the people, as a threat to stability. The crucial point is the restraint of both these elements in a constitution within which both enjoy limited 'liberties' under a prince whose will is law. Long before Harrington and the later English republicans, Heylyn had recovered – and distorted – Polybius' theory of governments and extolled the Spartan state as a model for a balanced commonwealth.

The Professor's Progress

In the very year that Heylyn published *Microcosmus*, the University of Oxford appointed its first history professor. Camden endowed a chair in civil history and, on the recommendation of the venerable astronomer and manuscript collector, Thomas Allen of Gloucester Hall, picked as his first incumbent Degory Whear (1573–1647). The nominee was a competent if uninspiring classicist, but no historian. His surviving letterbook, which begins in 1595, shows little interest in history and none in antiquarianism or philology prior to his appointment.[48] Yet this sort of dull pedagogue was exactly what Camden had in mind, and Whear was duly entrusted with the instruction of Oxford's youth in ancient history.

Ostensibly obeying the wishes of his patron, Whear based his lectures on the innocuous epitome by Lucius Florus. Though Camden had likely only intended that Florus serve as a text on which the lecturer would expand, Whear took his charge literally. By 1631 he had delivered nearly two hundred lectures on Florus; the Laudian statutes of the 1630s soon sanctioned his performances, and he continued to drone on through the civil war till his death in 1647, providing the history of academic tenure with an inauspicious beginning.[49] It is an insoluble mystery why Camden picked Whear, simply on Allen's advice, above the university archivist Brian Twyne, the author of a recent erudite contribution to the argument between Oxford and Cambridge over which university was older. It could not have been on the grounds that Twyne was an antiquary rather than an historian, since he had studied Roman political history as well as the antiquities of England.[50]

Whear's lecture-notes on Florus' *Epitome* give us an idea of what the ordinary undergraduate arts and civil law students were compelled to hear; they also provide a reminder that history was as much an oral as a written art, reliant on the human voice as well as the printed page to make its points. Whear would read to his charges in Latin – he never wrote in English – and make appropriate observations, adding illustrations from other ancient historians. His students learned of the evils of sedition, the nasty fate of rebels, the vicissitudes of fortune and the eternal presence of God in history: 'Man certainly thinks and acts according to his nature: but the plans and actions of men are overseen by the observing God, who through these secondary causes ... is himself the first cause of all things, and who turns, twists and directs all events to suit Himself.'[51]

Whear's only real contribution, important because of its great popularity as a text until well into the next century, was his plan for reading histories. Like Heylyn's *Microcosmus*, Whear's *De ratione & methodo legendi historias* offered a list of the best historians and advice on the most fruitful way of reading them. The work originated as a short inaugural lecture in 1623. In 1625 he revised it and sent copies to interested parties, including John Speed and the Abingdon schoolmaster, Thomas Godwyn.[52] Whear expanded the work enormously in 1637, adding a commentary on all civil and ecclesiastical historians from ancient Greece to the present, though English history received comparatively little attention. The *Relectiones hyemales*, as he called the extended version, was a huge list of historians, many of whom, one suspects, Whear himself may not have read, for he invariably relied on various continental examples of the *ars historica* as guides to the histories themselves.[53] Nevertheless, his deference to the critical works of Bodin, Bartholomew Keckermann, Justus Lipsius, and especially Gerard Vossius did something for the spread of these works in England; more, perhaps, than Bacon's equally derivative *Advancement*, which did not acknowledge its debts.

The *ars historica* had evolved in the sixteenth and seventeenth centuries, as various nations, communities, and families acquired an interest in the past. In 1579, an enterprising Basel bookseller named Johann Wolf reprinted several famous specimens as *Artis historicae penus*, a two-volume set which included Bodin's *Methodus*, François Baudouin's *De historia universa* and the classical texts of Dionysius of Halicarnassus and Lucian of Samosata, among others.[54] The genre continued to flourish in the early seventeenth century in the works of Keckermann and Vossius, though its vogue had really passed. Whear drew on many of these *artes*, but on Vossius in particular. In 1623 Vossius had produced a short *Ars historica* which asserted the independence of history from rhetoric, logic, grammar, and poetry, just in time for Whear to make reference to it in the *De ratione*.[55] By 1627, Vossius had filled out his brief work with two monumental studies of the Greek and Latin historians, and these provided the bulk of the material used by Whear in 1637.[56] Vossius himself visited England from 1629 to 1633. He had many English friends and sent his works to several of them, including Greville, William Laud, and William Herbert, the third earl of Pembroke (who was chancellor of Oxford before Laud), and John Rouse of the Bodleian Library.[57]

In his own method book, the *De ratione*, Whear related history to geography and chronology, its left and right eyes, since all histories are confined in space and time. He divided history into divine, human, and natural (after Bodin) but distinguished between divine history proper (the Bible and other works on God) and ecclesiastical history (affairs of the church) which was properly a subdivision of human history (figure 3). Like Bacon's, Whear's theory simply reflects common practice, since historians such as Camden and de Thou had integrated political and ecclesiastical history within a single narrative.

Whear took issue with Bodin on the contentious 'four monarchies,' an interpretive device which the Frenchman – who was in a minority – had rejected (16–17 [17–20]; 30–1 [32]; 296 [221]), but he was as certain as Bodin of the uncertainty of historical facts. Following the Roman historian Varro, whose writings survived in a summary by the late imperial writer, Censorinus, Whear split ancient history into three periods. Times to the Flood he deemed 'obscure'; events from then to the first Olympiad were 'unreliable'; history became clear only in the 'historical period' thereafter. The crises and vicissitudes of human affairs could even make later events, such as the era of barbarian invasions, obscure again, though for many periods the flawless history provided in the Bible could take the place of the fabulous tales of the mythical periods. The resemblance to Ralegh on this point is obvious, and it is not surprising that one of Whear's favourite recent works was the *History of the World* (21ff [22ff]; 42 [45]; 114 [117]).[58]

The most interesting feature of Whear's methodological tract is that it actually makes a formal theoretical distinction between two separate didactic functions of history. On the one hand, history has a *philosophical* function: 'Words, actions and counsels, or events of things, which

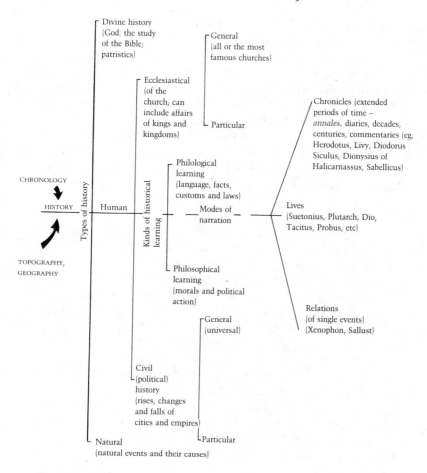

Figure 3   Degory Whear's Divisions of History (abstracted from *Relectiones* 1637 and *Method and Order* trans Bohun 1685)

history so plentifully supplies its readers with ... may be a sort of monitor for the governing and regulating the lives of men in publick, and private, in peace or war.' On the other, history also has a *philological* function. Whear concurs with Varro that histories can provide a valuable source for the origins and development of language. History, he says, teaches us good style and language and also restores to us 'the antient customs, all their rites, ceremonies and solemnities, of what sort soever they are' (322–3 [246–8]).[59] This distinction allows Whear to expand his definition of history to include in theory, as the early chapters of Speed's *History* had done in practice, elements of the social and cultural past; the *historian*, as opposed to the mere antiquary, can study the past by studying the meanings of words.

Yet by 1623, this was no longer as original as it sounds. Whear's acquaintance John Selden had already begun to approach history philologically. Whear had clearly been influenced by Selden's expansive definition of history and its proper method – the subject of the next chapter – and he quotes from an extremely important document in the history of English historiography, Selden's commendatory letter to the herald Augustine Vincent, published in 1622. Whear also, significantly, considered Camden's *Britannia* a 'history,' not simply a chorography (131–2 [130–1]). Though he still believed that 'the principal end of history is practice, and not knowledge or contemplation' (299 [223]), simply because his work was so popular, it helped to spread the idea that history could include more than politics and war. Nevertheless, his writings, like his lectures, were never intended to offer a theory of historical writing, but to provide the reader with a bibliography, 'a thread of histories disposed in such a right order, as he may from it learn the distinct changes, and varieties of times, and the series of the great transactions that have passed in the world, down to our own age' (131 [130]).

Ancient History and an Antiquary

So far we have seen little to challenge Arnaldo Momigliano's comments about the divorce between erudition and ancient history. Yet there is one obscure exception, a study of the reign of *Nero Caesar*, whose author, critical of the literary sources, attempted to supplement them by recourse to the physical remains of the past as found in inscriptions. Edmund Bolton, the author of this work, was born in 1575. Bolton, mentioned above as the associate of Speed, was an intellectual firefly who flitted from patron to patron and project to project, ending a life filled with bitter disappointments as an impoverished and persecuted recusant about 1635. He matriculated at Trinity College, Cambridge, in 1589, where he met John Coke, the future secretary of state who would provide him with one of several connections to the crown. Subsequently, Bolton studied at the Inner Temple, but literary pursuits distracted him; by 1600 he had abandoned the law for poetry, first appearing in the collection known as *England's Helicon* in that year. He was a friend of Camden and Cotton: how close it is difficult to say as we have only his letters to them and none that he received.[60]

In 1608, Bolton tried to improve his situation by attracting a patron. His first target, the earl of Salisbury, showed no interest in a 'litle, Latin work' which Bolton wished to dedicate to him, but Bolton managed to capture the attention of the earl of Northampton, to whom he dedicated his first major treatise, *The Elements of Armories* (1610), and to whom he provided legal precedents and historical information. But anticipated favours were not forthcoming and persistent requests fell on deaf ears. Bolton complained to Cotton in July 1610 that 'manifowld losses, and troubles have exercised, and daily do exercise [me],' asking Cotton to remind Northampton of his promise to help him.[61] About the same time, Cotton found him work as Speed's assistant.

Bolton's surviving letters, like his prose works, which have not been fully exploited, are interesting, informative, and interminable. He never said in two words what could be said in ten. One suspects that he was regarded with a mixture of amusement and impatience by Cotton, Camden, and his noble patrons: Northampton finally told Bolton to write to him only indirectly, through Cotton. If he was importunate, it was largely because he was perpetually in debt: the first in a long series of hard blows struck when Northampton died in 1614 and left him nothing. Yet despite his own misfortunes, Bolton could be generous to those in even worse straits. In 1610 he had asked Northampton, as usual through Cotton, to give an impoverished cousin some public office in lieu of a reward to Bolton himself, who as a Catholic felt himself 'publickly incapable of emploiment.' In 1617 we find him writing to Edward Alleyn, the famous actor, entreating him to show his 'Christian munificence' to the same cousin, whom Bolton sent with the letter.[62]

As luck would have it, Bolton managed to marry a well-connected wife in 1606. Margaret Bolton was the sister of Endymion Porter, who was to become the servant of his own kinsman George Villiers, the marquess and subsequently duke of Buckingham.[63] In 1617, Bolton enlisted Buckingham's support for his latest scheme, an 'academ roial' for the study of history, antiquities, heraldry, and polite letters in general. The background and fate of this plan have been well charted, most recently by R.W. Caudill.[64] It was more than simply a revived Society of Antiquaries, though many members of that group were to be prominent 'Essentials' in the academy. What Bolton wanted was not further disparate essays on aspects of antiquity but a new history, 'an entire and compleat body of English affairs, a *corpus rerum anglicarum*, a general history of England, to which not only the exquisite knowledge of our own matters is altogether necessary, but of all other our neighbours whatsoever, yea of all the world, for where our arms and armies have not been, our arts and navies have.'[65]

Bolton knew the deficiencies of Speed's history better than most, having himself contributed much of it. By a 'general history' he meant one that covered all aspects of the ancient and medieval English past, arts as well as arms. Though he is not as clear on this as one might wish, his debt to La Popelinière's *L'Idée de l'histoire accomplie* is apparent.[66] Bacon had made 'perfect history' a stylistic category: unbroken narrative as opposed to the chronicles and annals which provided source material. He envisaged a huge collection of histories on many different subjects, including literature and art; what Bolton had in mind was a different matter, an integrated general history of the realm.

Bolton's best-known work was a kind of *ars historica*. The *Hypercritica, or a Rule of Judgement, for Writing or Reading Our Histories* originated as an attempt to show that not *all* of Geoffrey of Monmouth's history was necessarily fabulous, in reaction to the increasing tendency to dismiss that work in its entirety as an imaginative fiction. Camden saw this part of the work in 1618 and Bolton referred to it in his translation of Florus the following year. But most of the tract was written in 1621, as a study of the original manuscripts reveals.[67] The complete work, which remained unpublished until the following century, was designed as a set of opening 'addresses' for the embryonic academy. Bolton may also have hoped to obtain, through his connection with Sir John Coke, Greville's chair in history at Cambridge, for in the final version he altered a reference to Greville's 'impious Mustapha' to read 'matchless Mustapha.'[68]

A treatise on style as much as on history, the *Hypercritica* differs from Heylyn's and Whear's *artes* in being aimed at the writer rather than the reader of histories. Although he cites Bodin's *Methodus*, his work is closer in spirit to La Popelinière.[69] Yet Bolton believed that the chronicles of the Middle Ages were not all as bad as Sir Henry Savile had once said. Bede and William of Malmesbury were perfectly respectable historians, even if they wrote in decayed Latin. The more recent 'vast, vulgar tomes' put forth by printers (by whom he probably meant Grafton and Holinshed) were neither learned nor elegant, but they contained good material for the historian. All of them had 'their uses towards the composition of an universal history for England.' Certainly, 'dry bloodless chronicles' and 'musty rolls' are dull, says Bolton, but they must be used by anyone 'who will obtain the crown and triumphal ensign of having compos'd a *Corpus Rerum Anglicarum*.' As for the style in which this new history should be written, Bolton's model was not his 'pretious Florus' but Polybius.[70] Tacitus troubled him, though he recognized the value of that historian's works and was familiar with the scholarship of continental Taciteans such as Justus Lipsius, Isaac Casaubon, and Traiano Boccalini.[71]

Part of the *Hypercritica* consisted of a short review of English history, modelled on the account in Florus, of whom Bolton was the first English translator. Just as Rome had gone through four ages or 'revolutions' (as Bolton translated *aetas*), so had England, though Bolton ignored the Florean body metaphor.[72] This section is rather disappointing, for while it offers useful comments on the organization of a future history according to these revolutions, it does not come close to showing the sense of social and constitutional development displayed by Samuel Daniel.[73] Nor does the tract ever approach the imaginative scope of La Popelinière's, which was thirty times as long; and unlike the French author, Bolton was quite obscure as to the nature of the 'arts' and 'laws' he would have his general historian discuss.

Even more than La Popelinière's and Bacon's longer schemes, Bolton's remained an outline, the application of which was unclear. Like them, he assumed that a definitive history could be written, even though the sources on which it was based continually contradicted one another. He thus took a bold stand against rabid pyrrhonism, but it was ultimately an unproductive one;[74] a more promising perspective would open up when historians began to distinguish between reasonable and unreasonable doubt, and to reconcile themselves to the idea of history as an ongoing process of research and revision. In Bolton's view, the sceptics could be answered by a single definitive account of the nation's past. Such a work would be 'superfluous, if [England] ever had an history,' and once one existed it need never be rewritten.[75] The possibility that new evidence might emerge or that some readers would disagree with the general historian's conclusions simply did not enter Bolton's head.

Bolton's best work was not the *Hypercritica* but his study of *Nero*

Caesar, or Monarchie Depraved, which first appeared in 1624. It may have been published in a hurry, because many of the spaces intended for sketches of Roman coins are left blank, a fault rectified with the second edition of 1627. Though it is, on one level, a shameless attempt to impress the crown and Buckingham with a defence of tyranny, it is also a serious effort to establish, from conflicting and incomplete sources, the *detailed* facts of Nero's reign. We are fortunate in the survival of Bolton's notebook for Nero's reign and for that of the emperor Tiberius. He had also written a vindication of Tiberius' reputation (now lost) which defended the emperor's severity towards authors who offended him.[76] In *Nero*, Bolton made no such attempt to exonerate his subject. Quite the contrary: Bolton's aim was first to contrast the evils of Nero's reign with Jacobean benevolence, and secondly to show that as bad as Nero was, the rebels who rose against him were worse. Alan Bradford is undoubtedly correct that the work was inspired by the king himself – Bolton admits as much in the preface – and that Bolton likely intended it as a justification for some of James's earlier statements in *The Trew Law of Free Monarchies.*[77]

Providing specific textual references to his sources, Bolton followed Nero's rule from its first five noble years to its cataclysmic end in the 'year of five emperors' (AD 68–9). In Bolton's interpretation, which dissents from that of Tacitus, Nero was less a naturally vicious monster than the victim of evil counsel. By dethroning him instead of trying to give him better advice, the Romans sealed their eventual fate. Henceforth the army would continue to make and break Caesars; it was 'at this breach [that] the empires fall first entred' (287).

But the most interesting feature of the work is not the story it tells; it is the way in which Bolton used non-literary evidence to tell it. He made no distinction between history and antiquarianism. For him the 'Gruterian fragments of Roman inscriptions' (a reference to Gruter's famous collection) were as good a source as Tacitus. Better, in fact, for inscriptions owe nothing to patron or party and thus hold 'the most certaine marks of facts.' In chapter XI of *Nero*, Bolton makes a plea for the use of coins in recalling the great events of the past. They should also be used by modern monarchs to preserve their own deeds, and those of their forebears, for the benefit of future historians. 'Coigns are so vital to memorie ... I may much wonder why sovereign princes (who doe hold of glory in chiefe) make either very little, or no historicall use at all, no not of their copper moneyes' (6, 14–15).[78] Yet Bolton did not make the mistake of failing to criticize non-literary evidence: although monuments and inscriptions were useful 'to revive the memorie of antient stories' he recognized that even they were not infallible. 'Nothing can be truer then that false writing is sometimes found in marbles, coignes, and other moniments,' for in antiquity coins were often minted to commemorate – or exaggerate – the deeds of earlier times (63). The historian must treat this sort of evidence with care. Bolton supplemented the inscriptions in *Britannia* with ones from a much earlier collection, Jacopo de Strada's *Epitome thesauri antiquitatum* (1553), and it was evidence from these sources that allowed him at one point to establish the thesis that London was the leading town of Britain before Caesar's arrival (134).[79]

Throughout *Nero* legends are dismissed wholesale for lack of evidence. Bolton slowly unravels the facts of the murder of Nero's mother, Agrippina, which are ambiguous 'because the text of the Cornelian Annals is at this place holden [by Justus Lipsius] somewhat depraved.' Tacitus claims that Nero sent assassins to kill Agrippina while on her ship, but that she swam to safety, only to be murdered later. With a dearth of evidence Bolton had to fall back on common sense; the tale seemed unlikely to him because he knew of no evidence in other historians that Roman women were particularly strong swimmers (35–8).

Boadicea and her rebellious Britons received little sympathy from Bolton, whose depiction of the Britons as barbarians was as hostile as Speed's. Britain had formerly been content under the 'peace of Tiberius,' and the Britons should not have rebelled simply because Nero's governors were bad. They were simply exchanging temporary inconvenience for a return to savagery. As usual, Bolton wrote more freely in his notebook than in the printed history: 'And though to serve as a captive bee simplie in itself worse then to dye, beecause it is unnatural; yet is it much better to live a protected subject in a civil, wise and valiant nation, where gentle arts and noble labors florish (for what is life itself without the life and savorie salt of good learning?) then to live a rude lord among the wild ...' Strong rule permitted scholars the freedom to study and write; weak rule meant chaos and a decline into barbarism. Bolton was more restrained in the printed *Nero*, but he still deflated the myth of 'Boadicia's quarrel' by casting doubt on the British *casus belli*, the rape and beating of the queen and her daughters. Dio Cassius (who had paraphrased Tacitus) did not repeat this tale, argued Bolton, and even Gildas, a Briton, had his doubts. The modern reader should therefore beware (128, 148, 151).[80]

This sort of criticism was not new, nor was the interest in non-literary evidence in itself: Bolton himself admitted having been inspired by 'that most modest, and antient good friend of mine, William Camden, Clarenceux' (88). What was different was his application of such sources to a chronological narrative. In this respect, *Nero* is unique as a work of ancient history in early Stuart England. Bolton's creed was simple: by all means draw lessons from the past, but first find out exactly what happened. 'The order of reason requires,' he informed his reader, 'that things should first bee known what they were, before wee declare what became of them.' One cannot generalize until one knows the facts. 'Right historie deals in particulars, and handles limb by limb. Generalities are for summists' (108).[81]

The "academ roial" died with James I, though Bolton continued to push the scheme in various forms through Buckingham and later Sir Kenelm Digby. In his last years he prospered even less. Under James he had enjoyed the right to practise his religion in peace, but the new reign, and parliamentary hostility toward recusancy, made life increasingly difficult. In February 1628, his world collapsed. He was fined as a recusant and, unable to pay either this or the recent subsidy, was thrown into the Fleet, whence he was moved to the Marshalsea. Buckingham was unable or unwilling to assist him; as for his brother-in-law, Endymion Porter ripped up Bolton's requests for help.[82]

It is unknown if or when Bolton was released from prison, but he did not remain idle, always seeking the right project to save him from his own improvidence. In 1629 he published *The Cities Advocate*, a work designed to show that apprenticeship did not extinguish gentle birth. Still later, he planned a life of the assassinated Buckingham. He also tried to get the city's support for his *Vindiciae Britannicae*, a chronological history of the city in Latin and English, which he hoped would supersede Stow's *Survay*, 'a good book indeed, but rude.' After investing ten months in the *Vindiciae* he was disappointed. The aldermen, 'startled at the mention of 3 or 4000 pounds,' the cost of publishing the work with elaborate maps, refused to pay. He suggested they send it out to readers who included Edward Coke, John Selden, Sir Henry Wotton, Digby, Ben Jonson, Sir Dudley Digges, and Degory Whear. But the aldermen had received a better offer: Jonson himself had agreed to draw up a chronicle of the last four years of the city's history at no charge.[83] We last hear of Bolton in 1634, when he sent his old friend Sir John Coke the finished life of Tiberius. Both the book and the author then vanish.

Bolton was neither a master philologist nor an especially good writer, but he has been undeservedly neglected. It is true that he was reluctant to dismiss the *British History* in its entirety: so, for that matter, was Camden. Although he had much sympathy for philological scholarship, he was slightly scornful of those who rejected every doubtful tale out of hand; he reproved those 'criticks [who] mark with their Αδηλον and their Μυθικόν their *ignotum* and *fabulosum*', useful works like Geoffrey of Monmouth's *Historia*, thereby removing what to Bolton was an important, if problematic, source for the ancient British past.[84] His forte was the study of physical remains; he had made antiquarian tours of England and Ireland and collected old documents.[85] Thomas Hearne, perhaps sympathizing with another scholar who had put religion before preferment, praised *Nero* and the *Hypercritica* highly in the next century, but most of Bolton's work was uninfluential.[86] As for the history of Rome, this remained for much longer a matter of recopying and digesting the ancients, though in 1649 another scholar, Richard Symonds, actually went to Rome to study its ancient buildings; throughout the rest of the century and into the next, young men on the Grand Tour were urged to visit the sites of historical events, to take notes, and sketch pictures of great monuments.[87] But until the development of a science of stratigraphy much later, even the use of Roman coins remained limited and subject to error.

The study of Roman history, and in particular the period of the late Republic and early Empire on which early Stuart authors dwelt, provides a kind of parallel or mirror image to the study of English history. Many of the themes which concerned English historians surface in the works of Greville, Fulbecke, and Heylyn, among them the relationship between monarchical authority and representative institutions, the benefits of absolute rule, and the horrors of civil unrest. Since Roman history lay at some distance, both temporal and geographical, from the English past, one might expect to find a wider variation in attitudes to the past – a greater freedom from the requirements of self-censorship – than in most writings on English history. This would certainly prove to be the case later in the century, as the transformation of England into a commonwealth excited new interest in the institutions of pre-imperial Rome and inspired the classical republicanism of James Harrington and his 'Augustan' and eighteenth-century successors.[88] At the same time that Harrington's denunciation of 'the execrable reign of the Roman emperors' would attract attention from exponents of the Good Old Cause, the pro-republican view of Rome would be rivalled by the Augustanism of the Restoration monarchy, an attitude which stressed order, peace, and the benefits of kingly authority, and whose strongest early Stuart exponent was Peter Heylyn.[89] But one looks in vain for signs of historical argument about Rome in the early seventeenth century. Heylyn might talk of the benefits of empire, Bolton discourse of the requirement that even evil princes be obeyed, and Fulbecke chronicle the strife of civil war and its implications for the Roman law. But these authors really do not lie very far from the reflective musings on the nature of good monarchy which we find in Greville. Perhaps the most 'radical' voice on Roman history in the period, Isaac Dorislaus is atypical in other regards as both a foreigner and the citizen of a republic; the uniqueness of his views (insofar as we can reconstruct what those were) as much as their swift silencing suggests that the consensus on the English past applied with equal strength to that of Rome.

This uniformity of perspective should not, on reflection, surprise us. It was natural within the context of the imperial rhetoric of Tudor and early Stuart art, ritual and propaganda, and especially in view of James I's consistent 'self-fashioning' into an Augustan figure of peace and political order. The tendency of Renaissance thinkers to conceive of the past, and particularly the remote past, simply as a mirror image of contemporary affairs, rather than as providing the roots from which all subsequent historical development sprang, further inhibited the writing of historical accounts whereby modernity could be traced from antiquity: there was no equivalent to Samuel Daniel for Roman history before Harrington decided to cast the history of government in a classical mould as the story of 'ancient' and 'modern' prudence.[90]

This reluctance to think in linear terms about the ancient past was not restricted to writers of historical narrative. The persistence of analogical thinking about the antiquities of Rome is demonstrated in a writer like Thomas Godwyn. Others managed to link the Roman and the national past through the reading of seminal texts like Tacitus' *Agricola*, or through the study of the physical remains of the Roman presence in Britain, as Camden had done in the *Britannia*. Only Edmund Bolton, it seems, was able to draw on both the historical and antiquarian traditions in writing a narrative of a single episode in Roman history, one which incidentally involved him in the discussion of matters British.

Bolton's virtuosity allowed him to slip over the traditional boundaries of history, into the realm of philological research, but the shortness of his attention span and the relative shallowness of his erudition prevented him from doing much of substance while he was there. And, like Bishop Francis Godwin, who had also called for a 'new' history of England, he had missed the essential point: one did not need to integrate antiquarian detail into a 'new' narrative history of England to be doing history. For that matter, one did not even have to write a history of

England or its rulers at all, for entities other than kingdoms or individuals have a past. One of Bolton's friends tried a different approach. From 1610 Bolton had lived in Whitefriars, a few hundred yards from John Selden, his junior by nine years. Selden visited Bolton – perhaps still residing in the Marshalsea – in 1632, whence he conveyed the lost *Vindiciae* to the city.[91] It is to Selden that we must turn to find the most striking signs of change in English historical writing during the first decades of the seventeenth century.

Selden: From Antiquarianism to History

What Fables have you vex'd! What Truth redeem'd!
Antiquities search'd! Opinions disesteem'd!
Impostures branded, and Authorities urg'd!
What Blots and Errors have you watch'd and purg'd
Records and Authors of! How rectified
Times, Manners, Customes! Innovations spied!
Sought out the Fountaines, Sources, Creeks, Paths, Wayes,
And noted the Beginnings and Decays!
    Ben Jonson 'To his Honord Friend Mr John Selden, Health'
(*Titles of Honor*, 1614)

The Limits of Antiquarianism

In the last decade of the sixteenth century, the Elizabethan Society of Antiquaries met regularly to discuss contemporary institutions such as Christianity, knights or the office of earl marshal, and their 'originalls,' often using non-literary sources such as coins and epitaphs to supplement the evidence of chronicles and documents. The antiquaries were severely limited by a mutual agreement which restricted them to English sources, and by the lack of focus to their inquiries.[1] The discourses in the Cottonian library, many of which were printed by Thomas Hearne in the early eighteenth century, vary considerably in quality. The best of the investigators, Francis Tate, Arthur Agard, John Dodderidge, Cotton, and Camden, often went beyond their fellows both in the depths of their inquiries and in their abilities to generalize about the past – to fit each piece into a larger puzzle.[2] Nevertheless, the 'collective' nature of their discussions is an illusion. Thinking like the common lawyers which many of them were, each antiquary drew up his own 'brief' and read it to his fellows; and that was the end of that. If an issue remained unresolved at the conclusion, it could stay that way. 'In a question which cannot be proved by authoritie, probabilities and conjectures are to be used,' said Dr Thomas Doylie. His colleague Arthur Agard, vexed by this situation, commented that 'there was not in anye of our former propositions anye judiciall or fynall conclusion sett down, wherby wee might say this is the judgement or right opynyon that is to be gathered out of every man's speache.' Linda Van Norden has noted the 'total lack of reciprocal adverse criticism' in the discourses.[3] In this regard, the antiquaries were not unlike narrative historians.

The antiquaries used histories, both medieval chronicles and even modern books like Clapham's *Historie*, as evidence in drawing up their discourses, but they did not consider the finished product as history. Discourses entitled, 'Of Dukes,' 'Of the Antiquity of Sterling Money,' and 'Of the Antiquity of Seals' were not – and this cannot be overstressed – called the *history* of dukes, sterling, or seals.[4] As we have seen, chorographical works from Lambarde's *Perambulation of Kent* through Camden's *Britannia* and Stow's *Survay of London* to Thomas Habington's *Worcestershire* were called by a variety of geographical titles, and referred constantly to histories as sources, but were never themselves called histories, topographical or otherwise.

In one short work, in some ways his most interesting, Camden came closer than anyone to breaking down the barrier between history and the philological study of antiquities, without actually regarding his work as a history. Beginning with leftovers from his chorographical researches, he published in 1605 the first edition of *The Remaines of a Greater Worke, concerning Britaine, the Inhabitants Thereof, Their Languages, Names, Surnames, Empreses, Wise Speeches, Poesies and Epitaphs*.

Although Camden restricted his discussions to the island of Britain, he also took advantage of continental work, in particular the researches of 'the wonderfull linguist Joseph Scaliger,' following whom he traced some of the roots of the ancient English language back to the Persian tongue.[5] The *Remaines* is among the earliest English works to draw its inspiration, at least in part, from the studies of Scaliger. The influence of that great grammarian and chronologer dictated that language would provide the key to Camden's own researches and to his own conception of changes in English society – an approach which is never more apparent than in this collection.

Language had been altered by usage, and by 'the tyranne time, which altereth all under heaven.'[6] Camden traced the origins of the development of Christian names and of surnames with reference to the work of earlier Anglo-Saxon scholars (Nowell and Lambarde) and to French, Norman, and English literary sources. The classicist in him could not avoid the temptation (in which Camden saw nothing wrong) to note patterns of historical recurrence, such as that the first and last emperors of Rome were called Augustus. More seriously, he did not have a plan of attack, a general set of rules by which to interpret words. A born pragmatist, he specifically rejected the creed of 'method,' preferring to trust his instincts and common sense. 'To reduce surnames to a methode,' he remarked, 'is matter for a Ramist.' With his usual timidity, he protected himself and begged forgiveness for any errors. 'Pardon me if it offend any, for it is but my conjecture.'[7]

Camden dedicated the *Remaines* to Sir Robert Cotton, who had also attracted the admiration of an English antiquary in exile, who sent Cotton, among other things, the petrified tongue of a fish. Richard Rowlands had changed his name to Verstegan on returning to his ancestral Holland, from whence he came, about 1587, to Paris.[8] In 1605, he published the first edition of *A Restitution of Decayed Intelligence*, which begins with a commendatory verse from his fellow Catholic, Richard White of Basingstoke.[9] Dedicating the book to King James, and describing him, unconventionally, as of Anglo-Saxon rather than British origins, Verstegan became the first writer to glorify the Saxons above all other English peoples. The British held no interest for him. He criticized French writers for confusing the British and English, though, he admitted, the English themselves did this as well: even John Foxe had confused the two names. Whether or not Verstegan can be said to have touched off a 'Saxon craze' leading straight to Leveller pseudo-history and 'the Norman yoke' is another question entirely, but his was nevertheless a significant departure from the adulation of the British and their Trojan ancestors.[10]

Less well acquainted with continental philology and with the origins of individual words than Camden, Verstegan concentrated on peoples and institutions rather than dwelling exclusively on language. From Tacitus' *Germania* and Justus Lipsius' Tacitean commentaries, he drew both his conviction that the Saxons, who had migrated to England, were a Germanic people, and his respect for their hardy, simple character: they were a tribe 'without fraud and subtiltie' (46).[11] While his conception of the social and cultural differences among ancient peoples owed much to Bodin, he rejected the latter's climatological determinism in favour of a simpler and more realistic explanation.

> I do confesse that certain nations have certain vertues and vices more apparently proper to them than to others, but this is not to be understood otherwise to proceed, then of some successive or heritable custome remaining among them, the case concerning learning and scyence beeing far different ... People are not ingenious according to their contrey aire. (51)[12]

Custom and heritable national character cause the endurance and development of a people; therefore, if they migrate to different climes, from the forests of Germany to the small windswept island of Britain, they will still retain their individuality as a race. Verstegan saw no need to make of England and Germany geographical duplicates.

The rejection of this aspect of Bodin's theories may also be found in La Popelinière. Verstegan drew this customary interpretation of social traits from the *Histoire des histoires,* concurring with its author's rejection of Trojan forebears: 'Popilinier a late French author, maketh it in his historie of histories a meer fable and foolery, for any man to imagin that ever the francks or frenchmen have issued from these miserable fugitives: notwithstanding it hath bin as long and as much believed, as that Brute and his Britains have also in lyke manner from them had their offspring' (92). Verstegan also adapted La Popelinière's anthropological explanation for the origins of such fables in a period before historical records were kept. The ancient Druids, having had no learning, became ignorant of their own origins, unlike the literate Anglo-Saxons, and were forced to invent a myth. Exposure to the Romans dictated that this should be a Trojan myth, based on Virgil. Yet tradition still forced Verstegan to accept the historicity of at least Brutus himself, since this was 'the common received opinion ... not now rashly to be rejected.' He compromised by postulating that Brutus was actually a Gaul, since Britain was once joined to France, a fact long accepted by geographers and supported by evidence of bones and fossils, some of which he adduced in illustrations (69, 89–93).[13]

Verstegan accepted a biblical explanation for the multiplicity of peoples and tongues, which originated at Babel in Asia, where 'mankynd had first beginning.' This was no great insight, and hardly, except accidentally, a discovery of the Mesopotamian roots of civilization; it was simply a recognition that the Germanic peoples could all be traced back to the ancient Teutonic tribe and its language, which was not, perhaps, older than Hebrew but was still 'one of the most ancientest of the world' (26, 191–2). Relating the Saxons to the Franks by their common German or 'Teutonick' origin, he gave an account of their eviction from the original 'England,' their region of Germany, by the Danes, and of their conquest of the Britons. Verstegan accepted Gildas' account of the Britons' extirpation and confinement to Wales and Corn-wall; the Anglo-Saxons he accredited with much greater endurance. They survived the invasions of the Danes and Normans (both of whom were Germanic cousins) to remain the predominant race. The Normans 'could not conquere the English language as they did the land.' The Conquest was purely political, and the invaders quickly adopted the Saxon language and custome, while the English 'soon began to grow in credit' and acquired offices, lands, and church livings (182–7, 203).

Verstegan appended to his historical account a glossary of English words and their etymologies, wherever possible preferring a Germanic to a Latin derivation, often painfully to the detriment of accuracy. The word 'constable,' for example, he traced to the German 'cuningstable,' ignoring both the more traditional derivation from *comes stabuli* and the fact that all European equivalents, Germanic and Romance, were descended from the Latin word (313). His linguistic knowledge did not rival the ex-schoolmaster Camden's, and Verstegan could not construct his whole treatise on such a basis, despite his lengthy glossary. In his eagerness to prove the occurrence of great change in England with the Saxons and continuity ever since, he rejected too easily the possibility of other influences; he had little understanding of the developments of the post-Norman period. He went further than Camden in writing a book not simply on language, but on cultural change. Yet, like Camden, he did not deem the final product to be history.

John Selden and French Scholarship

Before Elizabeth's reign was out, she had been petitioned by Sir Robert Cotton and two associates to establish a national 'library and an acad-emy for the study of antiquities and history.' The supplicants' goal was the preservation of 'the matter of history of this realm, original charters, and monuments.' This was a significant step. These suitors did not recognize the work of the antiquary as being history in a formal sense, but it is clear that they were ready to view antiquities as constituting the matter from which history should be written. A virtuoso himself, Cotton blurred the distinction between history and antiquities still further by building a huge library of both narrative (chronicle) and non-narrative sources for history, especially medieval history.[14]

It was in this library, under Cotton's aegis, that the young John Selden set to work in the 1610s, and it is probably these fortuitous circumstances, combined with the catholicity of his interests, that led Selden eventually to disregard the distinction entirely and, as a result, redefine 'history' in something like its modern sense. Selden cannot take all the credit for this. He worked within an environment and among other scholars sympathetic to his views – if he had not, then his most striking insights would have amounted to little. Yet it is in his works, read widely in ensuing decades, that we encounter the most profound, articulate, and original comments on the scope and purpose of history yet made by any Renaissance Englishman. If the laurel of 'discovering' feudalism is to go to Spelman, Selden at least deserves credit for recognizing that discoveries of this sort lay within the ambit of the historian.

Selden's profession was the law, but even before his call to the bar in 1612 he had shown himself far more interested in its study than in its practical application on a day-to-day basis.[15] His literary career began with a series of studies of English legal antiquities, such as the *Analecton Anglo-Britannicon* (completed by 1607, but not published till 1615), an essay on the successive nations which had inhabited the island. It ended, half a century later, with a magisterial series of studies of ancient Hebrew laws and government which set forth a theory of natural rights the originality and importance of which have recently been established.[16] In response to the political events in which he was prominent, Selden passed through a range of disciplines, from legal antiquarianism, through social and legal history, and finally to political thought. In the context of the present work, however, his most significant and lasting accomplishments are those made early in his career, before he left English history behind him.

John Selden was born in December 1584 in the Sussex parish of West Tarring. His father was recorded in the parish register as having been a 'ministrell,' though he appears to have been a man of some means, having married the daughter of a local gentleman. The relative prosperity of Selden's parents provided their intelligent son with the opportunity to obtain a university degree and a legal training. After receiving his early education at the Chichester Free School, the younger Selden matriculated at Hart Hall, Oxford, in 1600. Within two years he had departed, without a degree, for Clifford's Inn in London, going from there to the Inner Temple in 1603. It was while a student at the Temple (which many years later refused to house his legacy of books, to Oxford's gain) that he became acquainted with the older generation of antiquaries and men of letters living in London. Camden and Cotton became close friends and mentors, but Selden was never a member of the Society of Antiquaries, a fact which may have helped rather than hindered his development.

Selden's range of acquaintances, both in England and abroad was vast. Initially he owed a great deal to his acquaintance with Cotton, for all roads led to Sir Robert's library. Other scholars and noblemen soon wrote to him in his own right. The Scandinavian scholar, Olaus Wormius, went into mourning in 1637 upon hearing a rumour of Selden's death; it took a letter from Sir Henry Spelman to reassure him that Selden was alive and well and living in the library.[17] Christina of Sweden was well acquainted with his work, and he was one of the few intellectuals of Salmasius' and Descartes' calibre who resisted her call in the 1650s. Both Cotton's Howard patrons, the earls of Northampton and Arundel, retained Selden's services, and Northampton provided him with his own manuscript treatise on earls.[18] William Watts, chaplain to Arundel and the editor of Matthew Paris' *Historia major* (1640), translated Selden's *Mare clausum* into English, though the version has been lost.[19] Lord Herbert of Cherbury, a lifelong friend who shared his sceptical cast of thought, provided Selden both with a useful catalogue of oriental manuscripts and a sympathetic ear during his troubles over the *Historie of Tithes*. Robert Sidney, earl of Leicester, gave him transcripts of some Irish charters in 1622.[20] Selden served as steward to the earl of Kent and then as adviser to that 'most incomparable person,' Elizabeth, the earl's widow. For much of his life he dwelt in the earl's London home, Carmelite House in Whitefriars, not far from the Inner Temple.[21]

Among the literary and academic establishment he had the adulation, evident in dozens of letters, of Gerard Langbaine, Edward Pocock, and James Ussher. Pocock, his undoubted superior as an Arabist, and Ussher, his equal in biblical scholarship, both acknowledged the brilliance of his erudition.[22] Patrick Young, another scholar with continental connections, provided Selden with material from the Royal Library. Cotton's librarian, Richard James, helped Young and Selden decipher the Arundel marbles (including the famous 'Parian Chronicle') in 1628, and on James's death, Selden attempted to buy his large collection of books.[23] Selden's library pilgrimages carried him to both of England's universities as well, and he was not always scrupulous in returning borrowed books.[24]

Ben Jonson was a close friend whom Selden furnished with both commendatory verses to *Volpone* and, in 1616, notes on the historical and literal senses of the scriptural texts forbidding the counterfeiting of sexes by apparel. In this case, Selden examined the historical practice of such disguises from Hebrew and classical sources outside the Bible, but refused to pronounce on the justice of what the church fathers had written – not the last time he would equivocate in this way. Ironically, despite his literary connections, Selden was himself a stylist of limited abilities. His prose, whether in Latin or English, is always awkward and tentative, and quite often confusing; this perhaps accounts for the relative dearth, until recently, of research into his life and works. As the earl of Clarendon, one of Selden's associates from the days of the Great Tew Circle and an admirer of his learning, would later recall, 'His stile in all his writings seems harsh and sometimes obscure; which is not wholly to be imputed to the abstruse subjects of which he commonly treated, out of the paths trod by other men; but to a little undervaluing the beauty of a stile, and too much propensity to the language of antiquity.'[25]

Like Camden, Young, and Sir Henry Spelman, Selden soon made contact with continental scholars. His earliest work, the *Analecton*, was published at Frankfurt in 1615, a decade after he had written it, largely for the information of foreign readers. His tract on the gods of the ancient fertile crescent, *De dis Syris* (1617), which Selden had completed as early as 1605, drew him to the attention of Pierre Dupuy and Gaspar Gevaerts in Paris. It impressed both Peiresc, who later assisted him in his edition of Eadmer, and the Dutchman Daniel Heinsius.[26] The latter, who in 1628 would see a second edition of the work through the Elzevier press at Leiden, was the favourite pupil and successor of Selden's hero, Joseph Scaliger, and he became Selden's most intimate correspondent among the European philologists, although the two men never met.[27] Selden was able to maintain a good relationship with both Heinsius and his hated rival Claude Saumaise or Salmasius. That other great light of Dutch learning, Gerard Vossius, spoke highly of Selden's ability to stay on good terms with those with whose opinions he disagreed; as we shall see further on, the English scholar was not always able to maintain this polite stance towards his opponents, especially when, in his view, they appeared to be supporting incorrect arguments with flawed historical evidence.[28] So profound was the respect of European *literati* for the London lawyer and MP that his involvement in politics, which led twice to imprisonment, seemed to some a tragic waste of time and talent. Writing to Pierre Dupuy in 1629, Peter Paul Rubens regretted that Selden had abandoned his study of the Parian chronicle 'in order to involve himself in political dissensions'; the tireless correspondent Peiresc also lamented Selden's incarceration.[29]

As well as corresponding with French and Dutch scholars, Selden paid close attention to the work of their predecessors. Although he was well versed in Machiavelli and Guicciardini, the Florentines exercised relatively little influence on his thought, and even that small influence gradually declined as Selden aged. He owned the 1550 edition of Machiavelli's *Tutti l'opere*, the published letters of the Venetian humanist Pietro Bembo and many of Guicciardini's works, including the *Storia d'Italia*.[30] In both the *Analecton* and its successor, the *Jani Anglorum facies altera* of 1610, Selden cites Machiavelli's *Discorsi* approvingly to justify William the Conqueror's munificence as the best way to subdue a newly conquered country.[31] Such references diminished hand in hand with his growing belief in a superior natural law and in fundamental natural rights; a distaste for 'Reason of State' would emerge in his speech during the Petition of Right debates in 1628.[32] If one wishes to find an important Italian strain in Selden's thought, it is likely Venetian rather than Florentine. Selden would certainly have been familiar with the conflict between secular power and papal authority that had recently placed Venice under an interdict; and the writings of Paolo Sarpi, an outspoken opponent of the Counter-Reformation papacy, may have influenced Selden's own critique of clerical claims to a *jure divino* right to tithes and nurtured the pronounced Erastianism he would show in later life.[33]

The *Analecton* was largely based on printed sources, classical and medieval, and Selden did not take much care to distinguish earlier and original documents from later, derivative authorities. The work shows little sign of French influence, except the odd reference to Bodin and Andrea Alciato, Budé's successor at Bourges, who was Italian anyway. Selden doubted the myth of Trojan origins but he did not make Verstegan's useful comparison with similar French myths. His description of mythological Britain is drawn from 'the newest writer of the history of Britain,' Richard White; it does not make the distinction, fundamental to his later writings, between 'primitive' or 'heroic' ages, in which fact is difficult to distil from fiction, and the historical age, in which events can be documented and assigned a date from reliable sources.[34]

Selden's early interest in the collective development of England as a society organized under laws is significant, and implies rather more debt to Bodin than the few citations to him suggest. Having read both the *République* and the *Methodus*, Selden saw the value of studying the history of peoples and nations (and not simply kings) comparatively.

He also drew on Bodin's recognition that earlier historians, taken as sources, do not usually agree in their accounts, and must be judged critically, with an eye to their perspective and to any prejudices which may colour their accounts.

Another profound influence on Selden's methodology was Joseph Scaliger. Probably the most erudite scholar of his day, Scaliger had set new standards in textual editing, mastered a dozen languages, and then turned to the difficult task of emending the chronology of world history. His brilliant *magnum opus* of 1583, the *De emendatione temporum*, and his later edition of Eusebius were based on a careful comparison of all chronologies of the past in a variety of tongues.[35] Scaliger was held in deserved awe by his many admirers and fewer friends, and could be scathing in his denunciation of rivals. Selden's acquaintance, the English chronologer Thomas Lydiat, was dismissed by Scaliger as an incompetent charlatan, and the two carried on a heated if esoteric debate from which Selden stood aloof.[36] The young English philologist appears to have dreaded the 'divine Scaliger' as much as he worshipped him, and it is perhaps not surprising that he published nothing before his idol died in 1609.

Three lesser-known but equally important French scholars also influenced Selden's ideas and methods. The name of Pierre Pithou, admired by Camden and Scaliger as a great medievalist (though the latter considered Pithou a bad Greek scholar), appears fairly early in Selden's notes.[37] Pithou had made a career of the recovery and restoration of the past through textual editing, and he had explored the history of such institutions as the earldom of Champagne and the early Gallican church. His work was known to Camden and, by 1612, to Selden.[38] So was that of Jean du Tillet, another medievalist, whose 'inventories' of the contents of French archives were to prove useful to Selden. The English antiquary would commend du Tillet's lists of documents pertaining to Anglo-French relations, and he himself attempted to extend this work from the mid-sixteenth century to the reign of Elizabeth, thus anticipating the huge *Foedera* of Thomas Rymer at the turn of the century. Du Tillet's account of the anointing of French kings was the basis of Selden's study of the ceremony in the first edition of *Titles of Honor*, a book which also owed a great deal to the French scholar's *Recueil des rangs des grands de France*.[39]

Pithou was by nature more editor than historian, and du Tillet regarded his *Recueils* as providing the source material for history, rather than being history in their own right. Another French lawyer had no such reservations. Etienne Pasquier, a student of Baudouin and Hotman in the 1540s, died in 1615 at the ripe age of eighty-six. He had found in the celebration of the French church, language, customs, laws, and people a cause, and in history a battlefield.[40] His greatest work, the *Recherches de la France*, was the product of a lifetime in the archives, and it grew in successive editions from a slim one-book octavo in 1560 to the gargantuan posthumous folio of nine books published in 1621.

Pasquier's *Recherches* was no narrative, and though it handled nearly every conceivable aspect of the French past, it would not have fulfilled the requirements of his countryman La Popelinière for a definitive general narrative of the nation's history. His researches covered the political history of the fifteenth and sixteenth centuries (Books V, VI), the development of the French language and of French literature (Books VII, VIII), the early development of the French nation and church (Books I, II) and France's administrative institutions (Book II). This last item, founded on the documents Pasquier uncovered in the *Chambre des Comptes*, dealt with institutions such as the *parlements* which du Tillet, focusing on officers rather than offices, had neglected.[41]

For Pasquier, the archive-searching antiquary was an historian, and history was anything which described the past, reconstructing it from all available sources, and from it tracing the development of the present. It made no difference if the reader picked up moral *exempla*, though the glosses to the work make it clear that Pasquier himself was a thorough believer in the punishment of the wicked, in the direct intervention of God in history, and in patterns of historical recurrence.[42] The important thing was to reconstruct the past and compare it with the present: that was history. No one in England had yet said anything of the kind.

John Selden only slowly absorbed the work of these French scholars, making but one reference to Pasquier's *Recherches*, for instance, in the first edition of *Titles of Honor*. But read them he did, and though it is always difficult to know where 'influence' ends and originality begins, it is equally difficult to avoid the conclusion that Pasquier, Scaliger and the others provided a decisive contribution to Selden's later synthesis of antiquarianism, philology, and history.

Selden's Early Works

Selden's first published work, the *Duello* (1610), bears all the marks of an antiquarian discourse. In it he followed the single combat from its ancient origins to the England of his own time, when it had become a controversial practice, one which King James through much of his reign attempted to abolish. The lawyer in Selden instructed him that the key to understanding a custom such as the duel lay in its *use*, the various modes of its practice and the social functions it had performed at different times. 'Historical tradition of use, the succinct description of ceremony, are my ends.'[43] His praise of Varro (whose remains Scaliger had edited in 1578) and Selden's division of time into 'time historick' and what 'the philologers call mythick' show that he had grown better acquainted with 'that great linguist Joseph Scaliger' since writing the *Analecton*. Here, too, he began to compare England with other nations, citing French cases of duels from Bodin's *République* as well as Danish, Italian, and German examples. Ultimately he concluded that while combats of all sort originate in antiquity, the judicial combat of medieval England derived from the Lombards and other northern barbarians, 'whose posterity filled this kingdom's continent.'[44]

Rather more ambitious was the work Selden produced later that year. Essentially a refurbished but more sophisticated version of the still unpublished *Analecton*, Selden's *Jani Anglorum facies altera* was intended to outline the developments and mutations of English law. He divided it into two parts on either side of the Norman Conquest. Although he recognized the Conquest as an event of enormous significance, he asserted the continuity of English law, as modified gradually by a series of invasions, Roman, Anglo-Saxon, and Norman. The Anglo-Saxon period introduced Germanic institutions such as the *concilium*, where the nobles met to approve and assent to royal proclamations, but Selden avoided the elevation of the Anglo-Saxon period in importance, succumbing neither to Richard Verstegan's extreme Saxonism nor to George Saltern's devotion to British survivals.[45] He demonstrated that many laws had originated since the Conquest, especially such as pertained to the rights of tenancy or vassalage. Starting with the *Jani Anglorum* and continuing through subsequent works, Selden would eventually come to a complete understanding of the nature of feudal tenures after 1066 and of the great impact of the Conquest upon English landholding, and hence upon English social structure.[46]

Selden's attitude to historical disagreement in the *Jani Anglorum* is interesting. In the spirit of disinterested scholarship, he avoided cavilling at those whom he was correcting. Polydore Vergil was wrong to date jury trials and sheriffs from the Conquest, for juries originated with King Ethelred, and sheriffs even earlier. But he might be excused as a foreign writer since 'it is easy for an Italian to make mistakes in England.' He similarly addressed 'my dear Bodin' courteously before disputing his assertion that a government of women was against natural law.[47] Like Camden, whose *Britannia* was Selden's most important authority, he took no pleasure in showing his predecessor's errors, nor in departing from established views; but he did not hesitate to differ if the evidence warranted it.

Both the *Jani Anglorum* and the unpublished English abridgment of it, *England's Epinomis,* show Selden to have read extensively in the works of his fellow Englishmen, and to a limited degree those of continental authors. His notes and illustrations to Michael Drayton's *Poly-Olbion* (1612) carried this process further. Selden's task here was to fill out the poetic fancies of his friend's imaginative journey through Britain with cool, sober facts. Poetry and history were never split further apart than in this work where they alternate. Restraining himself from an explicit condemnation of Galfridian myths, Selden nevertheless made it clear that he spoke 'but as an advocat for the Muse ... disclaiming in it, if alleg'd for my own opinion.' Such myths belonging to the period before Julius Caesar were untrustworthy. After Caesar, one could turn to Roman historians and then to native ones such as Bede, Asser, and Malmesbury. In a passage which in some ways anticipates Herbert's later formulation of historical 'probability' in *De veritate,* Selden notes that most history rests upon 'tradition.' The reader must be careful to recognize the dependence of the earlier historians upon beliefs, conventions, and myths which they have inherited, the collective traditions which make up national history. Only those with personal experience in affairs of state (which the young Selden of 1614 still lacked) might escape dependence on the judgments of their predecessors and reach conclusions of their own. 'No nationall storie, except such as Thucydides, Xenophon, Polybius, Caesar, Tacitus, Procopius, Cantacuzen, the late Guicciardin, Commines, Macchiavel, and their like, which were employed in the state of their times, can justifie themselves but by tradition.'[48]

Although the above list of *historians* includes not one of the French philologists, the content of his notes demonstrates that Selden's familiarity with their work had increased substantially. In discussing the antiquity of the term 'Palatine' from Roman times, he was able to contribute a valuable comparison with the French earldom of Champagne, 'as Peter Pithou hath at large published.' He notes that an Italian like Polydore borrowed 'many odde pieces of his best context' from 'the judicious French historiographer P. Emilius.'[49] More important, it was here that Selden introduced a new word into English historical discourse: *synchronism.*

In the sense that Selden used it, the word meant the opposite of 'intollerable antichronismes,' or anachronisms. It implied strict adherence to principles of chronology in the use and interpretation of sources. Thus, a document purporting to be of the early eighth century but showing some trace of debt to a later period, either in handwriting or contents, was clearly a fake. In dealing with dubious legends such as Brutus, synchronism would invariably prove 'the best touch-stone' for the antiquary.[50] The idea that documents and entire legends resting upon them could be exposed this way goes back at least to Valla's exposure of the 'Donation of Constantine,' while the principles of strict chronology had been more recently established by Scaliger; although he never used the word 'synchronism,' it is likely to his works that Selden owed the idea, but it was Selden himself who would first apply the concept directly to historical research.[51]

Despite Selden's application of the philological method to British chronology, it is clear that he accepted, at least initially, the traditional distinction between antiquities and true history. This is revealed explicitly in a passage which recalls Camden's protestation in the *Britannia*. In his illustrations to the eleventh song of *Poly-Olbion*, Selden recorded the names of the seven original Anglo-Saxon kingdoms (the heptarchy), their dates, and the manuscript and printed authorities for these. But he stopped short of giving a narrative account of the process whereby the kingdom of Wessex gradually achieved hegemony, referring the reader elsewhere: 'How in time they successively came under the West-Saxon rule, I must not tell you, unless I should untimely put on the person of an historian. Our common annals manifest it.' Elsewhere, he commented that 'history, not this place, must informe the reader of more particulars of the Danes.'[52]

By the time he provided the illustrations for Drayton, Selden had all but finished his first major work of English history, *Titles of Honor*. After the famous physician Robert Fludd cured him of a serious illness about 1613, the young scholar – he was still under thirty – was able to complete and publish this study of titles of royalty, nobility, and gentility. Revealing a large debt to du Tillet's *Recueil des rangs de grands de France*, both as source and model, Selden sallied forth to show, from printed and manuscript material, the origins and changes in almost every conceivable title from emperor to esquire. In addition to the rigidly methodical system of marginal references which was by now the hallmark of his treatises, Selden included a bibliography of 'the more speciall autors' whom he had read, and many works, no longer extant, which they had cited, a list of over four hundred names in all. It comprised all the standard English and classical writers as well as a number of French legal humanists and scholars, including Cujas, Hotman, Scaliger, Bodin, du Tillet, du Haillan, and Pierre Pithou.[53]

Titles of Honor is organized on hierarchical lines, title by title, from emperor down to esquire, though within each title Selden follows chronological principles, tracing each rank from its origins to the present. The breadth of learning in this book, particularly in continental sources, is quite remarkable, but no more so than the prefatory statement containing Selden's views on the uses of philology. As Selden envisaged it, the purpose of all research and writing was the discovery of truth. Like the most erudite of his contemporaries – Bacon, Fludd, and Spelman, to name but a few – Selden believed that the pursuit of truth knew no disciplinary boundaries: or, at least, that whatever the nature of such boundaries in theory, they were not insurmountable in practice. Indeed, in the second edition of *Titles of Honor* (1631) he would expand on this view, using the metaphor of a world of learning divided into islands (one recalls Bacon's 'intellectual globe') to characterize the scholar's search for knowledge:

> It is said that all iles and continents (which are indeed but greater iles) are so seated, that there is none, but that, from some shore of it, another may be discovered ... Certainly the severd parts of good arts and learning, have that kind of site. And, as all are to be diligently sought to be possessed by mankind, so every one hath so much relation to some other, that it hath not only use often of the aide of what is next it, but, through that, also of what is out of ken to it.[54]

Selden allowed that the 'vast circle of knowledge' could be subdivided, but at the same time he asserted the freedom of one art to borrow from another.

Books, Selden argued, have one of two functions. These are *verum* and *bonum*, both contributing to 'man's best part.' *Titles of Honor* is a work 'of verum chiefly, in matter of story and philologie.'[55] Philology held the key to antiquities – one could not study an aspect of the past more closely than through the words signifying it. By associating philology so closely with 'story,' or history, Selden came within a hair's breadth of the position which equated the two in the *Histories of Tithes*. In the first part of *Titles of Honor*, which would be corrected and greatly expanded over a period of years prior to the second edition, Selden dealt with the honours belonging to sovereign monarchs, kings and emperors, pharaohs, shahs, and other titles of east and west, past and present.

The longer second part concerned marks of honour from prince to gentleman, and carried Selden's understanding of the impact of the Norman Conquest on landholding to a higher level than he had attained in the *Jani Anglorum.*

Selden never hid behind the curtain of Coke's immemorial laws. He knew that all forms of human organization had come into existence at a specific point in time (though not necessarily in their current forms), but the lack of sources for the 'heroick' age would not always allow this to be fixed. Institutions, titles, and customs constantly changed in name and form, and it was foolish to assume that the absence in the records of the past of a specific word denoting an office or rank meant that the thing itself did not exist under another name. The Saxon *ealdormen,* for instance, performed essentially the same role as the post-Norman sheriffs. On the other hand, some kinds of institutions did *not* exist in any similar form before 1066 – Anglo-Norman military institutions being an example. 'Those kind of militarie fiefs or fees as wee now have, were not till the Normans,' and it was the Normans who introduced related feudal practices such as wardship.[56] In every case, the clues to the course of historical change lay in close study and careful criticism of the relevant documents, in chronological sequence.

In his notes to the 1616 edition of Sir John Fortescue's *De laudibus legum Angliae,* the classic fifteenth-century apology for the antiquity and superiority of English law, Selden tackled the ancient constitution once again, steering clear of two sharp rocks. It was no more simple-minded to accept Fortescue's thesis that the constitution had endured unchanged through the centuries than to espouse the antithesis of this argument: that *all* modern laws and forms of English government originated with the Anglo-Saxons or the Normans. Both theories denied the importance in history of gradual change by usage and custom. To Selden the English constitution was a mixture of many ingredients. 'But questionlesse the Saxons made a mixture of the British customes with their own,' he argued. For that matter, so had 'the Danes with old British, the Saxon and their own; and the Normans the like.'

Invasions do not pass by without far-reaching effects on existing tradition. In a passage that echoes William Fulbecke's interpretation of the impact of the Conquest – and which derives from a similar ability to see the common law in comparative perspective – Selden noted that the Normans had grafted many of their own laws on to the law codes inherited from their Anglo-Saxon predecessors: 'But cleerly, divers Norman customes were in practice first mixt with them, and to these times continue; as succeeding ages, so new nations (comming in by a

Conquest, although mixt with a title, as of the Norman Conqueror, is to be affirmed) bring alwaies some alteration.'[57]

As always with Selden, there is a catch. The political theorist in him takes up where the legal philologist leaves off. In a sense, he argues, 'all laws in generall are originally equally ancient.' All are grounded ultimately on the law of nature, the *fons et origo* of all types of law. As he would later put it, the differences between various national customs and legal systems have resulted merely from variations and 'limitations' on a natural law imposed by God through Noah and his offspring.[58] Though sceptical of the supposed foundation of Britain by Noah's descendant Gomer, son of Japhet, Selden was reluctant to reject the legend in its entirety; it smacked less of 'poetick fictions' than did the tales of Brutus, and it was supported by the scholarship of Eusebius and, more recently, Scaliger. More important, it provided Selden with an easy explanation of the manner in which the world had been quickly repopulated after the Deluge, itself a scriptural 'fact' which Selden, along with all other scholars, had to take as a given. Time for the early modern historian and antiquary alike had a specific beginning, and biblical events could be assigned a specific date; if other events of those times were not equally fixable, this was either because they were legends invented by later ages or because the secular sources available were deficient.

A Philological History

Selden's *Historie of Tithes* must be read within the context of Elizabethan and Jacobean discussions of the proper methods and subjects of history; only then does the nature of the conceptual shift Selden helped to bring about become apparent. The *Historie* is not concerned with great events, nor with great men, except insofar as these figure incidentally in his account. It points no morals, nor any lessons useful to statesmen. It is devoid of a teleological outlook which assumes the present *must have* rather than *did* emerge from the past. It is not founded on the idea of historical recurrence but on that of gradual growth and mutation. It is an examination, through a chronological and critical comparison and analysis of all available sources, of the historical origins, development, changes, and social effects of a single *thing*, the institution known as tithe payment. As an account of its subject it has never been superseded, something which could not be said for any other work of history from the period.[59]

A detailed investigation of the customs and institutions of tithing in the history of the English church and in other countries from biblical times to the end of the sixteenth century, the *Historie* was inspired by a short essay of Scaliger which Selden had first read as early as 1612, and by a desire to correct a view of the past which asserted the clergy's right to tithes *jure divino*.[60] It is also just possible that Selden had read, in manuscript, Paolo Sarpi's tract *Delle materie beneficiarie*, written about 1609 but unpublished till after Sarpi's death. This work, usually referred to as the *History of Benefices*, has many similarities with Selden's *Historie*, though it is more openly polemical and, unlike Selden's, is concerned only secondarily with tithing practices.[61]

Selden was peering into something which was no dry academic dispute – not, we might say today, an example of irrelevant antiquarianism. Over and above the obvious economic implications of an attack on *jure divino* tithes, Selden's research demonstrated conclusively that the canon law could only be effective when it was incorporated, either by custom or statute, into the laws of individual nations. In his efforts to relate the true history of tithing practices Selden must have known that he was lighting a match to read the label on a barrel of gunpowder.

The consequence of this was to force Selden into calling his work a *history* so that he could pose as a neutral in the tithes controversy. Writing in different circumstances from Sarpi or Scaliger – he could scarcely criticize the English clergy with the same freedom enjoyed, with state support, by the Venetian renegade or the protestant philologist – Selden had to deny that he was penning a polemical tract, that he had a point to prove. A 'discourse on tithes,' or a 'treatise on tithes' would be taken as a partisan attack on the clergy. A history, on the other hand, being simply a narrative of what had happened in the past, might make its case without causing offence: in a sense, his very choice of genre offered Selden the same sort of opportunity to cloak criticism as history which we have already seen in politic historians like Bacon. As things turned out, this was almost incredible naiveté, though the results of this rhetorical sleight-of-hand proved to be important in the long term to the development of history in England. But to take at face value Selden's presentation of himself as an independent arbiter and objective recorder of events is fundamentally to misunderstand both the politico-theological context within which he wrote, and the reasons that impelled him to write the *Historie* in the first place.

Selden deliberately cast in chronological form a book that is manifestly a piece of erudite scholarship, of antiquarian philology, attempting the difficult task of representing in a narrative the findings of detailed research in non-narrative sources. In one way, he simply returned to the original, Herodotean sense of ἱστορία as inquiry, protesting that he was not arguing a case but simply writing a morally neutral history in the tradition of Pliny and Aristotle:

> Neither is it any thing else but it self, that is, a meer narration, and the *Historie of Tithes*. Nor is the law of God, whence tithes are commonly derivd, more disputed of in it, then the divine law, whence all creatures have their continuing subsistence, is inquired after in Aristotles historie of living creatures, in Plinies naturall historie, or in Theophrastus his historie of plants.[62]

Yet there was one important difference between Selden's work and a conventional natural history: *The Historie of Tithes* dealt with the past and its institutions, with a world of flux, not with the static realm of nature. Selden had successfully conflated several different modes of historical discourse, bringing the antiquary's sense of the past and the idea of history as 'inventory' under the same conceptual umbrella as the historian *qua* narrator of events. In short, he had seen both that a single institutional aspect of the present, tithing, had evolved in several stages over the centuries, and that the tale of that evolution merited being told in a history.

In his methodological preface, Selden asserts that he wishes to establish the veracity of the historical argument that tithes had always been paid to the clergy *jure divino*. This is not a matter of theology but of practice and custom. He admits that his book, the first of its kind, is likely to be unpopular, and reminds the reader that such earlier scholars as Reuchlin and Budé had also been resented for their erudition; such also was the fate of Erasmus, and of Roger Bacon (xvi), of whom Selden would later make a separate study for the benefit of Sir Kenelm Digby.[63] The same lack of modesty which is obvious in this implied comparison of himself with such a pantheon of learning no doubt also allowed Selden to avoid Camden's self-denying ordinance, the protestation that a scholar such as he would never presume to meddle in the writing of history. If continental authors such as Budé, Cujas, Pithou, and Pasquier can bring philology to the 'rectifying of storie,' asks Selden, 'why then may not equally a common lawier of England use this philologie?' (xx). A reliable miniature of even the narrowest corner of the past could not be drawn without an understanding of the complete picture, and that in turn could only be achieved through a synthesis of philology with history. Selden had arrived, in theory as well as practice, at a point reached earlier by the French scholars he cited, the alliance of different branches of knowledge in the pursuit of historical truth.[64]

All available evidence had to be found, criticized, and set in the scales. The investigation must be conducted chronologically, with close attention to synchronism, which will alert the investigator to bogus documents and the errors of fallible sources. Selden's bibliography includes records from the Tower, a large number of original cartularies from Cotton's library, which were more trustworthy than their printed versions, and other documents supplied from the libraries of Henry Savile of Banke (cousin of the more famous warden of Merton College) and Thomas Allen of Oxford, as well as Patrick Young's collections in the royal library, and the books and manuscripts of the Bodleian (491ff).

Yet all this effort had a purpose, without which it would have proven pointless. Selden distinguished between a constructive study of antiquities on the one hand and an unfocused love of old things on the other. He was careful to argue that he was not interested in the relics of the past for their own sake but in the production of a meaningful, useful narrative which would illuminate both the history of tithing practices and the entire institutional framework of the church as it had developed down to his own day.

> For, as on the one side, it cannot be doubted but that the too studious affectation of bare and sterile antiquitie, which is nothing els but to be exceeding busie about nothing, may soon descend to a dotage; so on the other, the neglect or only vulgar regard of the fruitfull and precious part of it, which gives necessarie light to the present in matter of state, law, historie, and the understanding of good autors [sic], is but preferring that kind of ignorant infancie, which our short life alone allows us, before the many ages of former experience and observation, which may so accumulat yeers to us as if we had livd even from the beginning of time' (sigs a2r–v).

Selden was not interested merely in 'what hath been' but in its relevance to 'the practice & doubts of the present' (II). Like many other politically active early Stuart antiquaries, he saw his erudition as a means of contributing to the common weal. Just as the painstaking examination of precedents and customs buried in the darkest recesses of the Tower provided guidance for MPs debating points of procedure and questions of law, so the close examination of the remote and recent past of the church and its institutions could sharpen and clarify the issues involved in the developing debate between laity and clergy over the possession of tithes. The very distinction between sacred and secular history, between the political and spiritual realm, which Camden had tried to safeguard only three years earlier, dissolves in Selden's analysis of an important outgrowth of the church as an institution created, modified, and changed by men over a period of centuries.

The effects of all this were threefold. First, Selden had given constructive and methodical antiquarian research a formal place in historical narrative. Second, he had asserted the freedom of the historian to alight on any topic he chose: to write the history of 'things' as well as of men and kingdoms. Third, he had also denied a place to the unmethodical antiquary, the man interested only in collecting coins or examining old documents for their own sake, without a larger concept of history against which to measure their importance. The long passage quoted immediately above puts Selden in precisely the same category as George Huppert's philosophical scholars; the words could have been written by Pasquier or La Popelinière. Selden lacked the burning love of the past for its own sake which in the seventeenth century would drive an increasing number of gentry and clergy on endless searches for coins and monuments while blinding them as to the meaning of their discoveries;[65] instead, he directed his research to the answering of broad questions.

Erudition and Argument

Selden's book would unquestionably help to redefine the relationship between history and erudite knowledge in England, but we should not suppose for a moment that this is why he wrote it; nor should we make the mistake of treating the *Historie of Tithes* as a model of objective, modern scholarship.[66] Precisely because Selden was politically engaged, because he researched and wrote with an eye on the present, the *Historie* is very much a work of its time. If it differs radically from much of the historical writing studied elsewhere in this volume it is not because it is less polemical but because it is in some ways more so, for all its author's protestations of neutrality. Like most of the historians we have encountered so far, Selden's view of the past was shaped by present concerns, political and religious. Unlike most of them, however, he openly acknowledged the possibility of different interpretations of history, while at the same time setting himself to rectify what he regarded as a fatal flaw in the accepted account of one aspect of the past. In no work of history published in the early seventeenth century does a particular point of view, a lawyer's urge to make a case, come across so clearly as in the *Historie of Tithes.*

It is because he was playing the barrister as well as the humanist scholar that the weight of evidence cited and even quoted *in extenso* is so great. There is a tendency to regard any historian who includes documents so that they may 'speak for themselves' as unbiased, and even to regard this as an anticipation of the techniques of modern scholars. But this is precisely the wrong way to look at it. As we have seen, such historians as Edward Ayscu quoted documents in their narratives with a view to making a point; even Camden, perhaps the least politically involved of all early Stuart historians, included documentary material as a means of lending authority to his picture of Queen Elizabeth, not for the sake of advancing historical methodology.[67]

The presentation of historical evidence within the text of a history should thus not be viewed as a foreshadowing of the enterprises of Enlightenment and nineteenth-century historiography; it is rather a harking back to an era of more virulent historical controversy. Few works of sixteenth-century historical writing make more use of documentary evidence, presented *ipsissima verba,* than John Foxe's *Acts and Monuments.* Whatever Foxe's great talents as an historian of the English Reformation, few readers would now consider him a precursor of objective scholarship. And looking ahead a few decades, to the historical writings of the 1640s, 1650s, and after, one can find ample evidence of historians, locked in combat over the past, printing various documents at length in order to provide authority for their arguments. For examples, one need only consider such works as Bulstrode Whitelocke's *Memorials of the English Affairs,* John Rushworth's *Historical Collections,* and John Nalson's *An Impartial Collection of the Great Affairs of State,* whose greatest weapons were documents selectively presented, often with minimal authorial commentary, in order to push the reader towards an intended conclusion.[68] Selden both echoes Foxe's polemical tone, masked as unbiased neutrality, at the same time that he anticipates not the techniques of modern documentary criticism but the ideologically motivated historiography of the period following the civil war. If these points are grasped, it then becomes easier to understand how and why Selden wrote the *Historie of Tithes* as he did, and why it is, nonetheless, an important document in the development of the idea of history without being anything like a fountain whence flowed modern 'scientific' research into the past.[69]

Tithes by Divine Right

Much has been made of Selden's 'Erastianism,' which became pronounced during the ecclesiastical debates of the 1640s, as remarks in his widely quoted *Table Talk* demonstrate.[70] But the Selden of the *Historie of Tithes* had not yet reached this position, and the *Historie* is not even especially anticlerical: it defends the distinction of layman and priest and at various points praises the primitive and early medieval clergy, noting their co-operation in such matters as the administration of justice. Selden's criticism of the clergy in the *Historie* must be understood not in the context of mid-century arguments over the character and powers of the priesthood, but as part of a series of Jacobean debates over legal *jurisdiction*.[71] The dispute between the common law courts and Chancery was one example of such conflicts, and the rivalry of the common and civil lawyers another. Throughout the period the common law courts frequently used such measures as writs of prohibition to restrain prerogative courts such as High Commission from proceeding in cases which were felt to fall properly within their own sphere.

Few such issues were as serious as the question of conflicting lay and clerical claims to property. This was a dispute which had medieval origins but which was given new urgency in the sixteenth century after the dissolution of the religious orders and the division of much of their property among the gentry and nobility. This loss of property was compounded by an inflationary reduction of clerical incomes which by the early seventeenth century had grown particularly acute. By 1618, several complaints had been made about the decaying position of the parish clergy, much of which was blamed on the impious practice of laymen impropriating tithes. Among these was a tract by George Carleton, the future bishop of Chichester. Carleton's appeal on behalf of tithes, published in 1606 and again in 1611, was among the more moderate advanced by clerical proponents; throughout it he was careful to emphasize that tithes were owed God by the 'moral law,' rather than merely according to the positive law of the realm or according to mere ceremonial practice; though such 'judiciall' obligations as that pertaining to the ancient Levites had expired with the authority of Hebraic law, a moral obligation to render a holy tenth to God still existed. Yet Carleton had some knowledge of both common and canon law, which he used to describe tithes, as a lawyer might, in terms of property: 'But when tithes are said to be the Lords, this is in respect of a proprietie and immediate right, that he hath in tithes, for otherwise why should the Lord say that tithes are his more then the other 9 parts?'[72]

On this argument, God had a theoretical right to *all* property simply as the overlord and Creator of all persons and things; but He had an immediate claim to one tenth which went beyond His ownership of the rest. There is an obvious similarity, which Carleton did not trouble to make explicit, between this distinction and that made by common lawyers between lands held immediately and mediately of the king. In England, where there was no allodial tenure, it was widely recognized that all land was held of the king by some form of service; yet the crown had a greater, and immediate, claim both to its own lands, and to a return (in the form of military service, wardship, and other feudal obligations), from those lands it granted to subjects.

The clergy were not alone in advancing such arguments; they could draw on some powerful lay support for their position in the person of so learned a scholar as Sir Henry Spelman, who attacked lay usage of churches for profane purposes in his *De non temerandis ecclesiis* (1613), and who would go on to write several further works on the issue of tithes.[73] One of these, *The Larger Treatise Concerning Tithes*, may have been completed before Selden wrote his book though it did not appear in print till the 1640s. In that work, Spelman argued that tithe payment was entirely in conformity with the 'old law of the land,' citing King Athelstan's ancient decree that both bishops and kings should pay tithes, and subsequent endorsements of these laws by later Saxon monarchs and by William the Conqueror: on not all fronts, clearly, was Spelman prepared to concede the importance of the Conquest.[74] Taking Carleton's analogy between human and divine property further, he could speak of God's claim to tithes in the same vocabulary as he might discuss a feudal title, as a sort of property devolving on God by that most ancient of legal charters, the covenant between God and Noah: 'To speak in the phrase of lawyers, and to make a case of it: God is originally seised of tithes to his owne use, *in dominico suo, ut de feodo,* in his own demesne, as of fee-simple.' While the ownership of land derives from human law, the whole world is ultimately God's *ex jure divino*. But Spelman was not content simply to argue for the divine-law sanction of tithes; he devotes a chapter to the argument that tithes had been, since very ancient times, sanctioned by custom and legislation as well.[75]

It was here that he differed from Selden, who likely had not read *The Larger Treatise* but had almost certainly read and absorbed Spelman's similar position, more briefly stated, in the published *De non temerandis ecclesiis*. Unlike Spelman, Selden was fundamentally convinced that clerical *jure divino* claims to property, and particularly to the right of tithing, were unjustified historically and had neither always been exercised nor even claimed under the laws of the realm. But in order to persuade the clergy, and his readers, that their version of the past was incorrect, it was not simply sufficient to construct an argument, or even to produce the appropriate documents in evidence. He had to present his case in the same mode of discourse that a cleric would adopt. The reason why the *Historie* is so successful at combining profound erudition with a biting argument is that Selden opted to fight the clergy on their own grounds, with their own scholarly weapons. In few contexts had learning been more widely used in the sixteenth century than in religious or theological debate, as protestants, puritans, and Catholics in England and across Europe used their knowledge to barrage opponents with citations, documents, and authorities. Selden now borrowed techniques of argumentative rhetoric honed in several generations of theological and ecclesiological controversy to prove, from a weight of critically examined evidence, that the appeal of the clergy to custom and practice was historically weak.

The Structure of the *Historie of Tithes*

It is a central argument of this study that historical writing in the early Stuart era, unlike many other genres of writing, was largely consensual rather than controversial. The corollary of this thesis is that the ideological differences which existed, and which render one historian's treatment of an issue like the Norman Conquest subtly different from another's, were not yet severe enough to make historical *narrative* into a suitable medium of polemic. Because most histories were so unargumentative, because they seemed, by and large, to support a generally accepted picture of the past, even the most panegyrical of early Stuart historians enjoyed a reputation for neutrality and objectivity; little need remained by 1603 for the sort of polemical history-writing practised by a Reformation historian such as John Foxe. Although Selden called his work a *history*, and though he claimed, like historians, simply to be presenting the past as his authorities and sources recorded it, his work has less in common with the historical narratives of the period than it does with the theological writings of learned clerics like Thomas Gataker and Lancelot Andrewes.[76] It is therefore no wonder that the clergy found his book so threatening, and why, with good reason, they challenged Selden's claim that he had merely written a 'history.'

Divided into fourteen chapters, the *Historie* traces the history of tithe laws and tithing customs from pre-Mosaic times to the present, examining the materials which illustrate this history, frequently comparing different copies of the same document, and critically assessing the motives of those who wrote them. The first seven chapters establish the European context of tithing before focusing on the practice in England and its differences. Along the way Selden attacks a number of subordinate issues, such as the reliability of certain sorts of documents, the gradual development of the parish, and the emergence of the ecclesiastical courts.

The work opens with an account of pre-Mosaic tithing, in which Selden put his knowledge of Hebrew to good use. He treats the Bible as an historical source, open to interpretation if not to contradiction. Melchizedek (long venerated both as the first priest and as an Old Testament type of Christ) received tithes, but only of the spoils of war; the offerings of Cain and Abel were made in no specified quantity, and could not therefore be considered as tithes; while Abraham and Jacob, who *had* paid tithes themselves, were both priests rather than laymen. There were no laws for tithes in those times, nor were any lasting tithing laws established by the Pentateuch, as chapter II reveals. Scaliger had already examined Hebrew tithing practices in the *Diatriba de decimis*, edited by Casaubon in 1610.[77] Selden went further, using the Talmud (the Hebrew canon law) to unlock the true sense of the Old Testament. He establishes that the Jews paid a first and second tithe to the Levites, who in turn passed on a tithe of this to the priests; the latter never received tithes directly from the people, although they did receive first fruits and a 'heave offering,' a voluntary donation.

This is a two-edged argument. On the one hand, Selden demonstrates that the priests had no claim to tithes in Jewish law. On the other, he sets up an implicit analogy between the Levites and the patrons, churchwardens, and lay impropriators of his own day: the modern recipients of tithes against whom Spelman and others had barked (12–21). After this, the *coup de grace* is rather an anti-climax: Selden falls back on the argument that the Jews themselves had not regarded tithing as mandatory since the destruction of the second Temple and the dispersion of the first century AD, and therefore, any tithing laws that ruled them could not be deemed binding on Christians. After a similar attack on Greek and Roman sacrificial practices, the third chapter concludes that Gentiles made *occasional* offerings to certain gods, voluntarily. They, too, had no general practice of obligatory tithing; a text of Festus which suggested the contrary Selden showed to be the result of poor editing by a medieval scholar, Paul the Deacon (28–9).[78]

The next four chapters consist of a chronological narrative and analysis of the growth of tithing in Christian Europe, relating it to the larger course of ecclesiastical history. There was no mention of tithing in the primitive church, to AD 400. Tithes of mines and quarries were paid to the emperors after Constantine, not to priests (39–40), while the church grew and thrived on voluntary offerings from its members. By AD 400, the priesthood may have presumed a divine right to tithes, but the evidence indicated that no custom had given them a prescriptive, historical right. Between 400 and 800, the first signs of tithing appear, in offerings made to abbots, the clergy at large, and the poor. These took the forms of arbitrary consecrations made by landowners at will. There was no agreement among the fathers as to the law supporting this: St Ambrose and St Augustine had said the tithe was due by God's law; St Jerome and Chrysostom had said only that in justice, no less than a tenth should be offered to God. No canon as yet demanded tithe payment, nor any secular law (64–7), and the infeudation of tithes (the sale or gift of them by clergy or laymen to other laymen) did not yet exist.

Among the developments of the period from 800 to 1200, Selden counted the capitularies of Charlemagne as the first secular laws enforcing tithe payment. He went on to demonstrate that by the late thirteenth century, both doctrine and canons 'had made the dutie of tithes of a known right among the clergie' (119). A historical turning point came with the third Lateran Council of 1179–80, in which tithes were explicitly named, and which condemned future infeudations *by laymen* without invalidating earlier ones. And this was only a general rule which, history showed, had admitted many exceptions; it suggested papal self-interest, not divine right, as the motivation. Alexander III's council still did not fully enforce the parochial right to tithes, that is, the doctrine that a parish priest has prior claim on the tithes of his parishioners' crops, livestock, and profits of business. This had to wait for the dramatic increase in papal authority, and in the influence of canon law, under Innocent III. From the fourth Lateran Council of 1215, parochial tithes became entrenched in canon law and eventually in the common laws of those countries which had received it (137–48).

The direction of tithing history changed so radically after 1200 that the clergy were able to pretend that they had always possessed a common right to parochial tithes. With the supremacy of the canon law, the practices of lay consecrations at will to churches and monasteries outside parish boundaries, and of the appropriation of churches, with tithes, by religious orders, fell into disuse. But there had still been no agreement even within the church on the question by what law tithes were due. The canonists held that tithes were due to the clergy by 'divine moral law,' though exceptions were possible. The scholastic theologians, less tied by papal strings, 'lookt much further into all that they medled with, then the canonists could do' (165). Many thought that as long as adequate maintenance was given to the parochial clergy, tithes *per se* were not mandatory. Others went even further and held tithes as voluntary alms only; the friars were prominent advocates of this view, arguing from self-interest since they could not receive tithes but could accept alms (154–78).[79]

Having painted the European background, Selden then focused on England. The eighth chapter presents a survey of the laws of tithes in England, generated by church councils, and by the Anglo-Saxon synods and witenagemotes. Selden quoted extensively from Saxon laws, offering translations as well as old English, for 'To have left out the originall, had prevented some freedom of the readers judgement, and tied it to the translators; to have added no translation, had been as a purpose to have troubled even the fittest readers with a strange tongue' (196). He modified, incidentally, his earlier position on the changes of the Norman Conquest, by identifying the Saxon micelne synod as 'a great synod, or councell, *a kind of parlament*, both of lay and spirituall men' (215, 220, my emphasis).[80] His account of the laws proceeds to the reign of Edward vi and shows how, little by little, the parochial right to tithes became entrenched in English common law, as recorded in the year-books.

Selden digressed in chapter ix to present a kind of history-within-a-history: a self-contained narrative of the early development of the parish, which by 1600 had supplanted the manor as the basic unit of secular as well as ecclesiastical administration. The word *parochia*, Selden demonstrates, initially meant province or bishopric, and tithes in the primitive church were therefore paid, at any church in the diocese, into a common fund held by the bishop, who divided it among the clergy, who resided with him and travelled to churches rather like Assize circuit judges (254).[81] Only about AD 700, a century after Augustine's arrival, as laymen started building and endowing churches in their area for service to their families and tenants, did clergy become resident and parish boundaries fixed, in order that the parishioner could tell to which church to pay his tithes. The bishops were forced to encourage this practice or risk dampening lay enthusiasm (259–68). To bring the whole system into uniformity, the bishops subsequently restricted the profits of the individual churches under their control to incumbent, resident priests. There was no law to limit profits parochially, until 970, when King Edgar ordained that any parishioner who had not erected a church of his own should pay tithe either to his local parish church or to a monastery, since religious houses still had in residence many secular clergy. In time, many small parishes were amalgamated and many larger ones split into two by granting dependent chapelries the right of burial (265–6).

The point of this long and brilliant chapter, in which Selden got to the root of medieval local ecclesiastical organization, is that if parishes themselves developed historically, and the word *parochia* had changed its meaning, how then could tithes have always been paid parochially? The parochial right only really became fully 'setled with us in practice' in the time of Edward I (288). Consequently, even if tithes *were* due *jure divino*, then the early Christians either did not realize this or went against their consciences, as did the clergy who eagerly sought and accepted arbitrary consecrations of tithes. Selden conceded that some early synodal and secular laws had ordained parochial rights in the Saxon era, but these laws were clearly either ignored, or perhaps settled and then discontinued, before AD 1200, when they were revived. Consequently, nothing in the law of tithes could be deemed immutable. 'For notwithstanding all those ordinances, both secular and synodall, anciently here made for due payment, it is cleer, that in the time before about that Innocent [III], it was not only usuall, in fact, for lay men to convey the right of their tithes, as rents-charge, or the like, to what church or monasterie they made choice of, but by the course and practice of the law also of that time (both common and canon, as it was here in use) such conveyances were cleerly good ...' (290)

The discovery of 'arbitrary consecrations' in the manuscript charters and cartularies of Cotton's library was the keystone to Selden's interpretation, and was a strikingly innovative concept. 'This of arbitrarie consecrations, I presume, is like strange doctrine to most men. It may well be, for the truth of it, I think, was never before so much as pointed at by any that hath writen of any part of our subject' (470). Chapter XI illustrates the prevalence of this practice 'in examples selected out of muniments of infallible credit.' They proved beyond all doubt what the year-books suggested: that laymen prior to 1179 had been perfectly free to convey the tithes arising from their lands to whatever church or monastery they chose. 'By the *practiced* law, cleerly every man gave the perpetuall right of his tithes to what church he would, although the canon law were against it' (359, my emphasis).

Even after the third Lateran Council, papal directives were largely ignored: 'whatever the pope wrote from Rome, we know the truth by a cloud of home-bred witnesses' (ibid). But papal supremacy in the next century changed things, and 'it soon came to be a receivd law, that all lands regularly were to pay tithes to the parish or mother church according to the provision of the canons' (362). This constituted a decisive break, an end to the practice of arbitrary consecrations and the establishment of a parochial right to tithes.[82] Even so, the canons were sufficiently moderated and limited by common law and local practice to permit many exceptions (365).[83]

In chapter xii, Selden examined another way in which tithes had long escaped the hands of the parish clergy. Monasteries and abbeys had often 'appropriated' smaller churches, along with their tithes. Such appropriations began in the eighth century and reached a peak between the Conquest and 1200, during which time about 370 monasteries were erected. A house then instituted a vicar in the parish, who received the 'small tithe' drawn on certain types of produce. Corn, grain, hay, and wood, the much more valuable 'great tithe,' remained the right of the rector, in this case the monastery. This distinction – which Selden fails to make very clearly – developed as a custom and was formalized by the statute 15 Richard ii, cap 6 (375–87).[84]

Selden went to some effort to point out one way in which tithing in England had developed differently than on the continent. Infeudations of tithes into lay hands, fairly common in Europe from the late eleventh century, did not appear in England, with a few exceptions, until the Reformation, in 'the age of our fathers.' Under Henry viii and his son, statutes were enacted enabling the crown to grant the tithes of the dissolved monasteries, by lease or sale, into lay hands. The seventeenth-century descendants of these tithe purchasers continued to hold them 'as they do other enheritances of lands or rents' (395). The treatment of tithes as property was new only to England, and had clearly been commonplace elsewhere in Christendom.

After giving further details of means by which frequent exemptions from parochial tithe payment had been made, Selden closed his *Historie* with a chapter on 'the historie also (but only the historie) of the jurisdiction of tithes in this kingdom' (411). Dividing this second mini-history into three periods – Anglo-Saxon, Norman (to Henry ii), and recent times – he described how tithe disputes gradually became a matter for the ecclesiastical courts. Under the Anglo-Saxons ecclesiastical cases (including tithes, though these are rarely mentioned then) had fallen under the jurisdiction of the hundred or county court; this was presided over jointly by the diocesan bishop and a sheriff or ealdorman, each judging the case according to his own sphere, divine or positive law.[85] The 'alteration at the Norman Conquest' broke this tradition by separating the episcopal jurisdiction (which subsequently evolved into the bishop's consistory court) from the shrieval. Both courts continued to judge tithe disputes, the court in which a suit originated taking precedence. But by the time of Henry II and John, increasing papal pressure on the monarchy established the practice which remained current in the seventeenth century, by which disputes were all initiated in ecclesiastical courts, unless prohibited by the king. Many remnants of the secular jurisdiction still existed in the early seventeenth century, in the form of writs of right of advowson and writs *scire facias* (412–13, 425–46), while the conflict of secular and ecclesiastical jurisdictions remained an unsolved problem.[86]

Shocked by early reaction to his masterpiece when only a few copies had been printed, Selden hastily drew up a fifty-page 'Review' and appended it to the text. The consequent delay in printing perturbed the anxious Peiresc, who eagerly awaited the book in France.[87] Selden's style is always tortuous, and the 'Review' lacks even the *Historie's* limited lucidity. But it afforded him an opportunity to restate his argument and it leaves no doubt that Selden held an interpretation of the history of tithing which was diametrically opposed to the traditional view. He defended his crucial discovery of the mechanism of arbitrary consecrations by accusing the clergy of having, since 1200, deliberately obscured or concealed the documentary evidence supporting it. He himself claimed to have seen 'catalogues' from the late thirteenth century which mention tithes clearly originating in lay consecrations, 'wherein not the least mention is of any grantor' (469). By the end of the thirteenth century, arbitrary consecrations were 'as much concealed in legall proceedings of the canon law, as they had been in the more ancient times desired and hunted after by such as were enricht by them' (470).

With more than a trace of annoyance in his tone, Selden concluded that after reading his book, 'no fit reader can be so blind as not to see necessarie and new assertions and consequents to be made out of them in every inquirie that tends to a full knowledge of the true and originall nature of tithes, as they are possest or detain by either lay or clergie man, in respect only of any humane positive law or civill title' (485). With that, the barrister rests his case.

Historical Controversy

The *Historie of Tithes* set off the biggest historical controversy in England since Polydore Vergil had called Geoffrey of Monmouth a liar. All the necessary ingredients were there: two opposed interpretations of the past, each with advocates committed to a point of view determined by their perceptions of the present; and an issue which threatened to cut holes in clerical pockets even more than it challenged historical and religious orthodoxy.

First to the lists was Sir James Sempill, a friend – and exact contemporary – of King James. Sempill feebly attacked Selden and his idol Scaliger in an appendix to a tract he had written some years earlier and chose now to publish, *Sacrilege Sacredly Handled* (1619). Sempill's approach was quite straightforwardly *sola scriptura:* Selden should, in his view, 'Cleave to the words of the text [rather] then thrust in commentaries for the overthrow of it; or practise against precept.' Confining himself to the first two chapters of Selden, he completely discounted the authority of the Talmud (which he had probably not read). Nervously praising the erudition of both Scaliger and Selden, he protested, 'Let no man thinke I doe glorie in differing from these men.' Sempill disbelieved the capacity of the historian to investigate such matters, since history was but 'a simple narration of what is done.'[88]

Following hard on Sempill's heels was the more pugnacious Doctor Richard Tillesley, archdeacon of Rochester. His *Animadversions upon M. Selden's History of Tithes, and His Review Thereof* was both much longer and more aggressive. He infuriated Selden by reporting that his opponent had recanted before the High Commission. In fact, Selden had merely apologized to some members of the commission for *publishing* the book, and had in no way revised his views. Tillesley praised Sempill's piety and learning, offering a catalogue of names of authors in support of the latter's work. Like Sempill, Tillesley snorted at Selden's admiration of Scaliger: 'Such flattering hyperboles proceed from ambitious love.' Refusing to accept Selden's distinction between first fruits and tithes, or his 'new opinion of arbitrary consecrations,' Tillesley also uniformly interpreted the Latin *decimae* as divinely due tithes, ignoring the historical fact that words change their meanings.[89] He called Selden a fraud who misquoted and manipulated documents to suit his case. Tillesley never denied Selden's claim that tithes were subject to custom; indeed, he fell back on a simple plea for the superiority of divine right over human custom, quoting St Augustine: 'Woe to thee thou flood of custome, who shall resist thee?' To discredit Selden's production of cartularies in chapter x, he claimed that Selden never allowed him to see them, and produced a few of his own which – as one might expect – had nothing to say on the subject of arbitary consecrations.[90]

It was at this point that the *rex pacificus* intervened. King James had no wish to see an ugly public debate over the history of clerical property;

still less, however, did he want to allow Selden the last word on the subject. Although the king forbade him to publish them, Selden's replies to Sempill and Tillesley circulated privately and have survived. Warming up on the mild Sempill, he asks why he has been attacked, defending himself and Scaliger as historians. 'Neither of us (being both laymen) were so bold, as to instruct the clergy, what should be done in a matter of divinity. My title is history only, so are the three parts of it, so is every line of the whole.'[91]

Sempill's argument that because something should have been so, it was so, was easily cut to shreds. 'What logick is this?' cried Selden: if he wished to use the same argument himself, he could prove that Sempill had not written his tract merely because he shouldn't have done so. Selden pointedly asked his opponent 'who think you is the greater for the certainty of the practised law in England? Are our year-books, or Hollingshead, or Polydore Vergil?' This remark seems like an apology for the superiority of original and contemporary documents over the printed accounts of a later age, and to a degree it is just that; but it also reflects the common lawyer's traditional antipathy to the derivation of the law from chronicles – even very old chronicles – rather than from legal records, a point made by Coke, as we saw in chapter 1, in the *Third Reports*.[92]

Sempill escaped with few bruises. Not so the hapless Tillesley, upon whose head descended the full fury of Selden. Denying his 'recantation,' he indicated that when the *Historie* was in the press, he had given Tillesley every liberty to examine his sources. Selden claimed to have rechecked his quotations and found them all accurate.[93] Putting his opponent on the defensive, he charged Tillesley with making 'innovation against the ancient positive laws of our own state, and of all other states of Christendom.' Why had his opponent relied on conjecture instead of examining Selden's cartularies? 'His lodging was near enough to those chartularies, and he might have seen them at his pleasure.' Tillesley's conclusions were even faultier than his minimal evidence. 'Is this your logick, doctor? We use no such in the inns of court.'[94]

Sempill and Tillesley were scholarly lightweights, readily dispatched, although one can imagine no worse punishment for Selden than the order which forbade him to publish these rebuttals. He was notably calmer in writing to James's young favourite, Buckingham, who had 'invited' him to restudy the issue. He reiterated his conclusion that tithes had never, in recent ages, been paid *jure divino*, even if they should have been, 'but only according as the secular laws made for tythes, or local customs, ordain or permit them.' But having been denied the freedom to defend his conclusions publicly, he declined to address himself to the question again.[95]

A much more formidable opponent reopened the attack in 1621. Richard Montagu, the future Arminian bishop, was a scholar in his own right, and a protégé of Sir Henry Savile. By 1621, Montagu had been the king's chaplain for four years. His *Diatribae upon the First Part of the Late History of Tithes*, in which he dealt with the first three chapters of Selden, is interesting because it attacks not simply Selden's historiography, but his very definition of the boundaries of history. Montagu had already commended Selden's abilities in a letter to Cotton – a strict neutral – who had furnished him with evidence for his counter-attack. 'You know I am sure, that his Majestie hath sett me upon business against him, whom you love, and I too protest unfeignedly, for his excellent good parts, saving the Churches quarrel, into which I would he had never entred.'[96]

Montagu responded directly to Selden's principal rhetorical strategy, his claim that he was only a historian, with an articulate reassertion of the traditional view of history's form and limits. He bowed to Selden's learning but discounted the argument that the *Historie* was only 'a meere narration of tithes': 'A meere narration is a plaine relation, nothing else. History disputeth not pro or con, concludeth what should be, or not be: censureth not what was well done, or done amisse: but proposeth accidents and occurrences as they fall out: examples and precedents unto posterity.'[97] Montagu's criticism of Selden's supposed pronunciation of rightness and wrongness in the *Historie* would at first seem to amount to a virtual reduction of history ('plaine relation') to chronicle, thereby denying the historian the didactic role that almost all parties agreed was an essential part of the rhetoric of history. But what he really intended by this was not to argue that history is amoral, but that its lessons should be so obvious from the narrative itself that the historian need not intrude, heavy-handed, with his own explication of them. Montagu challenged Selden's claim that the *Historie* belonged to the same genre as Camden's *Annales* and Bacon's *Henry VII*, two works with clear political messages but without overt polemical purpose. All Selden had done was make himself a party, 'which no historian doth or at least should do.' The reader must be left alone to judge the events and personages of the past for himself, following his own moral sense rather than the arguments of a prejudiced author.

In addition, Montagu continued, Selden had attempted to confound a straightforward narration with 'philology and humane learning.' Montagu denounced 'those French lawyers,' the continental philologists whom Selden had imitated, though he himself did not balk at using them to refute his opponent on specific points. Correcting the received view of the past was a 'morbus epidemicus' among the philologists, and Selden had only succeeded in undermining the *certainty* in history. Instead of recounting the past in its accepted form for the sake of edifying the reader, Selden had made of history a battle of 'text against text: translation against translation.' It is clear from these remarks that Montagu had failed to grasp the essence of Selden's methodology: the strict attention to synchronism which allowed the philologist to distinguish the best version of a source from among a number of extant copies. To Montagu this was mere pedantry which could do no more than confuse and mislead the innocent reader.

Montagu was particularly adamant on the dangers of digging up the remnants of antiquity which did not accord with the values and practices of the present: 'Whatsoever you have heaped and raked together out of chartularies, leigier books, moath-eaten evidences, records, remembrances, etc., wherein your greatest adventure is, and most glorious atchievement doth consist, is onely to bring in, set up, or ratifie and confirme a custome to undoe the clergie by, and to breake the necke, were it possible, of their *jus divinum,* by bearing up with, and giving life unto the *jus humanum positivum.'* This clash between canon and customary law therefore entailed a confrontation between two different outlooks on the nature and purpose of historical inquiry.[98] Montagu objected to Selden's book precisely because he perceived that it turned history, the great schoolroom of morality, toward the advocacy of a position that was *immoral.* His attack is the English counterpart of the charges of scepticism and atheism laid against the *érudits* in Richelieu's France.

Selden never replied to Montagu's assault, or to any of the subsequent attacks.[99] He returned to the issue in the 1650s, ironically to defend the continuance of tithes under the commonwealth on the grounds of prescription and positive law. Gerard Langbaine, writing to him in August 1652, told Selden that he 'was not able to give any better direction then by sending them to your history.' Langbaine hoped that the book which had 'struck deepest against the divine' would also supply arguments for the 'civill right' of tithes.[100] By this time, Selden's interpretation had achieved general acceptance among the laity and many clergy, for historically it was irrefutable, except on minor matters of detail. As for Montagu's counterattack, even the clergy eventually proved reluctant to place much stock in it. Selden's friend Bishop Brian

Duppa would later note in his copy of the *Diatribae*, 'Was ever so much learning, wit, and folly blended together as in this book!'[101]

From Tithes to Titles

The *Historie of Tithes* lay closer to the beginning than the end of Selden's career. He clarified aspects of his method in 1622, in the form of a prefatory letter 'To my singular good friend, Mr Augustine Vincent.' This appeared in Vincent's counterattack on Ralph Brooke's *Discoverie of Errours* in Camden's *Britannia*. The Brooke-Camden dispute which had festered for nearly thirty years had managed to involve nearly the whole College of Arms – almost to a man on Camden's side, for by 1622 the pugnacious Brooke had alienated most of his colleagues. Vincent, then Rouge-Croix pursuivant, had been the pupil and deputy of Camden since 1618.[102] The principal importance of his own *Discoverie*, for our purposes, is not the immediate heraldic dispute on the finer points of genealogy, but the occasion it gave for Selden, another disciple of Camden, to express his methodology concisely. His epistle to Vincent is one of the most interesting and important short documents in the history of English historiography.

Men will applaud Vincent's use of unprinted sources, which Selden deemed 'the more abstruse parts of history which lie hid, either in private manuscripts, or in the publick records of the kingdom.' Vincent shows good knowledge of published authors, but one cannot write history from printed sources alone. Selden rounded on the ignorant who rely on published material exclusively. 'They think nothing worthy the reading, but what is printed. As if the press gave first authority to whatsoever hath been written' (42). Vincent clearly knew, he added, 'what a deficiency must thence come into the knowledge of history.' Alluding to the work of French and Dutch scholars, Selden noted that 'such antient pieces of the history of other states, as being worthy of light, were preserved only in written copies, are of late for the most part made publick by divers learned men.' In England, by comparison, far more remained unprinted in a dozen different repositories from Cotton's huge armoury to the smaller university colleges. Little wonder that there was a dearth of good histories of England: the only exceptions were 'the annals of Queen Elizabeth and the life and reign of King Henry VII' which had been 'lately set forth by learned men of most excelling abilities.'[103]

Selden judged his predecessors primarily on their use of unprinted sources, not on matters of style and eloquence. By these demanding standards, only a few medieval English chroniclers were of use, in particular Henry Knighton, who had used some rolls of parliament which by Selden's day had long since disappeared. The ancients had been more successful: Polybius, Livy, Suetonius, and Tacitus all used the public records of their day, and Thucydides seems to have done so. To attempt to produce history without a command of the original sources was 'but to spend that time and cost in plaistering only, or painting, of a weak or poor building, which should be imployed in provision of timber and stone for the strengthening and enlarging it.'[104]

Selden continued his sketch of medieval historiography the following year, when he edited an invaluable authority for early Norman England, the *Historia novorum* of Eadmer. One of Selden's recurrent weaknesses was his conviction that the latest new text he had discovered could provide the answer to all an historian's questions. Like Coke before him, he had for years relied on the authority of the fifteenth-century forgery believed to be the work of the eleventh-century Ingulph of Croyland. He would make the same mistake again at the end of his career with 'Eutychius'; though this tenth-century patriarch was a legitimate historian, Selden uncritically and stubbornly insisted that he was a dependable authority for the early development of eastern Christianity, thereby violating his own practice of using only contemporary or near-contemporary documents.[105] With Eadmer, however, his enthusiasm was more than justified, for the *Historia novorum* provided an important alternative to the *Gesta regum* of William of Malmesbury. Selden dedicated this edition to Bishop John Williams, who would later be asked to reciprocate by lending him, through Cotton, the Babylonian Talmud in the library of Westminster Abbey.[106] Selden also acknowledged the help and advice of Peiresc and of the aged Thomas Allen, who had once again provided manuscripts against which Selden could check his edition.[107]

Selden wrote one last major work on English history before he embarked on a new and equally bright scholarly career as an interpreter of ancient Hebrew law and a political theorist. For years he had been wanting to revise and expand *Titles of Honor*. He had prepared a second edition for the press as early as 1621, but its publication had then been prevented, perhaps because of his activities during the parliament of that year. He had then told Ussher that the new version was 'in the press, and new written, but I hear it shall be staid.' It was finally published only a decade later, in 1631, after Selden had been imprisoned a second time for his perceived parliamentary opposition to the crown.[108]

One has only to compare the preface to this edition with that to the first to see that Selden had developed from an antiquarian lawyer into a philological historian, and that he had brought the two activities together. It is here that he offered the most concise and articulate formulation of his idea of history:

> Under histories, I comprehend here not only the numerous store of histories and annalls of severall states and ages, wherein the actions of them are put together in some continued discourse or thred of time, but those also that otherwise, being writen for some narrow particulars, *and sometimes under other names,* so shew us in example what was done in erecting or granting or otherwise, concerning the titles here medled with, that we may thence extract what conduces to the representation of the formes and patents of erections and grants and of the circumstances and nature of the being of them.[109]

This is a more deliberate and more thoroughly considered statement than anything in the *Historie of Tithes;* like the dedicatory epistle to Vincent, it formalized and summarized the tendencies that can be seen in Selden's work as far back as his notes to *Poly-Olbion,* twenty years earlier.

Yet the expanded *Titles of Honor* also went a step beyond *The Historie of Tithes,* both in its announced methods and in its structure. Selden had returned to the organization of his earlier works, whereby time was subordinated to topic, though he continued to discuss each title chronologically. But there is an important difference. Though he never called the whole book a history, he made it clear that it was *historical* simply because it pertained to the discovery and presentation of facts about the past. The presence or absence of a chronologically organized narrative structure was of no importance. Matter took precedence, at long last, over form. The public records, private archives, episcopal registers, and other sources, including non-documentary ones such as inscriptions, were not merely the materials from which a history could be composed. They were, in their totality, the essence of history itself: '[They] are to be reckond for historie or among the parts of it, and of necessary use in the search of it; though they beare other titles, and are too much neglected chiefly by compilers of annalls and historie, who for the most part seeke no other materials or helps, then what obvious volumes that beare but such kind of names as their owne shall, can easily afford them.'[110]

Although the revised *Titles of Honor* has not worn nearly as well as the *Historie of Tithes,* it was nevertheless a gargantuan piece of work, blazing a trail for later writers such as Burke and Debrett. Selden expanded almost every section of the first edition, and where before he had only quoted documents briefly, he now transcribed and printed them *in extenso.* Woodcuts provided pictorial illustrations of ancient and medieval robes, crowns, and ornaments used in creation ceremonies. His already extensive marginal references were fattened: a single point, the origin of the title 'peer,' is substantiated with references to ten different original sources and to French scholars including Pasquier, Pithou, du Haillan, Hotman, and Vignier.[111]

Recent scholarship has contravened the views of Sir Henry Spelman and his nineteenth-century successor, J.H. Round, that feudalism was superimposed at the Conquest, in a fully developed form, on an entirely different social system. Selden actually came nearer the truth than Round by equating the Anglo-Saxon thanes with post-Conquest tenants *in capite.* 'Those that were the kings immediate tenants of faire possessions, which they held by personall service as of his person ... were, I conceive, the thanes that had the honorary dignitie, and were part of the greater nobility of that time ... That is, they were all the kings feudall thanes.'[112] This was not a denial of the impact of the Conquest but a recognition of continuity. Selden understood the landholding system to have changed radically in 1066; but, like the law, parts of it survived from the previous era.

By 1631 Selden's political career was a decade old and he had already grown interested in suprahistorical disciplines. Political thought, classical philology, and oriental studies intertwined to draw him further and further from English history. The manuscript notes in his copies of his own books show that he never entirely abandoned interest in a topic, but it is clear that his later introductions to an edition of the medieval lawbook, *Fleta,* and to the *Historiae anglicanae scriptores decem* (1652), a collection of chronicles edited by his friend Sir Roger Twysden, were mere diversions from more important tasks.[113] During the civil war he held the key to the Cottonian library, serving the needs of younger scholars such as Meric Casaubon and Gerard Langbaine. Having once worshipped Scaliger, he died in 1654, a scholar of nearly equal rank, having remained active till the last months of his life.[114]

History and Antiquities after Selden

I have argued that Selden's marriage of erudition with history – in practice in *The Historie of Tithes,* and more systematically and reflectively in subsequent writings – was neither the product of one man's far-sighted originality, nor a sign that history was proceeding confidently along a road leading directly to its modern form. Although Selden had, under the influence of continental scholarship, clearly been working towards a philological conception of history well before he tackled the problem of tithes, the *Historie* itself clearly owes as much to Selden's desire to present himself as a disinterested narrator as it does to his sensitivity, however great, to the subtleties of historical change. But accident or not, Selden's conception of history *did* alter the common usage of terms such as history by contemporary and later writers.

The notoriety of *The Historie of Tithes,* as much as the quality of its scholarship, ensured it a wide readership, while *Titles of Honor* became a standard reference work for the rest of the century, time enough for Selden's more comprehensive concept of history and historical method to establish itself as a credible alternative to the older humanist notion. Philologists, antiquaries, and legal writers could now legitimately consider themselves to be doing history, and a gradually increasing number of works were devoted to the history of institutions instead of individuals. Sir John Dodderidge, the antiquary and judge who died in 1628, had completed in 1604 a 'discourse' on the development of the offices and institutions of the principality of Wales and its related honours, the duchy of Cornwall and the earldom of Chester. When this finally reached the press in 1630, its printer gave it a new title which belies its antiquarian content and its topical arrangement, *The History of the Ancient and Moderne Estate of the Principality of Wales.*[115] Dodderidge, like Selden, had seen that an institution of state could be described historically; it remained for his publisher to go a little further by selling the work as a history.

Peter Heylyn imitated the form of Selden's *Historie,* and his use of history as a medium for erudite discourse on a controversial subject, in his own study of another religious custom, the *History of the Sabbath* (1636). Commissioned by Charles I, the work was written and published within a period of four months; Heylyn described it as 'a story which shall represent unto you the constant practise of Gods church in the present busines, from the Creation to these daies.' Heylyn was not in Selden's league as a scholar, but there can be no doubt that his book, a polemic against the sabbatarian movement, is modelled on the lawyer's.[116] Though the two men came to their subjects from very different points of view, Heylyn imitated Selden's distinction between that which the divine law required and that which could be shown *historically* to have occurred. So, too, did Thomas Gataker, perhaps the most erudite biblical scholar in England, in his treatise *Of the Nature and Use of Lots*, described by its author as 'a treatise historicall and theologicall.'[117]

As more histories became concerned with traditionally extrahistorical subjects, so more works of scholarship laid claim to the dignity of histories. The antiquary William Burton, a friend of Selden (who had sent him documents from the Cottonian library), produced a *Description of Leicestershire* in 1622, which went beyond a description of local antiquities to include 'matters of historye, armoury and genealogy.' Burton made no apology for mixing history and chorography. Nor did William Bedwell, who considered his topographical account of Tottenham High Cross to be 'an historicall narration.'[118] John Philipot, another former deputy of Camden, and a man much influenced by French scholarship, seems to have been the first Englishman to refer to his master's *Britannia* as a 'history' of Britain.[119] William Dugdale, the greatest antiquary of the next generation, published his *Antiquities of Warwickshire* in 1656, two years after the death of Selden. He wrote in his preface, which quotes extensively from Selden's commendatory epistle to Vincent, of 'historie in general,' of which his book represented one sort; and when he cited Cicero's *De oratore*, as a traditional historian might do, the passage concerned the historian's duty to uncover the truth, not his need to moralize and instruct. In collaboration with Sir Edward Dering, Sir Thomas Shirley, and Sir Christopher Hatton, Dugdale had already attempted, in 1638, to revive the Society of Antiquaries. The twenty articles of the *Antiquitatis rediviva* included one under which the members agreed to collect everything needed for 'historicall illustration of this kingdome.'[120]

From the 1630s on, the words 'antiquary' and 'historian' were often used synonymously. In Shakerley Marmion's play, *The Antiquary* (1641), Leonardo comments that he has heard 'of an antiquary who, if he be as good at wine as at history, he is sure an excellent companion.'[121] By the early 1700s, it was possible for White Kennett to offer much the same argument in defence of 'historical antiquities' as they were often now called, that apologists for traditional history had raised a century earlier, an appeal to the moral succour it could provide:

I am sensible there be some who slight and despise this sort of learning, and represent it to be a dry, barren, monkish study. I leave such to their clear enjoyment of ignorance and ease. But I dare assure any wise and sober man, that historical antiquities, especially a search into the notices of our own nation, do deserve and will reward the pains of any English student, will make him understand the state of former ages, the constitution of governments, the fundamental reasons of equity and law, the rise and succession of doctrines and opinions, the original of ancient, and the composition of modern tongues, the tenures of property, the maxims of policy, the rites of religion, the characters of virtue and vice, and indeed the nature of mankind.[122]

A side-effect of this recognition of the close relationship between the historian and the antiquary was a growing tendency to discount the latter when he did not contribute to history-writing. The term 'antiquary' itself gradually evolved into 'antiquarian,' a more restricted term with connotations of pedantry, of mustiness, and of a perverse love of dead things.[123] Marmion's own description of Veterano, the aged antiquary, presents a good example:

He is grown obsolete,
And 'tis time he were out of date. They say he sits
All day in contemplation of a statue
With ne'er a nose, and doats on the decays ...[124]

John Earle provided an even more amusing caricature, in which the antiquary became one of his own hoary artifacts, 'one that hath that unnaturall disease to bee enamour'd of old age and wrincles.' The antiquary's estate 'consists much in shekels, and Roman coynes,' he sneered, 'and he hath more pictures of Caesar, then James, or Elizabeth.'[125] Thus, while antiquaries could now consider themselves to be researching and writing history, the terms 'antiquities' and 'antiquary' managed to maintain a separate identity only at the cost of acquiring a good deal of undesirable connotative baggage.

Whatever the relevance of constructive antiquarianism for history-writing, the two fields were never completely identified. The circles occupied by historian and antiquary now overlapped in a way that they had not before, but the overlap was never complete and never universally accepted. The resistance of the traditional definition of history as a narrative form dealing principally with important events did not collapse overnight; it remains even today the popular view.

History could now include antiquities among its sources, and could address antiquarian problems, but not every learned discourse about the past was a history. In the early eighteenth century, as good a scholar as Richard Rawlinson could still recognize a distinction between scholarship and narrative history; the difference between his view and the Elizabethan position was that he regarded research in antiquities as an indispensable preparation for history-writing. He even referred to non-narrative topographical works as 'histories,' but, like Selden, considered the true historian to be the man who could use his erudition to compose a whole greater than the sum of its parts. The ability to write elegantly and persuasively was still important, and this led Rawlinson to comment of Dugdale, who had dabbled in narrative history, that he was 'a better antiquary than historian.' Today, we would say that Dugdale was a better researcher than a writer.[126] In the early seventeenth century, many men laid claim to the title of antiquary, while comparatively few, as we have seen, considered themselves historians. The opposite is now true, and the beginnings of a tendency toward holding the scholar up to scorn are apparent in the Augustan age.[127] In the Europe of the late seventeenth and early eighteenth centuries, narrative histories whose sources were earlier narrative histories continued to draw more public attention than the erudite but dry works of the scholars.[128]

Yet for all this, it is equally clear that the relationship between scholarship and history had changed, and that with this shift, the meaning of the word 'history' had evolved into something close to its modern sense. If men now faced the prospect of the impossibility of a 'perfect' history such as that advocated by La Popelinière in France and Francis Bacon in England, they at least saw that they need no longer confine themselves to a single aspect of the past, that they could explain the world around them in the language of history. Later narrative historians could and did ignore the researches of the scholars, but Bishop William Nicolson's popular *The English Historical Library*, which was accepted as the standard bibliographical manual on historical research and writing for many decades, makes it clear that to do so was folly. Nicolson's inclusion of topographical, archival, numismatic, and bibliographical research under the rubric of history is a measure of just how much the meaning of the word had evolved in the seventeenth century.[129] Such developments are rarely the work of one individual or even a group, and this case is no exception. But any search for the origins of a broader, less rigid conception of history must begin with Selden and his contemporaries.

CHAPTER EIGHT

Through a Prism

Historical Writing in the 1630s

A cultivated king, Charles I saw as clearly as his father the uses to which history could be put. The court culture of the 1630s was built upon the representation of royal power poetically, dramatically and visually, in the form of masques and portraits casting Charles as the new Constantine or as St George. The artwork on the magnificent flagship the *Sovereign of the Seas* featured the image of the Anglo-Saxon king Edgar, celebrated by Samuel Daniel as the founder of English naval power. With artists like Van Dyck and Rubens and poets like Jonson and his cavalier followers gracing the court, it is little wonder that the 1630s is now acknowledged as one of the greatest decades in English cultural history.[1]

It is surprising then that narrative historical writing, which had flourished under Elizabeth and James, entered a period of doldrums under Charles. Publishers reprinted Speed, Daniel, and even Martyn. It was both easier and cheaper for publishers to update older works than to begin afresh: Stow's *Annales*, updated by Edmund Howes in 1615, was reissued once more in 1631, again with Buck's *The Third Universitie* appended. But the chronicle itself was rapidly declining in popularity, though occasional examples of the genre still cropped up from time to time, such as Sir Richard Baker's *Chronicle of the Kings of England*, which was first published in 1643 and ran through nine editions by 1696.[2]

A few politic histories and biographies appeared after 1630, though most – with the notable exceptions of Herbert of Cherbury and Habington – did not reach the mark set by Camden, Hayward, and Daniel.

John Trussell, a lawyer who served as mayor of Winchester in 1624 and 1633, and who was steward to its bishop, Walter Curle, wrote a continuation of Daniel's *Collection* which, like many sequels, failed to measure up to the original.[3] Trussell eulogized both Daniel and Bacon; although he modestly claimed only to be filling in the gap between them, he was not without talent, and he had antiquarian interests which extended to an investigation of his own town's history.[4] But for his additions to Daniel he depended completely on printed sources (mainly Hall and Holinshed), and his historical imagination was leaden in comparison with his exemplar's. Trussell's narration of the Wars of the Roses shows one innovation: a kind of score sheet in the margins which helped the reader keep track of the numbers of nobles and retainers slain on each side. Otherwise, his account of 1399 and its fifteenth-century aftermath was the usual battle of kites and crows, complete with the by now obligatory speech of the bishop of Carlisle against the deposition of God's anointed.[5]

Like Trussell, the Gloucestershire solicitor Robert Powell was connected with Bishop Curle, to whom he dedicated his *Life of Alfred, or Alured: The First Institutor of Subordinate Government in this Kingdome*. This included a discourse on Alfred's supposed creation of shires, hundreds, and tithings, a popular belief attacked by Selden in the second *Titles of Honor*, which Powell had not read.[6] The work also contained a 'parallel' of Alfred and Charles I showing how Charles, like Alfred, was militarily prepared by sea and land, and how both kings enjoyed stately entertainments. Since 1634 was the first year of ship money, Powell may have hoped to reap some reward by showing that naval preparation in peacetime and the maintenance of an expensive court were characteristics of good kingship.[7] He used Daniel's *First Part of the Historie of England*, Holinshed, and Godwin's *Catalogue of Bishops;* he acknowledged a heavy debt to Brian Twyne's work on the antiquity of Oxford, and to Noel Sparks, a lecturer in Greek at Corpus Christi College, Oxford, who furnished Powell with notes on Asser's biography of Alfred. As for Alfred's laws, Powell, who knew no Anglo-Saxon, was forced to rely on Lambarde's *Archaionomia*.[8]

Poets, poetasters, and playwrights also continued to churn out new versions of well-worn tales. John Taylor, the 'Water-Poet,' defiantly proclaimed his allegiance to the Trojan myth, answering scepticism with a kind of shoulder-shrugging historical fideism. 'Histories are obscured and clouded with ambiguities, some burnt, lost, defaced by antiquity, and some abused by the malice, ignorance or partialitie of writers so that truth is hard to be found,' wrote Taylor, mimicking

Speed, but with exactly the opposite results. 'Amongst all which variations of times and writers,' he declaimed with confidence, 'I must
conclude there was a Brute.'[9] Charles Aleyn and Thomas May (the
future historian of the Long Parliament) each wrote historical poems in
the 1620s and 1630s. One of Aleyn's works treated the now-legendary
English victories over the French at Crécy and Poitiers; the other was a
poetic recitation of the deeds of the ever-popular Henry VII. In 1634, the
reign of the first Tudor king would provide the subject of John Ford's
The Chronicle Historie of Perkin Warbeck.[10]

No study of early Stuart historical writing would be complete without
at least a glance at the work of a man whose literary career spanned
the entire period, Thomas Heywood. A poet, playwright, and prolific
'popularizer' of history, Heywood wrote at many levels, though generally
for a lay, unscholarly audience. Although his works remind us once
again that the motives underlying historical poetry and drama were
often very different from those impelling scholarship, Heywood nevertheless provides a good window into the state of 'popular' historical
thought on the eve of the civil war.

In 1599 Heywood had explored the consequences of rebellion and the
horrors of civil war in two plays on Edward IV's troubles.[11] His later
two-part play on Queen Elizabeth's life, *If You Know Not Me, You Know
No Bodie,* achieved high popularity at a time when the history play itself
was in decline, and he published a prose version of the first part which
made the queen's life accessible to those who could not afford Camden
or Speed.[12] He included part of Bodin's *Methodus* as a preface to his
translation of Sallust, but gave the problems of historiography little or
no thought. His lengthy poem *Troia Britanica* (1609) contained a potted
history of the kingdom from Brutus to the renewal of 'Great Brittaines
Empyre' under James, where he stopped. 'With ages past I have been
too little acquainted, and with this age present, I dare not bee too bold.'[13]
His thoughts had changed little in 1641 when he republished them in
his *Life of Merlin,* another epitome of ancient British history. Heywood
settled for repackaging the same goods in the form of a series of ancient
prophecies of the shape of kings to come, a device already used in
William Harbert's *Prophesie of Cadwallader* at the beginning of the
century. Again, his aim was to reach as wide an audience – primarily
an urban audience of merchants and well-to-do craftsmen – as possible
by providing a kind of Reader's Digest to more ponderous tomes. 'In
this small compendium or abstract,' he promised the reader, 'thou hast
Holinshed, Polychronicon, Fabian, Speed, or any of the rest, of more
giantlike bulke or binding.'[14]

We do well to remember that for every reader of a work by Selden or even Camden, dozens more would read Heywood and other popularizers such as Thomas Gainsford, Thomas Deloney, Anthony Munday, and the unsilenceable Taylor.[15] A broad spectrum lay between the extremes marked by the antiquaries on one side and the historical poetasters on the other, attesting to a division between scholarly and popular beliefs about the past which has only grown more pronounced over the centuries. How many times since the 1640s have historians revised, debated, and revaluated the character of innumerable events from the Roman invasions to the present? Yet some kings, such as Henry v, Richard iii, and Henry viii have retained a popular image (for which Shakespeare alone bears a great deal of responsibility) which no quantity of academic debate and writing can ever hope to alter. The stereotypes of the classic *1066 and All That* view of English history, first made commonplace in the sixteenth and seventeenth centuries, have enjoyed unending resale value ever since.

It is difficult to avoid the conclusion that by the mid-1630s English historiography had, on the whole, settled into a state of stagnation. Despite Selden's attempt to synthesize narrative and erudition, many scholars and antiquaries had gone elsewhere, and Selden himself would soon join Spelman and Ussher in abandoning English history for greener pastures of classical and oriental scholarship. The outstanding historians of James i's reign, Camden, Hayward, Bacon, Buck, and Daniel were all dead or inactive by the mid-1620s, while the closing of the Cottonian library in 1629 and the death of its owner two years later deprived antiquaries and historians alike of indispensable source material. Though many scholars, most notably Herbert of Cherbury, could and did continue to use its materials, the catalogue of the library prepared by William Boswell in the 1630s was a poor substitute for the knowledge of its great collector.[16]

But the deaths of a few individuals cannot adequately account for the apparent decline of humanist historiography in England. For that, there are a number of plausible explanations. The most obvious of these is that after nearly a century of existence, during which it had successively emancipated itself from the chronicle, defended its existence against the assault of poets and sceptics, and faced the emergence of a potent rival in antiquarianism, humanist historiography had, from one perspective, simply run out of steam. Much the same thing had happened in quattrocento Italy, before the horrific events of the French invasion of 1494 shocked historians into refocusing their attention on the recent past. As Eric Cochrane pointed out, it took only six or seven decades of the fifteenth century for humanist historical writing to come close to dying of 'inanition' – without a sense of direction it very nearly choked on its own eloquence.[17] In England, a similar process had taken less than half that time, hastened by the impact of print and by a continued political stability which only late in the 1630s seemed in serious jeopardy. With most of English history well described by the biographical historians, and no shortage of surveys of the whole, it might be said that by about 1630 (and certainly ten years later) historians were running out of things to write about.

It may be more helpful to note that the events of the late 1630s, and *a fortiori* the nightmare of civil war that followed, badly shook faith in the conventional view of history as the *magistra vitae*, the great schoolmistress of morality and teacher of politics. The type of historical advice book written by Bacon or, late in the period, by Habington had pushed that mode of historical narrative to its extreme, but the failure of history to provide counsel in a truly effective manner, to have real political influence, extended far beyond those particular writers to embrace the didactic tradition as far back as Thomas More and the Tudor chroniclers. Samuel Daniel, perhaps the most sensitive historical mind in early Stuart England to the ties between past and present, had composed his *Civil Wars* amid the *angst* of the 1590s, as a warning against the renewal of civil strife; many other authors, including Shakespeare, had done likewise. But after 1642 there was simply little point in repeating once again the lessons of 1399 and 1485; those of more recent weeks and months seemed much more pressing. It was no longer sufficient to describe the evils of rebellion and civil war; the task was rather to explain how civil war had once again come about.

The Collapse of Consensus

The 1640s and 1650s would witness a great deal of change in historiography as much as in political thought and religion, and the much greater prominence of an old but previously minor player: ideology. Enduring the experience of the French in the sixteenth-century wars of religion, English historians discovered that they could turn to the past not simply to find precedents or useful examples, but to explain the disasters of the present in such a way as to cast blame on their opponents.[18] The subjective character of historical interpretation really became clear, though not immediately to the writers themselves. When accused of bias in his *Church-History of Britain* (1655), Thomas Fuller protested that 'As for pleasing of parties, I never designed or endevoured it.' But he knew his complaints would fall on deaf ears. Surveying the state of historical writing at the end of the 1650s, he lamented the divisions that had sprung up among historians, and wistfully recalled a bygone era when differences of opinion remained below the surface:

> Happy those English historians who wrote some sixty years since, before our civil distempers were born or conceived; at least wise, before there were house-burnings (though some heart-burnings) amongst us: I mean, before mens latent animosities broke out into open hostility; seeing then there was a generall right understanding betwixt all of the nation.
>
> But alas! Such as wrote in or since our civil wars, are seldome apprehended truely and candidly, save of such of their owne persuasion, whilest others doe not (or what is worse *will not*) understand them aright.[19]

The first historiographical battlefield was the immediate past. In one of the earliest narratives of the civil war and its origins, the former court poet and student of Lucan, Thomas May (1595–1650), traced the conflict back to James I's failure to maintain the policies of his predecessor. At the beginning of his *The History of the Parliament of England, Which Began November 3, 1640*, published in 1647, May declared his belief that his account had to begin at 'precedent times,' namely with the reign of Queen Elizabeth, 'that prince (fresh in the memory of some yet living) who first established the reformed religion in this kingdom.' Elizabeth had 'woven the interest of her own state so inseparably into the cause of religion itself, that it was hard to overthrow one without the ruin of the other.' She left England at a height of prosperity from which it would soon come tumbling down. May blamed such policies as James's appeasement of Spain and the courting of Rome for arousing discontent; favourites such as Buckingham ('an unhappy vapour') ruled the king, and eventually his successor, causing both to become 'disaffected to parliaments.'[20] Under Charles, things got worse still: taxes increased, liberties were invaded and popery thrived. God frowned upon the land he had so recently blessed:

> It cannot but be thought, by all wise and honest men, that the sins of England were at a great height, that the injustice of governors and vices of private men were very great, which have since called down from Almighty God so sharp a judgment, and drawn on by degrees so calamitous and consuming a war. Those particular

crimes an English historian can take no pleasure to relate, but might rather desire to be silent in ... But to be silent in that were great injustice and impiety toward God; – to relate his judgments upon a kingdom, and forget the sins of that kingdom, which were the cause of them.

Under the Stuarts 'the manners of the people were corrupted' by novelty, luxury, and profanity, which soon incurred divine judgment. In a voice reminiscent of Ralegh thirty-three years earlier, but now openly critical of the Jacobean and Caroline courts, May argued that a general state of sin, brought on by a surfeit of prosperity, had occasioned the ruin of the nation. Like a biblical prophet, he could lay much of the responsibility for this moral and religious decay 'with the faults of the higher powers.'[21]

May is important because he is among the first historians to write a history that is, if not antimonarchical, at least openly critical of early Stuart government. But he is also of interest because he recognized the partisan direction which historical writing was taking under the pressure of war. As a secretary to the Long Parliament, May was in a good position to relate its history, but he realized that this gave him less than a complete view of events.

My residence hath been, during these wars, in the quarters and under the protection of the parliament; and whatsoever is briefly related of the soldiery, being toward the end of this book, is according to that light which I discerned there ... If in this discourse more particulars are set down concerning the actions of those men who defended the parliament than of those that warred against it, it was because my conversation gave me more light on that side.[22]

This was not an outright confession of partisanship, and still less an admission of the subjectivity of history – May was thoroughly convinced of the validity of his own case, and the parliamentary imprimatur to his book states that it conveys 'impartiall truth.' But it was at least a recognition that proximity to the events described often reduces the breadth of one's field of vision: to use May's own metaphor, history was a light upon the truth of the past and, like a light, it sometimes did not reach into every corner of a shadowy room. In the hope that 'those that write on the other side' would show the same restraint and candour that he had, he proclaimed his loyalty to the cause of truth. 'I will only profess to follow that one rule, Truth, to which all the rest (like the rest of moral virtues to that of justice) may be reduced.' But truth, he warned, can be offended by more than mere falsehood; the use by some writers of 'rhetorical disguises, partial concealments and invective expressions' can undermine veracity much more stealthfully than a bold-faced lie. This makes a partial history much more dangerous than a straightforward polemic. 'Against the unexpected stroke of partial history,' he observed acutely, 'the ward is not so ready, as against that polemic writing, in which hostility is professed with open face.'[23] Here we have an echo of the same concern voiced in Richard Montagu's attack on Selden in 1621. Polemical, argumentative writing was possible, and even desirable in some contexts (for instance when dealing with Catholic propagandists), but it had no place in history. Precisely because history was believed to present the unadorned truth, it had much greater potential to subvert that truth if written in a partisan spirit.

Like May, many other writers on the parliamentary side felt obliged to search further back than 1640 to find the origins of the war; others found themselves compelled to deny that this was necessary. May's former friend Clarendon, the well-known author of the *History of the Rebellion*, would denounce the historian of the Long Parliament as a man who had lost sight of the duty he owed his monarch and had 'prostituted himself to the vile office of celebrating the infamous acts of those who were in rebellion against the king.' Clarendon could agree with May that such horrible calamities 'have usually attended kingdoms swoln with long plenty, pride, and excess'; though he acknowledged God's hand in all occurrences, he felt it possible to describe the rebellion as the product of 'natural causes and means,' of which the decay produced by prosperity and peace was one factor.[24] As a reformer in the early days of the Long Parliament, Clarendon felt compelled to admit that all had not been right under Charles's rule, in spite of the king's virtue and good intentions. But he saw little need to go back beyond the succession of Charles to locate the roots of the recent troubles:

> I shall not then lead any man farther back in this journey, for the discovery of the entrance into these dark ways, than the beginning of this king's reign. For I am not so sharp-sighted as those who have discerned this rebellion contriving from, if not before, the death of Queen Elizabeth, and fomented by several princes and great ministers of state in Christendom to the time that it brake out.[25]

Pro-parliamentary historians did not agree, and they were able to set the historiographical agenda largely by articulating versions of the past which required an answer from royalist opponents. Attacks on and defences of Charles I appeared both during the war and especially after his execution; and throughout the 1650s authors such as Arthur Wilson and Anthony Weldon, William Sanderson and Godfrey Goodman, debated the character of James I and his responsibility for the civil wars, though in most cases the king's critics seemed unable to make a direct connection between the sins of the Jacobean court and the outbreak of the war, other than observing that God always punishes the wicked. In a scurrilous memoir of the *Court and Character of King James*, Weldon, a disgraced and disgruntled former royal servant, reviewed the sins, vices, and crimes that had beset James I's court, complete with implications of sexual impropriety and murder which have given Weldon claim to the dubious distinction of being the leading scandal-monger of the early Stuart court. It was almost certainly his book, published in 1651, which inspired Bishop Goodman shortly thereafter to set down his own much more favourable – but not uncritical – recollections of the king and his times, though he dared not publish them under the Cromwellian regime.[26] The puritan Arthur Wilson's *History of Great Britain* (1653), essentially another study of James's reign, is more restrained than Weldon's tract, but it too demanded systematic, point by point rebuttal, in this case from the royalist Sir William Sanderson.[27]

It was possible, of course, to look well beyond the beginning of the seventeenth century for the origins of the war, and to rethink the entire course of English history along the way. Rather like the case among modern historians of the civil war, the more radical a seventeenth-century author's political and religious views, the more likely he was to attribute the crises of the 1640s and 1650s to long-term causes.[28] Thus the Levellers and Diggers, while using the vocabulary of Coke and the other defenders of the common law, came to much more radical conclusions about the origins of the law and its usefulness. Where Coke had sought to deny and Selden to minimize the impact of the Norman Conquest on the English legal system, the radicals turned the Conquest into an event of epochal importance which had imposed a legal yoke on the freedom of the Anglo-Saxons to the benefit of a foreign monarchy and aristocracy; they thus denied the validity of most constitutional development since 1066.[29]

John Milton's *History of Britain* was researched between 1640 and 1644, and largely written before the execution of the king, though it would be extensively revised over the next twenty years in the wake of the several successive changes of regime which eventually led to the republic's collapse. In it, Milton looked afresh at the era of the Britons and Saxons less to trace the origins of the war than to shed light on the collapse of liberty in his own time. Drawing on the moralizing history of such early medieval writers as Gildas, he paid particular attention to the manner in which a sinful people might, through internecine squabbling, bring ruin on itself. In his mind, the period of 'intermission or change of government' between the Roman withdrawal and the Saxon invasion deserved highlighting, 'considering especially that the late civil broils had cast us into a condition not much unlike to what the Britans then were in ... which times by comparing seriously with these later, and that confused anarchy with this intereign, we may be able from two such remarkable turns of state, producing like events among us, to raise a knowledg of our selves both great and weighty ...'

Because the Britons lacked 'the wisdom, the virtue, the labour, to use and maintain true libertie,' Milton concluded, 'they soon remitted thir heat, and shrunk more wretchedly under the burden of their own libertie, then before under a forren yoke.'[30] Much the same fate awaited their successors; the Saxons would be civilized and converted to Christianity, but they too proved incapable of living virtuously and guarding their liberties. In a departure from early Stuart treatments of the issue, Milton actually saw the union of the Anglo-Saxon kingdoms under Wessex as the beginning of the Saxons' own enslavement. Far from strengthening the nation, this 'West-Saxon yoke' merely made the subordinate kingdoms fight among themselves and overlook the successive threats of the Danes and Normans: 'Men might with some reason have expected from such union, peace and plenty, greatness and the flourishing of all estates and degrees: but far the contrary fell out soon after, invasion, spoil, desolation, slaughter of many, slavery of the rest, by the forcible landing of a fierce nation.'[31]

For all his idealization of liberty and his regret in the 1660s over the collapse of the godly republic, the *History of Britain* is no attack on monarchy – and was therefore publishable under Charles II. The sad destinies of the Britons and then the Saxons were fulfilled through the failings of the peoples themselves, and not their rulers. The virtues of godly princes such as Egbert and Edgar simply proved an insufficient bulwark against corruption, and with the death of Edgar the glory of the Saxons was extinguished. 'From henceforth nothing is to be heard of but their decline and ruin under a double Conquest.'[32] Drawing, as Samuel Daniel had, on William of Malmesbury, Milton noted that the licentiousness of the nobles and the poor education of the clergy had allowed vice to run rampant, while the quarrelling English proved incapable of establishing a settled government. The final ignominy, beyond which Milton could not bear to proceed, was the conquest and enslave-ment of the English under William I. Again, the parallels with 1658–60 are difficult to miss, as the English, 'while they agreed not about the choice of thir native king, were constrain'd to take the yoke of an out-landish conqueror.' In concluding his account, Milton issued a warning to his contemporaries lest still worse calamities should follow: 'If these were the causes of such misery and thraldom to those our ancestors, with what better close can be concluded, then here in fit season to remember this age in the midst of her security, to fear from like vices without amendment the revolution of like calamities.'[33]

Milton's *History* thus harked back to earlier attempts to make of the past an analogue of the present, such as Bacon's or Cotton's, while at the same time calling into question such long-accepted notions as the benefits of union – one cannot help but wonder how Milton, had he proceeded as far as the thirteenth century, would have dealt with the issue of Anglo-Scottish unity. The *History* thus envisions the remote past, in the traditional manner of humanist historical narrative, as providing parallels for the present; Milton stopped short of drawing a direct line of development between the vicissitudes of ancient British history and the troubles of his own era.

In that regard, among others, Milton's way of looking at the past was quite different from that of a fellow republican, James Harrington. In *The Commonwealth of Oceana*, published in 1656, Harrington rewrote English history in the light of a new thesis, the relationship of land ownership to the shifting 'balance' of political power. Brief as his histori-cal remarks were, they signify a highly original and imaginative vision of the medieval past whose only real precursor is Daniel's *Collection*.[34]

In Harrington's account, the identities of English kings and queens are disguised by classical pseudonyms but are easily recognizable. It was the earliest invaders of the island, the Teutons, who had introduced 'the form of the late monarchy.' Many years later, 'Turbo' king of Neustria had conquered Oceana and placed it under feudal institutions, Harrington's discussion of which derives largely from the second edition of Selden's *Titles of Honor*. The introduction of baronage by letters patent in the reign of Dicotome (Richard II) made the nobility much more powerful; it gave them 'hands in the king's purse, and … no shoulders for his throne.' Soon, resenting Dicotome's generosity to newer nobles, the older peers 'deposed him, got the trick of it, and never gave over setting up and pulling down of their kings, according to their various interests and that faction of the white and red into which they had been thenceforth divided, till Panurgus, the eighteenth king from the conquest, was more by their favour than his right advanced unto the crown.'[35]

'Panurgus' was, of course, Henry VII. In this passage Harrington challenged the legitimacy of Henry VII's hereditary claim to authority, and thereby undermined the right of his Tudor and Stuart descendants to the throne. But he also saw that Panurgus' reign had had important social consequences. Using those arts of diplomacy and guile noted earlier by Bacon (another of Harrington's sources), he succeeded in disrupting the power of the nobility. The consequence of this, which Harrington could not have drawn from Bacon or any other early Stuart historian, was so severe a reduction in the economic and social position of the aristocracy that their political power soon 'came to fall into the hands of the people.' Under Panurgus' son, Coraunus, 'the declining estate of the nobility' worsened, as the king dissolved the abbeys and returned their wealth to the nation. This placed 'the balance of the commonwealth' in the hands of the 'popular party.' His heir, Queen Parthenia, in turn 'wholly neglected the nobility,' building her regime on the 'love tricks that passed between her and her people.' The outcome of this decay of noble wealth and power was the rise of the house of commons and the eventual collapse of the monarchy, now bereft of its natural aristocratic allies.[36]

One of Harrington's incidental targets was the author of *Leviathan*, Thomas Hobbes. After the Restoration, the aging former translator of Thucydides turned from the analysis of government and political power to the causes of civil unrest. *Behemoth, or the Long Parliament*, finished in 1668 when Hobbes was nearly eighty, is a set of dialogues exploring the relations of king and parliament, of secular and ecclesiastical authority, over a vast period of time, ending with the dissolution of the Rump and the Restoration of Charles II. More than simply an account of the war, it ranges from discussion of the donation of Constantine, to the founding of universities (which Hobbes principally blamed for nurturing religious dissent and political unrest), to the now much-controverted issue of whether the place of the commons in parliament predated the Conquest. On this last subject, Hobbes took a sceptical position reminiscent of his friend John Selden's view of the origins of tithe payment: 'It is a question of things so long past, that they are now forgotten. Nor have we any thing to conjecture by, but the records of our own nation, and some small and obscure fragments of Roman histories: and for the records, seeing they are of things done only, sometimes justly, sometimes unjustly, you can never by them know what right they had, but only what right they pretended.'[37]

Hobbes and Clarendon, though they wrote on the same side, came to differing views on the origins of the wars. Fuller, Heylyn, and later Gilbert Burnet were among those who debated the recent history of the English church. Ecclesiastical history had always been, more obviously than secular history, dangerous territory – one recalls Camden's reluctance to say any more about it than he absolutely had to in dealing with Elizabeth's reign. But in an era which had experienced, as closely related events, both violent political change and the utter uprooting of the established church, the distinction between these two types of history was apt to be lost: it was now even less possible than it had been a few decades earlier to separate the religious from the political past.

Discussions of the historical authority of episcopacy and attacks on or defences of presbyterianism, independency, and anabaptism might be even more venomous than those histories which stuck to political matters. Peter Heylyn's assault on the presbyterians, *Aerius Redivivus*, and Clement Walker's vicious attack on independency are by no means atypical in this regard.[38] Fuller's exasperation at the partisan character of post-war historical writing has already been mentioned. Embittered by Heylyn's animadversions on his *Church-History*, Fuller declared that his critic 'by his causeless carping hath allayed in me the delight in writing of histories; seeing nothing can be so unpartially and inoffensively written, but some will carp thereat.'[39] Fuller had many critics, including Sir William Dugdale, but none pursued him with the dogged pedantry shown by Heylyn, who may have been the most openly and unashamedly partisan historical writer on the royalist side. From the middle of the civil war until his death in 1662 the former royal chaplain and author of *Augustus* kept busy writing accounts of the church, of the reign of King Charles, and of the life of his hero, Archbishop Laud. The circumstances of the 1650s forced him to vent his spleen publicly against more moderate fellow royalists such as Hamon L'Estrange, whose *The Reign of King Charles* did not seem loyal enough, and Fuller, whom Heylyn accused of supporting presbyterianism.[40] Several of Heylyn's other works, such as his biography of Laud, *Cyprianus Anglicus*, had to await posthumous publication after the Restoration.[41]

With the collapse of censorship in 1641, polemic became the order of the day, though no writer would admit that he was arguing a disputable case. In fact, historians still refused to admit that two opposed accounts of the same series of events might be justified; each one continued to claim that his version, and his alone, provided the only 'true' account. I suggested earlier that the introduction of extensive documentation into English historiography in such works as Foxe's

Acts and Monuments and Selden's *Historie of Tithes* owes less to a spirit of impartial, critical enquiry and to the growth of modern standards of scholarship than it does to the requirements of polemic and to the infiltration of history by the controversial mode and argumentative techniques long associated with debates over religious issues. Most interregnum and Restoration historians still preferred to think of themselves as reasonable men, and while it would be a mistake to take any account, whether by Clarendon or Weldon, on face value, so too would it be an error to take their authors' professions of impartiality as entirely insincere.

The proceedings of the Long Parliament, followed by the war, the trial of the king, and the vicissitudes of the interregnum, generated an unprecedented quantity of printed pamphlet literature and newsbooks, as indicated by the massiveness of George Thomason's famous collection of tracts. Volumes of public documents, statutes, ordinances, and state correspondence began to appear in the mid-1640s as part of the propaganda war.[42] Extensive use of such documentation occurs in many of the longer accounts of the 1640s and 1650s precisely because historians wished to win their historical debates in the forum of readership, while at the same time preserving both a sense of their own impartiality and their belief that historical truth was not just knowable, but capable of balanced presentation.[43] Thus not every civil war history has the belligerent tones of Heylyn, or the lurid flavour of Weldon; quite often, in fact, a historian could go to considerable lengths to avoid both highly coloured language in the description of events and vehement attacks on his opponents. Yet despite the even-tempered, almost laconic presentation of affairs in works such as Bulstrode Whitelocke's *Memorials of the English Affairs,* the ideological thrust is difficult to miss, even if it must often be found between the lines, hinted at in asides and glosses, or in the memorialist's selection of letters, state papers, and newsbooks for reprinting.[44]

Two of the outstanding works of interregnum and Restoration historical writing illustrate this attempt to balance truth and controversy. John Rushworth's enormous *Historical Collections,* published in eight folio volumes over a forty-year period, provides a chronological study of events from the beginning of the ill-advised Spanish match to the execution of King Charles. Rushworth (1612?–90) had been a clerk assistant and a messenger in the Long Parliament, and later served as secretary first to Sir Thomas Fairfax and subsequently to Cromwell.[45] He exploited his access to state papers and parliamentary documents to include a vast quantity of printed material in support of his narrative.

Like Whitelocke, he was subtle enough to rely on documentation to make his points without too obviously pleading a case. His preface proclaims both the difficulty of ascertaining the truth and the perils of relating it; he quotes both Ralegh's definition of the purposes of writing history, and the latter's famous remark that those who follow truth too near the heels may have their teeth kicked out. As for himself, he finds it necessary, while concentrating on recent years, to push his account back to the reign of James, lest he omit events of crucial importance to the outbreak of the civil war: 'I hope this story begins with a distance of time, not so far off, as the footsteps of truth are worn out; nor yet so near, as the heels of it need to be feared. But this I am sure, that had I not gone so far back as I doe, I had not reached the fundamentals to the history of these times.' Rushworth believes his kind of presentation of evidence to be essential if the reader is to determine the truth about the unhappy events of the 1620s and 1630s, and their even more dire consequences in the following decades. It is simply not enough to read published accounts of affairs (such as the civil war newsbooks) since the reader will be unable to sort the truth from falshood. This problem will be rendered worse over time, he predicts, commenting on 'the impossibility for any man in after-ages to ground a true history, by relying on the printed pamphlets in our days, which passed the press whilst it was without controul.' It is for these reasons that he has made his *Collections,* in order to 'separate truth from falsehood.'[46] The subtitle of volume vii, the last to be published, declares that in it the reader will find events 'impartially related,' that it sets forth 'only matter of fact in order of time, without observation or reflection.'[47]

Although John Nalson (1637–86) predeceased Rushworth, he was a full generation younger; what Rushworth perceived as part of his own autobiography was to Nalson more remote, and belonged even more clearly to the realm of the past than it did for his opponent. Nalson's retrospective glance at the civil war was inspired less by personal memories than by his detestation of post-Restoration nonconformity and by his own support for the crown during the popish plot and exclusion crisis from 1679 to 1682, when he was a vigorous tory pamphleteer. Yet though he approached his subject from a perspective very different from Rushworth's, Nalson, too, believed that historical truth was a seamless garment, and that his own rendition would be both unprejudiced and accurate. Explicitly intending to refute Rushworth's volumes, Nalson could seriously call his greatest work *An Impartial Collection of the Great Affairs of State from the Beginning of the Scotch Rebellion in the Year 1639 to the Murther of King Charles.*

Like Rushworth, Nalson included much in the way of supportive documentation, but he was much less guarded in confessing his conviction that the historian must comment on events rather than simply relate them: 'I have not tied my self strictly to the rules of a bare collector, but indulged my self in the liberty of an historian, to tie up the loose and scattered papers with the circumstances, causes, and consequences of them; and should I have been singular therein, yet I think the light which it will give to the matters of fact, and the diversion and satisfaction it may afford the curious and inquisitive reader, may so far oblige him as to procure his pardon, if not his thanks.'[48] It is impossible, Nalson claims, to relate such an event as the trial and punishment of Dr John Bastwick without providing some account of 'the temper and genius of the man.' Without this 'light' – he again uses this favoured image – the reader might mistakenly conclude that Bastwick was the victim of a tyrannical government, rather than of his own folly and arrogance. Throughout the work, Nalson feels free to colour his prose with bright language; the opponents of the crown, for instance, are not simply rebels but 'brutish' rebels.[49]

But whatever the historian's liberty to gloss the events he recounts, Nalson is utterly clear on one point: he, unlike Rushworth, will present the unadulterated truth, 'matters of undeniable fact, drawn from the records and remains of those very men and times.' While he has endeavoured to provide 'a true account from the best authorities extant,' he believes that the weight of evidence is so overwhelming that it is 'evident beyond all contradiction' that ambitious politicians and religious malcontents, presbyterians, independents, and anabaptists 'were the first disturbers of the peace, settlement and happiness of the church and nation.' He loses no time in attacking Rushworth's credibility. Unlike Nalson himself, who is unbiased, Rushworth has written *ex parte*. Worse, Rushworth has selected only documents that support his own case, and abridged those that do not: he has 'concealed truth, [and] endeavoured to vindicate the prevailing detractions of the late times as well as their barbarous actions.'[50]

It is easy to dismiss such writers as Nalson as tory hacks. It is equally tempting to suppose that more balanced representations of the past can be found in the writings of antiquaries, though that again would be a mistake. Selden's disguising of erudite polemic behind the colourless mask of history in 1618, as much as his and other lawyers' use of the past in parliamentary debate, shows that the antiquaries were no less likely to allow partisan concerns to determine their representations of history than were tory historians like Nalson and puritan memorialists like Weldon. The breakdown of consensus that characterizes the period after 1640 can be found in the research and writings of antiquaries as well, as David Douglas's classic study of Augustan scholarship demonstrates. Sir William Dugdale is now remembered principally for his antiquarian studies of the medieval monasteries and for his *Antiquities of Warwickshire;* he is less often quoted as the author of works such as the learned, but unquestionably partisan, *A Short View of the Late Troubles in England.* This eight-hundred page study of the origins and course of the civil war employs language closer to Heylyn and Weldon than to Nalson and Rushworth, describing puritans as 'men of proud and peevish spirits, who had not light enough in themselves to discern the truth, because they wanted learning to search into antiquities.' Dugdale thereby made ignorance of the past, and specifically of the true antiquity of the episcopal church, a principal cause of the war, which was fomented by radicals who themselves were the descendants of sixteenth-century anabaptists. Borrowing heavily from Cotton's short study of Henry III, Dugdale turned the thirteenth-century revolt of the baronage into one of two explicit parallels with the civil war; another is provided by a more recent episode, the French wars of religion.[51]

The predominance of polemic in the writing of history after 1640 is surely more reminiscent of the religious debates of the sixteenth century, and of works like Foxe's Book of Martyrs, than it is of either the writings of the early seventeenth century or of the academically disinterested history that we in the modern West are supposed to practise. This hardly suggests that the biography of history in the seventeenth century is a success story of uninhibited progress toward unbiased, critical modern scholarship, for all the accomplishments of Selden, Camden, and others; rather, it serves as a cautionary reminder that change, in intellectual as much as political or social history, rarely proceeds in a straight line. The principal difference between the type of history written by Foxe in the 1560s and that by royalist and parliamentarian writers a century later lies not in the polemical character of the prose, but in the existence of competing points of view within the same national community. A stable consensus on the course of English history, challenged only from outside by Catholic critics such as Robert Parsons and Richard Broughton, had given way to a fully dialectical, and multipartisan set of debates about the past.

By the time that a limited control over the press was reasserted, in the 1650s and during the Restoration, the genie was out of the bottle. Despite the triumph of royalism in 1660 and the re-establishment of censorship, radically differing views of the past continued to proliferate –

even if they could often not be published. Lucy Hutchinson's biography of her husband, Colonel Thomas Hutchinson, which was written in the 1660s, remained unpublished until 1806; in addition to recounting briefly the crimes of the 'wicked queen,' Mary Stuart, Mrs Hutchinson elaborated (and distorted) Harrington's analysis of the balance of wealth and power into a vehement critique of absolute monarchy: 'But severall of the kings, not satisfied with their bounded monarchie, made attempts to convert it into an absolute soveraignety, attempts fatall both to themselves and their people, and ever unsuccessefull.'[52]

According to her perception of English history, the aristocracy had 'ever stood up in the people's defence and curb'd the wild ambition of the tyrants, whom they sometimes reduc'd to moderation, and sometimes depos'd for their misgovernments.' Eager to break this yoke, the kings gradually weakened the nobles financially and politically. Henry VIII, by dissolving the monasteries, returned their revenues to the people; he thereby 'cast the ballance cleare on their side, and left them now only to expect an opertunity to resume their power into their owne hands.' Only the religious quarrels of the sixteenth century and the wisdom of Queen Elizabeth had 'prolong'd the last gasps of expiring monarchy.' With James I came Arminianism, the decay of morality, and the financial ruin of the land: 'The honor, wealth and glory of the nation, wherein Queene Elizabeth left it, were soone prodigally wasted by this thriftlesse heire, the nobility of the land utterly debas'd by setting honors to publick sale, and conferring them on persons that had neither blood nor meritt fitt to weare, nor estates to beare up, their titles, but were faine to invent projects to pill the people, and pick their purses for the maintenance of vice and lewdnesse.' Despite Charles I's more upright character, he proved 'a worse encroacher upon the civill and spirituall liberties of his people by farre than his father.' But though she reserves most of her venom for the first two Stuarts, there can be little doubt that Mrs Hutchinson, as clearly as Harrington, saw the roots of the civil war springing from long-standing tensions between the monarchy, aristocracy, and people.[53]

A similar example of a radical perspective on the past, also unpublished by its author, is provided by the republican and sectary Edmund Ludlow's *Memoirs*.[54] Throughout this work, written in exile, Ludlow makes no attempt to disguise his contempt for the institution of monarchy; he refuses to acknowledge the legality of the Restoration, and refers to Charles II throughout as Charles Stuart. His father Charles I, if not Antichrist himself, was at the very least a king who 'gave his power to the beast'; Henry VIII is described as 'that monster of mankinde'; James duke of York, the heir to the throne, is a scoundrel and a tyrant in the making:

> I shall not mention heer anythinge of the falsehood and bloudyness of his [James's] disposition and practice, nor of the like quallifications of his ancestors, they being all well knowne to those amongst whom they lived in England and Scotland. And so are the judgements of the Lord which followed them where ever they went, a great plague succeeding the comming in of King James, and the like that of King Charles.

The legal system, wrote Ludlow, echoing the Levellers, was a yoke placed on the people by William the Bastard, dependent for its power on the co-operation of sheriffs and judges, who were incapable of exercising justice since they were in the king's pay.[55]

The writings of Lucy Hutchinson and Edmund Ludlow merely provide two well-known illustrations of an interpretation of England's monarchical past that was as different from the royalist views of a Dugdale or Nalson as it was alien from the historical accounts of the pre-war period. By the end of the century one can find royalist, whig, parliamentarian, and republican interpretations of the past; gone for good was the relatively narrow ideological corridor that had confined most formal history-writing in Tudor and early Stuart England, together with many elements in the constellation of archetypes that had populated it.

Conclusion

The modern process of historiography assumes error, deficiency, and subjectivity as occupational hazards, unavoidable in a discourse where the objective 'fact' has little meaning except when placed in a pattern subjectively designed and manipulated by the individual historical mind. Today, we continually seek to refine our level of knowledge and understanding of the past, in a dialectical process which takes place every day in the journals, monographs, and university seminar rooms of the scholarly world. No one for a moment imagines that we can ever 'perfect' the writing of history; the most confident positivist would today claim only that we can endeavour, by periodically refining our methods and asking new questions of our sources, to improve it.

In the early years of the seventeenth century, historians did not assume that debates about history could be productive; they avoided criticism of their contemporaries in precisely the way we now try to be 'original.' Most of them were uninterested in the potential of history as a tool for explaining the present, as an account of the emergence of contemporary man, his customs, and institutions. Of those who were, some, like Samuel Daniel, believed that complete truth was unobtainable and that the job of the historian was to teach; there was little to be gained in quibbling over details. Others, like Francis Bacon, believed in their very different ways that the last word could and would eventually be said. Only a few – Selden, Herbert, and perhaps Camden – realized not only that history was imperfect, but also that knowledge of the past could be increased through laborious research.

It seems also that a number of phenomena, usually cited in support of the modernity of Renaissance historians, simply did not occur or have been misunderstood. History was not severed from rhetoric: very few of the writers treated here did not prize eloquence as highly as knowledge, and they had no reservations about carefully crafting their sentences in order to gloss over the rough edges of the past. Of the major politic historians before 1640, only Camden explicitly refused to write fictional speeches for his historical characters, and he because many of them or their acquaintances were still alive. Those who failed to live up to the historian's duty to capture the past in clear, eloquent sentences often found their works either ignored or, worse (as in Selden's case), seriously misconstrued.

Nor will the traditional view that the supernatural had all but disappeared from historical writing bear close scrutiny. Most historians clearly and frequently invoked providence, fate, or fortune. As explanatory tools, these were indispensable in a universe where God's hand ultimately governed all. Historians – again with the exceptions of Camden, Selden, and Herbert – had only the most limited sense of contingency: if something had happened, there never existed any chance of it not happening, insofar as God foreknew and preordained it. Although such an event could be shown to result from human choice – historians never explicitly denied human free will – God himself had willed the very choice.

The later seventeenth-century revolt against strict predestinarianism would help to erode this attitude toward the role of chance, but it was not until the eighteenth century that God would really be made into a 'divine clockmaker' who allowed his creation to tick away from day to day, propelled for the most part by its own cogs. Then, though a scholar-chronologer such as Newton could continue to speak of providence as an overarching force in history, it at least became possible to see the past as a web of interlocking contingencies.[56] Whatever the views of Newton and his successors, it is anachronistic to read a later, more thoroughly secularized 'mechanics' of history into the early seventeenth century, even in the case of the exceptional historians who relied relatively little on providence for their explanations. Camden did not need to invoke divine intervention because a mountain of state papers told him in detail the immediate causes of events; this does not mean that he did not think that God was ultimately responsible for them. For him and his readers, God's involvement in history was a given. Selden similarly depicted the *Historie of Tithes* as a sequence of changes over a long time. He did not need to use God to explain what was visible in black ink.

In later decades, when God had been placed outside the realm of daily events by post-Newtonian science, concepts like fortune and chance could genuinely be used to denote the irrational, the die-roll of circumstance in an open-ended historical process where the future was merely possible. It was then that the *philosophes* and their eventual successors, the metahistorians of the late eighteenth and nineteenth centuries, could intervene to explain the nature of history in rational, not theological, terms. In the first few decades of the seventeenth century, however, the rationalization of history lay well in the future.

I said at the outset that I have no wish to reopen the debate on the alleged 'historical revolution.' Yet even if there were no revolution in the study of the past, surely it would be equally wrong to deny the occurrence of some fundamental changes, particularly in ideas about the purpose and scope of history and in the language used to denote these ideas. Antiquarianism and history have never become the same thing, but they grew closer in the first decades of the century. Selden's assertion that a man who studied the past was an historian, whether or not he taught a moral or political lesson, pointed to divine judgments or even wrote chronologically marked a small but significant conceptual shift. Equally significant were Selden's belief – shared by Camden, Herbert, and the leading antiquaries – that only persistent, painstaking research, criticism, and revision could recapture the past and his admission that his own interpretations were open to question. Historians were, albeit only gradually and reluctantly, coming to the realization that just as the past itself was a series of contingent events, so historical research was a task without end, its certainty limited by the inability of a single mind to apprehend all the relevant facts at once.

Similar realizations were being made across Europe, as Jean Mabillon and the Bollandists developed diplomatic and paleographic techniques and Muratori systematically edited the corpus of Italian chronicles. George Huppert is probably correct to point out that the later seventeenth century witnessed a renewed divorce between technical erudition and philosophical history after the age of Pasquier, Scaliger, and La Popelinière.[57] Nevertheless, few would now distinguish the two formally, and it was not doubted that the work of scholars such as Mabillon, Muratori, and Thomas Madox was essentially historical. The similarities between the French and English experiences, especially in the seventeenth century, must be qualified by the very different intellectual and political environments in the two countries. The reaction against erudite research in protestant England, both before and after the disturbances of the mid-century, never reached the proportions it had attained in absolutist France, which also evolved a stronger tradition of courtly, panegyrical history than ever developed in England. In the 1630s, the Trojan myth had been revived in England in an attempt to buttress the public image of the Stuart monarchy, but it is significant that this revival was restricted to poetry and to the masque; there was no revival of quasi-mythical prose history to compare with the belletristic renaissance of Brutus' Gallic cousin, Francion. The late and faint-hearted foundation of the post of Historiographer Royal, after the Restoration, could not succeed in dissolving the new relationship between critical learning and historical writing.[58]

Nor could it ever restore the atmosphere of general agreement about the past and the willingness of authors to confine themselves to a zone of publicly acceptable opinion that had characterized early Stuart historical writing. There had been subtle currents of dissent on the past in the early seventeenth century, which broadly mirrored developing disagreements over aspects of the governance of the commonwealth. Among the points of disagreement over the past we have seen, for instance, the differences of opinion that could exist over key episodes such as the Norman Conquest and on its implications for the development of the common law, though these differences occasioned little in the way of published debate. There had even occurred a major controversy, over the *Historie of Tithes:* again, Selden's unsuccessful attempt to present his arguments as *unargumentative* illustrates nothing so much as the generally accepted notion that history was and should be the least controversial of literary genres.

That assumption, which derived from the humanist education experienced by most Elizabethan and early Stuart historians, reflects the high degree of control over representations of the past – in art and ritual as much as in prose – that the Tudor regime had acquired through the sixteenth century, and which the Jacobean government was able to build upon by adapting such themes as the union of the Roses to its own ends. When that government lost the trust and eventually the support of a significant segment of the articulate population, as it had done by the 1640s, the conditions were right for a sharp alteration in the manner in which historical discourse occurred. Together with the instruments of official censorship, the need for self-censorship of unorthodox historical views soon disappeared; the creation of an atmosphere of open ideological conflict – an atmosphere which has outlived by several centuries the events in which it originated – ensured that thereafter the reader of any history would be well advised to take note of its author's political and religious perspective. The day had passed, as Thomas Fuller noted, when a work of historical writing could pass silently into the public realm without generating its own critics and challengers; and with it went much of that humanist faith in the study of the past as the fount of virtue and wisdom which had given history its status throughout the Renaissance. History might grow more erudite and it might still hold up a light to truth. Henceforth, however, that light would be passed through the prism of debate, and refracted into a multicoloured spectrum of ideological difference.

Notes

Preface

1 Arthur B. Ferguson *Clio Unbound: Perception of the Social and Cultural Past in Renaissance England* (Durham, NC 1979)

2 For the intellectual context of the Renaissance sense of the past, see Ricardo J. Quiñones *The Renaissance Discovery of Time* (Cambridge, Mass. 1972). Among the best-known works on the history plays, see E.M.W. Tillyard *Shakespeare's History Plays* (1980; first published 1944); Lily B. Campbell *Shakespeare's Histories: Mirrors of Elizabethan Policy* (San Marino, Cal. 1947); I. Ribner *The English History Play in the Age of Shakespeare* (Princeton, NJ 1957). Among more recent works the following, though not exclusively devoted to the history play, have proved of special value: Martin Butler *Theatre and Crisis, 1632–1642* (Cambridge 1984); Jerzy Limon *Dangerous Matter: English Drama and Politics in 1623–24* (Cambridge 1986). M. Heinemann *Puritanism and Theatre* (Cambridge 1980) has much useful material on the city drama of the 1620s, though its argument that there was such a thing as 'opposition' drama is unconvincing.

3 I have also avoided treating the small number of histories of contemporary foreign states written by Englishmen or translated by Englishmen from foreign works, for example, Richard Knolles *The Generall Historie of the Turkes* (1603); Thomas de Fougasses *The Generall Historie of the Magnificent State of Venice*, trans W. Shute (1612); Louis de Mayerne Turquet *The Generall Historie of Spaine* trans Edward Grimeston (1612); and Grimeston's *The General Historie of the Netherlands* (1608). These works constitute a genre unto themselves and the absence of a number of them on the same subject would render any conclusions tenuous at best.

4 J.G.A. Pocock *The Ancient Constitution and the Feudal Law: A Study of English Historical Thought in the Seventeenth Century* (Cambridge

1987). See also Pocock's stimulating essay 'The Origins of Study of the Past: A Comparative Approach,' *Comparative Studies in Society and History* 4 (1961–2) 209–46.

5 F.S. Fussner *The Historical Revolution: English Historical Writing and Thought 1580–1640* (1962); F.J. Levy, *Tudor Historical Thought* (San Marino, Cal. 1967); briefer surveys can be found in Herschel Baker *The Race of Time* (Toronto 1967) and Peter Burke *The Renaissance Sense of the Past* (1969).

6 Christopher Hill *Intellectual Origins of the English Revolution* (Oxford 1965). For attacks on the 'historical revolution' thesis, see Joseph M. Levine, 'Ancients, Moderns and the Continuity of English Historical Writing in the Later Seventeenth Century' in his *Humanism and History: Origins of Modern English Historiography* (Ithaca, NY 1987) 155–77; Joseph H. Preston 'Was There an Historical Revolution?' *Journal of the History of Ideas* 33 (1977) 353–64. In the light of this consensus against a 'revolution,' I find surprising the recent statement by W. Herendeen that 'modern historiographers are generally in agreement that the period covered by Camden's life ... is one of revolution' in his otherwise useful 'William Camden: Historian, Herald, and Antiquary' *Studies in Philology* 85 (1988) 192n2.

7 R. Flower 'Laurence Nowell and the Discovery of England in Tudor Times' *Proceedings of the British Academy* 21 (1935) 47–74; R.A. Caldwell 'Joseph Holland, Collector and Antiquary' *Modern Philology* 40 (1942–3) 295–301; J.W. Harris *John Bale* (Urbana, Ill. 1940) and H. McCusker *John Bale, Dramatist and Antiquary* (Bryn Mawr, Penn. 1942); Retha Warnicke *William Lambarde, Elizabethan Antiquary, 1536–1601* (1973)

8 May McKisack *Medieval History in the Tudor Age* (Oxford 1971); Levine *Humanism and History* and *Doctor Woodward's Shield: History, Science and Satire in Augustan England* (Berkeley and London 1977); T.D. Kendrick *British Antiquity* (2nd ed, 1970); D.C. Douglas *English Scholars, 1660–1730* (2nd ed, 1951); for important essays on various aspects of antiquarianism, see *English Historical Scholarship in the Sixteenth and Seventeenth Centuries* ed Levi Fox (1956) and two books by Stuart Piggott: *Ruins in a Landscape* (Edinburgh 1976), and *Ancient Britons and the Antiquarian Imagination* (New York 1989).

9 Keith Thomas *Religion and the Decline of Magic* (1971) chapters 3 and 4 passim; H.A. Kelly *Divine Providence in the England of Shakespeare's Histories* (Cambridge, Mass. 1970); C.A. Patrides *The Grand Design of God: The Literary Form of the Christian View of History* (1972), especially chapters 5 and 6, offers perhaps the best introduction to the literature, with a good bibliography.

10 Kevin Sharpe *Sir Robert Cotton, 1586–1631: History and Politics in Early Modern England* (Oxford 1979); Linda Levy Peck *Northampton: Patronage and Policy at the Court of James I* (1982); David Sandler Berkowitz

John Selden's Formative Years: Politics and Society in Early Seventeenth-Century England ed M. Jansson (Washington, DC 1988)

11 Felix Gilbert *Machiavelli and Guicciardini: Politics and History in Sixteenth-Century Florence* (Princeton, NJ 1965); J.G.A. Pocock *The Machiavellian Moment: Florentine Political Thought and the Atlantic Republican Tradition* (Princeton 1975). For a general survey of formal historical writing, see Eric Cochrane *Historians and Historiography in the Italian Renaissance* (Chicago 1981); for antiquarian activity, Roberto Weiss *The Renaissance Discovery of Classical Antiquity* (2nd ed, Oxford 1988).

12 Donald R. Kelley *Foundations of Modern Historical Scholarship: Language, Law and History in the French Renaissance* (New York 1970); George Huppert 'The Renaissance Background of Historicism' *History and Theory* 5 (1965) 48–60 and *The Idea of Perfect History: Historical Erudition and Historical Philosophy in Renaissance France* (Urbana, Ill. 1970). An earlier essay in the same direction is Julian Franklin *Jean Bodin and the Sixteenth-Century Revolution in the Methodology of Law and History* (New York, 1963); for a recent critique of these works, see Zachary S. Schiffman 'Renaissance Historicism Reconsidered' *History and Theory* 24 (1985) 170–82. The seventeenth century, in comparison, has been less well covered: see, however, Orest Ranum *Artisans of Glory: Writers and Historical Thought in Seventeenth-Century France* (Chapel Hill 1980).

13 The best survey of the late seventeenth-century *érudits* remains David Knowles' *Great Historical Enterprises* (1963). For the dichotomy between erudition and history see A.D. Momigliano 'Ancient History and the Antiquarian' in his *Studies in Historiography* (1966) 1–39; such a division was earlier hinted at by Paul Hazard in *The European Mind, 1680–1715* trans J.L. May (1953) 48–52.

14 For a similar definition of ideology as it relates to history, see Peter Novick *That Noble Dream: The 'Objectivity Question' and the American Historical Profession* (Cambridge 1988) 62.

15 On the political debates of the period, the best recent guide is J.P. Sommerville *Politics and Ideology in England, 1603–1640* (London and New York 1986).

16 Novick *That Noble Dream* 224

Chapter One

1 T. Blundeville *The True Order and Methode of Wryting and Reading Hystories* (1574) ed Dick. The tract was based on F. Patrizzi *Della historia diece dialoghi* (Venice 1560) and G. Aconcio *Delle osservationi et avvertimenti che haver si debbono nel legger delle historie*, an unpublished manuscript (PRO SP 12/13/53) now printed in Aconcio *De methodo e opuscoli religiosi e filosofici* ed Radetti 305–13. Further

references to this tract will be to Dick's edition, and will be given in the text. A general overview of concepts of the didactic value of history in the Renaissance may be found in Gilmore *Humanists and Jurists* 14ff.

2 Cf Aconcio *Delle osservationi* 306.

3 James VI of Scotland recommended that his son Prince Henry read histories: 'By reading of authenticke histories and chronicles, yee shall learne experience by theoricke, applying the by-past things to the present estate, *quia nihil novum sub sole;*' *Basilicon Doron* in *Political Works of James I* ed McIlwain 40.

4 Dean *Tudor Theories of History Writing* 6

5 Spenser *Faerie Queene* VII.vii.47, in *Works of Edmund Spenser* ed E. Greenlaw et al (Baltimore 1932–49) vol VI, p 177; Baker *The Race of Time* chapter 1; Weisinger 'Ideas of History during the Renaissance'

6 Patrides *The Grand Design of God;* Pocock *The Machiavellian Moment* chapter 3, 49–80; Trompf *The Idea of Historical Recurrence in Western Thought* chapters 2 and 5

7 Hence the popularity of almanacs, which through astrology and prophecy plotted history into the future, and of attempts to project apocalyptic history into the future. Both would have been impossible if writers assumed an open-ended future.

8 Melanchthon *Loci Communes* trans C.L. Hill (Boston 1944) 74, 81; Thomas Gataker *Of the Nature and Use of Lots* (1619). For useful discussions of this aspect of chance, see Barbara Donagan 'Providence, Chance and Explanation: Paradoxical Aspects of the Puritan View of Causation' *Journal of Religious History* 11 (1981) 385–403, especially 390–6. Ian Hacking in *The Emergence of Probability*, chapter 1, argues that there is little sign of an idea of random chance as probability before the 1660s, though he notes certain interesting exceptions.

9 Machiavelli *The Prince* chapter 25 (trans Bull, 130–3)

10 Boethius *The Consolation of Philosophy* 2.1.35–60 (trans Tester, 177–8); Thomas *Religion and the Decline of Magic* 90ff, 144, 784

11 John Webster *The White Devil* 1.1.4–5, in *Complete Works* ed F.L. Lucas (1927) IV, 111

12 Edward Hall *Hall's Chronicle* ed Ellis 15, 112; *The Raigne of King Edward the Third*, 3.1.124 and 3.4.136, in *Elizabethan History Plays* ed Armstrong; Tillyard *Shakespeare's History Plays* 40–50; Kelly *Divine Providence in the England of Shakespeare's Histories* passim

13 R. Holinshed *Chronicles* (2nd ed, 1587) III, 760–1; *The Mirror for Magistrates* ed Campbell 143, line 5 and 213, lines 17–18, 37–8; J. Norden *Vicissitudo rerum* (1600) stanza 28; L.D. Green 'Modes of Perception in *The Mirror for Magistrates' Huntington Library Quarterly* 44 (1981) 117–33

14 Providence, not fortune, ordains the death of Alexander VI in Guiccardini *The Historie of Guiccardin* trans Fenton (1579) 308. Fenton does retain fortune in its more formulaic usage, eg, 685.

15 V. Malvezzi *Romulus and Tarquin* trans Henry Carey (1637) 144

16 Holinshed *Chronicles* III, 761; J. Dodderidge *The History of the Ancient and Moderne Estate of the Principality of Wales* (1630) 28; Edward Ayscu *A Historie Contayning the Warres, Treaties, Marriages, and Other Occurrents betweene England & Scotland* (1607) 318; Todd 'Providence, Chance and the New Science in Early Stuart Cambridge' 700–5

17 Ayscu *Historie* 321; Sir Walter Ralegh *The History of the World* (1614) 1.1.12–14; 17–19); Boethius *Consolation of Philosophy* 5.3.20–100; 5.6.60–75 (trans Tester, 397–401, 427)

18 Blundeville *True Order* 157, 165; Holborn 'Greek and Modern Concepts of History' 3–29

19 Hall *Chronicle* 'Introduccion' 1–3; Tillyard *Shakespeare's History Plays* 43–5

20 Richard Grafton *An Abridgement of the Chronicles of England* (1563) sig B2r

21 Cicero *De oratore* 2.36

22 Sir Thomas Elyot *The Boke Named the Governour* (1531) ed H.H.S. Croft (1880) II, 384, 386; Roger Ascham *The Scholemaster* (1570) in *Whole Works* ed. J.A. Giles (1864) III, 142, 229. For the Renaissance background to the cult of Cicero as it relates to wisdom and eloquence, see Jerrold E. Seigel *Rhetoric and Philosophy in Renaissance Humanism* (Princeton 1968) 3–30; Gray 'Renaissance Humanism.'

23 A.D.B. *The Court of the Most Illustrious James, the First* (1619) 46, 160; Richard Brathwait *The Schollers Medley, or, an Intermixt Discourse upon Historicall and Poeticall Relations* (1614) sig A3v, p 3; Robert Powell *The Life of Alfred, or Alured* (1634) preface

24 Fulke Greville *An Inquisition upon Fame and Honour* stanza 7 in *Works* ed A.B. Grosart (4 vols 1870) II, 69

25 Ralegh *History of the World* (1614) frontispiece; Campbell *Shakespeare's Histories* Benjamin, 'Fame, Poetry and the Order of History in the Literature of the English Renaissance'

26 J. Hayward *Lives of the III. Normans* (1613) sig A2v

27 S. Goulart *Admirable and Memorable Histories* trans E. Grimeston (1606) sig b2r

28 Momigliano 'Ancient History and the Antiquarian'; but see the criticisms of Momigliano's thesis in Erasmus *The Origins of Rome in Historiography* 34, 36, 44, 58, 123.

29 Momigliano 'Gibbon's Contribution to Historical Method'

30 Levy *Tudor Historical Thought* chapter 7; Fueter *Geschichte der neueren Historiographie* 166–70

31 Momigliano 'Ancient History and the Antiquarian' 8

32 Pocock *Ancient Constitution* 6. For historical Pyrrhonism see Hazard *The European Mind* 48–52; Franklin *Jean Bodin* 83–102; Popkin *History of Scepticism* 111; Louis I. Bredvold *The Intellectual Milieu of John Dryden* (Ann Arbor, Mich. 1956) 16–46; Shapiro *Probability and Certainty* 119–62

33 Examples of these different terms may be found in a wide variety of

sources from actual histories to parliamentary debates: T.E. Hartley
Proceedings in the Parliaments of Elizabeth 1 vol 1 (Leicester 1981) 28;
Thomas Pie *An Houre Glasse Contayning a Computation from the
Beginning of Time to Christ* (1597) 85–6

34 For an Elizabethan instance of 'history' as a kind of register or record,
see the speech of Pisanio in Shakespeare's *Cymbeline* (3.5.98–9): 'This
paper is the history of my knowledge / Touching her flight.'

35 R.G. Collingwood *The Idea of History* (2nd ed, Oxford 1961) part one,
passim; Press *The Development of the Idea of History in Antiquity*; J.
Karl Keuck *Historia: Geschichte des Wortes und seiner Bedeutungen in
der Antike und der romanischen Sprachen* (Emsdetten 1934); Joachim
Knape *Historie im Mittelalter und früher Neuzeit* (Baden-Baden 1984).
I owe this last reference to the kindness of Fritz Levy.

36 Robert Fludd *Utriusque cosmi maioris scilicet et minoris metaphysica,
atque technica historia* (Oppenheim 1617–21); Hobbes *Leviathan* I,
ix. Similar taxonomies can be found in Grey Brydges, fifth Lord Chandos
(attribution questionable), *Horae Subsecivae: Observations and Discourses* (1620) 194–5; Peter Heylyn *Microcosmus, or a Little Description
of the Great World* (Oxford 1621); and Degory Whear *Relectiones hyemales, de ratione & methodo legendi utrasque historias, civiles et ecclesiasticas* (2nd ed, Oxford 1637; trans Edmund Bohun, 1685): Whear
and Heylyn are discussed below, in chapter 6.

37 Bacon *Works* IV, 303–4; Nadel 'History as Psychology in Francis Bacon's
Theory of History'; Fussner *Historical Revolution* 150–3, 253–62; Seif-
ert *Cognitio Historica* 116–38; Ferguson 'The Non-Political Past in
Bacon's Theory of History'

38 Reynolds 'Shifting Currents of Historical Criticism' 471–92 still offers
a good description of these works in English; it should now be supplemented by Cotroneo *I trattatisti del 'Ars historica.'*

39 Eg, Lewis Machin and Gervase Markham *The Dumbe Knight* (1608), a
'historicall comedy' which involves fictional personages; or John Ford
The Chronicle Historie of Perkin Warbeck (1634) which concerns real
ones. Shakespeare's 'histories' also provide an excellent example.

40 Samuel Daniel *The Civil Wars* (1595–1609) ed Michel, 1, 6 and introduction. Other examples include Francis Hubert's verse *Historie of Edward
the Second* (1629) and the historical poems of Michael Drayton and
Thomas May.

41 Eg, STC 3528, by 'N.C.': *The Modern History of the World. Or an Historicall Relation since the Beginning of 1635* (part eight of the *Swedish
Intelligencer* 1635)

42 Spufford *Small Books and Pleasant Histories* 219–57; R.S. Crane *The
Vogue of Medieval Chivalric Romance during the English Renaissance*
(Menasha, Wisc. 1919); Paul Salzman *English Prose Fiction 1558–1700:
A Critical History* (Oxford 1985) 186–9, 265–70

43 Aristotle *Poetics* 9.1–3; Cicero *De inventione* 1.19.27–21.30 (trans H.M. Hubbard, Loeb ed, 1960, pp 55–63); Nelson *Fact or Fiction* 5; Robert Scholes and Robert Kellogg *The Nature of Narrative* (Oxford 1966) 57–81, 99–105; Davis *Factual Fictions* 42–70

44 Cicero *De oratore* 2.36 (trans E.W. Sutton, Loeb ed, 1942, p 307), John Marbeck *A Booke of Notes and Common-Places* (1581) 492

45 Brian Melbancke *Philotimus* (1583) sig A2v; Richard White of Basingstoke *Historiarum Britanniae Libri (I-XI) cum notis antiquitatum Britannicarum* (Arras and Douai 1597–1607); John Speed *The History of Great Britaine* (1611). John Caius, however, used the terms *antiquarii* and *historici* indiscriminately to describe the sources for his *De antiquitate Cantabrigiensis academiae libri duo* (1568) and the *Historia Cantabrigiensis academiae ab urbe condita* (1574), but he seems to have been the exception rather than the rule.

46 Thomas Hearne *A Collection of Curious Discourses* (rev ed Joseph Ayloffe, 2 vols, 1771); on the society itself, see Van Norden 'The Elizabethan College of Antiquaries' passim and 'Sir Henry Spelman on the Chronology of the Elizabethan College of Antiquaries' 131–60; McKisack *Medieval History in the Tudor Age* 85–93; Evans *A History of the Society of Antiquaries* 7–13; Levine *Humanism and History* 73–122.

47 *Leland's Itinerary in England* ed Lucy Toulmin Smith (2nd ed, Carbondale, Ill. 1964) I, xlii; IV, 1–35; *Collectanea* ed Thomas Hearne (3 vols in 4 parts; Oxford 1715); Kendrick *British Antiquity* 45–64

48 Sir Philip Sidney *An Apology for Poetry* (1595) ed G. Shepherd (2nd ed, Manchester 1973) 105

49 Sidney's polemic was not entirely sincere, since in a letter to his brother, Robert, he accorded history limited usefulness as a teacher of political action, though not as a teacher of morality: *The Prose Works of Sir Philip Sidney* ed Feuillerat, III, 130–3; Levy 'Sir Philip Sidney and the Idea of History' 608ff.

50 William Lambarde *Archion, or a Comentary upon the High Courts of Justice in England* (1635) 53: the dedication to Sir Robert Cecil is dated 22 October 1591; on Lambarde see Warnicke *William Lambarde* 27–35; Alsop and Stevens 'William Lambarde and the Elizabethan Polity' 246–50; Murphy 'Methods in the Study of Old English' 344–5.

51 Lambarde *A Perambulation of Kent* (2nd ed, 1596) 23. Cf Lambarde's *Dictionarium Angliae topographicum & historicum* (1st ed, 1730). In the dedication to the *Perambulation* Lambarde explains that he called the other work a dictionary and not a history 'because it was digested into titles by order of alphabet, and concerned the description of places.'

52 Lambarde's friend, Sir Thomas Wotton, actually referred to the *Perambulation* as a history in his commendatory letter to the 1596 edition – but only because it did some of the things he thought a history should

do, such as recounting the deeds of the county's great men in 'good words well placed, eloquently.' Ibid, epistle dedicatory; Thomas Wotton 'To his Countriemen, the Gentlemen of Kent' ibid sigs A3r–4v

53 William Camden *Britain* trans Philemon Holland (1610) 340, 363, 369, 371. The corresponding passages in the 1607 Latin edition *Britannia, sive florentissimorum regnorum, Angliae, Scotiae, Hiberniae chorographica descriptio* are at 206, 239, 256, 260–1. Cf Piggott 'William Camden and the *Britannia*' 199–217; Levy 'The Making of Camden's *Britannia*.' For Camden's connection with Sidney and with the 'poetry versus history' debate, see Herendeen 'Wanton Discourse,' 146–8.

54 Nearly half a century after Camden's death, Milton would endorse his firm division of chorography and history from the historian's point of view. Just as he was reluctant to follow his chronicle sources in including lengthy lists of nobles and sheriffs, so Milton confessed that he did not wish to 'wrincle the smoothness of history with rugged names of places unknown, better harp'd at in Camden, and other chorographers': *The History of Britain* (1670) ed Fogle 239–40.

55 Thomas Habington *A Survey of Worcestershire* ed J. Amphlett (2 vols, Oxford 1893–9) I, 184; John Norden *Speculum Britanniae. The First Parte an Historicall Discription of Middlesex* (1593)

56 Ralph Brooke *A Discoverie of Certaine Errours Published in Print in the Much Commended Britannia, 1594* (nd [-1596?]) 'To Maister Camden'; Mark Noble *A History of the College of Arms* (1804) 240–5

57 Camden *Britain* (1610) 145; *Britannia* (1607) 104

58 Camden to de Thou, 10 August 1612: BN Coll Dup MS 632 fol 103r–v (a copy of this is in Bodl MS Smith 74 fols 25–8); De Molen 'The Library of William Camden' passim

59 John Stow *A Survay of London* ed C.L. Kingsford (2 vols, Oxford 1908) I, 3; Claxton to Stow, 10 April 1594, BL MS Harl 374 (D'Ewes papers) fol 21

60 Thomas Martin *Historica descriptio complectens vitam, ac res gestas beatissimi viri Gulielmi Wicami ...* (1597) sig c2r

61 A.D.B. *The Court of the Most Illustrious James, the First* 46; Henry Peacham *The Complete Gentleman* (1622, 1634) ed Virgil B. Heltzel (Ithaca, NY 1962) 62–3, 117–27; Brathwait *The Schollers Medley* 61, 80

62 Coke to Greville, 15 September 1615, printed in N. Farmer, Jr. 'Fulke Greville and Sir John Coke'

63 McKeon *Origins of the English Novel* 25, 39–47

64 Schoeck 'The Elizabethan Society of Antiquaries and Men of Law' 417–21; McKisack *Medieval History in the Tudor Age* 78–82

65 Pocock *Ancient Constitution* 91–123; Ferguson *Clio Unbound* 259–311

66 This is less the fault of Pocock himself, who has made it clear that he uses Coke and Sir John Davies purely as examples of the common-law mind, and who avoids assuming that their views are typical; see especially the 'retrospect' in the *Ancient Constitution* 274ff. Not all subsequent

scholars writing within the Pocockian framework have been so careful: for a particularly simplistic caricature of the Cokean view as a set of 'fantasies,' accompanied by a whiggish assessment of the common-law mind as 'anti-history,' see Rodgers 'Humanism, History and the Common Law.'

67 Sommerville *Politics and Ideology in England* 91 and 'History and Theory: The Norman Conquest in Early Stuart Political Thought'

68 Pawlisch *Sir John Davies and the Conquest of Ireland* 161–75; Christianson 'Young John Selden and the Ancient Constitution'

69 *Modus Tenendi Parliamentum: An Ancient Treatise on the Mode of Holding Parliament in England* ed T.D. Hardy (1846); F.W. Maitland 'Introduction' to *The Mirror of Justices* ed W.J. Whittaker (Selden Society VII, 1895) ix–lv; Pocock *Ancient Constitution* 43. Coke believed that though the *Mirror* in the text he possessed had been composed by one Andrew Horn in the early fourteenth century, 'the most of it was written before the conquest': *La Dix^{me} Part des Reports* (1614) sig d3r.

70 Coke *La Neuf^{me} Part des Reports* (1613) sigs C2r–3v: Coke was unwilling, however, even to concede that the name of parliament was a Norman innovation.

71 Coke *Le Tierce Part des Reportes* sig D2v; Coke *The Second Part of the Institutes of the Lawes of England* (1642) sig A6r; Pocock *Ancient Constitution* 42–5

72 Coke *La Size Part des Reports* (1607) no sig

73 Coke *Le Tierce Part des Reportes* (1602), 'To the Reader,' sig C3r

74 Coke, *La Size Part des Reports* (1607), 'To the Reader,' no sig; *Le Tierce Part* sig D2r

75 Coke *La huict^{me} part des reports* (1611), 'To the Reader,' no sig

76 Ibid, sig C3v. For Sir John Davies' similar statements on behalf of the great antiquity of the law, and the Conqueror's refusal to alter the laws (except for turning them into French), see the dedication to his *Le Primer Report des Cases et Matters en ley Resolves & Adjudges en les Courts del Roy en Ireland* (1615; 2nd ed, 1628).

77 Ibid, sig D1v–2r; *La Huict^{me} Part*, 'To the Reader,' no sig. Coke explained the apparent similarity of English and continental feudal institutions by arguing that William had so admired Anglo-Saxon laws that he had transplanted them to Normandy: the *Customes of Normandie* therefore derived from English law, not vice versa: *Le Tierce Part* sig E1r–v.

78 Coke *Le Second Part des Reports del Edward Coke* (1602), 'To the Learned Reader'

79 Sir Henry Spelman 'The Original, Growth, Propagation and Condition of Feuds and Tenures by Knight-service, in England,' *Reliquiae Spelmanniae: The Posthumous Works of Sir Henry Spelman Kt.* ed Edmund Gibson (Oxford 1698) 2, 6, 10–11, 46; 'Of Parliaments' ibid 63; but compare his statement, in the context of the tithes controversy, that King Edgar 'in a great parliament about the yeare 959' had confirmed the

practice of paying tithes: *The Larger Treatise concerning Tithes* ed J. Stephens (1647) 129–30.

80 See below, chapter 7, pp. 223–4.

81 Coke *The Fift Part of the Reports* (1605) sig A1v

82 Trimble 'Early Tudor Historiography' 30–41; Whibley 'Chroniclers and Historians' 2 remarks that many Tudor histories are 'not so much separate works as variations of the same legend.'

83 This remains true in spite of their devotion to rhetorical skills, since those skills were most often employed for persuasion and illustration rather than critical argument; one cannot help but be reminded of Socrates' objections to the sophists and of a long-standing conflict between philosophy and rhetoric which dates back to the Greek schools. On this relationship as it affected historical consciousness in the earlier Renaissance, see Nancy Struever *The Language of History in the Renaissance: Rhetoric and Historical Consciousness in Florentine Humanism* (Princeton 1970).

84 Ferguson *Clio Unbound* 3–27

85 The major exception to this is King John, who began the sixteenth century as the persecutor of the church and murderer of his nephew, and was then turned into a proto-protestant, anti-papal hero by John Bale's *King Johan* and Foxe's *Acts and Monuments*, two obviously different views. By the time of Shakespeare's *King John* the two opinions had converged somewhat, but there was no consensus as to whether he was a good or bad king. See Campbell *Shakespeare's Histories* 132, 140ff; Carole Levin *Propaganda in the English Reformation: Heroic and Villainous Images of King John* (Lewiston, NY 1988) passim.

86 Tillyard *Shakespeare's History Plays* 59–64

87 *Hist Mss Comm, 4th Report* (1874) col 300; Campbell *Shakespeare's Histories* 191; Charles Aleyn *The Historie of that Wise Prince Henrie the Seventh* (1638) 56

88 William Harbert *A Prophesie of Cadwallader, Last King of the Britaines* (1604); Robert Fletcher *The Nine English Worthies* (1606); Parry *The Golden Age Restor'd* 1–40

89 Patterson *Censorship and Interpretation;* cf Norbrook *Poetry and Politics in the English Renaissance* and Sharpe *Criticism and Compliment.*

90 T. Lake 'Of Sterling Money' (1590) in T. Hearne *A Collection of Curious Discourses* ed J. Ayloffe (1775) I, 10. Camden speaks of (and questions) the 'receaved opinion' that Joseph of Arimathea was the first Christian in England, ibid, II, 165. For a useful definition of opinion, see Hacking *The Emergence of Probability* 18–30.

91 A fact of which one of their number, Arthur Agard, complained. Hearne *Curious Discourses* II, 160 and below, chapter 7, p 201.

92 R. Brooke *A Discoverie of Certaine Errours* (1596); Stow made a collection of materials against faults in Grafton's chronicle, BL MS Harl 367 fols 1–4, 11.

93 Kendrick *British Antiquity* 78–98; Levy *Tudor Historical Thought* 130–3
94 Coke *The Fift Part of the Reports* sig A1v
95 Jewel *An Apology ... of the Church of England* in *Works* ed J. Ayre
(Cambridge, Parker Society 1848) III, 69; Conrad Russell 'Arguments
for Religious Unity in England, 1530–1650' *Journal of Ecclesiastical
History* 18 (1967) 201–26, at 202, 225; Isaiah Berlin 'The Divorce
between the Sciences and the Humanities' in *Against the Current* ed
Henry Hardy (Oxford 1981) 87
96 Edmund Campion in James Ware ed *Two Histories of Ireland* (1633) 21
97 Camden to Lipsius, 18 August 1604, *Camdeni Epistolae* 64
98 Sidney *Apology for Poetry* ed Shepherd 103–10; Nauert *Agrippa and the
Crisis of Renaissance Thought* 299, 326; Agrippa's *Of the Vanitie and
Uncertaintie of Artes and Sciences* was translated by James Sandford in
1569; Levy 'Sir Philip Sidney and the Idea of History'; A.C. Hamilton
'Sidney and Agrippa', *Review of English Studies* new ser 7 (1956) 151–7
99 Fulke Greville *A Treatise of Humane Learning* stanza 142, in *Works* II,
59
100 Robert Chester *The Anuals of Great Brittaine* (1611) 34; Richard Brathwait *A Survey of History* (1638) 241; cf the earlier version of the *Survey*
in Brathwait's *Schollers Medley* 28, 104. Brathwait's examples are all
classical, not contemporary.
101 Yates 'Paolo Sarpi's "History of the Council of Trent" '; Wootton *Paolo
Sarpi* 104–17
102 François Hotman *Francogallia* (1573) ed R.E. Giesey and trans J.H.M.
Salmon (Cambridge 1972) 371
103 *Table Talk of John Selden* ed F. Pollock (1927) 80
104 Sleidan's *De quatuor summis imperiis* was translated into English by S.
Wythers in 1563.
105 Hay *Annalists and Historians* 122–5; Cochrane *Historians and Historiography in the Italian Renaissance* 458–63
106 Barnes *Vitae Romanorum pontificum* (Basel 1535); C. Hill *Antichrist in
Seventeenth-Century England* (1971) 9; R. Pineas 'Robert Barnes's
Polemical Use of History' *Bibliothèque d'Humanisme et Renaissance*
26 (1964) 55–69
107 Hill *Antichrist* 13–14; Firth *Apocalyptic Tradition* 81–6
108 Jewel *Apology* in *Works* III, 69; Christianson *Reformers and Babylon*
32–3; Ferguson *Clio Unbound* 182–94. For a useful study of one Elizabethan's formulation of a 'protestant vision' of the past, see G.J.R. Parry
*A Protestant Vision: William Harrison and the Reformation of Elizabethan
England* (Cambridge 1987).
109 Camden *Historie of ... Princesse Elizabeth* trans Robert Norton (1630),
Preface, sig B2v
110 *DNB* sv 'Camden, William'; Thomas Fuller *The Church-History of Britain* (1655) Book x, pp 50–3; according to Fuller (51) the two historiographers were 'learnedly to record, and publish to posterity all memorable

passages in Church, and Commonwealth.' Their function, in short, was less to promote an interpretation of the ecclesiastical past (already accepted within the church) than to describe events of the present for the benefit of future readers. They might have just as accurately been called 'chroniclers.'

111 On some of the uses of arguments from sacred history by Catholics and puritans to challenge orthodox positions, see Cragg *Freedom and Authority* 193–218, 281–90.

112 N. Sanders *Rise and Growth of the Anglican Schism* (1585) trans David Lewis (1877) 25, 237; *DNB* sv 'Sanders, Nicholas.' It is precisely this bluntly polemical note which reveals that works like Sanders' are much closer to the scurrilous Suetonian-style 'court histories' of mid-seventeenth-century writers such as Sir Anthony Weldon than they are to the equally political, but uncontroversial, histories of the early seventeenth century.

113 Robert Parsons *An Answere to the Fifth Part of Reportes Lately Set Forth by Syr Edward Cooke* (St Omer 1606), Epistle Dedicatory

114 Ibid 143

115 Ibid 165

116 Ibid 341, 374; Parsons never mentions such inconvenient examples as the execution by Henry IV of Archbishop Scrope.

117 R. Doleman (alias Parsons) *A Conference about the Next Succession to the Crowne of Ingland* (Antwerp 1594)

118 Ibid Part One, p 56; Part Two, pp 57, 67

119 Most notably in John Hayward *An Answer to the First Part of a Certaine Conference* (1603), for which see below, p 110

120 *DNB* sv 'White, Richard'; Fuller *Worthies* I, 413

121 *Richardi Viti Basinstochii ad leges decem virorum* (Antwerp 1597); Richard White *Historiarum Britanniae libri (I-XI) ... cum notis antiquitatum Britannicarum* (Arras and Douai 1597–1607). For Selden's use of White see below, chapter 7: Fuller in *Worthies* I, 413 notes that White was 'often cited by Mr Selden, which makes me believe much merit therein.'

122 Baronius to White, 2 July 1600, printed in White *Historiarum libri* IX, 172

123 Eg, ibid VIII, 17

124 White *Historiarum libri* III, 382–3; Bede *Ecclesiastical History* 1.4 (ed V.D. Scudder, 1910, p 9); Foxe *Acts and Monuments* ed Josiah Pratt (1877) I, 308–10; Jewel *Reply to Mr. Harding's Answer* in *Works* I (1845) 306. George Saltern *Of the Antient Lawes of Great Britaine* (1605) sig H3r. The legend of Lucius was not exposed until the nineteenth century; Kendrick *British Antiquity* 113.

125 Lambarde printed it in *Archaionomia* (1568) fol 131

126 White *Historiarum libri* v, 401

127 Book VIII, for example, is completely Arthurian, culling material of such wide-ranging reliability as Geoffrey, his medieval critic William of New-

burgh, Polydore, and Camden's *Britannia*. White did try to round off a few of Arthur's sharper edges by rejecting – on religious rather than historical grounds – elements such as the prophecies of Merlin, 'rightly prohibited by the recent Council of Trent,' and Arthur's supposed future return: ibid VII, 76 (*nota* 21); VIII, 58–60.

128 Ayloffe, editing Hearne, *Curious Discourses* II, 424, disputes this suggestion by Hearne, but Broughton cites a manuscript by John Leland in his *An Ecclesiastical Protestant Historie* (St Omer 1624) 105, which he can only have had from Camden or another of Cotton's associates, a number of whom he refers to by name frequently.

129 Wood *Fasti Oxonienses* I, 428–9

130 R. Parsons *A Treatise of Three Conversions of England* (3 vols, St Omer 1603–4) I, 8, 160; Broughton *An Ecclesiastical Protestant Historie* 8

131 Broughton *An Ecclesiastical Protestant Historie* 29, 64–8

132 Ibid 109, 117

133 Broughton *The Ecclesiasticall Historie of Great Britaine, Deduced by Ages* (Douai 1633)

134 Broughton *Ecclesiasticall Historie* 252, 295–304, 386–406 passim

Chapter Two

1 Sir Walter Ralegh *The History of the World* Part One (1614). All references to the *History* will be to this edition and given in parentheses in the text by book, chapter, section, and page (eg, IV.i.1: 158), and by signature to the preface. The *History* is divided into five books, of which books I and II are consecutively paginated from 1 to 651, and books III, IV, and V from 1 to 776. References to Ralegh's other writings will be to his *Works* ed William Oldys (8 vols, Oxford 1829).

2 In the eighteenth century William Oldys compiled a list of writers cited in the *History*: *Works* I, following p ccl (no page no); even more useful is Oakeshott 'Sir Walter Ralegh's Library,' which includes works of Vignier (no 287), Scaliger (no 402), Jean de Serres (no 82) and three by La Popelinière (nos 70, 91, 510). Of the plethora of studies of Ralegh or his *History*, the following have proven especially useful: Firth, 'Sir Walter Raleigh's History of the World'; Strathmann *Sir Walter Ralegh: A Study in Elizabethan Skepticism* 219–53; Hardy 'The Idea of Providence in Sir Walter Ralegh's *History of the World*'; Greenblatt *Sir Walter Ralegh* 127–54. Christopher Hill *Intellectual Origins* chapter IV offers a fascinating if contentious account of the intellectual environment within which Ralegh wrote his book.

3 Ralegh devotes a section of Book III to the connection between sacred and profane history, especially where the two conflict as to the date of an event. *History* III.i.1: 1–2

4 Firth *Apocalyptic Tradition* 180–91

5 Ralegh *The Sceptic*, in *Works* VIII, 548–56

6 Compare the discussion in Bodin *Method* trans Reynolds 85. Bodin does not appear in the *History* or in Oakeshott's Library List, but Ralegh would undoubtedly have been familiar with the *Methodus* and *République*, at least via their critics, such as La Popelinière.

7 Ralegh cites approvingly the 'goodlie pollicie' of Machiavelli in *History* v.ii.3:380; v.vi.1:711; but contradicts Machiavelli on the importance of rulers taking counsel in *Maxims of State*, in *Works* VIII, 16, no 15. Like Machiavelli, Ralegh confines his discussion in *Maxims* and *History* to the six Aristotelian states.

8 Oakeshott 'Ralegh's Library' no 294; Firth *Apocalyptic Tradition* 183

9 Compare Bodin *Method* 291–302.

10 Compare Boethius *Consolation* 5.6.60–80 (trans Tester, 427).

11 The seventeenth-century owner of the Bodleian Library copy of the *History* (shelfmark K.3.6.Art) wrote, at p 20, 'Note nothing doon by chance or fortune but by God himself.'

12 On the pseudo-Berosus see Kendrick *British Antiquity* 71–2.

13 Greenblatt *Sir Walter Ralegh* 140

14 Philinus was the Carthaginian author of a lost history used by Polybius *History* 1.13–64

15 Ralegh is 'overkilling' the Tudors here. On Ralegh's own terms, Henry VII's Machiavellianism had *already* merited the Tudors' eventual extinction before Henry VIII was born.

16 On Ralegh's self-fashioning, see Greenblatt *Sir Walter Ralegh* passim.

17 Ralegh *Maxims of State* in *Works* VIII, 1–36; *The Cabinet-Council* in *Works* VIII, 37ff.; Nadja Kempner *Raleghs staatstheoretische Schriften: Die Einführung des Machiavellismus in England* (Leipzig 1928) 43–136

18 Firth 'Raleigh's *History of the World*' 442 advances the interesting if unprovable theory that Ralegh's name was excised because he was 'civilly dead' as a convicted traitor. On the 'king/tyrant' distinction and its use in Elizabethan literature see W.A. Armstrong 'The Elizabethan Conception of the Tyrant' *Review of English Studies* 22 (1946) 161–81.

19 Another factor may well be its relative compactness, compared with the bulky Speed and Holinshed who were, however, covering a different part of history. As late as 1655, Ralegh was still popular with undergraduates: he is the only non-classical historian in the book list of one John Legg of Cambridge (Inner Temple Library, Barrington MS 84, fols 3–7).

20 Bacon *Letters and Life* III, 249–52

21 Ibid; Bacon *A Brief Discourse Touching the Happy Union of the Kingdoms of England and Scotland* (1603?) in *Letters and Life* III, 90–9. Bacon was also one of the commissioners appointed to negotiate the union.

22 Levack 'Toward a More Perfect Union' 70; Levack *The Formation of the British State* 1–30; Galloway *The Union of England and Scotland*; Willson 'King James I and Anglo-Scottish Unity'

23 J. Thornborough *A Discourse Plainely Proving the Evident Utilitie and Urgent Necessitie of the Desired Happie Union of the Two Famous*

Kingdomes of England and Scotland (1604) 28–33; Henry Savile 'Historicall Collections' in *The Jacobean Union: Six Tracts of 1604* ed Bruce
R. Galloway and Brian P. Levack (Edinburgh 1985) 185–239; J. Dodderidge 'A Breif Consideracion of the Unyon' in ibid 143–60; Henry Spelman 'Of the Union' in ibid 161–84; John Hayward *A Treatise of Union
of the Two Realmes of England and Scotland* (1604) 55; William
Cornwallis *The Miraculous and Happie Union of England and Scotland*
(1604) sig E1r; Levack *Formation of the British State* 31–67

24 *Gray's Inn Admission Register, 1521–1889* (1889) 103; *Hist Mss Comm,
Salisbury* VIII (1899) 103, 255, 296, 328; *Hist Mss Comm, Salisbury*
XVIII (1940) 44; T.D. Hardy *Catalogue of Lords Chancellors* (1843) 109;
PRO *Lists and Indexes* no 31 (1909), Inquisitions post mortem, 76

25 Friedländer 'Growth in the Resources for Studies in Earlier English History' 143; W.D. Macray *Annals of the Bodleian Library* (2nd ed, 1890)
28; for the best biography see the introduction to J. Clapham *Elizabeth
of England* ed E.P. and C. Read (Philadelphia 1951) 4–11; *Hist Mss
Comm, Salisbury* XVII (1938) 359.

26 J. Clapham (trans) *A Philosophical Treatise concerning the Quietness
of the Mind* (1590); *Narcissus* (1591); *The Historie of England* (1602);
The Historie of Great Britannie (1606). This second edition adds a short
preface at sig A3r and omits the longer preface in the first edition.

27 *Historie of England* preface, sigs A3r–B2r; *Historie of Great Britannie*
199, 302

28 Clapham *Verses Gratulatory upon the King's Majesty's Entrance* in 2nd
draft MS of *Certain Observations*, printed in *Elizabeth of England*
118–19; ibid 105; *Historie* (1606) 4. All further references will be to the
1606 edition of the *Historie* and will be given in the text.

29 The DNB entry, sv 'Ayscu, Edward,' is to be disregarded, for it confuses
two, possibly three Ayscoughs. There were many in Lincolnshire at
this time, including one who corresponded with Sir Robert Cotton in
1627 (BL MS Cott Julius C.III, fol 9); this man is referred to as a knight
in another letter to Cotton from William Bedell (ibid, fol 16) and can be
ruled out: he was the sheriff of Lincoln in 1632. The historian was the
Edward Ayscu (1550–1616) of Cotham, Lincolnshire, whose grandson,
Sir George, would rise to become an admiral during the Interregnum.
Information on the historian and his several namesakes may be found
in Venn *Alum Cant;* A.R. Maddison *Lincolnshire Pedigrees* (1902) I,
61ff; PCC *Wills* (Index Library vol XLIII) 24; *Cal SP Dom, 1627–28* 81;
Hist Mss Comm, Cowper II (1888–9) 70. For further details, see my
unpublished DPhil thesis, 'Change and Continuity in English Historical
Thought, c. 1590–1640' (Oxford 1983) 331–3.

30 Ayscu *Historie* 'To the Reader' sig A7v, dated 24 March 1606/7 at
Cotham. Further references will be given in the text.

31 *Chronica magistri Rogeri de Houedene* ed W. Stubbs, Rolls Series, li
(1869) ii.80–2

32 James I had himself spoken of Henry's union of the two houses and of

his descent from Henry in providential terms in his first speech to the
parliament of 1604 and in the proclamation of his new style: *Political
Works of James I* ed McIlwain, 271–3; T. Rymer and R. Sanderson
Foedera (1727–35) XVI, 526, 603.

33 S.T. Bindoff 'The Stuarts and Their Style' *English Historical Review* 60
(1945) 192–216

34 Per Palme *The Triumph of Peace* (Stockholm 1956) plates IV, V; Patrick
Hannay *Two Elegies on the Death of Queen Anne* (1619) sig C2r

35 BL MS Royal 17B.VI, fol 1; George Saltern *Of the Antient Lawes of Great
Britaine* (1605). Saltern is even more obscure than Clapham. The son
of William Salterne of Bristol, he was admitted to the Middle Temple 15
July 1584 and called to the bar 20 November 1590. His contemporaries
at the Temple would have included William Martyn and George Buck.
J. Hutchinson *A Catalogue of Notable Middle Templars* (1902) 214;
Middle Temple Admission Register (1949) I, 53. Edmund Howes
acknowledged Saltern's help in revising John Stow's *Annales* (1615)
1087. A George Salter or Saltern of Bristol who had commercial dealings
turns up contemporaneously in *Hist Mss Comm, Salisbury* x (1904) 215;
Merchants and Merchandise in Seventeenth-Century Bristol ed P.
McGrath (Bristol Record Society Publications, vol XIX, 1955) 120–1;
City Chamberlain's Accounts in the Sixteenth and Seventeenth Centuries ed D.M. Livock (Bristol Record Society Publications, vol XXIV,
1966) 81. In 1631 a George Saltern was steward of the court at Bristol:
Cal SP Dom, 1631–3, 192.

36 Levack 'The Proposed Union of English Law and Scots Law in the
Seventeenth Century' 97–115 and *Formation of the British State*
68–101

37 Saltern *Antient Lawes* sig L4r even goes so far as to suggest that every
calamity to hit Britain since Lucius resulted from temporary deviations
from his laws, which constituted a convenant with God.

38 John Lewis *The History of Great-Britain* ed [Hugh Thomas] (1729); BL
MS Royal 18.A.XXXVII, fols 1–20 (proposals for a history of Britain).
Since 1729 the MS has disappeared, a copy of the first part (to Brutus)
surviving as MS Harl 4872, fols 242–341. The work cites Camden's
Remaines (1605) and refers to Prince Henry as prince of Great Britain,
not Wales, the title he acquired in 1610; but in Harl 4872, fol 247v,
Lewis lists Samuel Daniel's history, the first part of which appeared in
1612, suggesting that he spent several years writing the work.

39 Lewis *History* I, 39 (where he claims to know Camden personally); II, 3,
14; V, 158; VI, 179–96

40 *Alum Ox* 696; DNB sv 'Herbert, William'; Harbert *A Prophesie of Cadwallader, Last King of the Britaines* (1604) sig A3r, H1v. Harbert was not
the only poet inspired by the union: in 1605 the prolific tailor-chronicler
Anthony Munday (or Mundy) wrote and staged a pageant entitled *The
Triumphes of Reunited Britania.*

41 Farmer 'Fulke Greville and Sir John Coke' 217–36

42 Lewis *History* III, 57, 77; Harry *Genealogy* (1604) 39-40; a manuscript of this is BL MS Add 6928, fols 29-68

43 Colman to Burghley, 2 January 1587 and 12 October 1588, BL MS Lans XCIX (Burghley letters) fols 139, 141; BL MS Add 38139 (Manwood papers) fol 218v shows Colman living at York House in 1592; Wood *Ath Ox* II, 198.

44 Bodl MS Rawl D.506 (Egerton accounts) fols 1-55; genealogies and heraldic MSS by Colman are BL MS Stowe 75, fol 22, and Bodl MS Lat Misc a.1, executed respectively in 1592 and 1604: the first version was included in a single sheet digest of Camden in 1592, *Angliae et Hiberniae nova descriptio ad G. Camdeni Britanniam accomodata*; in revised form, it became Colman's *Genealogies of King James I and Queen Anne, His Wife, from the Conquest* (1608).

45 Lewis *History* III, 23. Lewis also entitled the first chapter of Book I 'Of the Uncertainty of Antiquity.'

46 As critical and self-assured a scholar as John Selden, writing notes to his friend Michael Drayton's *Poly-Olbion* in 1612, refused absolutely to commit himself in print, though 'disclaiming in it, if alleg'd for my own opinion.' Whether Drayton himself believed in the literal (as opposed to the poetic) truth of all he wrote is quite doubtful: Drayton *Works* IV, viii*; I. Gourvitch 'Drayton's Debt to Geoffrey of Monmouth' *Review of English Studies* 4 (1928) 394-403.

47 Henry Savile, ed, *Rerum anglicarum scriptores post Bedam* (1596), epistle dedicatory; Edmund Bolton *Hypercritica* in *Critical Essays of the Seventeenth Century* ed Joel Spingarn (Oxford 1907) I, 96, and chapter 6 below

48 Bacon *De augmentis scientiarum* in *Works* IV, 301. John Speed and John Barkham, for instance, reject the monastic view of King John as a murderous tyrant but are forced to rely on such chroniclers as the staple of the *History of Great Britaine* (1611) 483-507; for a fuller account of the decline of the chronicle and a theory of its eclipse by other historical genres, see Woolf 'Genre into Artifact.'

49 *Cal SP Dom, 1598-1601* 62; *Theatre of the Empire of Great Britaine* Warwickshire, 53; *DNB* sv 'Speed, John.' The number of tailors practising history is worth further discussion; one thinks also of Anthony Munday, author of *A Briefe Chronicle of the Successe of Times from the Creation* (1611).

50 Speed *The History of Great Britaine* (1611) sig 6P2r; further references will be given in the text.

51 This statement of acknowledgments by Speed is incomplete and must be supplemented by Speed's marginal notes and Bolton's later remarks in *Hypercritica* 98; Speed to Cotton, nd (1610?) *Original Letters of Eminent Literary Men* 108-9.

52 Bolton *Hypercritica* 98

53 Fuller *Worthies* I, 306; Philip King *The Surfeit to A.B.C.* (1656) 21-2; Bolton *Hypercritica* 98

54 Bolton *Hypercritica* 98; *History* 660: 'the copy whereof I had from the

learned Mr. John Clapham'; ibid 733; *Theatre* Norfolk, 35. In *History*, sig 6P3r, Speed credits Smith but not Carew; Speed asked Cotton for help with the life of Henry v (written by Carew, according to Bolton, who may have been mistaken) in a letter to Cotton, nd *Original Letters of Eminent Literary Men* 113

55 Speed comments that Gildas was not a 'perfect historian', *History* 321, using the phrase in the sense given it by Bacon in the *Advancement of Learning*, published a few years earlier. Camden, without considering the problem, casually referred to 'Speedes Chronicle' in a draft list of books: Trinity College, Cambridge, MS R.5.20, fol 115v. Though Speed has no specific classical model, he was clearly familiar enough with classical histories and follows the structure of Polydore much more than that of Holinshed or Stow. The conscious use of Roman type instead of the black letter common to chroniclers may also have been a deliberate attempt both to set his book apart from similar works, such as Stow's *Annales*, and to appeal to a more refined audience rapidly growing accustomed to that form of print: on the social differences between black letter and Roman type in this period as they relate to literacy, see Keith Thomas 'The Meaning of Literacy in Early Modern England' in *The Written Word: Literacy in Transition* ed Gerd Baumann (Oxford 1986) 97–131.

56 Speed to Cotton, nd *Original Letters of Eminent Literary Men* 108–9, 111–13

57 Cf *History* 179, where Speed draws an analogy between the nakedness of the Britons and that of 'the wilder Irish, and Virgineans.' For the influence of New World exploration on historical thought, particularly concerning the Britons, see Piggott *Ancient Britons and the Antiquarian Imagination* 54–86.

58 This passage seems directly inspired by Clapham *Historie* (1606) 4, 22.

59 Speed may have derived this model of ancient government from a contemporary example such as the Holy Roman Empire.

60 Cf Bodin *Method* 336.

61 BL MS Add 57336, fols 26v, 55r. These notes are incorporated in *History* 714, 717.

62 MS Add 57336, fol 61

63 *Cal SP Dom, 1603–10* 639; BL MS Add Egerton 2255. Montagu was bishop from 1616 till his death in 1618, confining the date of the MS to these years.

64 Eg, *History* 421, 557, where he ascribes the defeat of Edward II at Bannockburn to 'Gods anger against the English.' Speed reports natural phenomena such as earthquakes, 'prophesies and prodigies' without necessarily accepting them, eg, ibid 432, 616, 725.

65 'The Florentine secretary was scarse born at this time [1460], but the divell was as great a master then as afterward'; cf 614 for an explicit rejection of 'reason of state.'

66 Speed compares Elizabeth with Deborah, for instance, ibid 831, and likens Lanfranc to Rehoboam's sage in 1 Kings 12.6, at 418.

67 The allusion to Camden extricates Speed from a detailed discussion of Mary Stuart's troubles.

68 BL MS Titus B.I. fols 6–53 (Cotton's notes from Guicciardini on the reign of Henry VIII); Sharpe *Sir Robert Cotton* 240; Speed does use the word 'politicke' to describe Henry IV, but also has him offer his son advice 'prudently and Christianly,' *History* 621.

69 D. MacLeane *Oxford College Histories: Pembroke College* (1900) 34; *Hist Mss Comm, Exeter* (1916) 55, 132. The DNB date of Martyn's recordership, 1605, is based on an error in Wood *Ath Ox* II, 199; Fuller *Worthies* I, 306; J. Hutchinson *Catalogue of Notable Middle Templars* 159; *Middle Temple Admission Register* I, 53; Wallace MacCaffrey *Exeter, 1540–1640* (2nd ed, Cambridge, Mass. 1975) 255, 262–3.

70 William Martyn *Youths Instruction* (1612, rpt. 1613)

71 Martyn *The Historie, and Lives, of the Kings of England* (1615; 2nd ed with continuation, 1638). All references will be to the expanded edition of 1638 and will be given in the text.

72 Cf Holinshed *Chronicles* III, 735; Speed had addressed questions to his characters, eg Henry IV in *History* 614, though not with such moral fervour.

73 Ralegh skips lightly over Edward's reign, *History of the World* (1614) Preface, sig A3v. Of other portraits of Edward II, compare Drayton *The Barons Warres* in *Works* II, canto v, verses 62–9, and Sir Francis Hubert's *The Deplorable Life and Death of Edward the Second* (1628, revised ed 1629). Hubert rewrote the pirated 1628 version of his poem in 1629, and is more sympathetic to Edward than Martyn. The Hubert poem was widely circulated in manuscript copies such as the present BL MSS Add 28021 and 34316. I exclude here the extremely damning portrait by 'E.F.' *The Historie of the Life and Raigne of King Edward II* (1680) usually thought to be taken from a manuscript written in 1627 by Henry Cary, first Viscount Falkland. This is almost certainly a bogus work contrived by polemicists in the Exclusion Crisis of 1680. For the case against this work, see my 'The True Date and Authorship of Henry, Viscount Falkland's *History of the Life, Reign and Death of King Edward II' Bodleian Library Record* 12 (1988) 440–52. While the evidence is not without ambiguities, I am unpersuaded by the response of Isobel Grundy (*Bodleian Library Record* 13 [1989] 82–3) who asserts this work to be a legitimate Caroline product, composed by Falkland's estranged wife, Elizabeth Cary.

74 Ayscu *Historie* 247–8, 289; J. Ford *Perkin Warbeck* 4.3 in *Elizabethan History Plays* ed W.A. Armstrong (1965). Interestingly, Martyn has nothing to say about the union – probably not because he rejected it, but because there is no connecting theme in his work.

75 Fuller *Worthies* I, 306; Wood *Ath Ox* II, 199; *Acts of the Privy Council*

in the Reign of James I, II [1615–16] (1925) 62, 67, 73, 100. Martyn was ordered to acknowledge his fault in writing and allowed to go free. A bond he had issued as surety for his appearance was returned to him.

76 Arber IV, 393. A comparison of texts indicates that B.R. largely plagiarized the Robert Norton translation of Camden's *Historie* (1630) and Morgan Godwin's 1630 translation of his father Francis' *Annales*.

Chapter Three

1 Jonson *Sejanus His Fall,* in *Ben Jonson* ed C.H. Herford and P. and E. Simpson (11 vols, Oxford 1925–52) IV, 350, 473–85; Drayton *Poly-Olbion* in *Works* IV. For evidence that the debate between poetry and history was not always adversarial, see Herendeen 'Wanton Discourse' 144–8.

2 William Slatyer *The History of Great Britanie [Palae-Albion]* (1621) Preface, no sig; Kendrick *British Antiquity* 74–5; Bodl MS Smith 17 (Camden's commonplace book) fol 75v

3 'To Henry Reynolds' line 126, in *Works* III, 229. Jonson, Conversation with Drummond of Hawthornden, in *Ben Jonson* I, 132, 138

4 For general studies of Daniel's career and thought, see the works by Joan Rees, C.C. Seronsy, and Pierre Spriet listed in the bibliography. Useful accounts of the historical works may be found in the following articles: McKisack 'Samuel Daniel as Historian'; Blissett 'Samuel Daniel's Sense of the Past'; Godschalk 'Daniel's *History*'; Gottfried 'Samuel Daniel's Method of Writing History'; Levy 'Hayward, Daniel, and the Beginnings of Politic History in England.'

5 Ferguson 'Historical Thought of Samuel Daniel' and *Clio Unbound* 64–8, 340–3; Hulse 'Samuel Daniel: The Poet as Literary Historian' and *Metamorphic Verse* 195–220

6 Throughout this chapter references to Daniel's works will be as follows: *Musophilus,* 'To Sir Thomas Egerton,' 'To the Reader,' *Delia, The Complaint of Rosamond,* and *A Defence of Ryme* are all from *Poems and a Defence of Ryme* (= *Poems*) ed Arthur Colby Sprague (3rd ed, Chicago 1965); 'To Prince Henrie' from John Pitcher *Samuel Daniel: The Brotherton Manuscript. A Study in Authorship* (Leeds 1981); *The Civil Wars* in the edition of Laurence Michel (New Haven 1958); all other poems and plays from *Complete Works in Verse and Prose of Samuel Daniel* ed Alexander B. Grosart (5 vols, 1885–96). Reference to the prose history is in general to *The Collection of the History of England* (= *Coll*) (1618), or to the earlier *The First Part of the Historie of England* (= *First Part*) (limited edition, 1612; 1st full ed, 1613).

7 I owe this point to Professor James Keller of the University of Manitoba.

8 On the idea of Nemesis, see Robert B. Pierce *Shakespeare's History Plays: The Individual and the State* (Columbus, Ohio 1971) chapter 3; T.F. Driver *The Sense of History in Greek and Shakespearean Drama* (New

York, 1960). Nemesis was defined by Archbishop Whitgift as 'a disdain for the prosperity or felicity of some man, which he is unworthy of'; Whitgift *Works* ed John Ayre (3 vols, London 1851–3) I, 167–8. Something of this sense carries over into Daniel's usage of the Greek goddess.

9 G.R. Elton *The Tudor Constitution: Documents and Commentary* (2nd ed, Cambridge 1982) 353–8

10 Sommerville *Politics and Ideology in England* 86–95

11 Sir John Davies *Le Primer Report des Cases ... en les Courts del Roy en Ireland* (1615; 2nd ed, 1628), dedication

12 On Ellesmere and his relationship with Daniel, see Knafla *Law and Politics in Jacobean England* 41, 58, 62, 128, 152, 164–7; Pitcher 'Samuel Daniel's Letter to Sir Thomas Egerton' 55–61.

13 Ellesmere *The Speech of the Lord Chancellor of England, in the Exchequer Chamber, Touching the Post-Nati* (1608), reprinted in Knafla *Law and Politics in Jacobean England* 247

14 Loys (or Louis) Le Roy *Of the Interchangeable Course, or Variety of Things in the Whole World* trans R. Ashley (1594), fol 125 and passim; Seronsy 'The Doctrine of Cyclical Recurrence and Related Ideas in the Works of Samuel Daniel' 387–407; Hulse 'Samuel Daniel' 58ff

15 Eccles 'Samuel Daniel in France and Italy' 148ff. The influence may be direct, or indirect, via other thinkers – for example, Ellesmere, who does cite Bodin explicitly (Knafla *Law and Politics in Jacobean England* 49, 69, 72, 74–5) – or more likely both. Bodin's *Methodus* was known in England by the 1570s; the Elizabethan antiquary William Fleetwood cited it as early as 1575, four years before Bodin's visit to England: J.D. Alsop 'William Fleetwood and Elizabethan Historical Scholarship' (unpublished paper) 13. I am indebted to Jim Alsop for allowing me to read and cite this illuminating essay.

16 Compare this passage with Bodin *République* (1576), trans Richard Knolles as *Six Bookes of a Commonweale* (1606) VI, ii, 652–3; cf *Coll*, 50, 96, 111.

17 Bodin *Method* 86, 142, 302; Tooley 'Bodin and the Medieval Theory of Climate'

18 Skinner *Foundations of Modern Political Thought* II, 355–8

19 On microcosm and macrocosm in seventeenth-century thought, see James Daly 'Cosmic Harmony and Political Thinking in Early Stuart England' *Transactions of the American Philosophical Society* 69, part 7 (1979) 1–10; Don Parry Norford 'Microcosm and Macrocosm in Seventeenth-Century Literature' *Journal of the History of Ideas* 38 (1977) 409–28.

20 Compare BL MS Royal 18 A.LXXII with *A Panegyrike Congratulatory* stanza 2 (*Complete Works* I, 143).

21 Brents Stirling 'Daniel's *Philotas* and the Essex Case' *Modern Language Quarterly* 3 (1942) 583–94; G. Wilkes 'Daniel's *Philotas* and the Essex Case: A Reconsideration' *Modern Language Quarterly* 23 (1962)

233–42; most recently, see Levy 'Hayward, Daniel, and the Beginnings of Politic History' 21–3.

22 Daniel left unpublished what appears to be a short summary of his projected history, the tract contained in Bodl MS Tanner 84 and known as *An Introduction to a Breviary of the History of England*; this was first published in 1693 and has been ascribed, wrongly in the view of most modern scholars, to Ralegh: see Gottfried 'Authorship of *A Breviary of the History of England*' 172–90.

23 It is likely that one of his intended readers was Prince Henry, to whom the printed edition of *Philotas* had been dedicated in 1607, and who patronized both Sir Robert Cotton and Sir John Hayward. Daniel's *First Part* was also clearly directed at Salisbury, to whom it was initially dedicated; on Salisbury's death (May 1612), the royal favourite Robert Carr, later earl of Somerset, stepped into the breach as the work's new patron without Daniel having actually sought his support: see Pitcher *Samuel Daniel: The Brotherton Manuscript* 28, 70, 173–7.

24 'To My Deare Brother and Friend M. John Florio, One of the Gentlemen of Hir Majesties Most Royall Privie Chamber' (2nd ed, 1613) in *Complete Works* I, 285, lines 1–4. Compare the slightly different version of this in the 1603 edition of Florio's translation (ibid I, 290–3).

25 Montaigne 'Of Conscience' *Complete Essays of Montaigne* trans Donald M. Frame (3rd ed, Stanford, Cal. 1965) 2.5, 266; R. Himelick 'Montaigne and Daniel's To Sir Thomas Egerton' *Philological Quarterly* 36 (1957) 500–4; J.I.M. Stewart 'Montaigne's *Essays* and a *Defence of Ryme*' *Review of English Studies* 9 (1933) 311–12; Anthony LaBranche 'Samuel Daniel: A Voice of Thoughtfulness' in *The Rhetoric of Renaissance Poetry from Wyatt to Milton* ed Thomas O. Sloan and Raymond B. Waddington (Berkeley, Los Angeles, and London 1974) 123–39

26 What appears to be a large section of this appendix exists in a manuscript in the National Library of Scotland, Edinburgh, MS 5736, fols 22–80, the 'Kerr manuscript' recently unearthed by Pitcher *Samuel Daniel: The Brotherton Manuscript* Appendix D, 178–89. It shows that Daniel made direct reference to original sources – chronicles and charters available in Sir Robert Cotton's library and through friends such as Camden – rather than relying principally on a recent history such as Speed's or on Tudor chronicles.

27 Montaigne 'Of Experience' *Essays* 3.13, 819

28 Montaigne *Essays* 2.10, 438

29 Du Haillan, historiographer royal to Henri III, is among the historians listed by Daniel in his prefatory 'Certaine Advertisements to the Reader' *Collection* sigs A3r–4. His *L'Histoire de France* (Paris 1577) presents an interpretation of French history which closely resembles Daniel's of English; the debt is especially clear in Daniel's description of the 'election' of William I after Hastings (*First Part* 96–7, 102–3), which almost

certainly derives from du Haillan, 352. On du Haillan, see P.M. Bondois 'Henry III et l'historiographe du Haillan' *Revue d'histoire littéraire de la France* 30 (1930) 507–9; Kelley *Foundations of Modern Historical Scholarship* 233–7; Salmon 'Bodin and the Monarchomachs' in *Jean Bodin* ed Denzer 359–78; Ranum *Artisans of Glory* 96–102.

30 Knafla *Law and Politics in Jacobean England* 228

31 Daniel's concept of sovereignty might be described as a moderate Bodinian one: he speaks of the restriction of kings 'within those bounds wherein by the law of the state they are placed' (*Coll*, 138), but regards kings as sovereign nonetheless; indeed, he goes so far as to criticize Henry II for erecting a 'devided soveraignty' by crowning his son as joint king in his own lifetime – a point made by Bodin (*Six Bookes* II, iii, 209) with precisely the same example (though Bodin confuses Henries I and II).

32 Among the antiquaries with whom Daniel was acquainted were William Camden and Sir Robert Cotton (see above, note 26): *First Part* 240; Rees *Samuel Daniel* 133, 147, 152, 155. Not all contemporary antiquaries, as we have seen, agreed with this assessment, including John Selden, for whom see below, chapter 7. Sommerville 'History and Theory: The Norman Conquest in Early Stuart Political Thought' provides a good recent survey of contemporary attitudes to the Conquest.

33 Knafla *Law and Politics in Jacobean England* introduction, 70, and *Postnati* 217

34 Of Fergus James had written that 'a wise king comming in among barbares, first established the estate and forme of government and thereafter made lawes by himselfe, and his successours according thereto': *The Trew Law of Free Monarchies* in *Political Works of James I* ed McIlwain 61–2. The *Collection*, by removing extreme antiquity as a requirement for the limitation of kings by national law, is able to admit as one of the consequences of the Norman Conquest strong monarchical power; it thereby goes some way towards bridging the gap between royalist and common law interpretations of the ancient constitution.

35 Thomas Hedley, in *Proceedings in Parliament, 1610* ed Elizabeth Read Foster (New Haven and London 1966) II, 170–97, especially 175, 182, 186, 190. Though it may only be a coincidence, Hedley also cites Craterus, the villain of *Philotas*, as his example of the sycophantic councillor (197). I wish to thank Paul Christianson for drawing Hedley's speech to my attention.

36 My emphasis: the editions of 1621 and 1634 retain the revised gloss.

37 I have found no other such statement about Richard I in this period.

38 Knafla *Law and Politics in Jacobean England* 251. Speaking in the Great Chamber at Whitehall on the last day of March in 1607, King James VI and I informed his English parliament that he intended to effect a

union with Scotland, 'as if you had got it by Conquest, but such a Conquest as may be cemented by love': *Political Works of James I* ed McIlwain 292.

39 Bodin *Method* 282-6; *Six Bookes* VI, v, 723; II, iii, 207; W.H. Greenleaf 'Bodin and the Idea of Order' in *Jean Bodin* ed Denzer 23-38

40 Kliger *Goths in England* 142; Seaberg 'Remembering the Past' 42-3, 150-2; Inner Temple Library, MS Petyt 512, vol E, fol 170; MS Petyt 533, vol 1, fol 345 contains Petyt's excerpts from Daniel on Magna Carta; *A Complete History of England* ed. J. Hughes with White Kennett (2nd ed, 1719) vol I. Later seventeenth century editions were published in 1621 (2), 1626, 1634, 1650 and 1685; for the rather pedestrian *Continuation* of the *Collection* by John Trussell (1636), see chapter 8, below.

Chapter Four

1 Van Norden 'Sir Henry Spelman on the Chronology of the Elizabethan College of Antiquaries'; Anne Barton, 'Harking Back to Elizabeth: Ben Jonson and Caroline Nostalgia' *English Literary History* 48 (1981) 706-31

2 Spelman's *Archaeologus* was written under James, though it remained unpublished until 1626. Camden to Spelman, 19 September 1619, BL MS Add 25384 (Spelman correspondence) fol 5; BN Coll Dup MS 663 fols 13-19v; *Joannis Seldenis jurisconsulti opera omnia* ed D. Wilkins (3 vols in 6 parts, 1726) III, cols 140, 1451-8; Norbrook 'Macbeth and the Politics of Historiography' 82ff

3 For life-writing and its relationship to history in the early seventeenth century, see Stauffer *English Biography before 1700* 4-32, 235-7; Anderson *Biographical Truth* passim; McKeon *Origins of the English Novel* 90-6.

4 Sidney Lee 'Hayward, John' in *DNB*; more favourably, Goldberg 'Sir John Hayward'; Scarfe 'Sir John Hayward'

5 Levack *Civil Lawyers* 237-8; Thomas, earl of Arundel to Cotton, 19 August and 13 September [1609 or 1610, from Padua], Bodl MS Smith 71, fols 95, 125

6 Hayward *The Sanctuarie of a Troubled Soule* (1st complete ed, 1616); *Davids Teares* (1622); T.D. Hardy *Catalogue of Lords Chancellors* (1843) 109; Wood *Fasti Oxonienses* I, 368; Levack *Civil Lawyers* 96-7, 103-6, 134, 221, 232. On 22 June 1604, Hayward and the antiquary Francis Tate debated at the Middle Temple 'Of the Precedency of Doctors and Masters of the Chancery before Serjaunts att Lawe,' BL MS Add 22587, fols 33-6.

7 Roger Williams *Actions of the Lowe Countries* ed J. Hayward (1618) sig A2r

8 PRO SP 12/274/58-62; 12/275/25, 28, 33; 12/278/17; Dowling 'Sir John

Hayward's *Troubles over His Life of Henry IV'* 212ff.; Campbell *Shakespeare's Histories* 186–90. Bacon pointed out that Hayward was guilty of felony not treason, having lifted many of his *sententiae* from Tacitus: *Works* VII, 133.

9 Hayward *The First Part of the Life and Raigne of King Henrie the IIII* (1599) sig A3r. Hayward's book was brought up at Essex's trial. Campbell *Shakespeare's Histories* 190; R. Heffner 'Shakespeare, Hayward, and Essex' *Publications of the Modern Language Association* 45 (1930) 754–80.

10 Hayward *Henrie IIII* 50, 55, 66, 77; Machiavelli *The Prince* chapters 17, 24

11 Ibid 65, 100, 106; Levack *Civil Lawyers* 113–14

12 Hayward *Henrie IIII* 134, where Hayward falls back on Hall's scheme of the deposition of every third king from Henry IV to Henry VII

13 Ibid 107

14 Folger Shakespeare Library, MS G.a.12, fols 1–79. I have seen no other discussion of this MS, which remains unpublished, and am grateful to the Folger Library for allowing me to read and quote from it. On fol 79 is written, in an early seventeenth-century hand, 'I found this peece among Sir John Haiwoods papers which I bought, written in his owne hands. 1628.' The copy includes underscored passages and seems intended for print. The original owner may have been John Bill, the king's printer, who witnessed Hayward's will, which is printed in Hayward *Annals of the First Four Years of Queen Elizabeth* ed J. Bruce (Camden Society, 1st ser, VII, 1840) xli–xlvi.

15 Folger MS G.a.12, fol 2v; Hayward *Annals of ... Elizabeth*, introduction xvii

16 Folger MS G.a.12, fol 46v

17 Folger MS G.a.12, fol 60, underscored in MS. The specific lesson derives from Machiavelli *Discourses* II, 12; III, 12 (ed Bernard Crick and trans L.J. Walker, 1970) 305–10, 440–3; cf Machiavelli *The Art of War* trans E. Farneworth and ed N. Wood (Indianapolis 1965) 124. Hayward may have been exposed to Machiavelli through his printer, John Wolfe, who had published several surreptitious editions of the Florentine's works: H. Sellers 'Italian Books Printed in England before 1640' *The Library* 4th ser 5 (1924–5) 107.

18 Folger MS G.a.12, fols 42–46v; Hayward's account in the continuation is based mainly on Walsingham's *Historia Anglicana*, but the parliamentary sequence derives directly from the Rolls of Parliament, for which see *Rotuli Parliamentorum* III, 485–521. The statutes involved were 1 Edw III St 2 cap 5; 18 Edw III cap 7; and 24 Edw III St 5 cap 8, all confirmed by 4 Hen IV cap 13: *Statutes of the Realm* (1816) II, 137.

19 J. Hayward *An Answer to the First Part of a Certaine Conference, concerning the Succession* (1603) sigs B2r, K1r–2r, R3r; Campbell *Shakespeare's Histories* 185 plausibly suggests that the bishop of Carlisle's speech in *Henry IIII* was Hayward's first answer to Parsons.

20 Hayward to King James 6 June 1603: Bodl MS Smith 70, fols 23–5. His choice of Sallust is interesting and undoubtedly reflects the same fear of civil war over a disputed succession which preoccupied Daniel. It is also entirely possible, of course, that after his earlier misadventures Hayward was much more cautious about invoking Tacitus explicitly.

21 Hayward *A Treatise of Union of the Two Realmes of England and Scotland* (1604) 1–13, 55

22 Hayward *Treatise of Union* 11, 13, expanding on a position in *An Answer* sig F1v. Hayward seems to be twisting Sir Thomas Smith's Polybian statement that mutations of governments are natural into an argument for their deliberate change, a point explicitly rejected by Smith *De republica Anglorum* (1583) 5, 17.

23 Hayward *Treatise of Union* 51

24 Mosse 'The Influence of Jean Bodin's *République*' 73–83. Hayward makes numerous references to Bodin. In his council examination in 1601, he had cited Bodin (not 'Bodius' or 'Boethius' as misread in *Cal. SP Dom, 1598–1601* 540) on the subject's duty to the king in a monarchy: PRO SP 12/278/17. Hayward specifically cites Bodin (probably the *Six Bookes of a Commonweale*) in *An answer* sig D3r, and *A Reporte of a Discourse concerning Supreme Power in Affaires of Religion* (1606) 13. The Bodinian text distinguishing between a state and a government is *Six Bookes* trans Knolles (1606) II, vii, 249.

25 Hayward *Reporte* 7–8; Levack *Civil Lawyers* 100, 114

26 Hayward *The Lives of the III. Normans, Kings of England* sig A3r; further references will be given in the text.

27 Goldberg 'Sir John Hayward' 238; Bruce's introduction to *Annals of ... Elizabeth* xxii erroneously suggests that Hayward used a manuscript of the Anglo-Saxon chronicle.

28 Hayward's opinion that the Conquest was merely the restoration of the kingship to its proper heir echoes the later statement of Sir Edward Coke that Harold, as a usurper, should not be listed in the succession of rulers: *The Second Part of the Institutes of the Lawes of England* (1642) sig A6r. But it also comes surprisingly close to Robert Parsons' statement, in response to Coke, that the Normans were simply carrying out a just war on behalf of the papacy against a usurper: see *An Answere to the Fifth Part of Reportes Lately Set Forth by Syr Edward Cooke* (St Omer 1606) 160, discussed above, chapter 1.

29 Smith *De republica Anglorum* 1. Smith, however, believed that sovereignty in England, while 'absolute,' was divided among the estates: see J. Daly 'The Idea of Absolute Monarchy in Seventeenth-Century England' *Historical Journal* 21 (1978) 227–50, at 228.

30 *The Trew Law of Free Monarchies* in *Political Works of James I* ed McIlwain 61–2

31 Despite the justice of his title, William II was – Hayward is clear on this – an oppressive and rapacious king who ultimately paid the price

for his and his father's sins, being struck down by divine intervention in the New Forest. Hayward calls 'the secret working and will of God' the 'cause of all causes,' ibid 46, 218.

32 Hayward's model in all his histories was Tacitus. In *Davids Teares* (1622), 'To the Reader,' sig [A7r] he extolled the ancients in general as superior to the writers of his own age, 'which cannot neerely approach them'; Benjamin 'Sir John Hayward and Tacitus' 275–6.

33 Cf Hayward *Reporte* 8.

34 Hayward *Annals of ... Elizabeth* 15, 42, 67, 90

35 Folger Shakespeare Library MS 1467.2 is a presentation copy bearing James I's arms.

36 Hayward *The Life, and Raigne of King Edward the Sixt* (1630) 3; BL MS Cott Nero C.X

37 Hayward *Edward VI* 77, 143

38 For a recent survey of Camden's interests, see Herendeen 'William Camden.' Professor Herendeen is engaged on a full-scale biography of Camden which promises to add much to our knowledge of his earlier career as a schoolmaster as well as his antiquarian work.

39 Levy *Tudor Historical Thought* 125–34; Kendrick *British Antiquity* 134–67; Mendyk 'Early British Chorography'

40 Ortelius was not the last Dutchman to visit Camden. The poet Janus Douza the elder visited in 1572: Leiden University MS BPL 1406 (Douza's *album amicorum*) fol 141v. The virtuoso Bernardus Paladinus (Berend ten Broecke, d 1633) came at an unknown date: Royal Library, The Hague, MS 133, M.63 (Paladinus' *album amicorum*), fol 281v.

41 BL MS Cott Jul F.VI fol 408; 'Of Epitaphs', 3 November 1600, printed in Hearne *Curious Discourses* I, 228–32; Camden *Reges, reginae, nobiles, et alii in ecclesia collegiata B. Petri Westmonasterii sepulti* (1600)

42 J. Gruter *Inscriptiones antiquae totius orbis Romanae* 2 vols (Heidelberg 1602–3); L. Forster *Janus Gruter's English Years* (1967) 4–5. By 1607 the *Britannia* itself contained an extensive collection of inscriptions.

43 Camden *Britannia, sive florentissimorum regnorum Angliae, Scotiae, Hiberniae chorographica descriptio* (1586, 1587, 1590, 1594, 1600, 1607) translated by Philemon Holland as *Britain* (1610). All references unless otherwise indicated will be to the translation, which Camden personally supervised.

44 *Camdeni epistolae* App 85; Kendrick *British Antiquity* 49; Levy 'The Making of Camden's *Britannia*'; DeMolen 'The Library of William Camden.' Stan Mendyk's full-length study of Leland, Camden, and other chorographers, '*Speculum Britanniae*' (Toronto 1989), appeared too late for me to consult for my argument here.

45 Brooke *A Discoverie of Certain Errours Published in Print in the Much Commended Britannia, 1594* (nd, 1596?), 'To Maister Camden.' Camden first replied in 'Ad Lectorem,' appended to the 1600 edition of *Britannia*, 1–3, 16–18, 29.

46 Camden *Britain* (1610) 5; Piggott 'William Camden and the *Britannia*'

47 Camden *Annales rerum Anglicarum et Hibernicarum regnante Eliza-betha* (1615); Trevor-Roper 'Queen Elizabeth's First Historian: William Camden and the Beginnings of English "Civil" History' provides an excellent account of the work and its background, though it seems to me to misinterpret the extent of and reasons for the king's involvement.

48 Camden to de Thou, 16 April 1605, BN Coll Dup MS 632 (de Thou correspondence) fols 101r–2v

49 De Thou to Camden, 10 February 1605 (ns), *Camdeni epistolae* 68f; Young to the king, (nd, 1608?) Bodl MS Smith 76 (Young correspondence) fol 5, printed in *Patricius Junius: Bibliothekar der Könige Jacob I und Carl I von England* (Leipzig 1898) 3, my translation from Latin. The lack of a date makes it impossible to guess exactly when Camden came under the king's command; it is possible that the individual spoken of in Young's letter is Cotton, though this seems unlikely since the king and Sir Robert were already well acquainted.

50 Camden *The Historie of the Most Renowned and Victorious Princesse Elizabeth, Late Queene of England* trans Robert Norton (1630) sig B1r–3v, the first complete English edition. For convenience, all references, provided in the text, will be to this translation, with corresponding pages of the first London Latin editions (Books I–III, 1615; Book IV, 1627) in brackets; Camden remarked that his history was 'Inchoatio invidia, continuatio labor finis odium': Camden to de Thou, 10 August 1612, Bodl MS Smith 74 fols 25–8, a copy of BN Coll Dup MS 632, fols 103r–v.

51 Camden to de Thou, 22 November 1607, BN Coll Dup MS 836 (de Thou correspondence) fol 145

52 G. Carew to Salisbury, 2/12 September 1606, PRO SP 78/53/155c; Trevor-Roper 'William Camden' 128

53 Casaubon to de Thou, 20 June 1612, and 1 July 1612, *Isaaci Casauboni epistolae* (The Hague 1638) 345–6, 349; Bacon *Works* VI, 349–64. John Chamberlain, a close friend of Camden, told Dudley Carleton as early as 29 January 1612, that the *Annales* were 'collected with the help of Sir Robert Cotton and written by Mr Clarenceaux' *Chamberlain Letters* ed N.E. McClure (Philadelphia 1939) I, 332.

54 Camden to de Thou, 16 April 1605 and 10 August 1612, BN Coll Dup MS 632, fols 101–3v; Sharpe *Sir Robert Cotton* 89–95

55 King James to Camden and Cotton, 25 February 1615, Trinity College, Cambridge, MS R.5.20, fols 14r–v (copy in Camden's hand); Camden to de Laet, 18 June 1616, *Camdeni epistolae* 167

56 Trevor Roper 'William Camden' 133ff. Kenyon *The History Men* 10, similarly supposes that the king only very reluctantly permitted the work to go ahead; for a fuller account of James's attitude to Elizabeth after her death, see D.R. Woolf 'Two Elizabeths? James I and the Late

Queen's Famous Memory' *Canadian Journal of History* 18 (1985) 167–91.

57 Camden to 'Right Honourable,' nd, *Camdeni epistolae* 351; Dupuy to Camden, 5 December 1619, ibid 293; Camden to Dupuy, 29 August 1620, Bodl MS Smith 74, fols 53–4; Dupuy to Camden, 22 November 1620, *Camdeni epistolae* 310–11; Camden to Dupuy, 17 December 1620, BN Coll Dup MS 699 fol 210; Trevor-Roper 'William Camden' 19ff

58 Conway to the wardens of the Stationers' Company, 25 June 1624, PRO SP 14/168/41, restrains the stationers from printing the *Annales* as translated by Abraham Darcie until Camden's corrections are inserted by Cotton and he has examined the second part (Book IV). Cotton took only five days, apparently, for Conway lifted the restraint on 30 June; SP 14/214, 132.

59 Burke 'Survey of the Popularity of Ancient Historians'; Casaubon to Camden, 5 September 1609, *Camdeni epistolae* 126

60 Camden prepared his material under appropriate years in a workbook, now part of Trinity College, Cambridge, MS R.5.20, fols 81–93.

61 Eg, *Historie* I, 106 [1615, 132], where Hugh O'Neal is introduced as a young man 'who proved afterward the disturber, yea the plague of his country'

62 He did not, unfortunately for us, document his statements with precise references. A modern critical edition would be most welcome.

63 Camden to 'Right Honourable,' nd, *Camdeni epistolae* 351

64 Norfolk was the brother of the earl of Northampton and grandfather of the second earl of Arundel, successively earls marshal and patrons of Cotton and Camden.

65 *Historie* IV, 27–9 [1627, 34ff] presents an exception, Hacket's 'blasphemous madnesse' of 1591. Cf ibid II, 98 [1615, 285] for 'the execrable impietie of Matthew Hamont.'

66 Camden praises the Edwardian reformation in his letter to James Ussher of 10 July 1618; *Camdeni epistolae* 246–8. His view of the supremacy of the king-in-parliament in ecclesiastical matters is in accordance with Richard Hooker's *Laws of Ecclesiastical Polity* ed R. Houk (New York 1931) VIII, vi, 214ff. Elements of his political thought may derive from Fortescue's idea of 'politique' government, especially in 'William Camden's "Discourse concerning the Prerogative of the Crown" ' ed F.S. Fussner, *Proceedings of the American Philosophical Society* 101, no 2 (April 1957) 204–15. Whether this tract is really by Camden or not remains uncertain.

67 Camden's own attitude to Spain was one of suspicion and, as he told Dupuy in 1620, he thought the *Annales'* fourth book might not be published if times changed 'et Anglia in Hispanos propendeat': Camden to Dupuy, 29 August 1620, Bodl MS Smith 74, fol 53.

68 Lake to Salisbury, 2 December 1610, PRO SP 14/58/54

69 Besides the personal information available to Camden concerning the
king's involvement with Essex, there are many Cottonian, Salisbury,
and state papers which give a more accurate picture of the monarchs'
relations. See the sources listed by H.G. Stafford *James VI and the
Throne of England* (New York 1940) 210–24, 253.

70 *Vox Coeli* (1624); revised STC attributes the tract to Reynolds, a merchant. On Scott himself, see P.G. Lake 'Constitutional Consensus and
Puritan Opposition in the 1620s: Thomas Scott and the Spanish Match'
Historical Journal 25 (1982) 805–25. For works actually by Scott, such
as *Vox Populi* (part one, 1620), *Robert Earle of Essex His Ghost* (Paradise
[ie London] 1624), and *Sir Walter Rawleighs Ghost, or Englands Forewarner* (Utrecht [London] 1626) see M.A. Breslow *A Mirror of England:
English Puritan Views of Foreign Nations, 1618–40* (Cambridge, Mass.
1970) chapter 3 passim; Louis B. Wright 'Propaganda against James I's
"Appeasement" of Spain' *Huntington Library Quarterly* 6 (1943)
49–72. More offensive statements than Scott's, also appealing to Elizabeth's reign, are the anonymous *Tom Tell-Troath, or a Free Discourse
Touching the Manners of the Tyme* (1621?), *Harleian Miscellany* II
(1809) 419–38; and anon 'To the Blessed Saint Q. Elizabeth' PRO SP
14/180/107.

71 Rebholz *Fulke Greville* 1, 219

72 Cf Bodin *Method* 86.

73 See below, chapter 7.

74 BL MS Lans DCCCCLXXXIV, fol 204 (biographical notice by White Kennett);
E. Gibson 'Life of Camden' in *Britannia* (1695 ed) sig D1r; *Camdeni
epistolae* App 85; Hearne *Curious Discourses* II, 390; DBN sv 'Godwin,
Francis'; Godwin to Camden, 27 May 1608, *Camdeni epistolae* 109;
Godwin to Camden, 9 October 1620, ibid 308; Levack *Civil Lawyers*
63–4

75 Godwin *A Catalogue of the Bishops of England* (1601); Broughton, *Ecclesiasticall Historie of Great Britain* 255ff; Merchant 'Bishop Francis
Godwin' 45–7

76 Godwin, *Rerum Anglicarum Henrico VIII, Edwardo VI et Maria regnantibus, annales* (1616). All references, given parenthetically, will be to
the enlarged and corrected translation by Morgan Godwin, *Annales of
England* (1630). The bishop's own corrections may be seen in BL MS
Add 45140 (Scudamore papers, vol I) fols 6–9 (1616). The autograph MS
of the Latin version is BL MS Cott Titus C.XI.

77 Godwin here cites unspecified 'publique records' on Anne Boleyn's trial
and death, probably those in BL MS Cott Otho C.III and *Letters and
Papers Foreign and Domestic of the Reign of Henry VIII* ed J.S. Brewer,
J. Gairdner, et al (1887) x, no 876. Godwin does not name his sources,
but they can be pieced together from his occasional marginal references.
The Scottish writers who best suited him were George Buchanan
Rerum Scoticarum historia (Edinburgh 1582) and John Leslie *De rebus*

gestis scotorum posteriores, libri tres (Rome 1578). Cavendish had already been used by Holinshed, but Godwin's excerpts do not follow the text of the *Chronicles* (1587).

78 Eccles 'Sir George Buc' 411–506

79 Excluding, of course, the rehabilitation of King John at the Reformation by authors like John Bale, which was not nearly as sophisticated, since it relied largely on simple denials that the 'monkish chroniclers' could be trusted

80 Christopher Brooke *The Ghost of Richard the Third* (1614); Brooke was MP for York in every parliament from 1604 to 1626, and was a friend of Cotton, Selden, Jonson, and Drayton: DNB sv 'Brooke, Christopher'; Sharpe *Sir Robert Cotton* 198.

81 Sir George Buck *The History of King Richard the Third* ed A.N. Kincaid (Gloucester 1979) introduction, xviff, lxiv–lxxxvi: all references are to this edition.

82 Buck *History* introduction, passim, 7, 110–18, 204. Buck contributed *The Third Universitie of England* to the continuation of Stow's *The Annales of England* ed Edmund Howes (1615).

83 Buck *History* introduction, xxiii; Buck Δαφνις Πολυστεφανος (1605), again pirated by the younger George Buck as *The Great Plantagenet or a Continued Succession of that Royal Name* (1635). Buck's kinsman, friend, and patron, Charles Howard, was one of the union commissioners in 1604.

84 Bodl MS Eng misc b.106, fols 19, 31, 386v, 389

85 William Cornwallis *The Prayse of King Richard III* in *Essayes of Certaine Paradoxes* (1616)

86 Daniel's views on monarchical election may be an influence here, though Daniel believed it could supplant a title, while Buck is at pains to stress that Richard's title was legitimate. Buck cites Daniel in MS notes on page 26 of his copy of Godwin's *Catalogue of the Bishops of England* (1601), Bodl shelfmark 4° Rawl 569.

87 *A Complete History of England* ed J. Hughes with W. Kennett (2nd ed, 1719) I, preface, sig A1v

88 For Herbert's life and thought see, most recently, Bedford *Defence of Truth* and Hill *Herbert of Cherbury*.

89 Montaigne's *Essaies* and *Apologie de Raimond de Sebond* were translated by John Florio in 1603 (see above, chapter 3); Pierre Charron *Of Wisdome Three Bookes* trans Samson Lennard (1608) developed and popularized many of Montaigne's ideas: cf Popkin, *History of Scepticism* 42–65, 84ff.

90 Selden to Herbert, February 1620, BL MS Add 32092, fol 314; M. Rossi *La vita, le opere, i tempi di Edoardo Herbert di Cherbury* I, 179, the fullest biographical study, links Herbert to Selden's patroness the countess of Kent, though Sidney Lee (DNB sv 'Herbert, Edward, first baron of Cherbury') believes that the Herbert mentioned by Selden in *Table Talk*

ed F. Pollock (1927) 37, in connection with the countess was Sir Edward Herbert (d 1657), the historian's cousin. Either identification seems possible.

91 Camden to Dupuy, nd [1619?], BN Coll Dup MS 699, fol 204; *The Life of Edward, First Lord Herbert of Cherbury* ed J.M. Shuttleworth (1976) 49, 120–1; Popkin *History of Scepticism* 129–50; Bedford *Defence of Truth* 48–50, 55–8

92 Herbert *De Veritate* trans M.H. Carré (Bristol 1937) introduction, 24–5, 42–4; text 115–45, 289–307; Bedford *Defence of Truth* 21–2

93 Bedford *Defence of Truth* 248; Hill *Herbert of Cherbury* 18–35, believes Herbert to have been a deist. For a recent definition of the varieties of unbelief in this era see D. Wootton 'Lucien Febvre and the Problem of Unbelief in the Early Modern Period' *Journal of Modern History* 60 (1988) 695–730.

94 *Life of Herbert* 120–21; Loys Le Roy's *Of the Interchangeable Course, or Variety of Things* trans R. Ashley (1594), fols 5v–7, seems a likely source of Herbert's theory of contrary principals.

95 Herbert *De Religione Laici* (1645) ed and trans H.R. Hutcheson (New Haven, Conn. 1944) 116–19 (which also contains a good bibliography of Herbert's works); cf *De Veritate* 120: 'It is clear, therefore, that in so far as there is necessity it is only a means; for Grace allows us to use it as we will.'

96 Hacking *Emergence of Probability* 19–24, 46. The differences between early modern and modern ideas of probability are sometimes insufficiently stressed in Shapiro's generally very useful *Probability and Certainty in Seventeenth-Century England* p 150ff, whose discussion of historical writing unfortunately follows Fussner's *Historical Revolution* in looking to the seventeenth century for modern attitudes to truth, empirical research, and hypothesis-making.

97 Popkin *History of Scepticism* 126; Van Leeuwen *Problem of Certainty in English Thought* 1–12; Shapiro *Probability and Certainty in Seventeenth-Century England* 119–62

98 Herbert owned Selden's *De anno civili, Uxor ebraica, De dis Syris* and *Analecton Anglo-Britannicon*: C.J. Fordyce and T.M. Knox 'The Books Bequeathed to Jesus College, Oxford, by Lord Herbert of Cherbury' *Proceedings and Papers of the Oxford Bibliographical Society* 5 (1936–9) 71–115, at 101, 109, 113.

99 Bedford *Defence of Truth* 179. Vossius read the first draft of *De religione gentilium* and his son Isaac edited the first edition (Amsterdam 1663): Vossius to Herbert, 30 December 1645, Bodl MS Rawl lett 84(c) (Vossius correspondence), fol 264; Vossius to Herbert, 16 June 1646, ibid fol 262. For Herbert's later religious writings, see Hill *Herbert of Cherbury* 36–50.

100 Herbert to Francis Windebanke, 19 January 1635, *Cal SP Dom, 1634–35* 468; Herbert to Sir John Coke, 25 February 1636, *Cal SP Dom, 1635–36*

254; Herbert to Windebanke, 9 February 1639, *Cal sp Dom, 1638–39*
441–2

101 Herbert *The Life and Raigne of King Henry the Eighth* (1649) sig F4r.
The pagination of this edition is highly erratic; references will therefore
be by signature.

102 For a recent example of the continued usefulness of Herbert, see E.W.
Ives *Anne Boleyn* (Oxford 1987) passim.

103 Hill *Herbert of Cherbury* 37, 51–65

104 BL MS Cott Cleo C.V, art 3

105 Herbert's most important continental sources include de Thou's *Historia
sui temporis* and Sarpi's *History of the Council of Trent* trans N. Brent
(1620).

106 *Proceedings in Parliament, 1610* (3 May 1610) ed Elizabeth Read Foster
(New Haven, Conn. 1966) I, 232. Salisbury added cynically that 'the worst
kings make the best laws,' citing Richard III the tyrant and Henry IV the
usurper as examples.

107 *Letters and Papers ... of Henry VIII* x (1887) 341

108 The passage is presented as a speech by an anonymous MP in the parliamentary session of November 1529.

109 Cf Godwin *Annales* (1630 ed) 149. Also unlike Godwin, Herbert refuses
to cite providence to explain the death of Thomas Howard, fiancé of
Henry VIII's niece Margaret.

110 Fisher 'The Speeches in Lord Herbert of Cherbury's *Life and Reign of
Henry VIII*' 498; Merchant 'Herbert of Cherbury and Seventeenth-Century Historical Writing'; Rossi *Edoardo Herbert* III, 472–5

111 Anderson *Biographical Truth* passim

Chapter Five

1 Sir Thomas Hoby 'A Breef Rehersall of the Chiefe Conditions and Qualities in a Courtier' appended to Baldassare Castiglione *The Book of the
Courtier* trans T. Hoby (1562) ed W. Raleigh (1900) 372–3

2 On Machiavelli see A.H. Gilbert *Machiavelli's Prince and Its Forerun-
ners* (Durham, N.C. 1938) vi, 15, 234; F. Gilbert *Machiavelli and
Guicciardini* passim; Raab *The English Face of Machiavelli*; Orsini
' "Policy" or the Language of Elizabethan Machiavellianism.'

3 G. Botero *Reason of State* ed P.J. and D.P. Waley (1956) xiii, 80f; R.
Polin 'Le concept de Raison d'Etat avant la lettre d'après Machiavel' in
Staatsräson ed R. Schnur (Berlin 1975) 27–42

4 Huppert *Perfect History* 178; Brown *The Methodus ... of Jean Bodin* 65

5 Edmund Bolton *Hypercritica* in Spingarn (ed) *Critical Essays* I, 85

6 Howell *Logic and Rhetoric in England* 116ff, 319ff

7 Smuts *Court Culture* 82

8 *Book of the Courtier* trans Hoby 180–3. But Castiglione also notes the
fate of Alexander's adviser Calisthenes, who 'bicause he was a right

philosopher and so sharpe a minister of the bare truth without mynglinge it with courtlinesse, he lost his lief and profited not, but rather gave a sclaunder to Alexander'; ibid 339.

9 All references in this chapter to the *Works* will be given in the text by volume and page number. References to the *Henry VII* will be by page number to *The History of the Reign of King Henry the Seventh* ed F.J. Levy (Indianapolis 1972).

10 The literature on Bacon's historical thought or on the *Henry VII* is quite voluminous: see especially Nadel 'History as Psychology in Francis Bacon's Theory of History'; Dean 'Bacon's Theory of Civil History-Writing'; Clark 'Francis Bacon: The Study of History and the Science of Man' and 'Bacon's Henry VII: A Case-Study in the Science of Man'; White 'The English Solomon'; Wheeler 'The Purpose of Bacon's *History of Henry VII*' and 'Bacon's Henry VII as a Machiavellian Prince.' Among more recent works, Jardine *Francis Bacon* 163ff contains an excellent discussion of Bacon's relationship to the rhetorical treatises of his time. Guibbory *Map of Time* 43–67 examines Bacon's attitude to the topos of historical recurrence; Marwil *Trials of Counsel* 149–202 studies the *Henry VII* in the context of the events of Bacon's career; it is revised somewhat by Anderson *Biographical Truth* 157–203, which now stands as the most thorough discussion of Bacon's manipulation of literal truth for political purposes.

11 Vico *New Science* secs 404–10, ed T.G. Bergin and M.H. Fisch (Ithaca, NY, and London 1968) 129–31. Vico acknowledged a debt to Bacon at several points in the *New Science* (secs 163, 359, 499) and listed him in his *Autobiography* as one of four authors (with Plato, Tacitus, and Grotius) who had most influenced him: Enrico de Mas 'Vico's Four Authors' in *Giambattista Vico: An International Symposium* ed Giorgio Tagliacozzo and Hayden V. White (Baltimore 1969) 3–13.

12 For example, Bacon says that knowledge is '*as* water' (IV, 16) and that the philosophies of Plato and Aristotle are *like* lightweight planks floating on the waves of time (VIII, 108). For the place of resemblance and correspondence in the 'episteme' of early modern Europe, see Michel Foucault's classic *The Order of Things* (1970) 50–67. I have dealt with the problem of historical 'difference' and 'similitude' (or, to use J.H. Hexter's famous terms, 'lumping' and 'splitting') more extensively elsewhere: 'Rethinking Renaissance Historical Thought: Time, Narrative, and the Structure of History' *Studies in History and Politics* 6 (1989) 179–200.

13 Seifert *Cognitio Historica* 52, 98ff, 116–38; on the question of Bacon's 'modernity' and his attitude toward innovation, see Charles Whitney *Francis Bacon and Modernity* (New Haven, Conn, and London 1986) 55–75.

14 Fussner *Historical Revolution* 255–63; Bodin *Method* 15–19; Bartholo-

mew Keckermann *De natura et proprietatibus historiae, commentarius* (Hanover 1610) 114

15 La Popelinière *L'Histoire des histoires, avec l'idée de l'histoire accomplie* (Paris 1599) Book II. Bacon's debt to La Popelinière has been hitherto unexplored. Sypher 'Similarities between the Scientific and the Historical Revolutions' 353–68, draws several parallels between them but mistakenly asserts that Bacon had not read the Frenchman's works. For an explicit reference by Bacon to La Popelinière, see Snow 'Francis Bacon's Advice to Fulke Greville' 371.

16 La Popelinière *L'Idée* 85. Closer to Bacon's meaning is Keckermann's statement, 'Historia politica est vel perfectioris status, vel imperfectioris', *De natura ... historiae* 106. But Bacon had used the term several years earlier in the *Advancement* (1605), in *Works* III, 333.

17 Levy 'Bacon and the Style of Politics' is the most recent discussion of Bacon's attitude to politics and its relationship to history.

18 Howell *Logic and Rhetoric* pp. 368–72; Harrison 'Bacon's View of Rhetoric, Poetry and the Imagination'; E. Berry 'History and Rhetoric in Bacon's Henry VII' in *Seventeenth Century Prose* ed S.E. Fish (New York 1971) 281–308; Tinkler 'The Rhetorical Method of Bacon's *History*'

19 The figure and the following summary are derived from the *De augmentis scientiarum*, Book II, in *Works* IV, 292–314; cf La Popelinière's call (*L'Idée* 191, 359–63) for a cultural history of 'les offices, les loix, coustumes, les formes de vivre, de parler, guerroier et autres choses necessaires à la forme de l'estat.'

20 The remark is made specifically about natural history, but it is not difficult to see its application to civil history.

21 Van Leeuwen *Problem of Certainty in English Thought* 1–12

22 Hayden White 'The Value of Narrativity in the Representation of Reality' in *The Content of the Form: Narrative Discourse and Historical Representation* (Baltimore 1987) 1–25

23 In accordance with his admiration of Machiavelli, Bacon allows as an exception the kind of non-narrative 'observations' exemplified by the Florentine's *Discourses on Livy* (III, 453; IV, 310; V, 56).

24 Cf *Letters and Life* III, 249–52; for Harrington, see below, chapter 8, and Pocock *Ancient Constitution* 142.

25 Ibid III, 335, 358; IV, 301; Snow 'Bacon's Advice to Greville' 373; Dean 'Bacon's Theory of Civil History-Writing' 222; Bouwsma 'Three Types of Historiography in Post-Renaissance Italy'

26 V. Luciani 'Bacon and Guicciardini' *Publications of the Modern Language Association* 62 (1947) 96–113

27 For example, *Works* III, 271 (emphasis in text), 345, 471; VI, 403, 408, 470, 473; VII, 55

28 Bacon *Letters and Life* VII, 405, 436; Quentin Skinner *Machiavelli* 21–4

29 Bacon criticizes as 'midwives' those who interrupt their narratives with

sentences and aphorisms: *Works* IV, 311. In the *Advancement* (III, 339) he thought that such works were not history at all but belonged 'amongst books of policy.'

30 Bacon *Essays* 'Of Boldness' (VI, 402). Cf his similar statement in 'Of Vain-glory' (VI, 505): 'Glorious men are the scorn of wise men, the admiration of fools, the idols of parasites, and the slaves of their own vaunts.' The incidental description of Henry VIII in the *De augmentis scientiarum* (VIII, 427) seems to fit this bill. Cf the opening paragraph of the aborted 'History of the Reign of King Henry the Eighth' printed in Bacon *Henry VII* appendix, 264–5. Here Bacon describes Henry VIII in glowing terms at the beginning of his reign: is it possible that Bacon ended his planned account of the Tudors in 1509 because he soon found Henry VIII 'fitter for a satire' than a history?

31 Bacon *Works* III, 336; VI, 275–9; Galloway *Union of England and Scotland* 28–9, 62ff

32 Anderson *Biographical Truth* 194–6

33 Cf *Works* III, 266, 298, 448; VI, 423; Parry *Golden Age Restor'd* 21, 26.

34 Bacon is less attentive to the problems of counsel (such as faction) than Machiavelli: cf *The Prince*, chapter 23 (trans Bull, 127); Marwil *Trials of Counsel* 181–3, 195.

35 Tinkler 'Rhetorical Method of Bacon's *History*.' Castiglione recommends that the prince choose a council 'of the noblest and wisest, wyth whom he shoulde debate all matters, and give them authority and free leave to uttre their minde francklye unto him without respect'; he also suggests, however, that the prince be advised by others of 'a baser degree': *The Book of the Courtier* 322.

36 Marwil *Trials of Counsel* 154

37 Selden to Bacon, 20 August 1621, Leiden University Library, MS Pap 2 [no fol], reproduced in Woolf 'John Selden, John Borough, and Bacon's *History*' 53. Sir Geoffrey Elton has been kind enough to point out two errors in my transcription of this document. In Selden's hand, it is contained in a collection of Anglo-Dutch correspondence. It effectively disproves the suggestion of Marwil *Trials of Counsel* 153 that Bacon felt no need for documentary sources from the capital. Selden had already acted as a legal adviser to the chancellor in February 1621: Bacon *Letters and Life* VII, 332–3.

38 Selden 'To my singular good friend, Mr Augustine Vincent' in Vincent's *Discoverie of Errours* (1622) sigs a1r–2r

39 Pocock *Ancient Constitution* 135, 202; Douglas *The Norman Conquest and British Historians* 27; Sharpe *Sir Robert Cotton* 24. Cotton may have correctly understood the nature of the knight's fee, but it seems to be pushing the evidence contained in his notes on escuage (BL MS Cott Titus F.IV, fols 60–2v) and elsewhere to say that he had the same understanding of the problem to be found in Spelman's 'Feuds and Tenures by Knight Service' in *Reliquiae Spelmanniae* ed E. Gibson (1698) 1–46.

Compare Cotton 'That the Kings of England have been pleased usually to consult with their Peers in the Great Council, and Commons in Parliament of Marriage, Peace, and War' (1621) in *Cottoni posthuma* ed James Howell (2nd ed, 1672) 14.

40 'Tenures,' 28 November 1591, BL MS Cott Faustina E.V (antiquarian discourses) fol 67; BL MS Stowe 1045 (Tate collections) fol 29; 'Of th'Antiquity, Services and Duties Appertaining to a Knights Fee,' 9 February 1599, MS Stowe 1045, fol 60. Cf Cotton and Camden's discourses on 'The Antiquity, Authority and Succession of the High Steward of England' in Hearne *Curious Discourses* II, 3, 8, 38–40.

41 Many were reprinted by Howell in *Cottoni posthuma*.

42 This work, described as a topographical 'history' by Sharpe *Sir Robert Cotton* 256, is BL MS Sloane 241. By early seventeenth-century standards, however, it was no more a 'history' than Camden's *Britannia*.

43 Bolton *Hypercritica* 98; BL MS Cott Titus B.I fols 6–53

44 PRO SP 16/54/4, 5

45 Cambridge University Library MS Dd 14 28 (2), fol 1; Thomas Crosfield noted the application of the tract to 'our state at this present': *Diary of Thomas Crosfield* ed F.S. Boas (1935) 12 (3 March 1627). BL MS Add 60284, fols 1–16v concludes with the remark 'Finis: AD, 1622' but is not written in Cotton's hand. Other manuscript copies of the work include: PRO SP 16/88/1; BL MS Harl 252, fols 129–36; and BL MS Royal App 7, fols 72–7.

46 Cotton *A Short View of the Long Life and Raigne of Henry the Third* (1627) 5; compare Bacon 'Of Ambition' in *Works* VI, 465–7.

47 The reference to Norfolk, restored as lord steward by Henry III only months before his death in 1221, after his opposition to John, suggests an oblique reference to Cotton's last patron, the earl of Arundel, heir to the defunct Norfolk dukedom.

48 Is it likely that Cotton would have presented such a sentence to the 'stranger' King James or the Scottish Robert Carr in 1614?

49 Cotton used at least ten different sources, including rolls from the tower, which are cited in the margins in the same manner as in his antiquarian and political tracts in *Cottoni posthuma*. The main authority used is Matthew Paris' *Chronica maiora*, first published in 1575, a thirteenth-century account which is highly uncomplimentary to the king.

50 *Cottoni posthuma* 308–20

51 'A Colectyone of Preceptes' Bodl MS Tanner 103, fols 196–8v. This criticizes not favourites per se, but 'too absolute inward favorits.' The list contains many precepts not included in the *Henry III*, suggesting that the history was written around the list rather than the list derived from the history; cf Sharpe *Sir Robert Cotton* 239–40.

52 T. Habington *A Survey of Worcestershire* ed J. Amphlett (Oxford 1893) I, 16–17; *Poems of William Habington* ed K. Allott (1948) introduction, xi–xliv, contains the best lives of Thomas and William, but nothing on

their historical works; among contemporary accounts, see especially
Wood *Ath Ox* III, 222–5, who received his information from Thomas
Habington the younger, William's son.

53 Sir Henry Herbert, another relative, also spoke of 'my cozen Abington':
Dramatic Records of Sir Henry Herbert ed J.Q. Adams (1917) 58;
Habington *Poems* xxixff, xxxiv, 154, 156–7; Gordon Albion *Charles I
and the Court of Rome* (1938) 157; Caroline Hibbard *Charles I and
the Popish Plot* (Chapel Hill, NC 1983) 140–7.

54 For Pembroke see *DNB* sv 'Herbert, Philip'; *Cal SP Dom, 1639* 319, 360,
398, 401, 432; Michael G. Brennan *Literary Patronage in the English
Renaissance: The Pembroke Family* (London and New York 1988)
195–8. Habington praises Pembroke's ancestor, William Herbert, executed by the Lancastrians in 1469, in his *Historie of Edward the Fourth*
(1640) 29, 46. There is no hard evidence for the theory that Thomas,
not William, was the real author of the *Historie;* though it is highly likely
that father assisted son, the *Historie* is sufficiently remote from
Thomas Habington's interests to suggest that William was in fact the
principal author.

55 Habington's son refers to the life of Henry V in a letter to Wood, 5 June
1672, Bodl MS Wood F.39, vol A–A, fol 2.

56 Habington *The Queene of Arragon* (1640) sig A2v refers to *The Prince;*
Poems 96 cites the *Discourses.*

57 Compare Machiavelli's commendation of Cesare Borgia's necessary cruelty in the Romagna *The Prince* chapter 17; Machiavelli *Discourses* III,
ch 4 (ed Crick 1970) 394–5.

58 Ibid III, chapter 26, 477. Habington points out (*Edward IV* 33) that
'Reason of state argued sharply against a marriage so uncquale to
majestie.'

59 This follows Hall's *Chronicle* (1809 ed, 276).

60 Compare *The Prince,* chapter 18.

61 Commynes *Mémoires sur Louis XI* ed J. Dufournet (Collection Folio no
1078, Paris 1979) 497

62 Hall's *Chronicle* 308, makes no such comment; Speed *Historie* 686
ignores the benevolence entirely; cf remarks by Bacon *Henry VII* 240.

63 Hall's *Chronicle* 331–3; Speed *History* 689

64 *The Prince* chapter 7, 58. If so, the analogy is tenuous, since Tiptoft was
executed by the Lancastrians, not by his master.

65 Patterson *Censorship and Interpretation* 10–20

66 S.R. Gardiner *History of England, 1603–1642* (10 vols, 1884) IX, passim;
Brian Manning 'The Aristocracy and the Downfall of Charles I' in *Politics,
Religion and the English Civil War* ed B. Manning (1973) 51

67 Habington to Mary Habington, 22 May 1640, printed in *Poems* xxxiii;
Hist Mss Comm, Various Collections I (1901) 316; ibid II (1903) 320

68 Habington refers to history as 'that great instructor of the present, and

certaine prophete of the future' in *Observations upon Historie* (1641)
sigs A3v–A4r.
69 *Hist Mss Comm, Various Collections* I, 319; *Cal sp Dom, 1645–47* 456;
Wood *Ath Ox* III, 225

Chapter Six

1 A. Duchesne *Histoire générale d'Angleterre, d'Ecosse et d'Irlande* (Paris
1614); Peiresc to Dupuy, 28 April 1624 (ns), *Lettres de Peiresc* I, 31;
BN Coll Dup MS 447 fols 77–101 (Dupuy's *Histoire de plus illustres
favoris*); Hotman to Camden, 21 October and 12 November 1617 (ns),
Camdeni epistolae 201, 202–3; Peiresc to Camden, 1 September 1617
(ns), *Lettres de Peiresc* VII, 761; Van Norden 'Peiresc and the English
Scholars' 369–89; Vossius to James Ussher, nd [c 1634] Bodl MS Rawl
lett 84 (f) (Vossius letters) fol 59; Spelman to Wheloc, 13, 17, and 20
September 1639, CUL MS Add 7596 (Spelman-Wheloc letters) fol 15, 24,
25 (unfoliated)
2 D.O. McNeil *Guillaume Budé and Humanism in the Reign of Francis
I* (Geneva 1975) 29; Weiss *Renaissance Discovery of Classical Antiquity* 177–8
3 Kelley *Foundations of Modern Historical Scholarship* 106–28; Grafton
Joseph Scaliger I, 101–33, 180–226; Pfeiffer *History of Classical Scholarship* 117–19
4 *Scaligerana, Thuana, Perroniana, Pithoeana, et Colomesiana* (Amsterdam 1740) II, 39
5 This incident is the subject of several amusing exchanges between
Peiresc, on behalf of Fronto, and Camden, between 11 December 1617
and 21 December 1622; *Lettres de Peiresc* VII, 763, 770, 781–3, 799–823
passim; Camden to Peiresc 12 December 1618, BN Coll Dup MS 699,
fol 202; Camden to Dupuy (nd), BN Coll Dup MS 699, fol 209.
6 Pfeiffer *History of Classical Scholarship* 144–58
7 P. Dupuy to Camden, 13 July 1619 (ns), *Camdeni epistolae* 277; Degory
Whear to Camden, 12 August 1622, *Camdeni epistolae* 331; Selden
to Peiresc, 8 February 1618, Bodl MS Smith 74, fols 163–4
8 T. Godwyn *Romanae historiae anthologia recognita et aucta. An English
Exposition of the Romane Antiquities* (Oxford 1623; 1st ed Oxford
1614) 160; notes on Godwyn, 1641, by S. Millington, BL MS Harl 5748,
fols 109–11. Godwyn's book was in use as late as 1705: Bodl MS Rawl
D 171, art 1, notes by Henry Bigge.
9 Dean 'Tudor Humanism and the Roman Past' 84–111
10 Fishel 'Image of Rome' 179–81; for a useful discussion of Elizabethan
views of Rome in the context of Shakespeare's Roman plays, see R.S.
Miola *Shakespeare's Rome* (Cambridge 1983).
11 Livy (Titus Livius) *The Romane Historie: Also the Breviaries of L. Florus*

trans P. Holland (1600) 1234. Holland also translated Suetonius in 1606 and Ammianus Marcellinus in 1609.

12 Lathrop *Translations from the Classics into English* 311–18; T. Lodge *The Wounds of Civil War* (1594) in *Complete Works* III (Glasgow 1883; rpt New York 1966); C. Edmonds *Observations upon Caesars Commentaries* (1600; 2nd ed, 1604)

13 Pedro Mexia *The Historie of All the Romane Emperours* trans William Traheron (1604; 2nd ed, trans Edward Grimeston, 1623); Thomas Milles published extracts from Mexia as *The Treasurie of Auncient and Moderne Times* (1613); Robert Basset *The Lives of All the Roman Emperors* (1636), sometimes attributed to Richard Brathwait.

14 Anon *Here Beginneth Thystory of the Seven Wyse Maysters of Rome* (various eds, 1555–1633); R. Robinson *A Record of Auncient Histories* (1620). The *Seven Wyse Maysters* was still popular in 1658: William London *A Catalogue of the Most Vendible Books in England* (2nd ed, 1658) 91.

15 John Barston *The Safeguarde of Societie: Describing the Institution of Lawes and Policies* (1576) fols 16v–17v; DNB sv 'Becon, Richard'; Beacon, *Solon His Follie, or a Politique Discourse, Touching the Reformation of Common-Weales Conquered, Declined or Corrupted* (1594). Machiavelli's own *Discorsi* on Livy were themselves translated by Edward Dacres in 1636.

16 Fishel 'Image of Rome' 89–100; Goldberg *James I and the Politics of Literature* 33–50; Smuts *Court Culture* 85–95

17 Sallust *Two Most Worthy and Notable Histories* trans T. Heywood (1608); *Lucan's Pharsalia: Or the Civill Warres of Rome* trans T. May (1626); May *A Continuation of ... Lucan's Historicall Poem till the Death of Julius Caesar* (1630); Hartman 'Contemporary Explanations of the English Revolution' 117–53; R. Schlatter 'Thomas Hobbes and Thucydides' *Journal of the History of Ideas* 6 (1945) 350–62

18 Florus *Roman Histories* (1619, 2nd ed, 1621) sig A3r; the Latin editions appeared at Oxford in 1631 and 1638 (STC 11101, 11102); *The Autobiography and Correspondence of Sir Simonds D'Ewes* ed J.O. Halliwell (1845) I, 121; W.T. Costello *The Scholastic Curriculum at Early Seventeenth-Century Cambridge* (Cambridge, Mass. 1958) 43, 177; H.F. Fletcher *The Intellectual Development of John Milton* (Urbana, Ill. 1956–1961) II, 327.

19 Gerd Oestreich *Neostoicism and the Early Modern State* trans D. McLintock (Cambridge 1982); J.H.M. Salmon 'Cicero and Tacitus in Sixteenth-Century France' in *Renaissance and Revolt: Essays in the Intellectual and Social History of Early Modern France* (Cambridge 1987) 27–53. Adriana McCrea of Queen's University at Kingston, Ontario, is completing a study of the English neostoics; I am indebted to her for several helpful discussions of the subject.

20 Burke 'Tacitism' 149–171; Schellhase *Tacitus in Renaissance Political*

Thought 157–65; Bradford 'Stuart Absolutism and the "Utility" of Tacitus'

21 Vossius to Greville, 13 September 1624, *G.J. Vossii et clarorum virorum ad eum epistolae* ed P. Colomesius (London 1690) 89; Vossius to Greville, 1 June 1625, ibid 93; Vossius to Greville, 8 August 1627, ibid 108; Matthew Wren to Wm. Laud, 16 December 1627, PRO SP 16/86/87

22 Bodl MS Auct F.5.9, presented by Camden in 1601; W.H. Allison 'The First Endowed Professorship of History and Its First Incumbent' *American Historical Review* 27 (1922) 733–7

23 I.B.B. [ie, G. Botero] *Observations upon the Lives of Alexander Caesar Scipio* (1602) sigs G1r, G3r

24 Pierre Matthieu *The Powerfull Favorite* (1628), two different editions (STC 17664, 17665); Mary Tenney 'Tacitus in the Politics of Early Stuart England' *Classical Journal* 37 (1941) 151–63; this last has been largely superseded by Bradford 'Stuart Absolutism and the "Utility" of Tacitus.'

25 G. Manzini *Politicall Observations upon the Fall of Sejanus* trans T. Hawkins (1634)

26 Virgilio Malvezzi *Romulus and Tarquin* (2nd ed, 1638) 136; the MS of a life of Numa by Malvezzi is BL MS Add 20028, fols 148–66. Malvezzi was also the author of *Discourses upon Cornelius Tacitus* trans Sir Richard Baker (1642).

27 DNB sv 'Leigh, Edward'; Leigh *Selected and Choice Observations concerning the Twelve First Caesars,* epistle dedicatory, no sig; Leigh to D'Ewes, nd, BL MS Harl 255 (D'Ewes correspondence), fol 63v. Leigh's orthodox opinion that the Caesars after Augustus were for the most part bad is little different from the anonymous *Romes Monarchie* (1596) sig I3v; and anon 'The Twelve Caesars' BL MS Sloane 2521, fols 101–12v.

28 Greville *A Treatise of Monarchy* stanzas 83, 304, in *Remains* ed Wilkes: all further references to this work will be given, by stanza number, in the text; Norbrook *Poetry and Politics in the English Renaissance* 157–74; Rebholz *Fulke Greville* 340ff; Charles Larson *Fulke Greville* (Boston, Mass. 1980) 71–7.

29 Greville here pinpoints the immediate causes of ruin as the election of Caesars and the lack of crown lands.

30 Greville *Of Humane Learning* stanza 43, *Works* II, 22–3

31 H.N. Maclean 'Fulke Greville: Kingship and Sovereignty' *Huntington Library Quarterly* 16 (1952–3) 237–71; Rebholz *Greville* 322–3

32 R. Eccleshall *Order and Reason in Politics* (Oxford 1978) 152; M. Mendle *Dangerous Positions: Mixed Government, the Estates of the Realm, and the Making of the 'Answer to the xix propositions'* (University, Alabama 1985) 111–13. There are, however, some exceptions to the rule, of which Samuel Daniel's vision of an 'absolute' king who is nevertheless bound by the laws provides an instance.

33 *DNB* sv 'Fulbecke, William'; Levack *Civil Lawyers* 136; Terrill 'William Fulbecke and Thomas Ridley' 169–85; on neo-Bartolism, see Pocock *Ancient Constitution* 23–5.

34 Fulbecke *A Parallele or Conference of the Civill law, the Canon Law and the Common Law of England* (2 parts, 1601–2), part one, sig 2*1r; *The Pandectes of the Law of Nations* (1602) fol 69v; Sommerville *Politics and Ideology in England* 69, 161; Glen Burgess 'Common Law and Political Theory in Early Stuart England' *Political Science* 40 (1988) 4–17. Fulbecke's attitude to the Conquest and to the rights of imposition which the monarchy could derive therefrom bear a close resemblance to Hayward's discussion of such issues a decade later in *The III. Normans.*

35 Fulbecke *Pandectes* fols 9v, 29r–v. Fulbecke suggested (specifically citing Bodin's *République*) that monarchy is the best of constitutions. He explicitly undercut the arguments in favour of popular government in Machiavelli's *Discourses* by showing that Machiavelli himself had preferred monarchy in *The Prince* and a mixed state such as Venice elsewhere in the *Discourses.*

36 Fulbecke *Historicall Collection* 'Preface,' sig A1v (dated 13 October 1600, at which time Essex's troubles would have been well known to a client of Buckhurst) 83–104

37 Cf Florus *Roman Histories* 2.17.7, trans Edmund Bolton (1619) 445. All references to Florus are to Bolton's translation.

38 Cf Florus *Roman Histories* Preface, sig B2r–3v; Trompf *Idea of Historical Recurrence* 212–13.

39 For Heylyn's life, see *DNB* sv 'Heylyn, Peter'; John Barnard *Theologo-historicus, or the True Life of the Most Reverend Divine, and Excellent Historian Peter Heylyn* (1683) 73–90; MacGillivray *Restoration Historians* 29–32.

40 Heylyn *Microcosmus, or a Little Description of the Great World* (Oxford 1621) 11–13; J. Freigius *Historiae synopsis* (Basel 1580) 9–10. Heylyn's own further exercises on the same line include the greatly expanded *Cosmographie* and the much smaller *A Help to English History*, both published in 1652.

41 Heylyn *Microcosmus* 18. Barnard *Theologo-historicus* 95ff notes that King James took exception to Heylyn's implication in the first edition of *Microcosmus* that France was a more famous kingdom than England; Heylyn apologized to the king through the intercession of the dean of Winchester, and removed the offending passage in subsequent editions.

42 Bodl MS Rawl D.353, fol 93, warrant dated 14 January 1629/30, by Philip Herbert, earl of Montgomery and lord chamberlain; Barnard *Theologo-historicus* 120–2, 155. It was out of gratitude to Danby that Heylyn would write his defence of St George, patron saint of England and of the Order of the Garter, *The Historie of that Most Famous Saynt and Souldier of Christ Jesus St George of Cappadocia* (1631).

43 Heylyn admits his authorship of *Augustus* in *Cosmographie* 44, where it is reprinted; as usual with tracts that have contemporary reference, he makes the claim that it was written many years before 1632. I refer throughout to the first edition of *Augustus* (1632); see p 50 for a citation of Guicciardini. Machiavelli is never cited by name, but some of Heylyn's observations are drawn from *The Prince*, eg the ability of virtue or 'valour' to dictate to fortune (9), and the relationship of the new prince to his nobility (122, mispaginated as 120).

44 Polybius does not describe the Decemvirate as an oligarchy, but Heylyn was able to find some authority for this in Dionysius of Halicarnassus, according to whom the Decemvirate preceded a mixed state (*Augustus* 27); Dionysius of Halicarnassus *Roman Antiquities* 11.2.1–3.1, trans E. Cary (1937–51) VII, 9–11). Interestingly, Heylyn also notes (7) that 'the commons' rather than the ruler were 'desirous of novelties.'

45 Cf Howard D. Weinbrot *Augustus Caesar in Augustan England* (Princeton 1978) 54–9, 100n.

46 Fink *Classical Republicans* 4–6 and passim

47 Barnard *Theologo-historicus* 155; Heylyn would help Noy draw up the charges against William Prynne's *Histriomastix* in 1633.

48 Savile to Camden, 25 October 1621, *Camdeni epistolae* 313; Allen to Camden, 19 November 1621, ibid 315; Whear to Camden, 27 December 1621, ibid 317–18; Bodl MS Seld Supra 81 (Whear's letterbook)

49 For the ordinances governing the chair, see *Camdeni epistolae* lxi–lxiv; Oxford University *Statuta selecta e corpore statutorum Universitatis Oxoniensis* (Oxford 1638) 12; several of Whear's lectures on the Punic wars survive as Bodl MS Auct F.2.21, beginning 21 October 1631.

50 Twyne, notes on Livy, Bodl MS Rawl D.692, fols 234–5; *Antiquitatis academiae Oxoniensis apologia* (Oxford 1608). Twyne (d 1644) of Corpus Christi, Oxford, also corresponded with Camden: Twyne to Camden, 24 February 1623, *Camdeni epistolae* 335–7. Camden offered Twyne the reversion, though Whear would outlive him.

51 Bodl MS Auct F.2.21, p 28

52 Whear *De ratione & methodo legendi historias dissertatio* (1623); Whear to Speed, nd [1625 or 1626], Bodl MS Seld Supra 81, fol 73; Whear to Thomas Godwyn, 24 April 1626, fol 81

53 Whear *Relectiones hyemales, de ratione & methodo legendi utrasque historias, civiles et ecclesiasticas* (Oxford 1637) trans Edmund Bohun as *Method and Order of Reading Both Civil and Ecclesiastical Histories* (1685). All references will be to the second edition of Bohun's translation (1694); corresponding passages in the 1637 *Relectiones* will be given in brackets, a necessary measure because of Bohun's frequent failure to inform the reader where he has added passages of his own.

54 *Artis historicae penus octodecim scriptorum tam veterum quam recentiorum monumentis ... instructa* ed J. Wolf (2nd ed, Basel 1579, 2 vols)

55 G.J. Vossius *Ars historica* (1st ed, Leiden 1623) in *Opera* (Amsterdam

1695–1701) IV, 1–48, p 4. Whear draws on Keckermann's *De natura et proprietatibus historiae, commentarius* (1610) to refute Vossius's suggestion (made against Keckermann) that the reader of histories, as opposed to the writer, need not possess, a priori, ethical and political precepts before studying the examples in histories: Whear *Method and Order* 297–310 (*Relectiones* 222–35).

56 Vossius *De historicis graecis* (Leiden 1624) and *De historicis latinis* (Leiden 1627) in *Opera* IV

57 Vossius to John Rous, 14 May 1634, Bodl MS Rawl lett 84(f), fol 81; Vossius provided a list of the recipients of *De historicis latinis* in a letter to Francis Junius, 13 August 1627, Bodl MS Rawl lett 84(b), fol 58.

58 Speed made the same division of time: see above, chapter 2, p 67; the common source is Censorinus' *De die natali liber* 21.1–6, ed O. Jahn (Berlin 1845) 62.

59 Varro *De lingua latina* 8.6, trans R.G. Kent (1938) II, 375

60 *Alum Cant* I, 175 records that Bolton was subsequently admitted to the Inner Temple. His name does not appear in the register, but he tells us he was there in a brief autobiography, BL MS Harl 6521, fol 247. There is no full study of Bolton's work. The only biography is by Thompson Cooper in the *DNB* sv 'Bolton, Edmund.' It should be used cautiously and supplemented by Joseph Hunter's life 'Chorus vatum Anglicanorum' BL MS Add 24488, fols 113–45; *Englands Helicon* (1600) ed H.E. Rollins (Cambridge, Mass. 1935) I, nos 2, 4, 8, 88, 97.

61 Bolton to Salisbury, 18 April 1608, 'from my Lodging at Templebarr,' BL MS Lans XC (Hicks papers) fol 180; Bolton *The Elements of Armories* (1610); Bolton to Cotton, 19 July 1610, BL MS Cott Jul C.III, fol 28; Peck *Northampton* 119–20

62 Bolton to Cotton, 19 July 1610, 16 October 1612, 16 July 1616, BL MS Cott Jul C.III, fols 28, 30, 32; Bolton to Alleyn, 13 August 1617, Folger Shakespeare Library, MS 916.1:x.c.8

63 Bolton to Hugh Hamersley, nd (1631), BL MS Harl 6521, fol 247

64 For the academy proposals in various forms see Bodl MS Tanner XCIV, art 6; BL MSS Add 39177, fol lv; Harl 6103 and 6143; Cott Titus B.V, fol 201 (project for raising money); and Royal 18.A.LXXI. Caudill 'Some Literary Evidence of the Development of English Virtuoso Interests in the Seventeenth Century' 279–86 largely supersedes Portal 'The Academ Roial of King James I.'

65 Bolton *Hypercritica: Or a Rule of Judgement for Writing or Reading Our Histories* in *Critical Essays of the Seventeenth Century* ed J. Spingarn (Oxford 1907) I, 114. I refer to this edition as the most available, though it contains numerous errors. The original MSS of the tract are Bodl MSS Rawl D.1 (draft) and Wood F.9 (presentation copy, presumably for Buckingham). On the history of the manuscripts and their correct date (1621) see Woolf 'Making of the *Hypercritica*' 162ff.

66 La Popelinière *L'Histoire des histoires, avec l'idée de l'histoire accomplie:*

part II, *L'Idée* 36, 191, 359–63; Myriam Yardeni 'La conception de l'histoire dans l'oeuvre de La Popelinière' *Revue d'Histoire Moderne et Contemporaine* 11 (1964) 109–26

67 Bodl MS Smith 17 (Camden's commonplace book), fols 64–7v, 'Decembris 1618'; Florus *Roman Histories* trans Bolton [1619], sig A5r. The translation of Florus was entered on the Stationers' Register 19 October 1619, but no date appears on the title page: Arber III, 658.

68 Compare Bodl MS Rawl D.1, fol 15r–v with MS Wood F.9, 37, 39; Bolton to Coke, 29 August 1634, *Hist Mss Comm Cowper* II (1888–9) 65. Bolton was a suitor to Buckingham in 1623 for the provostship of Eton, for which Bacon also applied. Bolton to Buckingham, nd (1624), Bodl MS Tanner 73, fols 418–22, contains a list of favours done Bolton by the duke. The provostship is not explicitly mentioned, but seems the likeliest subject of Bolton's request (which Buckingham could not grant having already awarded it to Sir Henry Wotton).

69 Bolton *Hypercritica* 93

70 Ibid 83, 96–7; Savile, ed *Rerum anglicarum scriptores post Bedam* (1596), epistle dedicatory; Bolton 'An historicall parallel,' dedicated to Endymion Porter, appended to the second edition of *Nero Caesar* (1627) 1, 12

71 Ibid 16; *Hypercritica* 84; Bolton comments on the dangers of Tacitus' antimonarchical tendencies corrupting youth in his letter to Coke, cited above, note 68. Boccalini was translated by John Florio in 1626 as *The New-Found Politicke*, of which pages 14–32 deal specifically with Tacitus.

72 Bolton *Hypercritica* 100–3; Florus *Roman Histories* sig B2v

73 Bolton *Hypercritica* 110 makes a rather disparaging reference to Daniel's poetry but not to his history. However, his concept of an 'English Revolution' (ibid 102) during which the English swallowed up the Norman invaders resembles Daniel's view in *The First Part of the Historie of England*.

74 Bolton *Hypercritica* 86; Cf La Popelinière's direct attack on pyrrhonism, *L'Histoire* 6.

75 Bolton *Hypercritica* 83

76 Bolton to Sir John Coke, 29 August 1634, *Hist Mss Comm Cowper* II, 65, concerns the *Tiberius*, with which it was sent; BL MS Harl 6521, fol 66; Bolton *Nero Caesar, or Monarchie Depraved* (1624) 81–2, 240–2, 287: further references are to this edition. Like many of Bolton's works, this was published under the pseudonym 'Philanactophil.'

77 Bradford 'Stuart Absolutism and the 'Utility' of Tacitus' 141–3

78 Cf J. Gruter *Inscriptiones antiquae totius orbis Romani* (Heidelberg 1603). On the Renaissance background to numismatics and epigraphy, see Weiss *Renaissance Discovery of Classical Antiquity* 145–79.

79 J. de Strada *Epitome thesauri antiquitatum* (Lyons 1553)

80 BL MS Harl 6521, fol 132r: Bolton digresses to incorporate antiquarian

discussions on subjects like the etymology of 'Verulam' and the difference between a Roman colony and a *municipium.*

81 BL MS Harl 6521, fol 127r
82 Bolton to Edward Conway, 30(?) December 1625, PRO SP 16/12/86; Bolton to Buckingham, 7 August 1628, SP 16/112/43; Bolton to Porter, 13 May and 2 July 1630, SP 16/166/63; 16/170/15
83 Bolton *The Cities Advocate* (1629); Bolton to Lord Keeper Coventry, nd (1631) BL MS Harl 6521, fols 243v, 247r, 248r
84 Bolton *Hypercritica* 83. This passage implies a rejection of extreme scepticism, not a lack of critical faculties.
85 Eg, Bodl MS Dodsworth 102, fols 89–95, extracts from the Halliwell register
86 T. Hearne *Reliquiae Hearnianae* ed P. Bliss (1857) I, 299, 306
87 BL MS Add 17919 (Symonds' notes); *DNB* sv 'Symonds, Richard' (1617–92?)
88 Caroline Robbins *Two English Republican Tracts* (Cambridge 1969), introduction, 40–59; Pocock *Machiavellian Moment* part three; Fink *Classical Republicans* chapters 4 and 5
89 James Harrington *The Commonwealth of Oceana* (1656) in *The Political Works of James Harrington* ed J.G.A. Pocock (Cambridge 1977) 188
90 Harrington *Political Works* 18off
91 Bolton to Sir Hugh Hamersley, nd 1631, BL MS Harl 6521, fol 247

Chapter Seven

1 'As neere as might be, thee moste proufes of our questions should be produced from our home writers, evidences, lawes, and deedes, and not from forregners, and straungers ignorant of the state and government of oure country ...': Arthur Agard 'Of the Same [the antiquity of the Christian religion in Britain]' (29 November 1604) in Hearne *Curious Discourses* II, 160. Agard's reminder of this rule, 'agreed at our first assemblies,' nearly twenty years later suggests some reluctance on his part to restrict himself to English sources: Evans *History of the Society of Antiquaries* 7–13.
2 Compare, for example, anon 'Of the Antiquity and Dignity of Knights' (6 May 1592) BL MS Stowe 1045 (Tate collections), fols 29–31, which cites *Britannia* and a few other English sources, with some of the material in the same MS, which contains references to Andrea Alciato (fol 84), Lipsius (fols 69, 70) and Bodin (fols 60–63v). Even more sophisticated (though from a later period, c 1629–31) is anon 'Origo feudorum' BL MS Stowe 1046 (antiquarian discourses), fols 2–5v, by an author who had clearly absorbed both the continental writers and Selden's early conclusions on feudal tenure in *Titles of Honor* (1614), for which see below.
3 T. Doylie 'Armes' (nd) BL MS Cott Faustina E.V, fol 101v; A. Agard 'Of

the Etymology, Dignity and Antiquity of Dukes in England' (nd) in Hearne *Curious Discourses* I, 184–5; McKisack *Medieval History in the Tudor Age* 85–93; Van Norden 'Elizabethan College of Antiquaries' 403–4

4 Clapham is cited in the anonymous tract 'Of the Diversity of Names of this Islande' (29 June 1604) BL MS Cott Faustina E.V, fol 64.

5 W. Camden *Remaines of a Greater Worke, concerning Britaine ...* (1605) 14, 40–75. The editor of the most recent edition of this text points out that Camden dropped all reference to the 'greater worke' in the title of the revised and expanded edition of 1614, thereby indicating that what began as a collection of material unused in *Britannia* eventually became a work in its own right: *Remains concerning Britain* ed R.D. Dunn (Toronto 1984), introduction xvff.

6 Camden *Remaines* (1605) 20, 130

7 Ibid 34, 95, 114, 139

8 Verstegan to Cotton, 15 June 1609 (ns), Bodl MS Smith 71, fol 57; same to same, 6 October 1619 (ns) ibid, fols 105–6; *DNB* sv 'Rowlands, Richard'; Kliger *Goths in England* 115ff

9 Verstegan *A Restitution of Decayed Intelligence* (Antwerp and London 1605). The work was reissued in 1628 and 1634.

10 Verstegan *Restitution* sig † 4r; J. Foxe *Acts and Monuments* ed Pratt I, 224; Schoeck 'Early Anglo-Saxon Studies and Legal Scholarship in the Renaissance;' For further background, see the following: Hill, Murphy 'Methods in the Study of Old English' 346. 'The Norman Yoke'; Richard T. Vann 'The Free Anglo-Saxons: A Historical Myth' *Journal of the History of Ideas* 19 (1958) 259–72; R.F. Jones *The Triumph of the English Language* (Stanford, Cal. 1953) 270; MacDougall *Racial Myth in English History* 31–70; Piggott *Ancient Britons and the Antiquarian Imagination* 578.

11 On the other hand, he believed that the German contribution to technology and learning was significant, including 'sundry most rare inventions': ibid 52.

12 Cf Bodin *Method* 86, 142: strictly speaking, even Bodin admitted that 'air' was only one of several geographical factors and did not exercise 'final control.'

13 Cf La Popelinière *L'Histoire des histoires* 27–30; Huppert *Perfect History* 137–8.

14 Hearne *Curious Discourses* II, 324; on the Cottonian library, see Sharpe *Sir Robert Cotton* chapter 2; Fussner *Historical Revolution* chapter 3; and C.E. Wright 'Elizabethan Society of Antiquaries and the Formation of the Cottonian Library' 176–212.

15 The single page of Selden's autobiography is Lincoln's Inn, Hale MSS, vol 12, fol 236. Selden awaits a full-length study, but in the meantime see David Berkowitz's 1946 Harvard PH D dissertation, 'Young Mr Selden: Essays in Seventeenth-Century Learning and Politics, Being Prolego-

mena to Parliament.' On legal issues, the best treatment remains the now very old article by H. Hazeltine 'Selden as Legal Historian.' The best short biography, revising the account in *DNB* by Edward Fry, is Berkowitz 'Selden, John' in *Biographical Dictionary of British Radicals in the Seventeenth Century* ed Greaves and Zaller III, 153–60; a longer treatment of the first stage of Selden's career is in Berkowitz's posthumously published monograph, *John Selden's Formative Years* ed Jansson, which does not, however, entirely supersede his earlier dissertation. Selden's significance in legal-historical studies is recognized by Kelley 'History, English Law and the Renaissance' 24–51; cf Brooks and Sharpe 'Debate: History, English Law and the Renaissance' 133–42. Professor Paul Christianson is currently completing a study of Selden's treatment of the 'ancient constitution' in relationship to his political career, which I am grateful to have been able to consult in typescript: in the meantime, see his essays 'Young John Selden and the Ancient Constitution' and 'John Selden ... and Discretionary Imprisonment.'

16 Tuck *Natural Rights Theories* 82–100; but cf Sommerville 'John Selden, the Law of Nature and the Origins of Government.'

17 Spelman to Wormius, 1 July 1637, *Olai Wormii et ad eum doctorum virorum epistolae* (Copenhagen 1751) 466; Wormius to Spelman, 22 May 1638, ibid 447

18 Selden to Bulstrode Whitelocke, 2 March 1654, BL MS Add 32093, fol 328. Selden helped to decipher Arundel's collection of marbles in 1628; for 'My Lord of Northampton's discourse of earls and dukes' see the Selden collections in Lincoln's Inn, Hale MSS, vol 12, fols 217–32v; Peck *Northampton* 101–21; David Howarth *Lord Arundel and His Circle* (New Haven and London 1985) 92, 97.

19 William Watts to Selden, 11 July 1636, Bodl MS Seld Supra 108 (Selden correspondence, vol I), fol 82; *DNB* sv 'Watts, William'

20 Lincoln's Inn, Hale MSS, vol 12, fols 360–70v; vol 11, fol 54; Selden to Herbert, February 1620, BL MS Add 32092, fol 314; Berkowitz *John Selden's Formative Years* 24

21 Selden acted as executor of her will in 1651, three years before his own death: BL MS Add 6489, fol 5v (copy of Selden's will); Selden to Francis Junius, 7 December 1651, Leiden University MS Pap 2 (unfoliated).

22 This is indicated in the vast quantity of letters from these men to Selden, especially in Bodl MS Seld Supra 109 (Selden correspondence, vol II). Langbaine provided Elias Ashmole with an introduction to Selden in April 1653 (fol 337). Pocock assisted Selden with his edition of 'Eutychius' and completed the work on the latter's death: Pocock to Selden, 5 August 1653, ibid, fol 351.

23 Selden *Historie of Tithes* (1618), following p 491; *Marmora Arundeliana*, in *Joannis Seldenis jurisconsulti opera omnia* ed D. Wilkins (3 vols in 6, 1726) II, 1439; Selden to unknown recipient, 13 December 1638, Huntington Library MS 2946, unfoliated (for a copy of which I am indebted to the Huntington Library). Except where indicated otherwise,

I have cited from original editions of Selden's works rather than Wilkins' collection. A shelfmark in square brackets (e.g. [8° L7.Art.Seld.]) following the date of publication denotes that Selden's own copy of a book, in the Bodleian Library, has been used.

24 CUL MS Oo.7.51, fol 161 contains a list of Latin and oriental manuscripts borrowed by Selden from the Lambeth Palace Library and never returned there by him. After his death, they were sent by his executors to Cambridge, 'to be added to ye rest of the Lambeth Librarie.' Selden often had other scholars do his spadework, such as the Cambridge musicologist Peter Turner: Turner to Selden, 19 August 1627, Bodl MS Seld Supra 108, fol 228.

25 Selden to Jonson, 28 February, *Opera* II, 1690ffv; Edward Hyde, earl of Clarendon *The Life of Edward Earl of Clarendon* (2 vols, Dublin 1759) I, 30–1. Clarendon adds, however, that 'in his conversation he was the most clear discourser ... of any man that hath been known,' a point borne out by his recorded parliamentary speeches and by the pungent clarity of the often-cited *Table Talk of John Selden* ed F. Pollock (1927).

26 G. Gevaerts to P. Young, 3 March 1618 (ns), in *Patricius Junius* ed Kemke 30; Pierre Dupuy to Camden, 30 August 1617 (ns), in *Camdeni epistolae* 194; Peiresc to Camden, 29 January 1618 (ns), ibid 212–13; Selden *Opera* II, 1600; Van Norden 'Peiresc and the English Scholars'; Berkowitz *John Selden's Formative Years* 18

27 P.R. Sellin *Daniel Heinsius and Stuart England* (Leiden 1968) 90

28 G.J. Vossius to Selden, 2 January 1648 (ns), Bodl MS Rawl lett 79, fol 109. In August 1627 Vossius entrusted Selden with an unpolished draft of his commentary on Roman history: Bodl MS Rawl lett 84 (b), fol 53.

29 Rubens to Dupuy, 8 August 1629, *Correspondance de Rubens* ed Ch. Ruelens (Anvers 1887–1909) V, 148; Peiresc to Dupuy, 21 July 1629 (ns) in *Lettres de Peiresc* ed P. Tamizey de Larroque (Paris 1888–98) II, 136

30 Bodl MS Seld Supra 111 (Selden's library list). Excerpts from this have been printed by Barratt 'The Library of John Selden,' appendix C; cf Sparrow 'The Earlier Owners of Books in John Selden's Library' 263–71.

31 Selden *Analecton Anglo-Britannicon libri duo* (1615) in *Opera* II, 948–9; *Jani Anglorum facies altera* in *Opera* II, 964

32 'We have a new law, the law of state ...': Selden, speech in the Commons, 19 April 1628 in *Opera* III, 1989; Berkowitz 'Reason of State in England and the Petition of Right' in *Staatsräson* ed Schnur 165–212

33 Wootton *Paolo Sarpi* 45–76. I thank David Wootton for having suggested to me the possibility of a connection between the Venetian interdict of 1606–7, Sarpi's writings, and Selden's position on clerical temporals in *The Historie of Tithes*, explored below.

34 *Analecton* in *Opera* II, 865, 870. Selden refers to Verstegan's account of the pagan gods of the Saxons.

35 J.J. Scaliger *Opus novum de emendatione temporum in octo libros* (Paris

1583) [G.2.12.Art.Seld.]; Scaliger, *Thesaurus temporum, Eusebii Pamphili Caesareae Palaestinae episcopi, chronicorum canonum* (Paris 1605); Grafton 'Joseph Scaliger and Historical Chronology' Wilcox *Measure of Times Past* 195–208

36 Scaliger to Casaubon, 1 January 1606 (ns), *Illustrissimi viri Josephi Scaligeri ... epistolae* (Leiden 1627) 306; DNB sv 'Lydiat, Thomas'; *Scaligeri epistolae* 337. Camden sent Scaliger a copy of the *Britannia* in 1594 through the peripatetic Cambridge scholar, Richard Thomson: Thomson to Camden, 1 July 1594, *Camdeni epistolae* 54.

37 J.E. Sandys *A History of Classical Scholarship* (3 vols, Cambridge 1903–08) II, 192; Kelley *Foundations of Modern Historical Scholarship* 257; Selden owned Pithou's posthumously published *Opera, sacra, juridica, historica, miscellanea* (Paris 1609) ed Ch. Labbé [4° P.36.Art.Seld.].

38 Camden was in correspondence with Pithou's younger brother, François, who lived till 1621: Thomas Savile to Camden, nd, *Camdeni epistolae* 4.

39 Jean du Tillet *Recueil, des guerres et traictez d'entre les roys de France et d'Angleterre* (Paris 1588) [E.1.1.Art.Seld., a gift from Cotton]; Selden 'To my singular good friend, Mr. Augustine Vincent' in Vincent *A Discoverie of Errours* (1622) sig a1r; Lincoln's Inn, Hale MSS, vol 34, fols 1–114; Selden, *Titles of Honor* (1614) 128–67

40 E. Pasquier *Recherches de la France* in *Oeuvres* (Amsterdam 1723) I. Paul Bouteiller 'Un historien du XVI siècle: Etienne Pasquier' *Bibliothèque d'Humanisme et Renaissance* 6 (1945) 357–92; Dorothy Thickett *Estienne Pasquier (1529–1615): The Versatile Barrister of Sixteenth Century France* (1979) chapter 7; Kelley *Foundations of Modern Historical Scholarship* 271–300; Huppert *Perfect History* 28–71

41 Pasquier *Recherches* col iii; Thickett *Pasquier* 162

42 Pasquier frequently draws 'diverses leçons' from his stories, a practice which Selden avoids. For a critical re-evaluation of the contributions of Pasquier and other French *érudits* to Renaissance 'historicism,' see Schiffman 'Renaissance Historicism Reconsidered.'

43 Selden *The Duello, or Single Combat: From Antiquity Derived into this Kingdom of England* in *Opera* III: 'To the Reader'

44 Ibid III, 66, 77, 84

45 Selden *Jani Anglorum facies altera* in *Opera* II, 989

46 *Jani Anglorum* in *Opera* II, 964; Christianson 'Young John Selden and the Ancient Constitution'; Pocock *Ancient Constitution* 286–305. *Jani Anglorum* was translated in 1682 by 'Redman Westcot' (pseudonym for Adam Littleton) as *The Reverse or Back-face of the English Janus.*

47 Ibid II, 981, 1003

48 Selden 'Illustrations' to Michael Drayton *Poly-Olbion* (part one, 1612) in *Works* ed J.W. Hebel (2nd ed, 5 vols, Oxford 1961) IV, viii*, 22–3

49 Ibid 231, 290; the reference is to Pithou's *Memoires des comtes heredi-taires de Champagne et Brie* (Paris 1572).

50 Ibid viii*

51 Lydiat *Defensio tractatus de variis annorum formis praesertim antiquissima & optima contra Josephi Scaligeri* (1607) [8° L.6.Art.Seld.]; Lydiat *Emendatio temporum compendio facta ab initio mundi ad praesens usque* (1609) [8° L.7.Art.Seld.]. The sixteenth-century Dutch scholar Merula referred to 'synchronismo' in describing his chronological arrangement of the events of the sixteenth century in the different realms of Europe, and various English writers used the word in a variety of different senses. P. Merula to Camden, 7 November 1595, *Camdeni epistolae* 58; for 'Synchronism' see *Oxford English Dictionary*. On the importance of the principal of synchronism for early modern chronologers see Wilcox *Measure of Times Past* 200ff.

52 Selden 'Illustrations' to Drayton *Poly-Olbion*, in *Works* IV, 246, 272

53 Selden *Titles of Honor* (1614), epistle dedicatory, sigs a3r, 3D4v–3F1v, 353

54 Ibid, epistle dedicatory, sig a3r; *Titles of Honor* (2nd ed, 1631), epistle dedicatory, sigs †3v–4r

55 Selden *Titles of Honor* (1614), sig a2v

56 Ibid 301. This passage appears nowhere in the 1631 edition. Spelman quotes it in order to show Selden's agreement with him: 'Feuds and Tenures by Knight-Service' in *Reliquiae Spelmanniae* ed E. Gibson (1698) 26. Selden's position here approximates that of the late Victorian authority J.H. Round. Subsequent scholarship has revised this picture and emphasized the continuity of some feudal institutions from the pre- to the post-Conquest period: see C. Warren Hollister *Anglo-Saxon Military Institutions on the Eve of the Norman Conquest* (Oxford 1962), introduction.

57 Sir John Fortescue *De laudibus legum Angliae* ed Selden (1616), Notes, pp 7, 9

58 Ibid 17; Tuck 'The Ancient Law of Freedom' 143

59 See, for example, Easterby *History of the Law of Tithes*; H.W. Clarke *A History of Tithes* (1891); Roundell Palmer, first earl of Selborne, *Ancient Facts and Fictions concerning Churches and Tithes* (1892). All merely offer variations to Selden's themes, citing him as their final authority.

60 Joseph Justus Scaliger *Diatriba de decimis* in *Opuscula varia antehac non edita* ed Isaac Casaubon (Paris 1610) 61–70. Selden cites this in his illustrations to *Poly-Olbion* (*Works of Michael Drayton* IV, 186), and some notes in his hand on Scaliger's essay are to be found in Bodl MS Seld Supra 108, fols 187–90v.

61 Paolo Sarpi *History of Benefices and Selections from History of the Council of Trent* ed and trans P. Burke (New York 1967) 34–8 discusses

tithing practices in the primitive and medieval church. I have found no direct evidence that Selden read Sarpi's manuscript or even knew of its existence. Given the relatively free flow of manuscript writings across Europe in this period, however, and the points of similarity between the two works, such a connection is by no means impossible.

62 Selden, *The Historie of Tithes* (1618), facing p 1, italicized in original. All further references to the *Historie* will be given as page or signature numbers in parentheses.

63 Digby to Selden, 11 February 1637 (ns), Bodl MS Seld Supra 108, fol 78

64 Compare François Baudouin *De institutione historiae universae et ejus cum jurisprudentia conjunctione* (Paris 1561) cited by Kelley *Foundations of Modern Historical Scholarship* 116.

65 Houghton 'The English Virtuoso' 51–73

66 This error is perpetuated by Berkowitz in *John Selden's Formative Years* 32–50.

67 There were, of course, other reasons for the presentation of documentary evidence than the requirements of argument. Herbert of Cherbury and Daniel, for instance, seem to have been motivated less by any political message they hoped to convey than by the need to mitigate their own scepticism as to the certainty or, in Herbert's case, the 'probability' of the past.

68 For a brief discussion of some of these works and of the multipartisan character of post-1640 historical writing, see chapter 8 below. On the proliferation of documentary collections in historical writing, see MacGillivray *Restoration Historians* 97.

69 Wootton *Paolo Sarpi* 105 observes that the research conducted and presented by his subject was also scarcely impartial.

70 See, eg, *Table Talk* 100–1: 'Divines ought to doe no more then what the state permitts; before the state became Christian they made their owne lawes, & those y^t did not observe them they excommunicated (naughty men) ... By what lawe, by what power? They were still subject to the state, wch was heathen': this is typical of Selden's later erastianism, but it seems unwise to read such undated remarks back into Selden's earlier writings.

71 Tuck *Natural Rights Theories* 58–81, 86–94. It was in a similar jurisdictional dispute, over the control of the seas, that Selden would engage his most learned opponent, Hugo Grotius, in erudite debate, responding to Grotius' 1609 work *Mare liberum* with his own *J. Seldeni mare clausum*, largely written in 1618–19 but not published till 1635. It was translated by Marchamont Nedham in 1652 as *Of the Dominion, or Ownership of the Sea*.

72 George Carleton *Tithes Examined and Proved to Bee Due to the Clergie by a Divine Right* (1606) fols 14, 20; other works which may have attracted Selden's attention in the 1610s likely include Foulke Robartes *The Revenue of the Gospel Is Tythes, Due to the Ministerie of the Word, by that Word* (Cambridge 1613).

73 Sir Henry Spelman *De Non Temerandis Ecclesiis: A Tract of the Rights and Respect Due unto Churches* (1613) rpt in *The English Works of Sir Henry Spelman Kt.* ed Edmund Gibson (2nd ed, 1727)

74 Spelman *The Larger Treatise concerning Tithes* ed J. Stephens (1647) 79, 129ff. Spelman implied in 1613 that he had already written this work: see *De non temerandis ecclesiis* 3.

75 Spelman *Larger Treatise* 6, 93. For Spelman's further development of the case against lay invasion of clerical property, see his posthumously published *Tithes too Hot to Be Touched* (1646) and *The History and Fate of Sacrilege* (1698 and Bodl MS Cherry 18). All three of these works (and especially the last, which relates many graphic tales of the punishments inflicted on those who invade ecclesiastical property) are even more openly polemical than Selden's work. Spelman's ability to write forcefully in order to make a case is a point that is easily overlooked if one remains intent on seeing him, as much as Selden, strictly as a pioneer of modern historical scholarship.

76 It is possible, too, that in choosing to cast his argument as history, he was following Carleton, who referred to his own work as having recounted the 'story of tithes from the beginning': *Tithes Examined* fol 35.

77 J.J. Scaliger *Opuscula varia antehac non edita* ed Isaac Casaubon (Paris 1610) 61–70 points out (61) that Moses 'non unum genus decimarum proponit.'

78 Selden here further amends a correction by Scaliger.

79 Paolo Sarpi also made the important distinction between the views of the canonists and those of theologians, who do not argue that clerical property is held *jure divino: History of Benefices* 35, 37. Unlike Selden he was again more open in declaring flatly that the law of tithes did *not* rest on divine law: 'In general, we can say that the goods of the Church, of whatever sort, are possessed by their owners in virtue of human laws.' Selden as usual stopped short of this and protected himself by arguing only that such *jure divino* claims had little historical basis, not that they were actually invalid.

80 Christianson 'Young John Selden and the Ancient Constitution' 290–3, 302

81 Compare Sarpi *History of Benefices* 12.

82 Selden notes (364) that English monks at the council of Lyons in 1274 affirmed an arbitrary conveyance, implying the practice to be of long standing 'both of fact and positive law.'

83 For example, such lands which fell outside the boundaries of a parish retained the 'ancient libertie' of consecration; and the king could still give tithes of crown lands, as Edward I conveyed the tithes of the Forest of Dean to the diocese of Llandaff in 1280.

84 Selden is rather obscure on the division of tithes among rectors and vicars, and does not use the terms 'great' and 'small.' See Easterby *History of the Law of Tithes* 21–6.

85 Selden's commendatory attitude to the cooperation of lay and cleric in the pre-Conquest administration of justice provides a further caution against considering him an erastian, or even an anticlerical, at this stage in his career.

86 As chief justice, Coke had already fought a long battle with Archbishop Richard Bancroft a decade earlier: Hill *Economic Problems* 121–39, and *Intellectual Origins of the English Revolution* 247–8; N. Adams 'The Judicial Conflict over Tithes' *English Historical Review* 52 (1937) 1–22.

87 Peiresc to Camden, 4 March 1618 (ns) in *Camdeni epistolae* 221, also in *Lettres de Peiresc* VII, 773

88 James Sempill *Sacrilege Sacredly Handled* (1619), appendix, 19, 29, 34–5

89 Richard Tillesley *Animadversions upon M. Selden's History of Tithes, and His Review Thereof* (1619) sig b4r, 1–29, 33, 61, 81

90 Tillesley *Animadversions* 162, 192

91 Selden *An Admonition to the Reader of Sir James Sempill's Appendix* in *Opera* III, 1351, 1356

92 Ibid III, 1351, 1356; Coke *Le Tierce Part des Reportes*, 'To the reader', sig C3r. This was not, however, a universal opinion even among lawyers, many of whom (including Selden if occasion served) could cite chronicles in support of arguments (though mainly not involving points of law) in parliamentary debate; for some exceptions see Woolf 'Genre into Artifact' 330, 354.

93 Selden *A Reply to Dr Tillesley's Animadversions upon the History of Tythes* in *Opera* III, 1370–71. Selden also staked the loss of all his books on the accuracy of his quotations in 'Of My Purpose and End in Writing the "History of Tythes" ' in *Opera* III, 1452. This was not a wise wager. Selden was prone to careless citations, as a random check of his references reveals: for example, *Historie* 13 cites the statute of 26 Hen VIII c 3 as 16 Hen VIII c 3; some, such as this, were likely printers' errors. His transcriptions of cartularies include many contractions and lacunae which he does not indicate. Compare *Historie* 330 with William Dugdale *Monasticon Anglicanum* (1817–30) IV, 646–7; *Historie* 339–41 with *Monasticon* V, 14–15. He was either unaware of, or chose to ignore, a thirteenth-century tract *De decimis* (now Bodl MS Auct D.212), against the detaining of tithes, although the manuscript had been in the Bodleian since 1608.

94 Selden *Opera* III, 1380–1, 1386. Tillesley responded to Selden's unpublished, but circulated, reply in a second edition of the *Animadversions* in 1621.

95 Selden to Buckingham, 5 May 1620, Lincoln's Inn, Hale MSS, vol 12, fols 245–6 (also in *Opera* III, 1394–5)

96 Montagu to Cotton, nd (1620?), Bodl MS Smith 71, fol 107; on the organization of the attack on the *Historie*, see Berkowitz *John Selden's Formative Years* 35–8, 305n23. There is no reason to suspect the sincer-

ity of Montagu's admiration for Selden, whom he would later ask to serve as 'arbitrator' between him and his parliamentary critics in 1626: Nicholas Tyacke *Anti-Calvinists: The Rise of English Arminianism, c. 1590–1640* (Oxford 1987) 145–6; Sheila Lambert 'Richard Montagu, Arminianism and Censorship' *Past and Present* 124 (1989) 36–68, at 45.

97 Richard Montagu *Diatribae upon the First Part of the Late History of Tithes* (1621) 16

98 Montagu *Diatribae* 17, 24, 29, 73, 120, 123, 125–6, 217

99 Other works on the issue, each written in the light of and opposed to Selden's interpretation, include William Sclater the elder *The Quaestion of Tythes Revised* (1623); Richard Perrot *Jacobs Vowe, or the True Historie of Tithes* (Cambridge 1627). Bartholomew Parsons, the incumbent of Ludgershall, Wiltshire, addressed the issue once more in a brief pamphlet entitled *The Historie of Tithes: or, Tithes Vindicated* (Oxford 1637), which does not refer directly to Selden's book.

100 Langbaine to Selden, 22 August 1653, Bodl MS Seld Supra 109, fol 463. Cf Langbaine's letter to Selden on some fifteenth-century tithe documents, 27 September 1652, MS Seld Supra 109, fol 390.

101 Duppa's MS notes on page 369 of the Bodleian copy of the *Diatribae* [shelfmark 4° Rawl.455]

102 On Brooke, Vincent, and the 'controversy' over the accuracy of Camden's genealogical work in *Britannia*, see Mark Noble *A History of the College of Arms* (1804) 240–5.

103 Selden 'To My Singular Good Friend, Mr Augustine Vincent' in Vincent's *A Discoverie of Errours in the First Edition of the Catalogue of Nobility, Published by Ralph Brooke, Yorke Herald, 1619* (1622) [s.1.11.Jur.Seld. contains MS notes by Selden] sig a1r–v.

104 Ibid sigs a1r–2r; F.J. Levy notes that a similar remark can be found thirty-five years earlier, in the preface to the second edition of Raphael Holinshed's *Chronicles;* this may have been written by the antiquary Francis Thynne: 'Hayward, Daniel, and the Beginnings of Politic History in England' 29.

105 For Ingulph, or Ingulf, see, eg *Analecton* in *Opera* II, 922; *Jani Anglorum* in *Opera* II, 992; notes to *Poly-Olbion* in Drayton *Works* IV, 28. For 'Eutychius,' see Fry's article, 'John Selden,' in *DNB* and the letters from Pocock to Selden, Bodl MS Seld Supra 109, fols 390–400. Selden considered Eutychius to be 'the Bede of Egypt,' *Eutychii Aegyptii, patriarchae orthodoxorum Alexandrini, scriptoris ... ecclesiae suae origines* (1642) in *Opera* II, 418.

106 Selden to Cotton, 4 July 1629, BL MS Cott Julius C.III, fol 343

107 Selden *Notae et spicilegium in Eadmeri* in *Opera* II, 1600, 1667

108 Selden to Ussher, 4 March 1621, *Opera* II, 1707; Berkowitz *John Selden's Formative Years* 60–4, 231ff

109 *Titles of Honor* (2nd ed, 1631) [T.1.10.Jur.Seld. with MS corrections by Selden] sig §4r (my emphasis)

110 Selden *Titles of Honor* (1631) sigs §4–¶2
111 Selden *Titles* (1631) 525 note 's'
112 Ibid 612, 622–5. R.H.C. Davis points out the doubts which have arisen concerning Round's views: 'From Scandinavians into Franks' *Times Literary Supplement* 4164 (21 January 1983) 62.
113 As he himself tells us, his introduction was fit only for 'a period of domestic leisure incompatible with more extensive studies or more weighty affairs': *Joannis Seldeni ad Fletam dissertatio* trans David Ogg (Cambridge 1925) 3.
114 See eg Langbaine to Selden, nd (1654), BL MS Add 34727, fol 93; Selden to Meric Casaubon, 16 September 1653, BL MS Burney 369, fol 122. As late as 23 July 1654, Selden was discussing the astrological writings of Vettius Valens (2nd century AD) with the scholar P.D. Huet: Leiden Univ Lib, MS Burm Q.22.II (Huet letters) fol 235.
115 Compare this title with the autograph MS, 'a discourse or relation both of the auncyent and modern estate of the principality of Wales, dutchie of Cornewall, and earledom of Chester,' Inner Temple Library, London, Petyt MS 538, vol 39, fols 205–64v, signed and dated by Dodderidge (fol 206), 1 January 1 Jas. 1 (ie, 1604).
116 Peter Heylyn *The History of the Sabbath* (1636) sig A6r; K.L. Parker *The English Sabbath: A Study of Doctrine and Discipline from the Reformation to the Civil War* (Cambridge 1988) 1, 17, 198–204
117 Thomas Gataker *Of the Nature and Use of Lots* (1619)
118 William Burton *The Description of Leicestershire* (1622) 8–9; William Bedwell *A Briefe Description of the Towne of Tottenham High-Crosse in Middlesex* (1631) sig E3v
119 John Philipot *The Catalogue of the Chancellors of England, the Lord Keepers of the Greate Seale, and the Lord Treasurers of England* (1636) sig B1v; Philipot appears to have modelled his book on the *Recueil des roys de France, leur couronne et maison* (7th ed, 3 parts, Paris 1607) by the French archivist Jean du Tillet, for whom see Kelley *Foundations of Modern Historical Scholarship* 222–33.
120 Dugdale *The Antiquities of Warwickshire Illustrated* (1656), preface; Van Norden 'Elizabethan College of Antiquaries' 482–3
121 Shakerley Marmion *The Antiquary* Act 1 in his *Dramatic Works* (Edinburgh and London nd) 216
122 White Kennett *Parochial Antiquities, Attempted in the History of Ambrosden, Burcester, and Other Adjacent Parts in the Counties of Oxford and Bucks* ed B. Bandinel (2 vols, Oxford 1818) 1, xvii. Interestingly, Kennett tried to arrange his antiquities in chronological order, proceeding like an annalist year by year from the Norman Conquest.
123 The *Oxford English Dictionary* lists the first known instance of 'antiquarian' as a noun as early as 1610, though it did not enjoy much use till considerably later; the adjective, however, did not become current before the middle of the eighteenth century.

124 Marmion *The Antiquary* Act I in *Dramatic Works* 210
125 John Earle *Micro-cosmographie* (6th ed, 1633) no 9. For later examples, see *A New Dictionary of the Canting Crew* (1690) and James Puckle *The Club: Or a Dialogue between Father and Son* (1711) 10–11.
126 Richard Rawlinson *A New Method of Studying History, Geography and Cosmology* (2 vols, 1730) II, 460–2
127 Levine *Doctor Woodward's Shield* 114–29
128 On Augustan scholarship, see Douglas *English Scholars*; Levine *Doctor Woodward's Shield* 93–150, 291–3 and *Humanism and History* chapter 4; Michael Hunter *John Aubrey and the Realm of Learning* (1975).
129 William Nicolson *The English Historical Library* (1714)

Chapter Eight

1 Thomas Heywood *A True Description of His Majesties Royall Ship Built at Woolwitch* (1637) 29; Roy Strong *Van Dyck: Charles I on Horseback* (1972) 47, 59–63; Parry *Golden Age Restor'd* 249. For good general discussions of the court culture of the 1630s see Smuts *Court Culture* chapter 7; Norbrook *Poetry and Politics in the English Renaissance* chapters 9 and 10; Sharpe *Criticism and Compliment* chapter 1.
2 Sir Richard Baker *Chronicle of the Kings of England* (1643, 1653, 1660, 1665, 1670, 1674, 1679, 1684, 1696). On the decline of the chronicle, see Woolf 'Genre into Artifact.'
3 *DNB* sv 'Trussell, John'; Wood *Ath Ox* II, 270; in 1639 Trussell tried to obtain the patronage of Sir John Finch for his unpublished 'Epitome of the Forest Law,' Bodl MS Eng hist d242, fols 71–138v.
4 C.W. Brooks *Pettyfoggers and Vipers of the Commonwealth: The 'Lower Branch' of the Legal Profession in Early Modern England* (Cambridge 1986) 223
5 Trussell *A Continuation of the Collection of the History of England, Beginning Where Samuel Daniell Esquier Ended* (1636) sig A3r, 51
6 Powell *The Life of Alfred* (1634) 70; *DNB* sv 'Powell, Robert'
7 Powell *Alfred* 147–9; Smuts *Court Culture* 132ff provides a valuable corrective to the notion that the Caroline court spent an inordinate amount of money on art, architecture, music, and entertainments; using the accounts of the Exchequer he demonstrates that, if anything, money was spent more selectively and frugally on culture under Charles than under James, though wastage continued to occur in other areas of the household.
8 Ibid sig a6r; Twyne *Antiquitatis academiae Oxoniensis apologia* (1608). None of the several Robert Powells in *Alum Ox* 1193, or *Alum Cant* III, 388 fits the age of our man, who tells us in his preface that he had practised law for twenty-five years before 1634.
9 J. Taylor *A Memoriall of All the English Monarchs* in *All the Workes of John Taylor the Water-Poet* (1630) 269

10 Charles Aleyn *The Battailes of Crescey, and Poictiers* (1631; 2nd ed, 1633) and *The Historie of that Wise Prince, Henrie the Seventh* (1638); Thomas May *The Reigne of King Henry the Second* (1633) and *The Victorious Reigne of King Edward the Third* (1635); John Ford *The Chronicle Historie of Perkin Warbeck* (1634)

11 Thomas Heywood *The First and Second Partes of King Edward the Fourth* (1599)

12 Heywood *If You Know Not Me, You Know No Bodie* (Part I: 1605, 1606, 1608 [2], 1610, 1613, 1623, 1632, 1639; part II: 1606, 1609, 1623, 1633); idem *Englands Elizabeth; Her Life and Troubles* (1631); for background, see A.M. Clark *Thomas Heywood* (Oxford 1931) and L.B. Wright 'Heywood and the Popularizing of History' 287–93.

13 Sallust *Histories* trans Heywood (1608), Preface (no sig); Heywood *Troia Britanica, or Great Britaines Troy* (1609), cantos 16, 17, pp 413–66

14 Heywood *Life of Merlin* (1641) 'To the Reader'

15 L.B. Wright *Middle-Class Culture in Elizabethan England* 297–338; Levy *Tudor Historical Thought* 202–36

16 Sharpe *Sir Robert Cotton* 81–2. Spelman continued to foster scholarship by founding an Anglo-Saxon lectureship in 1638: Douglas *English Scholars* 53.

17 Cochrane *Historians and Historiography in the Italian Renaissance* 163

18 MacGillivray *Restoration Historians* is the only full-length study of the topic, and it concentrates mainly on the period after 1660; cf the briefer survey in Richardson *Debate on the English Revolution* 8–32; also Hartman 'Contemporary Explanations of the English Revolution' for detailed studies of Clarendon, Hobbes, Harrington, and, especially useful, Thomas May. To these works I owe much of the following brief survey of the post-war historiography.

19 Thomas Fuller *The Appeal of Injured Innocence: Unto the Learned and Ingenuous Reader* (1659) 1, 10

20 Thomas May *The History of the Parliament of England, Which Began November 3, 1640, with a Short and Necessary View of Some Precedent Years* (1647) ed F. Maseres (Oxford 1854) xix–xx, 2–3, 6–7. In his *A Discourse concerning the Successe of Former Parliaments* (1642) 4–5, 12, May had taken an altogether more moderate stance, shrinking from criticizing even past monarchs and even regarding some parliaments as bad (for example, that which had deposed Richard II). His opinions had changed by 1647, and they grew even more radical three years later, when in his *A Breviary of the History of the Parliament of England* (2nd ed, 1655) he was even more critical of the king and praised the Independents for their victory over the Presbyterians in parliament. May is a much more complex figure than has been assumed, and deserves further attention.

21 May *History of the Parliament* 16. The praising of Elizabeth as a means of blackening James's reputation by contrast is a strategy found in

many pro-parliamentary histories, for instance Francis Osborne's *Historical Memoires* on the reigns of the two monarchs, first published in 1658, and reprinted by Sir Walter Scott (under the title *Traditional Memoirs*) as part of his two-volume collection *Secret History of the Court of James the First* (2 vols, Edinburgh 1811) vol I. Modern historians, anxious to read back into James's own reign these unfavourable opinions, often fail to recognize that such works are *not* contemporary observations but histories or reminiscences, and should be treated with appropriate caution.

22 May *History of the Parliament* xix

23 Ibid xv

24 Edward Hyde, earl of Clarendon *The History of the Rebellion and Civil Wars in England Begun in the Year 1641* ed W.D. Macray (6 vols, Oxford 1888) I, 2; *The Life of Edward Earl of Clarendon* (2 vols, Dublin 1759) 35. R.W. Harris *Clarendon and the English Revolution* (Stanford, Cal. 1983) 7 argues that Clarendon could not have conceived of his history as a response to May since he nowhere mentions it and commenced it a year before his former companion's work appeared. This seems convincing, though it does not rule out Clarendon's having revised his history (as we know he did) in later years with parliamentarian accounts such as May's in mind.

25 Clarendon *History* I, 3. On Clarendon's religious and political views, the best study remains B.H.G. Wormald *Clarendon: Politics, History and Religion, 1640–1660* (Cambridge 1951); most recently, see Martine Watson Brownley *Clarendon and the Rhetoric of Historical Form* (Philadelphia 1985) 2–18, for an interesting discussion of Clarendon's literary artistry in the context of mid-seventeenth-century historical writing.

26 Sir Anthony Weldon *The Court and Character of King James* (1650) in *Secret History* ed Scott I, 313–482; Godfrey Goodman *Court of King James the First* ed J.S. Brewer (2 vols, 1839). For a view of James's reign only marginally less hostile than Weldon's, see the account by the bookseller Michael Sparke *The Narrative History of King James, for the First Fourteen Years* (1651). In contrast, royalist historians after the Restoration reverted, not surprisingly, to a highly commendatory position on both James and Charles I: see, for instance, George Meriton *Anglorum Gesta, or, a Brief History of England* (1675) 320ff; Francis Sandford *A Genealogical History of the Kings of England, and Monarchs of Great Britain, &c, from the Conquest, Anno 1066, to the Year 1677* (1677) 519–27.

27 Arthur Wilson *The History of Great Britain* (1653); Sir William Sanderson *Aulicus Coquinariae* (1650) in *Secret History* II; Sanderson *A Compleat History of the Lives and Reigns of Mary Queen of Scotland, and of Her Son and Successor, James the Sixth, King of Scotland ... in Vindication of Him against Two Scandalous Authors* (1656)

28 There are, naturally, exceptions to this. Not every historian had Harring-

ton's sensitivity to long-term causes, and two of the earliest pro-parliamentary historians, John Vicars and Joshua Sprigg, chose to narrate only recent events. Vicars started his *Magnalia Dei Anglicana. Or, Englands Parliamentary-Chronicle* (1646) with the commencement of the Long Parliament. Sprigg's *Anglia Rediviva. Englands Recovery* (1647), which is largely a panegyric of Sir Thomas Fairfax, has an even shorter perspective, briefly beginning with 'a general account of the miserable condition of this kingdome, before this present parliament' but concentrating almost entirely on narrating the period of the war after the creation of the New Model Army.

29 Hill 'The Norman Yoke' 81-92
30 John Milton *The History of Britain* ed French Fogle in *Complete Prose Works* v, part i (New Haven, Conn. 1971) 129, 131
31 Ibid 257
32 Ibid 327-8
33 Ibid 402-3
34 James Harrington *The Commonwealth of Oceana* (1656) in *Political Works* ed Pocock 190-8. The principal similarity between Harrington and Daniel lies in their assertion of a break in political traditions at 1485 with the advent of the Tudors. But in other ways their views were strikingly different. Harrington's historical thought is suffused with a classicism lacking in Daniel. Where Daniel praised the Vandals, Huns, and other barbarians for their contributions to language and culture, and generally extolled the Middle Ages, Harrington preferred the era of the Roman republic to either the tyrannical reign of the emperors or the barbarian migrations, which in his view had 'overwhelmed ancient languages, learning, prudence, manners, cities, changing the names of rivers, countries, seas, mountains and men; Camillus, Caesar and Pompey being come to Edmund, Richard and Geoffrey': *Political Works* 188, 190.
35 Ibid 196-7
36 Ibid 197-8
37 Thomas Hobbes *Behemoth, or the Long Parliament* ed Ferdinand Tönnies (2nd ed, 1969) 10-13, 40-56, 76. Hobbes concluded that the commons did not become part of parliament by right until after the baronial troubles of Henry III's reign.
38 Peter Heylyn *Aerius Redivivus: or, the History of the Presbyterians. Containing the Beginnings, Progress and Successes of that Active Sect ... from the Year 1536, to the Year 1647* (Oxford 1670); Clement Walker *The History of Independency, with the Rise, Growth, and Practices of that Powerfull and Restlesse Faction* (2 parts, 1648-9) II, 255 blames the war on the Independents, who wished to 'enslave the people with an oligarchicall, military, and arbitary government.' Charles I, on the other hand, 'from the beginning took up defensive arms to maintain religion, laws, liberties, and the ancient fundamentall being of parliaments and this kingdome' (ibid). Walker's book shows just how

thoroughly religious and political issues were interwoven in many accounts of the war. Richardson *Debate on the English Revolution* 9 seems to me to undervalue this point by asserting that historical controversy in the seventeenth century was 'primarily political and constitutional.'

39 Thomas Fuller *The Appeal of Injured Innocence* (1659) 11. Although he admits to having expected criticism of the *Church-History*, Fuller was surprised that Heylyn would attack 'one who had been his fellow-servant to, and sufferer for, the same lord and master, King Charles': ibid 2.

40 Peter Heylyn *Examen Historicum: or a Discovery and Examination of the Religious Learned and Ingenuous reader. In a Controversie betwixt the Animadvertor Dr. Peter Heylyn and the Author Thomas Fuller* (1659). Fuller responded to this in his *Appeal of Injured Innocence*, inciting Heylyn to reply in *Certamen Epistolare, or the Letter-Combate ... in Answer to Some Passages in Mr. Fullers Late Appeal* (1659); MacGillivray *Restoration Historians* 41 notes that the two writers were eventually reconciled. Heylyn had a nose for controversy: he had already been criticized by Sir William Sanderson in *Peter Pursued; or Dr. Heylin Overtaken, Arrested, and Arraigned upon His Three Appendixes* (1658). Not one to worry that he had too many opponents, Heylyn attacked L'Estrange's *The Reign of King Charles* (1655) in his own *Observations on the Historie of King Charles* (1656); within the same year a second edition of L'Estrange's work had appeared, with a rejoinder, to which Heylyn replied in *Extraneus Vapulans: or the Observator Rescued from the Violent but Vaine Assaults of Hamon L'Estrange, Esq.* (1656). On the various controversies, see Barnard *Theologo-historicus* 223ff.

41 MacGillivray *Restoration Historians* 30 suggests that Heylyn may have resigned himself to the permanence of the Cromwellian regime, a point that is borne out in his *Observations on the Historie of King Charles* 26 where he attacks L'Estrange for implying that parliaments are necessary to legitimize all acts of state. 'Were it so, a parliament must be co-ordinate to kings (*or such as have the power of kings*) not subordinate to them' (emphasis is mine).

42 *A Collection of All the Publicke Orders Ordinances and Declarations of Both Houses of Parliament, from the Ninth of March 1642. Untill December 1646* ed Edward Husbands (1646); cf the collection of letters and other 'secret' documents published in *Cabala: Sive Scrinia Sacra* (1654); MacGillivray *Restoration Historians* 96–7.

43 Preston 'English Ecclesiastical Historians and the Problem of Bias'

44 Bulstrode Whitelocke *Memorials of the English Affairs* (1682). Like Clarendon, Whitelocke begins his account of the revolution with the accession of Charles. In the published *Memorials* he maintained a position of apparent neutrality, while shaping his account to support the

moderate reforms of the Long Parliament. He was capable even of a generous assessment of Strafford (44), whom he had helped prosecute, and he offers an unemotional account of the execution of the king (370). But in his unpublished *Annals* (BL MSS Add 53726, 37343, 37344, 37345, and 4992), which contain much more about his life and place in affairs, he proved much less guarded: for discussion see MacGillivray *Restoration Historians* 120–44.

45 MacGillivray *Restoration Historians* 96–109

46 John Rushworth *Historical Collections* (8 vols, 1659–1701) I, sigs b1v–3r

47 Volume VII appeared in 1701, eleven years after Rushworth's death; volume VIII, published in 1680, is a separate part devoted to the trial of the earl of Strafford in 1641, at which Rushworth had taken notes.

48 John Nalson *An Impartial Collection of the Great Affairs of State from the Beginning of the Scotch Rebellion ... to the Murther of King Charles* (2 vols, 1682–3) I, ii; MacGillivray *Restoration Historians* 109–19. Despite its title, Nalson's book only reaches January 1642.

49 Nalson *Impartial Collection* I, ii; II, ii

50 Nalson *Impartial Collection* I, lxxviii; on Rushworth and Nalson in the context of late seventeenth-century debates over the 'historicity' of accounts of the recent past, see McKeon *Origins of the English Novel* 49–50.

51 Sir William Dugdale *A Short View of the Late Troubles in England* (Oxford 1681) 1, 6–7, 592–608

52 Lucy Hutchinson *Memoirs of the Life of Colonel Hutchinson* ed James Sutherland (1973) 40

53 Ibid 40–2

54 Ludlow's unknown seventeenth-century editor, who was likely the deist John Toland, turned Ludlow's manuscript into a published version which scarcely resembles it, as Dr Worden has convincingly shown in his recent study of the original memoirs: *A Voyce from the Watch Tower* ed A.B. Worden (Camden Society, 4th ser, 21, 1978) 22–5.

55 Ibid 7, 144, 208, 273. Ludlow also records (222) the regicide and republican Thomas Scott as having voiced the opinion, at his trial in 1660, that 'there was no more but a house of Commons, in the Saxons' tyme,' to which the court had replied that 'he spake of tymes wherein thinges were obscure.'

56 For Newton's attitude to the relationship between providence and history, and a salutary reminder of the continuing role played by God in the early eighteenth-century view of the past, see Frank E. Manuel *Isaac Newton, Historian* (Cambridge, Mass. 1963) passim.

57 Huppert *Perfect History* 170–82; Ranum *Artisans of Glory* chapter 1

58 Hay 'The Historiographers Royal'; Baker *Race of Time* 95

Bibliography

Manuscript Sources

London

Public Record Office, Chancery Lane
SP 12, 14, 16, 78

British Library
Additional Manuscripts

6489	Copy of Selden's will
6928	George Harry's genealogy and epitome of history
12497	Bolton's poem on the Roman emperors
17919	Richard Symonds's notes on Roman buildings
20028	Virgilio Malvezzi's life of King Numa
22587	John Hayward's tract on precedence of doctors of law over serjeants
24487–92	Joseph Hunter's lives of literary men
28021	Francis Hubert's *Edward II*
32092–3	Selden correspondence
34316	Hubert's *Edward II*
34599	Spelman correspondence
34727	Selden correspondence
35841	Selden correspondence
36294	Camden's letterbook
38139	Manwood papers (correspondence of Morgan Colman)
39177	Bolton 'academ roial' proposal
45140	Francis Godwin's notes on his *Annales*
57336	Speed's notebook on Yorkist kings
60284	Cotton's *Henry III*, copy dated 1622

Burney MSS
369   Selden correspondence with Meric Casaubon

Cottonian MSS
Julius C.III   Letters to Cotton
Julius C.V   Letters to Camden
Vespasian C.XIV   Bolton poem on Mary Stuart
Titus B.I   Cotton's notes on Guicciardini
Titus B.V   Bolton's 'academ' papers
Titus C.XI   Godwin's *Annales*
Faustina E.V   Discourses of the Society of Antiquaries

Egerton MSS
2255   Speed's tract on Christ
2711   Selden correspondence

Harleian MSS
255   D'Ewes correspondence
286   Selden correspondence
367   John Stow's collections
782   Ralph Brooke's notebook
4872   John Lewis' history of Britain
5748   17th-century notes on Thomas Godwyn
6018   Cotton's book-lending list, 1621
6021   Hayward's *Edward* VI
6103, 6143   Bolton 'academ' scheme
6521   Bolton's letterbook and notes on Roman history
7523   Bolton correspondence

Lansdowne MSS
XC   Hicks papers (Bolton correspondence)
XCIX   Colman correspondence
DCCCCLXXXIV   White Kennett's historical collections

Royal MSS
App 7   Cotton's *Henry* III
17.B.VI   Saltern's *Antient lawes*
18.A.XXXVII   John Lewis' proposals for a history of Britain
18.A.LXXI   Bolton 'academ' proposals

Sloane MSS
241   Geographical description of England by Cotton and an
              anonymous associate
2521   17th-century notes on Roman imperial history
3371   17th-century notes on Lucius Florus' epitome

Stowe MSS
75   Colman's genealogy of James I

76	*Gesta Britannici* by Roger Ley, c 1655 (contains biographical accounts of John Hayward and others)
1045	Francis Tate's antiquarian collections
1046	Miscellaneous antiquarian papers

Inner Temple Library
Barrington MSS

| 84 | Cambridge undergraduate's notebook, c 1655 |

Petyt MSS

512, vol A	Extracts on the Anglo-Saxon invasions
vol E	Petyt's notes on English history from Samuel Daniel and others
533, vol 1	Petyt's notes on Daniel concerning Magna Carta
538, vol 24	Miscellaneous transcripts from English histories and antiquarian discourses, on the antiquity of parliament
vol 39	Dodderidge's 'discourse' on the principality of Wales

Lincoln's Inn Library
Hale MSS

11	Selden collectanea (mainly for *Titles of Honor*)
12	Miscellaneous Selden collections
34	Idem
84	Idem
86	Commonplace book, possibly belonging to Selden

Maynard MSS

| 15 | Anonymous catalogue of kings of England from Egbert |

Oxford

Bodleian Library
Ashmolean MSS

837	Bolton correspondence
1113	Bolton dialogue on St George
1116	Miscellaneous heraldic and historical papers

Rawlinson MSS

D.1	Bolton's *Hypercritica*, first draft
D.353	Heylyn's warrant as royal chaplain
D.360, 368	17th-century notes on Samuel Daniel's *Collection*
D.396	Camden correspondence
D.692	Brian Twyne's notes on Livy
D.1062	Hayward's dedication of *Henry IIII* to the earl of Essex
lett 79	Vossius correspondence
lett 84:a–f	Idem

Selden MSS

Supra 81	Degory Whear's letters and poems
Supra 108–9, 123	Selden correspondence
Supra 111	Selden's library list

Smith MSS

17	Camden's commonplace book
70	Hayward's letter to James I
71, 74	Copies of Camden and Cotton letters
76	Letters of Patrick Young

Tanner MSS

73	Miscellaneous papers of Edmund Bolton
84	Archbishop Sancroft's copy of Daniel's Breviary
89	Bolton correspondence
94	Bolton 'academ' proposals

Miscellaneous Western MSS

Auct F.2.21	Whear's lectures on Florus
Auct F.9	Camden's manuscript of Florus
Cherry 18	Spelman's *History of Sacrilege*
Don.c.79	Camden correspondence
Eng hist d.242	Trussell's treatise on forest laws
Eng lett b.27	George Buck correspondence
Eng misc b.106	Buck's 'Commentary'
Eng poet d.3	17th-century notes on Fulbecke's history of Rome
Lat misc a.1	Colman's genealogy of James I
Laud misc 614	17th-century notes on Camden's *Annales*
Wood F.9	Bolton's *Hypercritica* (final version)
Wood F.39	Anthony Wood's correspondence

Cambridge

University Library

Add 7596	Spelman-Wheloc correspondence
Dd.3.63	Earl of Northampton's correspondence
Dd.14.28 (2)	Cotton's *Henry III* (dated 1614)
Oo.7.51	Lambeth Palace Library lending list

Trinity College

R.5.20	Camden's *Annales of England* 1603–23; notes for and royal licence to print first part of *Annales* of Elizabeth's reign

Washington, DC

Folger Shakespeare Library
MS 916.1   Bolton correspondence
MS G.a.12   Continuation of *Henry IIII* by Sir John Hayward

San Marino, California

Huntington Library
MS 2946   Miscellaneous correspondence, including a letter of
                  Selden

Paris

Bibliothèque Nationale
Collection Dupuy
632   De Thou correspondence
663   Peiresc correspondence
699   Dupuy correspondence
836   De Thou correspondence

The Hague

Royal Dutch Library
MS 130.E.32   Album amicorum of J.F. Gronovius
MS 133.M.63   Album amicorum of Bernardus Paladinus

Leiden

University Library
Pap. 2   Miscellaneous correspondence of English and Dutch
                  scholars
BPL.1406   Album amicorum of Janus Douza the elder
Gronov 55   Correspondence of J.F. Gronovius with Selden
Burm Q.22   Correspondence of P.D. Huet with Selden and others

Printed Works

For ease of reference, I have not followed the usual practice of dividing 'primary' and 'secondary' works, but have instead integrated them into the following list of printed works. As in the notes, place of publication of all items is London, except where otherwise specified. Two or more dates of publication indicates that more than one edition has been consulted. For books printed between 1500 and 1700 STC and *Wing* numbers are included following the date.

Aconcio, Giacomo *De methodo e opuscoli religiosi e filosofici* ed G. Radetti (Florence 1944)

Adams, E.N. *Old English Scholarship in England from 1566 to 1800* (1937)

Agrippa, Henry Cornelius *Of the Vanitie and Uncertaintie of Artes and Sciences* trans J. Sandford (1569) 204

Aleyn, Charles *The Battailes of Crescey, and Poictiers* (1631) 351

– *The Historie of that Wise Prince, Henrie the Seventh* (1638) 353

Allison, A.F., and D.M. Rogers *A Catalogue of Catholic Books in English* (Bognor Regis 1956)

Allison, A.F., and V.F. Goldsmith *Titles of English Books and of Foreign Books Printed in England* (2 vols, Folkestone 1976–7)

Alsop, James D., and Wesley M. Stevens 'William Lambarde and the Elizabethan Polity' *Studies in Medieval and Renaissance History* new ser 8 (1987) 231–65

Anderson, Judith H. *Biographical Truth: The Representation of Historical Persons in Tudor-Stuart Writing* (New Haven, Conn. 1984)

Anglo, Sydney 'The British History in Early Tudor Propaganda' *Bulletin of the John Rylands Library* 54 (1961–2) 17–48

Anonymous *The Most Ancient and Famous History of Prince Arthur* (1634) 806

Arber, Edward *A Transcript of the Registers of the Company of Stationers of London, 1554–1640* (5 vols, 1875–94)

Armstrong, W.A., ed *Elizabethan History Plays* (1965)

Ayscu, Edward *A Historie Contayning the Warres, Treaties, Marriages, and Other Occurrents betweene England and Scotland from King William the Conqueror, untill the Happy Union of Them Both in Our Gratious King James* (1607) 1014

B., A.D. *The Court of the Most Illustrious James, the First* (1619) 1022

Bacon, Francis *The History of the Reign of King Henry the Seventh* ed F.J. Levy (Indianapolis 1972)

– *Lord Bacon's Letters and Life* ed J. Spedding (7 vols, 1861–74)

– *Works of Francis Bacon* ed. J. Spedding, R.L. Ellis, and D.D. Heath (7 vols, 1858–61)

Baker, Herschel *The Race of Time: Three Lectures on Renaissance Historiography* (Toronto 1967)

Barnard, John *Theologo-historicus, or the True Life of the Most Reverend Divine, and Excellent Historian Peter Heylyn* (1683) B854

Barnes, H.E. *A History of Historical Writing* (2nd ed, New York 1963)

Barnes, Robert *Vitae Romanorum pontificum* (Basel 1535)

Baron, Hans *The Crisis of the Early Italian Renaissance: Civic Humanism and Republican Liberty in an Age of Classicism and Tyranny* (revised one volume ed, Princeton, NJ 1966)

Barratt, D.M. 'The Library of John Selden and Its Later History' *Bodleian Library Record* 3 (1950–1) 128–42, 208–13, 256–74

Barston, John *The Safeguarde of Societie: Describing the Institution of Lawes and Policies* (1576) 1532

Basset, Robert *The Lives of All the Roman Emperors* (1636) 1558

Beacon, Richard *Solon His Follie* (Oxford 1594) 1653

Bedford, R.D. *The Defence of Truth: Herbert of Cherbury and the Seventeenth Century* (Manchester 1979)

Benjamin, E.B. 'Bacon and Tacitus' *Classical Philology* 60 (1965) 102–10

– 'Fame, Poetry, and the Order of History in the Literature of the English Renaissance' *Studies in the Renaissance* 6 (1959) 64–84

– 'Sir John Hayward and Tacitus' *Review of English Studies* new ser 8 (1957) 275–6

Berger, T.L., and W.C. Bradford *An Index of Characters in English Printed Drama to the Restoration* (Englewood, Colorado 1975)

Berkowitz, David S. *John Selden's Formative Years: Politics and Society in Early Seventeenth-Century England* ed M. Jansson (Washington, DC 1988)

– 'Reason of State in England and the Petition of Right, 1603–1629' in *Staatsräson: Studien zur Geschichte eines politischen Begriffs* ed R. Schnur (Berlin 1975) 165–212

– 'Selden, John' in *Biographical Dictionary of British Radicals in the Seventeenth Century* ed R.L. Greaves and R. Zaller (Brighton 1984) III, 153–6

– 'Young Mr Selden, Essays in Seventeenth Century Learning and Politics, Being Prolegomena to Parliament' (PH D Harvard University 1946)

Biographia Britannica (6 vols in 7, 1747–66)

Blissett, William 'Samuel Daniel's Sense of the Past' *English Studies* 38 (1957) 49–63

Blundeville, Thomas *The True Order and Methode of Writing and Reading Hystories* ed H.G. Dick *Huntington Library Quarterly* 3 (1939–40) 149–70

Bodin, Jean *Method for the Easy Comprehension of History* trans Beatrice Reynolds (New York 1945)

– *Six Bookes of a Commonweale* trans R. Knolles (1606) 3193

Boethius *The Consolation of Philosophy* trans S.J. Tester (1973)

Bolgar, R.R. *The Classical Heritage and Its Beneficiaries* (Cambridge 1954)

– ed *Classical Influences on European Culture, A.D. 1500–1700* (Cambridge 1976)

Bolton, Edmund *The Cities Advocate* (1629) 3219

– *The Elements of Armories* (1610) 3220

– *Hypercritica, or a Rule of Judgment for Writing or Reading Our Histories* in *Critical Essays of the Seventeenth Century* ed J.E. Spingarn (3 vols, Oxford 1907) vol I

– *Nero Caesar, or Monarchie Depraved* (1624, 1627) 3221; 3222

Botero, Giovanni *An Historicall Description of the Most Famous Kingdoms* (1603) 3400

– *Observations upon the Lives of Alexander, Caesar, Scipio* (1602) 3397
– *Reason of State* trans P.J. and D.P. Waley (1956)
Bouwsma, William J. 'Three Types of Historiography in Post-Renaissance Italy' *History and Theory* 4 (1965) 303–14
Bradford, Alan T. 'Stuart Absolutism and the "Utility" of Tacitus' *Huntington Library Quarterly* 46 (1983) 127–55
Brathwait, Richard *The Schollers Medley, or, an Intermixt Discourse upon Historicall and Poeticall Relations* (1614) 3583
– *A Survey of History* (1638) 3583a
Breisach, Ernst *Historiography: Ancient, Medieval and Modern* (Chicago 1983)
Brinkley, R.F. *Arthurian Legend in the Seventeenth Century* (Baltimore 1932)
Brooke, Christopher *The Ghost of Richard the Third* (1614) 3830
Brooke, Ralph *A Catalogue and Succession of the Kings, Princes ... of this Realme* (1619) 3832
– *A Discoverie of Certaine Errours Published in Print in the Much Commended Britannia, 1594* (nd [1596?]) 3834
Brooks, C.W., and K.M. Sharpe 'Debate: History, English Law and the Renaissance' *Past and Present* 72 (1976) 133–42
Broughton, Richard *The Ecclesiasticall Historie of Great Britaine Deduced by Ages* (Douai 1633) 3894
– *An Ecclesiastical Protestant Historie* (St Omer 1624) 3895
Brown, J.L. 'Bodin et Ben Jonson' *Revue de littérature comparée* 20 (1940) 66–81
– *The "Methodus ad facilem historiarum cognitionem' of Jean Bodin: A Critical Study* (Washington, DC 1939)
Brushfield, T.N. *The Bibliography of the 'History of the World' and of the 'Remains' of Sir Walter Ralegh* (1886)
– 'Sir Walter Ralegh and His *History of the World' Reports and Transactions of the Devonshire Association for the Advancement of Science, Literature and Art* 19 (1887) 389–418
Bryant, J.A., Jr 'John Stow's Continuator and the Defense of Brute' *Modern Language Review* 45 (1950) 352–54
Buck, Sir George *The Great Plantagenet* ed G. Buck, gent. (1635) 3997
– *The History of King Richard the Third* ed A.N. Kincaid (Gloucester 1979)
– *The Third Universitie of England* in J. Stow *Annales* ed Edmund Howes (1615, 1631) 23338, 23340
Bullough, G. 'Fulke Greville, First Lord Brooke' *Modern Language Review* 28 (1933) 1–20
Burke, Peter *The Renaissance Sense of the Past* (1969)
– 'A Survey of the Popularity of Ancient Historians, 1450–1700' *History and Theory* 5 (1966) 135–52
– 'Tacitism' in *Tacitus* ed T.A. Dorey (1969) 149–71
Butterfield, Herbert *The Englishman and His History* (Cambridge 1944)

- *Man on His Past* (Cambridge 1955)
- *The Origins of History* (1981)
- *The Whig Interpretation of History* (Harmondsworth 1973)
Caldwell, R.A. 'Joseph Holland, Collector and Antiquary' *Modern Philology*
  40 (1942–3) 295–301
Calendar of State Papers, Domestic Series ed M.A.E. Green, vols 1591–1640
  (1867–82)
Camden, William *Annales rerum Anglicarum et Hibernicarum regnante
  Elizabetha* (Part 1, 1615; Part 2, 1627) 4496, 4496.5
- *Britain* trans Philemon Holland (1610) 4509
- *Britannia, sive florentissimorum regnorum Angliae, Scotiae, Hiberniae
  chorographica descriptio* (1586, 1607) 4503, 4508
- *Gulielmi Camdeni et illustrium virorum ad G. Camdenum epistolae* ed
  Thomas Smith (1691) c361
- *The Historie of the Most Renowned and Victorious Princesse Elizabeth*
  trans R. Norton (1630) 4500
- *Reges, reginae, nobiles, et alii in ecclesia collegiata B. Petri Westmonasterii
  sepulti* (1600) 4518
- *Remains Concerning Britain* ed R.D. Dunn (Toronto 1984)
- *Remaines of a Greater Worke, concerning Britaine* (1605) 4521
- 'William Camden's "Discourse concerning the Prerogative of the Crown" '
  ed F. Smith Fussner *Proceedings of the American Philosophical Society*
  101 (1957) 204–15 (attribution questionable)
Campbell, Lily Bess, ed *The Mirror for Magistrates* (Cambridge, 1938)
- *Shakespeare's Histories: Mirrors of Elizabethan Policy* (San Marino, Cal.
  1947)
- 'The Use of Historical Patterns in the Reign of Elizabeth' *Huntington
  Library Quarterly* 1 (1938) 135–67
Carew, Richard *The Survey of Cornwall* (1602) 4615
Cary, Henry, first Viscount Falkland *The History of the Most Unfortunate
  Prince King Edward the Second* (1680) F313 (attribution questionable:
  see Woolf 'Falkland,' below)
Casaubon, Isaac *Isaaci Casauboni epistolae* (The Hague 1638)
Caudill, R.W. 'Some Literary Evidence of the Development of English Virtu-
  oso Interests in the Seventeenth Century' (DPhil Oxford University 1975)
Chamberlain, John *The Letters of John Chamberlain* ed N.E. McClure (2
  vols, Philadelphia 1939)
Chapman, Raymond 'Fortune and Mutability in Elizabethan Literature'
  Cambridge Journal 5 (1952) 374–82
Charron, Pierre *Of Wisdome Three Bookes* trans S. Lennard (1608) 5051
Chester, Robert *The Anuals of Great Brittaine* (1611) 5120
Christianson, Paul 'John Selden, the Five Knights' Case, and Discretionary
  Imprisonment in Early Stuart England' *Criminal Justice History* 6 (1985)
  65–87
- *Reformers and Babylon* (Toronto 1978)

- 'Young John Selden and the Ancient Constitution, 1610–1618' *Proceedings of the American Philosophical Society* 128 (1984) 271–315
Clapham, John *Elizabeth of England* ed E. and C. Read (Philadelphia 1951)
- *The Historie of England* (1602) 5347
- *The Historie of Great Britannie* (1606) 5348
Clark, D.S.T. 'Bacon's Henry VII: A Case-Study in the Science of Man' *History and Theory* 13 (1974) 97–118
- 'Francis Bacon: The Study of History and the Science of Man' (PH D Cambridge University 1971)
Cochrane, Eric *Historians and Historiography in the Italian Renaissance* (Chicago 1981)
Coke, Sir Edward *Reports* (11 parts, 1600–15) 5493, 5495, 5499, 5502, 5504, 5509, 5511, 5513, 5515, 5518, 5521
- *The Second Part of the Institutes of the Lawes of England* (1642) C4948
Colman, Morgan *Genealogies of King James I and Queen Anne, His Wife, from the Conquest* (1608) 5568
Cornwallis, William *The Prayse of King Richard III* in *Essayes of Certaine Paradoxes* (1616) 5779
- *The Miraculous and Happie Union of England and Scotland* (1604) 5782
Cotroneo, Girolamo *I trattatisti del 'Ars Historica'* (Naples 1971)
Cotton, Sir Robert *Cottoni posthuma* ed James Howell (1651, 1672) C6485, C6486
- *A Short View of the Long Life and Raigne of Henry the Third* (1627) 5864
Cowell, John *The Interpreter: or Booke Containing the Signification of Words* (Cambridge 1607) 5900
Cragg, G.R. *Freedom and Authority: A Study of English Thought in the Early Seventeenth Century* (Philadelphia 1975)
Curtius, E.R. *European Literature and the Latin Middle Ages* trans W.R. Trask (1953)
Dallington, Sir Robert *Aphorismes Civill and Militarie* (1613) 6197
Daniel, Samuel *The Civil Wars* ed Laurence Michel (New Haven 1958)
- *The Collection of the Historie of England* (1618) 6248
- *Complete Works in Verse and Prose of Samuel Daniel* ed A.B. Grosart (5 vols, 1885–96)
- *The First Part of the Historie of England* (1612, 1613) 6246, 6247
- *An Introduction to a Breviary of the History of England* (1693) R169 (misattributed to Sir Walter Ralegh)
- *Poems and a Defence of Ryme* ed A.C. Sprague (2nd ed, 1950)
- *Samuel Daniel: The Brotherton Manuscript. A Study in Authorship* ed John Pitcher (Leeds 1981)
Danto, Arthur C. *Analytical Philosophy of History* (Cambridge 1965)
Dasent, J.R. ed *Acts of the Privy Council of England* vols xx–xlvi, 1590–1631 (1900–64)
Davies, Sir John *Le Primer Report des Cases et Matters en ley Resolves &*

Adjudges en les Courts del Rey en Ireland (1615; 2nd ed, 1628) 6361,
6362

Davis, Lennard J. *Factual Fictions: The Origins of the English Novel* (New
York 1983)

Dean, Leonard F. 'Bodin's Methodus in England before 1625' *Studies in
Philology* 39 (1942) 160–6

– 'Sir Francis Bacon's Theory of Civil History-Writing' in *Essential Articles
for the Study of Francis Bacon* ed B.W. Vickers (Hamden, Conn. 1968)
211–35

– *Tudor Theories of History Writing* (University of Michigan Contributions
in Modern Philology, no 1, April 1947)

Dean, Paul 'Tudor Humanism and the Roman Past: A Background to Shakespeare' *Huntington Library Quarterly* 51 (1988) 84–111

DeMolen, Richard L. 'The Library of William Camden' *Proceedings of the
American Philosophical Society* 128 (1984) 327–409

Denzer, Horst, ed *Jean Bodin* (Munich 1973)

D'Ewes, Simonds *The Autobiography and Correspondence of Sir Simonds
D'Ewes* ed J.O. Halliwell (2 vols, 1845)

Dictionary of National Biography ed L. Stephen and S. Lee (24 vols, 1921–2)

Dio Cassius *Dio's Roman History* trans E. Cary (9 vols, 1914)

Dionysius of Halicarnassus *The Roman Antiquities* trans E. Cary (7 vols,
1937)

Dodderidge, Sir John *The History of the Ancient and Moderne Estate of the
Principality of Wales* (1630) 6982

Douglas, David C. *English Scholars, 1660–1730* (2nd ed, 1951)

– *The Norman Conquest and British Historians* (Murray Lecture, Glasgow
1946)

Dowling, Margaret 'Sir John Hayward's Troubles over His Life of Henry IV'
The Library 4th series 11 (1930–1) 212–24

Drayton, Michael *Works of Michael Drayton* ed J.W. Hebel, Kathleen Tillot-
son, and B.H. Newdigate (2nd ed, 5 vols, Oxford 1961)

Duchesne, André *Histoire générale d'Angleterre, d'Ecosse, et d'Irlande* (Paris
1614)

– *Bibliothèque des autheurs qui ont escript l'histoire et topographie de la
France* (Paris 1618)

Dugdale, Sir William *The Antiquities of Warwickshire* (1656) D2479

– *Monasticon anglicanum* (revised ed, 1817–30)

– *A Short View of the Late Troubles in England* (Oxford 1681) D2492

Du Haillan, Bernard Girard *L'Histoire de France* (Paris 1576)

Du Tillet, Jean *Recueil, des guerres et traictez d'entre les roys de France et
d'Angleterre* (Paris 1588)

– *Recueil des roys de France* (Paris 1602)

Dunn, F.S. 'Julius Caesar in the English Chronicles' *Classical Journal* 14
(1918–19) 280–94

Earle, John *Micro-cosmographie* (6th ed, 1633) 7444

Easterby, W. *The History of the Law of Tithes in England* (Cambridge 1888)

Eccles, Mark 'Samuel Daniel in France and Italy' *Studies in Philology* 34 (1937) 148–67

– 'Sir George Buc, Master of the Revels' in *Thomas Lodge and Other Elizabethans* ed C.J. Sisson (Cambridge, Mass. 1933) 411–506

Edmonds, Clement *Observations upon Caesars Commentaries* (2nd ed, 1604) 7490

Ellis, Henry, ed *Original Letters of Eminent Literary Men of the Sixteenth, Seventeenth and Eighteenth Centuries* (Camden Society, original series 23, 1843)

Englands Helicon ed H.E. Rollins (Cambridge, Mass. 1935)

Erasmus, H.J. *The Origins of Rome in Historiography from Petrarch to Perizonius* (Assen 1962)

Erdeswicke, Sampson *A Survey of Staffordshire* (1717)

Evans, E. 'Of the Antiquity of Parliaments in England: Some Elizabethan and Early Stuart Opinions' *History* new series 23 (1938–9) 207–21

Evans, Joan *A History of the Society of Antiquaries* (Oxford 1956)

Farmer, N., Jr 'Fulke Greville and Sir John Coke: An Exchange of Letters on a History Lectureship and Certain Latin Verses on Sir Philip Sidney' *Huntington Library Quarterly* 33 (1969–70) 217–36

Ferguson, Arthur B. *Clio Unbound: Perception of the Social and Cultural Past in Renaissance England* (Durham, NC 1979)

– 'The Historical Thought of Samuel Daniel: A Study in Renaissance Ambivalence' *Journal of the History of Ideas* 32 (1971) 185–202

– 'The Non-Political Past in Bacon's Theory of History' *Journal of British Studies* 14 (1974) 4–20

Fink, Zera S. *The Classical Republicans* (Evanston, Ill. 1945)

Firth, C.H. 'Sir Walter Raleigh's *History of the World*' *Proceedings of the British Academy* 8 (1918) 427–46

Firth, Katherine R. *The Apocalyptic Tradition in Reformation Britain, 1530–1645* (Oxford 1979)

Fishel, D.N. 'The Image of Rome in Elizabethan and Jacobean Drama' (MLitt Oxford University 1978)

Fisher, H.A.L. 'The Speeches in Lord Herbert of Cherbury's *Life and Reign of Henry VIII*' *English Historical Review* 20 (1905) 498

Fitzsimons, M.A. 'Politics and Men of Learning in England, 1540–1640' *Review of Politics* 6 (1944) 452–83

Fletcher, R.H. *The Arthurian Material in the Chronicles* (2nd ed revised by R.S. Loomis, New York 1966)

Fletcher, Robert *The Nine English Worthies* (1606) 11087

Florus, Lucius Annaeus *The Roman Histories* trans Edmund Bolton (1619) 11103

Flower, Robin 'Laurence Nowell and the Discovery of England in Tudor Times' *Proceedings of the British Academy* 21 (1935) 47–74

Fordyce, C.J., and T.M. Knox 'The Books Bequeathed to Jesus College Library, Oxford, by Lord Herbert of Cherbury' *Proceedings and Papers of the Oxford Bibliographical Society* 5 (1936–9) 71–115

Fortescue, Sir John *De laudibus legum Angliae* ed John Selden (1616) 11197

Foster, Joseph *Alumni Oxonienses: The Members of the University of Oxford, 1500–1714* (4 vols, 1891–2)

– *Register of Admissions to Gray's Inn, 1521–1889* (1889)

Fox, Levi, ed *English Historical Scholarship in the Sixteenth and Seventeenth Centuries* (1956)

Foxe, John *Acts and Monuments of these Latter and Perilous Dayes* ed Josiah Pratt (8 vols, 1877)

Franklin, Julian *Jean Bodin and the Sixteenth Century Revolution in the Methodology of Law and History* (New York 1963)

Friedländer, M. 'Growth in the Resources for Studies in Earlier English History, 1534–1625' (PH D University of Chicago 1938)

Fueter, Eduard *Geschichte der neueren Historiographie* (Munich and Berlin 1911)

Fulbecke, William *An Historicall Collection of the Continuall Factions, Tumults, and Massacres of the Romans and Italians during the Space of One Hundred and Twentie Yeares Next before the Peaceable Empire of Augustus Caesar* (1601) 11412

– *A Parallele or Conference of the Civill law, the Canon Law and the Common Law of England* (Part 1, 1601; Part 2, 1602) 11415, 11415a

– *The Pandectes of the Law of Nations* (1602) 11414

Fuller, Thomas *The Appeal of Injured Innocence: Unto the Learned and Ingenuous Reader. In a Controversie betwixt the Animadvertor Dr Peter Heylyn and the Author Thomas Fuller* (1659) F2410

– *The Church-history of Britain* (1655) F2416

– *Worthies of England* ed J. Nichols (2 vols, 1811)

Fussner, F. Smith *The Historical Revolution: English Historical Writing and Thought, 1580–1640* (1962)

– *Tudor History and the Historians* (New York 1970)

Galbraith, V.H. *Historical Research in Medieval England* (1951)

Galloway, Bruce *The Union of England and Scotland, 1603–1608* (Edinburgh 1986)

Galloway, Bruce, and Brian P. Levack eds *The Jacobean Union: Six Tracts of 1604* (Edinburgh 1985)

Gilbert, Felix *Machiavelli and Guicciardini: Politics and History in Sixteenth-Century Florence* (Princeton, NJ 1965)

– 'The Renaissance Interest in History' in *Art, Science and History in the Renaissance* ed C.S. Singleton (Baltimore 1967)

Gilbert, Neal W. *Renaissance Concepts of Method* (New York 1960)

Gilmore, Myron P. *Humanists and Jurists* (Cambridge, Mass. 1963)

Giordano-Orsini, G.N. 'Thomas Heywood's Play on "The Troubles of Queen Elizabeth"' *The Library* 4th series 14 (1934–5) 313–38

Godschalk, W.L. 'Daniel's History' *Journal of English and Germanic Philology* 63 (1964) 45–57

Godwin, Francis *Annales of England* trans Morgan Godwin (1630) 11947

– *A Catalogue of the Bishops of England* (1601) 11937

– *De praesulibus Angliae commentarius* (1616) 11941

– *Rerum Anglicarum Henrico VIII, Edwardo VI et Maria regnantibus, annales* (1616) 11945

Godwyn, Thomas *Romanae historiae anthologia recognita et aucta. An English Exposition of the Romane Antiquities* (Oxford 1614, 4th ed 1623) 11956, 11959

Goldberg, Jonathan *James I and the Politics of Literature: Jonson, Shakespeare, Donne and Their Contemporaries* (Baltimore 1983)

Goldberg, S.L. 'Sir John Hayward, "Politic" Historian' *Review of English Studies* new series 6 (1955) 233–44

Goodman, Godfrey *Court of King James the First* ed J.S. Brewer (2 vols, 1839)

Gottfried, Rudolph B. 'The Authorship of *A Breviary of the History of England*' *Studies in Philology* 53 (1956) 172–90

– 'The Early Development of the Section on Ireland in Camden's *Britannia*' *English Literary History* 10 (1943) 117–30

– 'Samuel Daniel's Method of Writing History' *Studies in the Renaissance* 3 (1956) 157–74

Grafton, Anthony *Joseph Scaliger: A Study in the History of Classical Scholarship* I (Oxford 1983)

– 'Joseph Scaliger and Historical Chronology: The Rise and Fall of a Discipline' *History and Theory* 14 (1975) 156–85

Gransden, Antonia *Historical Writing in England* (2 vols, 1974–82)

Gray, H. 'Renaissance Humanism: The Pursuit of Eloquence" *Journal of the History of Ideas* 24 (1963) 497–514

Great Britain, Historical Manuscripts Commission *Fourth Report of the Royal Commission on Historical Manuscripts* (1874)

– *The Manuscripts of the Earl Cowper, K.G., Preserved at Melbourne Hall* II (1888–9)

– *Calendar of the Manuscripts of the Most Hon. the Marquis of Salisbury* V (1894), IX (1904), XVII (1938), XVIII (1940)

– *Report on Manuscripts in Various Collections* I (1901), II (1903)

– *Report on Records of the City of Exeter* (1916)

Great Britain, Public Record Office *Inquisitions Post Mortem* (PRO Lists and Indexes, No 31, 1909)

Greenblatt, Stephen *Sir Walter Ralegh: The Renaissance Man and His Roles* (New Haven, Conn 1973)

Greenleaf, W.H. *Order, Empiricism and Politics* (1964)

Greg, W.W. 'Samuel Harsnett and Hayward's *Henry IV*' *The Library* 5th series 11 (1956) 1–10

Greville, Fulke *The Remains, being Poems of Monarchy and Religion* ed G.A. Wilkes (1965)

- *Works of Fulke Greville, Lord Brooke* ed A.B. Grosart (4 vols, 1870)
Guibbory, Achsah *The Map of Time: Seventeenth-Century English Literature and Ideas of Pattern in History* (Urbana and Chicago 1986)
Guicciardini, Francesco *The Historie of Guicciardin, Conteining the Warres of Italie and Other Partes* trans G. Fenton (1579) 12458
- *The History of Italy* trans S. Alexander (New York 1972)
Gundersheimer, Werner L., ed *French Humanism: 1470–1600* (1969)
Habington, Thomas *A Survey of Worcestershire* ed J. Amphlett (2 vols, Oxford 1893–9)
Habington, William *The Historie of Edward the Fourth* (1640) 12586
- *Observations upon Historie* (1641) H166
- *Poems of William Habington* ed K. Allott (1948)
Hacking, Ian *The Emergence of Probability* (Cambridge 1975)
Haddock, B.A. *An Introduction to Historical Thought* (1980)
Halkett, S., and J. Laing *Dictionary of Anonymous and Pseudonymous Publications in the English Language, 1475–1640* (3rd ed rev J. Horden et al, 1980)
Hall, Edward *The Union of the Two Noble and Illustre Famelies of Lancastre and Yorke* (1548) 12722
- *Hall's Chronicle* ed H. Ellis (1809)
Harbert, William *A Prophesie of Cadwallader, Last King of the Britaines* (1604) 12752
Hardy, Linda R. 'The Idea of Providence in Sir Walter Ralegh's *History of the World*' (MPhil Oxford University 1979)
Harrington, James *The Political Works of James Harrington* ed J.G.A. Pocock (Cambridge 1977)
Harrison, J.L. 'Bacon's View of Rhetoric, Poetry and the Imagination' *Huntington Library Quarterly* 20 (1956–7) 107–25
Harry, George Owen *The Genealogy of James King of Great Brittayne* (1604) 12872
Hartman, M.P. 'Contemporary Explanations of the English Revolution, 1640–1660' (PH D Cambridge University 1978)
Hay, Denys *Annalists and Historians* (1975)
- 'Flavio Biondo and the Middle Ages' *Proceedings of the British Academy* 45 (1959) 97–125
- 'The Historiographers Royal in England and Scotland' *Scottish Historical Review* 30 (1951) 15–29
- *Polydore Vergil: Renaissance Historian and Man of Letters* (1952)
Hayward, Sir John *Annals of the First Four Years of Queen Elizabeth* ed J. Bruce (Camden Society, original series 7, 1840)
- *An Answer to the First Part of a Certaine Conference* (1603) 12988
- *The First Part of the Life and Raigne of King Henrie the IIII* (1599) 12995
- Introduction to Sir Roger Williams *Actions of the Lowe Countries* (1618) 25731
- *The Life, and Raigne of King Edward the Sixt* (1630) 12998

- *The Lives of the III. Normans, Kings of England* (1613) 13000
- *A Treatise of Union of the Two Realmes of England and Scotland* (1604) 13011
Hazard, Paul *The European Mind, 1680–1715* trans J.L. May (1953)
Hazeltine, H.D. 'Selden as Legal Historian' in *Festschrift Heinrich Brünner* (Weimar 1910) 579–630
Hearne, Thomas *A Collection of Curious Discourses* ed J. Ayloffe (2 vols, 1775)
- *Reliquiae Hearnianae* ed P. Bliss (2 vols, 1857)
- *Remarks and Collections of Thomas Hearne* ed C.E. Doble et al (10 vols, Oxford 1885–1915)
Heltzel, V.B. 'Sir Thomas Egerton and William Lambarde' *Huntington Library Quarterly* 11 (1947–8) 201–3
Heninger, S.K., Jr 'The Tudor Myth of Troy-novant' *South Atlantic Quarterly* 41 (1962) 378–87
Herbert, Edward, first baron of Cherbury *The Antient Religion of the Gentiles* trans W. Lewis (1705; first published in Latin, 1663)
- *De Religione Laici* trans H.R. Hutcheson (New Haven, Conn. 1944)
- *De Veritate* trans M.H. Carré (Bristol 1937)
- *The Life and Raigne of King Henry the Eighth* (1649) H1504
- *The Life of Edward, First Lord Herbert of Cherbury, Written by Himself* ed J.M. Shuttleworth (1976)
Herendeen, W.H. 'Wanton Discourse and the Engines of Time: William Camden – Historian Among Poets-Historical' in *Renaissance Rereadings: Intertext and Context* ed M.C. Horowitz, A.J. Cruz, and W.A. Furman (Urbana, Ill. 1988) 142–56
- 'William Camden: Historian, Herald and Antiquary' *Studies in Philology* 85 (1988) 192–210
Heylyn, Peter *Aerius Redivivus* (Oxford and London 1670) H1681
- *Augustus, or an Essay of those Meanes and Counsells Whereby the Commonwealth of Rome was Reduced unto a Monarchy* (1632) 13268
- *Certamen Epistolare, or the Letter-Combate ... in Answer to Some Passages in Mr Fullers Late appeal* (1659) H1687
- *Cosmographie* (1652) H1689
- *Examen Historicum; or a Discovery and Examination of the Religious Learned and Ingenuous Reader* (1659) H1706
- *Extraneus Vapulans; or the Observator Rescued from the Violent but Vaine Assaults of Hamon L'Estrange, Esq.* (1656) H1708
- *A Help to English History* (1652) H1715
- *The Historie of that Most Famous Saynt and Souldier of Christ Jesus St. George of Cappadocia* (1631) 13272
- *The History of the Sabbath* (1636) 13274
- *Microcosmus, or a Little Description of the Great World* (Oxford 1621) 13276
- *Observations on the Historie of the Reign of King Charles* (1656) H1727

Heywood, Thomas *Dramatic Works of Thomas Heywood* ed J. Pearson (4 vols, 1874)
- *Englands Elizabeth: Her Life and Troubles* (1631) 13313
- *The First and Second Partes of King Edward the Fourth* (1599) 13341
- *If You Know Not Me, You Know No Bodie, or the Troubles of Queene Elizabeth* (2 parts, 1605–6) 13328, 13336
- *The Life of Merlin* (1641) H1786
- *Troia Britanica, or Great Britaines Troy* (1609) 13366
Hill, Christopher *Economic Problems of the Church from Archbishop Whitgift to the Long Parliament* (Oxford 1956)
- *Intellectual Origins of the English Revolution* (Oxford 1965)
- 'The Norman Yoke' in *Puritanism and Revolution* (1958) 50–122
Hill, Eugene D. *Edward, Lord Herbert of Cherbury* (Boston 1987)
Hobbes, Thomas *Behemoth, or the Long Parliament* ed Ferdinand Tönnies (2nd ed, 1969)
Holborn, Hajo 'Greek and Modern Concepts of History' *Journal of the History of Ideas* 10 (1949) 3–29
Holinshed, Raphael *Chronicles* (2nd ed, 1587) 13569
Hotman, François *Francogallia* ed R.E. Giesey, trans J.H.M. Salmon (Cambridge 1972)
Houghton, Walter E. 'The English Virtuoso in the Seventeenth Century' *Journal of the History of Ideas* 3 (1942) 51–73, 190–219
Howell, W.S. *Logic and Rhetoric in England, 1500–1700* (Princeton, NJ 1956)
Hubert, Francis *The Deplorable Life and Death of Edward the Second* (1628) 13900 (revised 1629 as *The Historie of Edward the Second* 13901)
Hughes, John, and White Kennett eds *A Complete History of England* (2nd ed, 3 vols, 1719)
Hulse, Clark *Metamorphic Verse: The Elizabethan Minor Epic* (Princeton, NJ 1981)
- 'Samuel Daniel: The Poet as Literary Historian' *Studies in English Literature* 19 (1979) 55–69
Huppert, George *The Idea of Perfect History: Historical Erudition and Historical Philosophy in Renaissance France* (Urbana, Ill. 1970)
- 'The Renaissance Background of Historicism' *History and Theory* 5 (1965) 48–60
Hutchinson, John *A Catalogue of Notable Middle Templars* (1902)
Hutchinson, Lucy *Memoirs of the Life of Colonel Hutchinson* ed James Sutherland (1973)
Hyde, Edward, earl of Clarendon *The History of the Rebellion and Civil Wars in England Begun in the Year 1641* ed W.D. Macray (6 vols, Oxford 1888)
- *The Life of Edward Earl of Clarendon* (2 vols, Dublin 1759)
James VI and I *Political Works of James I* ed C.H. McIlwain (2nd ed, New York 1965)
Jardine, Lisa *Francis Bacon: Discovery and the Art of Discourse* (Cambridge 1974)

Jayne, Sears *Library Catalogues of the English Renaissance* (1956)

Jewel, John *An Apology, or Answer, in Defence of the Church of England* in *Works of John Jewel* ed J. Ayre (Parker Society, Cambridge 1848)

Johnson, J.W. 'Chronological Writing: Its Concept and Development' *History and Theory* 2 (1962) 124–43

Jones, H.S. 'The Foundation and History of the Camden Chair' *Oxoniensia* 8–9 (1943–4) 169–92

Jonson, Ben *Ben Jonson* ed C.H. Herford, Percy Simpson, and Evelyn Simpson (11 vols, Oxford 1925–52)

Keckermann, Bartholomew *De natura et proprietatibus historiae, commentarius* (Hanover 1610)

Kelley, Donald R. 'Budé and the First Historical School of Law' *American Historical Review* 72 (1967) 807–34

– 'De Origine Feudorum: The Beginnings of an Historical Problem' *Speculum* 39 (1964) 207–28

– 'The Development and Context of Bodin's Method' in *Jean Bodin* ed Horst Denzer (Munich 1973) 123–50

– *Foundations of Modern Historical Scholarship: Language, Law and History in the French Renaissance* (New York 1970)

– 'History, English Law and the Renaissance' *Past and Present* 65 (1974) 24–51

Kelly, H.A. *Divine Providence in the England of Shakespeare's Histories* (Cambridge, Mass. 1970)

Kendrick, T.D. *British Antiquity* (2nd ed, 1970)

Kennett, White [see also Hughes, John] *Parochial Antiquities, Attempted in the History of Ambrosden, Burcester, and other Adjacent Parts in the Counties of Oxford and Bucks* ed B. Bandinel (2 vols, Oxford 1818)

Kenyon, J.P. *The History Men: The Historical Profession in England since the Renaissance* (1983)

Kingsford, C.L. *English Historical Literature in the Fifteenth Century* (1913)

Kirkwood, James J. 'Bacon's Henry VII: A Model of a Theory of Historiography' *Renaissance Papers* (1965) 51–6

Kliger, S. *The Goths in England: A Study in Seventeenth and Eighteenth Century Thought* (Cambridge, Mass. 1952)

Klotz, Edith 'Subject Analysis of English Imprints for Every Tenth Year from 1480 to 1640' *Huntington Library Quarterly* 1 (1937–8) 417–19

Knafla, Louis A. *Law and Politics in Jacobean England: The Tracts of Lord Chancellor Ellesmere* (Cambridge 1977)

Knowles, David *Great Historical Enterprises* (1963)

Lambarde, William *Archaionomia* (1568) 15142

– *Archion, or a Comentary upon the High Courts of Justice in England* (1635) 15143

– *Dictionarium Angliae topographicum & historicum* (1730)

– *A Perambulation of Kent* (1576, 1596) 15175, 15176

Lathrop, H.B. *Translations from the Classics into English from Caxton to Chapman, 1477–1620* (2nd ed, New York 1967)

La Popelinière, Henri Lancelot Voisin *Histoire des histoires: avec L'Idée de l'histoire accomplie* (3 parts, Paris 1599)

Lee, Sidney *The French Renaissance in England* (Oxford 1910)

Leigh, Edward *Selected and Choice Observations concerning the Twelve First Caesars, Emperours of Rome* (Oxford 1635) 15410

Le Roy, Loys or Louis *Of the Interchangeable Course, or Variety of Things in the Whole World* trans Robert Ashley (1594) 15488

L'Estrange, Hamon *The Reign of King Charles* (1655) L1189

Levack, Brian P. *The Civil Lawyers in England, 1603–1641* (Oxford 1973)

– *The Formation of the British State: England, Scotland and the Union, 1603–1707* (Oxford 1987)

– 'The Proposed Union of English Law and Scottish Law in the Seventeenth Century' *Juridical Review* new series 20 (1975) 97–115

– 'Toward a More Perfect Union' in *After the Reformation: Essays in Honour of J.H. Hexter* ed Barbara C. Malament (Manchester 1980) 57–74

Levich, M. 'Disagreement and Controversy in History' *History and Theory* 2 (1962) 41–51

Levine, Joseph M. *Doctor Woodward's Shield: History, Science and Satire in Augustan England* (Berkeley and London 1977)

– *Humanism and History: Origins of Modern English Historiography* (Ithaca, NY 1987)

Levy, F.J. 'Francis Bacon and the Style of Politics' *English Literary Renaissance* 16 (1986) 101–22

– 'Hayward, Daniel, and the Beginnings of Politic History in England' *Huntington Library Quarterly* 50 (1987) 1–34

– 'The Making of Camden's *Britannia*' *Bibliothèque d'humanisme et renaissance* 26 (1964) 70–97

– 'Sir Philip Sidney and the Idea of History' *Bibliothèque d'humanisme et renaissance* 26 (1964) 608–17

– *Tudor Historical Thought* (San Marino, Cal. 1967)

Lewis, John *The History of Great-Britain from the First Inhabitants Thereof, 'till the Death of Cadwallader, Last King of the Britains, and of the Kings of Scotland to Eugene v* (1729)

Livius, Titus *The Romane Historie: Also the Breviaries of L. Florus* trans Philemon Holland (1600) 16613

Lodge, Thomas *The Wounds of Civill War* (1594) in *The Complete Works of Thomas Lodge* (5 vols, Glasgow 1883 rpt New York 1966) vol 3

London, William *Catalogue of the Most Vendible Books in England* (2nd ed, 1658) L2850

Lucan *Lucan's Pharsalia: or the Civill Warres of Rome* trans Thomas May (1627) 16887

Lucian of Samosata *How to Write History* trans R. Kilburn in *Lucian* vol VI (1959)

Ludlow, Edmund *A Voyce from the Watch Tower* ed A.B. Worden (Camden Society, 4th series 21, 1978)

Lydiat, Thomas *Defensio tractatus de variis annorum formis praesertim antiquissima & optima contra Josephi Scaligeri* (1607) 17040

– *Emendatio temporum compendio facta ab initio mundi ad praesens usque* (1609) 17041

MacDougall, Hugh A. *Racial Myth in English History: Trojans, Teutons, and Anglo-Saxons* (Hanover, NH, and Montreal 1982)

MacGillivray, Royce *Restoration Historians and the English Civil War* (The Hague 1974)

Machiavelli, Niccolo *The Art of War* trans E. Farneworth (Indianapolis, 1965)

– *The Discourses* trans L.J. Walker, ed B. Crick (1970)

– *History of Florence* trans F. Gilbert (New York 1960)

– *The Prince* trans G. Bull (1961)

Macray, W.D. *Annals of the Bodleian Library* (2nd ed, 1890)

Maitland, F.W. *English Law and the Renaissance* (Cambridge 1901)

Malvezzi, Virgilio *Romulus and Tarquin* trans Henry Carey (2nd ed, 1638) 17220

Manzini, Giovanni *Politicall Observations upon the Fall of Sejanus* trans T. Hawkins (1634) 17293

Martin, Thomas *Historica descriptio complectens vitam, ac res gestas beatissimi viri Gulielmi Wicami ...* (1597) 17516

Martyn, William *The Historie, and Lives, of the Kings of England* (1615, 1638) 17526, 17529

– *Youths Instruction* (1612) 17530

Marwil, Jonathan *The Trials of Counsel: Francis Bacon in 1621* (Detroit 1976)

Matthieu, Pierre *The Powerfull Favorite, or the Life of Aelius Sejanus* (2 separate translations, 1628) 17664, 17665

May, Thomas *A Breviary of the History of the Parliament of England* (2nd ed, 1655) M1396

– *A Continuation of ... Lucan's Historicall Poem till the Death of Julius Caesar* (1630) 17711

– *A Discourse concerning the Successe of Former Parliaments* (1642) M1404

– *The History of the Parliament of England, Which Began November 3, 1640, with a Short and Necessary View of Some Precedent Years* (1647) ed F. Maseres (Oxford 1854)

– *The Reigne of King Henry the Second* (1633) 17715

– *The Victorious Reigne of King Edward the Third* (1635) 17719

McCusker, Honor *John Bale, Dramatist and Antiquary* (Bryn Mawr, Pa. 1942)

McKeon, Michael *The Origins of the English Novel, 1600–1740* (Baltimore 1987)

McKisack, May *Medieval History in the Tudor Age* (Oxford 1971)
– 'Samuel Daniel as Historian' *Review of English Studies* 23 (1947) 226–43
Melanchthon, Philip *Loci Communes* trans C.L. Hill (Boston, Mass. 1944)
Mendyk, Stan 'Early British Chorography' *Sixteenth Century Journal* 17 (1986) 459–81
– *'Speculum Britanniae': Regional Study, Antiquarianism, and Science in Britain to 1700* (Toronto 1989)
Merchant, W.M. 'Bishop Francis Godwin, Historian and Novelist' *Journal of the Historical Society of the Church in Wales* 5 (1955) 45–51
– 'Lord Herbert of Cherbury and Seventeenth-Century Historical Writing' *Transactions of the Honourable Society of Cymmrodorion* (1956) 47–63
Meriton, George *Anglorum Gesta, or, a Brief History of England* (1675) M1787
Mexia, Pedro *The Historie of All the Romane Emperours* trans W. Traheron (1604) 17851; continued and trans Edward Grimeston (1623) 17852
Milton, John *The History of Britain* (1670) ed French Fogle in *Complete Prose Works of John Milton* v, part 1 (New Haven, Conn. 1971)
Momigliano, A.D. 'Ancient History and the Antiquarian' in his *Studies in Historiography* (1966) 1–39
– 'Gibbon's Contribution to Historical Method' in his *Studies in Historiography* (1966) 40–55
Montagu, Richard *Diatribae upon the First Part of the Late History of Tithes* (1621) 18037
Montaigne, Michel de *Complete Essays of Montaigne* trans Donald M. Frame (3rd ed, Stanford, Cal. 1965)
Mosse, G.L. 'The Influence of Jean Bodin's *République* in English Political Thought' *Medievalia et Humanistica* 5 (1948) 73–83
Munday, Anthony *A Briefe Chronicle, of the Successe of Times, from the Creation* (1611) 18263
– *The Triumphes of Re-united Britania* (1605) 18279
Murphy, Michael 'Methods in the Study of Old English in the Sixteenth and Seventeenth Centuries' *Mediaeval Studies* 30 (1968) 345–50
Nadel, George 'History as Psychology in Francis Bacon's Theory of History' *History and Theory* 5 (1966) 275–8
– 'Philosophy of History before Historicism' *History and Theory* 3 (1963) 291–315
Nalson, John *An Impartial Collection of the Great Affairs of State from the Beginning of the Scotch Rebellion ... to the Murther of King Charles* (2 vols, 1682–3) N106, N107
Nauert, Charles G. *Agrippa and the Crisis of Renaissance Thought* (Urbana, Ill. 1965)
Nelson, William *Fact or Fiction: The Dilemma of the Renaissance Storyteller* (Cambridge, Mass. 1973)
Nicholson, G.D. 'The Nature and Function of Historical Argument in the Henrician Reformation' (PH D Cambridge University 1977)

Nicolson, William *The English Historical Library* (1714)

Norbrook, David '*Macbeth* and the Politics of Historiography' in *Politics of Discourse* ed Kevin Sharpe and Steven N. Zwicker (Berkeley 1987) 78–116

– *Poetry and Politics in the English Renaissance* (1984)

Norden, John *Nordens Preparative to His Speculum Britanniae* (1596) 18638

– *Speculum Britanniae. The First Parte an Historicall Discription of Middlesex* (1593) 18635

– *Vicissitudo Rerum. An Elegiacall Poeme, of the Interchangeable Courses and Varietie of Things in this World* (1600) 18642

Oakeshott, Walter 'Sir Walter Ralegh's Library' *The Library* 5th series 23 (1968) 285–327

Orsini, N. ' "Policy," or the Language of Elizabethan Machiavellianism' *Journal of the Warburg and Courtauld Institutes* 9 (1946) 122–34

Oxford University *Statuta selecta è corpore statutorum Universitatis Oxoniensis* (Oxford 1638) 19007

Parry, Graham *The Golden Age Restor'd: The Culture of the Early Stuart Court, 1603–1640* (Manchester 1981)

Parsons, A.E. 'The Trojan Legend in England' *Modern Language Review* 24 (1929) 253–64, 394–408

Parsons, Bartholomew *The Historie of Tithes; or, Tithes Vindicated* (Oxford 1637) 19347.5

Parsons, Robert *An Answere to the Fifth Part of Reportes Lately Set Forth by Syr E. Cooke* (St Omer 1606) 19352

– *A Treatise of Three Conversions of England* (3 vols, St Omer 1603–4) 19416

– et al *A Conference about the Next Succession to the Crowne of Ingland* (Antwerp 1594) 19398

Pasquier, Etienne *Oeuvres* (2 vols, Amsterdam 1723)

Patch, Howard R. *The Goddess Fortuna in Medieval Literature* (Cambridge, Mass. 1927)

Patrides, C.A. *The Grand Design of God: The Literary Form of the Christian View of History* (London and Toronto 1972)

Patterson, Annabel *Censorship and Interpretation: The Conditions of Writing and Reading in Early Modern England* (Madison, Wisc. 1984)

Pattison, Mark *Isaac Casaubon* (2nd ed, Oxford 1892)

Pawlisch, Hans *Sir John Davies and the Conquest of Ireland: A Study in Legal Imperialism* (Cambridge 1985)

Peacham, Henry *The Complete Gentleman* ed V.B. Heltzel (Ithaca, NY 1962)

Peck, Linda Levy *Northampton: Patronage and Policy at the Court of James I* (1982)

Peiresc, Nicolas Fabri de *Lettres de Peiresc* ed Philippe Tamizey de Larroque (Documents inédits, 7 vols, Paris 1888–98)

Perrot, Richard *Jacobs Vowe, or the True Historie of Tithes* (Cambridge 1627) 19770

Pfeiffer, Rudolf *History of Classical Scholarship, 1300–1850* (Oxford 1976)

Philipot, John *The Catalogue of the Chancellors of England* (1636) 19846

Piggott, Stuart *Ancient Britons and the Antiquarian Imagination: Ideas from the Renaissance to the Regency* (New York 1989)

– *Ruins in a Landscape: Essays in Antiquarianism* (Edinburgh 1976)

– 'William Camden and the *Britannia*' *Proceedings of the British Academy* 37 (1951) 199–217

Pitcher, John 'Samuel Daniel's Letter to Sir Thomas Egerton' *Huntington Library Quarterly* 47 (1984) 55–61

Pithou, Pierre *Opera, sacra, juridica, historica, miscellanea* (Paris 1609)

Plomer, H.R. 'An Examination of Some Existing Copies of Hayward's "Life and Raigne of Henrie IV"' *The Library* new series 3 (1902) 13–23

– 'The Importation of Books into England in the Fifteenth and Sixteenth Centuries' *The Library* 4th series 4 (1923–4) 146–50

Pocock, J.G.A. *The Ancient Constitution and the Feudal Law: A Study of English Historical Thought in the Seventeenth Century. A Reissue with a Retrospect* (Cambridge 1987; first published in 1957)

– *The Machiavellian Moment: Florentine Political Thought and the Atlantic Republican Tradition* (Princeton, NJ 1975)

– 'The Origins of Study of the Past: A Comparative Approach' *Comparative Studies in Society and History* 4 (1961–2) 209–46

Pollard, A.W., and G.R. Redgrave *A Short-Title Catalogue of Books Printed in England, Scotland and Ireland and of English Books Printed Abroad, 1475–1640* (1926; 2nd ed revised by W.A. Jackson, F.S. Ferguson, and K.F. Pantzer, 2 vols, London 1976–86

Polybius *The Histories* trans W.R. Paton (6 vols, 1972)

Popkin, Richard *The History of Scepticism from Erasmus to Spinoza* (2nd ed, Berkeley, Cal. 1979)

Portal, Ethel M. 'The Academ Roial of King James I' *Proceedings of the British Academy* 7 (1915–16) 189–208

Powell, Robert *The Life of Alfred* (1634) 20161

Powicke, F.M. 'Sir Henry Spelman and the "Concilia"' *Proceedings of the British Academy* 16 (1931) 1–37

– 'William Camden' in *Essays and Studies Collected for the English Association* ed F.P. Wilson 1 (1948)

Press, Gerald A. *The Development of the Idea of History in Antiquity* (Kingston and Montreal 1982)

Preston, J.H. 'English Ecclesiastical Historians and the Problem of Bias, 1559–1742' *Journal of the History of Ideas* 32 (1971) 203–20

– 'Was There an Historical Revolution?' *Journal of the History of Ideas* 38 (1977) 353–64

Raab, Felix *The English Face of Machiavelli* (1964)

Ralegh, Sir Walter *The History of the World* (1614) 20637

– *Works of Sir Walter Ralegh* (8 vols, Oxford 1829)

Ranum, Orest *Artisans of Glory: Writers and Historical Thought in Seventeenth-Century France* (Chapel Hill 1980)

Rebholz, R.A. *The Life of Fulke Greville, First Lord Brooke* (Oxford 1971)

Rees, Joan *Samuel Daniel: A Critical and Biographical Study* (Liverpool 1964)

Reynolds, Beatrice 'Latin Historiography: A Survey, 1400–1600' *Studies in the Renaissance* 2 (1955) 1–66

– 'Shifting Currents of Historical Criticism' *Journal of the History of Ideas* 14 (1953) 471–92

Reynolds, John *Vox Coeli, or Newes from Heaven* (1624) 20946.4

Ribner, I. *The English History Play in the Age of Shakespeare* (Princeton, NJ 1957)

Richardson, R.C. *The Debate on the English Revolution* (1977)

Rodgers, C.P. 'Humanism, History, and the Common Law' *Journal of Legal History* 6 (1985) 129–56

Rossi, Mario M. *La vita, le opere, i tempi di Edoardo Herbert di Cherbury* (3 vols, Florence 1946)

Rubens, P.P. *Correspondance de Rubens et documents epistolaires concernant sa vie et ses oeuvres* ed Charles Ruelens (6 vols, Anvers 1887–1909)

Rushworth, John *Historical Collections* (8 vols, 1659–1701) R2316 et seq, R2333

Rymer, Thomas, and Robert Sanderson *Foedera, conventiones, literae, et cuiuscunque generis acta publica inter reges Angliae* (20 vols, 1704–35)

Salmon, J.H.M. 'Bodin and the Monarchomachs' in *Jean Bodin* ed H. Denzer (Munich 1973) 359–78

Saltern, George *Of the Antient Lawes of Great Britaine* (1605) 21635

Sallust *The Two Most Worthy and Notable Histories* trans Thomas Heywood (1608) 21625

Sanders, Nicholas *Rise and Growth of the Anglican Schism* trans D. Lewis (1877)

Sanderson, William *A Compleat History of the Lives and Reigns of Mary Queen of Scotland, and of Her Son and Successor, James the Sixth, King of Scotland ... in Vindication of Him against Two Scandalous Authors* (1656) s647

– *Peter Pursued; or Dr Heylin Overtaken, Arrested, and Arraigned upon His Three Appendixes* (1658) s649

Sandford, Francis *A Genealogical History of the Kings of England, and Monarchs of Great Britain, &c, from the Conquest, Anno 1066, to the Year 1677* (1677) s651

Sanford, Eva 'The Study of Ancient History in the Middle Ages' *Journal of the History of Ideas* 5 (1944) 21–43

Sarpi, Paolo (Pietro Soave, pseud) *The Historie of the Councel of Trent* trans N. Brent (1620) 21761

– *History of Benefices and Selections from History of the Council of Trent* ed and trans P. Burke (New York 1967)

Savile, Sir Henry, ed *Rerum anglicarum scriptores post Bedam* (1596) 21783

Scaliger, Joseph *Diatriba de decimis in lege Dei* in *Opuscula varia antehac non edita* ed Isaac Casaubon (Paris 1610)

– *Illustrissimi viri Josephi Scaligeri ... epistolae* (Leiden 1627)
– *Opus novum de emendatione temporum* (Paris 1583)
– *Scaligerana, Thuana, Perroniana, Pithoeana, et Colomesiana* vol II (Amsterdam 1740)
– *Thesaurus temporum, Eusebii Pamphili Caesareae Palaestinae Episcopi, Chronicorum Canonum* (Paris 1658)
Scarfe, N. 'Sir John Hayward, an Elizabethan Historian, His Life and Disappointments' *Proceedings of the Suffolk Institute of Archaeology and Natural History* 25 (1950) 79–97
Schellhase, K.C. *Tacitus in Renaissance Political Thought* (Chicago and London 1976)
Schiffman, Zachary S. 'Renaissance Historicism Reconsidered' *History and Theory* 24 (1985) 170–82
Schoeck, R. 'Early Anglo-Saxon Studies and Legal Scholarship in the Renaissance' *Studies in the Renaissance* 5 (1958) 102–10
– 'The Elizabethan Society of Antiquaries and Men of Law' *Notes and Queries* new series 1 (1954) 417–21
Sclater, William, the elder *The Quaestion of Tythes Revised* (1623) 21842
Scott, Thomas *Robert Earle of Essex His Ghost* (Paradise [ie, London] 1624) 22084
– *Sir Walter Rawleighs Ghost, or Englands Forewarner* (Utrecht [ie, London?] 1626) 22085
– *Vox Populi* (1620) 22098
Scott, Walter, ed *Secret History of the Court of James the First* (2 vols, Edinburgh 1811)
Seaberg, Robert B. 'Remembering the Past: Historical Aspects of Leveller Political Thought' (PH D Syracuse University 1977)
Sée, Henri 'La philosophie de l'histoire de Jean Bodin' *Revue Historique* 175 (1935) 497–505
Seifert, Arno *Cognitio Historica: Die Geschichte als Namengeberin der frühneuzeitlichen Empirie* (Berlin 1976)
Selden, John *The Historie of Tithes* (1618) 22172
– *Joannis Seldenis jurisconsulti opera omnia* ed David Wilkins (3 vols in 6 parts, 1726)
– *Table Talk of John Selden* ed F. Pollock (1927)
– *Titles of Honor* (1614, 1631) 22177, 22178
Sellers, Harry 'Bibliography of the Works of Samuel Daniel' *Proceedings and Papers of the Oxford Bibliographical Society* 2 (1927–30) 29–54
Sempill, Sir James *Sacrilege Sacredly Handled* (1619) 22186
Seronsy, C.C. 'The Doctrine of Cyclical Recurrence and Related Ideas in the Works of Samuel Daniel' *Studies in Philology* 54 (1957) 387–407
– *Samuel Daniel* (New York 1967)
Shapiro, Barbara J. *Probability and Certainty in Seventeenth-Century England* (Princeton, NJ 1983)

Sharpe, Kevin *Criticism and Compliment: The Politics of Literature in the England of Charles 1* (Cambridge 1987)
- 'The Foundation of the Chairs of History at Oxford and Cambridge: An Episode in Jacobean Politics' *History of Universities* 2 (1982) 127–52
- *Sir Robert Cotton, 1586–1631: History and Politics in Early Modern England* (Oxford 1979)
Sharpe, Kevin, and Steven N. Zwicker, eds *Politics of Discourse: The Literature and History of Seventeenth-Century England* (Berkeley 1987)
Shotwell, J.T. *An Introduction to the History of History* (New York 1922)
Sidney, Sir Philip *An Apology for Poetry* (1595) ed G. Shepherd (2nd ed, Manchester 1973)
- *The Prose Works of Sir Philip Sidney* ed Albert Feuillerat (4 vols, rpt Cambridge 1962) vol III
Skinner, Quentin *Foundations of Modern Political Thought* (2 vols, Cambridge 1978)
- 'History and Ideology in the English Revolution' *Historical Journal* 8 (1965) 151–78
- *Machiavelli* (Oxford 1981)
Slatyer, William *The History of Great Britanie [Palae-Albion]* (1621) 22634
Smalley, Beryl *Historians in the Middle Ages* (1974)
Smith, Sir Thomas *De republica Anglorum* (1583) 22857
Smuts, R. Malcolm *Court Culture and the Origins of a Royalist Tradition in Early Stuart England* (Philadelphia 1987)
Snow, Vernon F. 'Francis Bacon's Advice to Fulke Greville on Research Techniques' *Huntington Library Quarterly* 23 (1960) 369–78
Sommerville, J.P. 'History and Theory: The Norman Conquest in Early Stuart Political Thought' *Political Studies* 34 (1986) 234–61
- 'John Selden, the Law of Nature and the Origins of Government' *Historical Journal* 27 (1984) 437–47
- *Politics and Ideology in England, 1603–1640* (London and New York 1986)
Somner, William *The Antiquities of Canterbury* (1640) 22918
Sparke, Michael *The Narrative History of King James, for the First Fourteen Years* (1651) s4818
Sparrow, John 'The Earlier Owners of Books in John Selden's Library' *Bodleian Quarterly Record* 6 (1931) 263–71
Speed, John *The History of Great Britaine* (1611) 23045
- *Theatre of the Empire of Great Britaine* (1611) 23041
Spelman, Sir Henry *Archaeologus; in modum glossarii ad rem antiquam posteriorem* (1626) 23065
- *De Non Temerandis Ecclesiis: A Tract of the Rights and Respect Due unto Churches* (1613) rpt in *The English Works of Sir Henry Spelman Kt.* ed Edmund Gibson (2nd ed, 1727)
- *The History and Fate of Sacrilege* (1698) s4927
- *The Larger Treatise concerning Tithes* ed J. Stephens (1647) s4928
- *Reliquiae Spelmanniae* ed E. Gibson (Oxford 1698) s4930

– *Tithes too Hot to Be Touched* (1646) s4931

Spriet, Pierre *Samuel Daniel (1563–1619): sa vie – son oeuvre* (Paris 1968)

Sprigg, Joshua *Anglia Rediviva. Englands Recovery* (1647) s5070

Spufford, Margaret *Small Books and Pleasant Histories: Popular Fiction and Its Readership in Seventeenth-Century England* (1981)

Stauffer, Donald A. *English Biography before 1700* (2nd ed, New York 1964)

Stow, John *The Annales of England* ed Edmund Howes (1615, 1631) 23338, 23340

– *A Survay of London* (1598); ed C.L. Kingsford (2 vols, Oxford 1908)

Strathmann, Ernest A. 'The History of the World and Ralegh's Skepticism' *Huntington Library Quarterly* 3 (1939–40) 265–87

– *Sir Walter Ralegh: A Study in Elizabethan Skepticism* (New York 1951)

Strauss, Gerald 'Topographical-Historical Method in Sixteenth-Century German Scholarship' *Studies in the Renaissance* 5 (1958) 87–101

Sturgess, H.A.C. *Register of Admissions to the Honourable Society of the Middle Temple* (3 vols, 1949)

Suetonius *The Twelve Caesars* trans Robert Graves (1957)

Sypher, G.W. 'Similarities between the Scientific and the Historical Revolutions at the End of the Renaissance' *Journal of the History of Ideas* 26 (1965) 353–68

Tacitus *The Annals of Imperial Rome* trans Michael Grant (1956)

Taylor, E.G.R. *Late Tudor and Early Stuart Geography, 1583–1650* (1934)

Taylor, John *All the Workes of John Taylor the Water-Poet* (1630) 23725

Terrill, Richard J. 'The Application of the Comparative Method by English Civilians: The Case of William Fulbecke and Thomas Ridley' *Journal of Legal History* 2 (1981) 169–85

Thomas, Keith *The Perception of the Past in Early Modern England* (Creighton Lecture, 1983)

– *Religion and the Decline of Magic* (1971)

Thompson, J.W. *A History of Historical Writing* (2 vols, New York 1942)

Thornborough, John *A Discourse Plainely Proving the Evident Utilitie and Urgent Necessitie of the Desired Happie Union of the Two Famous Kingdomes of England and Scotland* (1604) 24035

De Thou, Jacques-Auguste *Histoire universelle de Jacques-Auguste de Thou* ed A. de la Haye (11 vols, Paris 1740)

– *Monsieur de Thou's History of His Own Time* trans B. Wilson (2 vols, 1730)

Tillesley, Richard *Animadversions upon M. Seldens History of Tithes and His Review Thereof* (1619; 2nd ed, 1621) 24073, 24074

Tillyard, E.M.W. *Shakespeare's History Plays* (1980; first published London 1944)

Tinkler, John F. 'The Rhetorical Method of Francis Bacon's *History of the Reign of King Henry the VII' History and Theory* 26 (1987) 32–52

Todd, Margo *Christian Humanism and the Puritan Social Order* (Cambridge 1987)

- 'Providence, Chance and the New Science in Early Stuart Cambridge' *Historical Journal* 29 (1986) 697–711
Tooley, M.J. 'Bodin and the Mediaeval Theory of Climate' *Speculum* 28 (1953) 64–83
Trevor-Roper, H.R. 'Queen Elizabeth's First Historian: William Camden and the Beginnings of English "Civil" History' in his *Renaissance Essays* (1985) 121–48
Trimble, W.R. 'Early Tudor Historiography, 1485–1548' *Journal of the History of Ideas* 11 (1950) 30–41
Trompf, G.W. *The Idea of Historical Recurrence in Western Thought: From Antiquity to the Reformation* (Berkeley 1979)
Trussell, John *A Continuation of the Collection of the History of England, Beginning Where S. Daniell Ended* (1636) 24297
Tuck, Richard ' "The Ancient Law of Freedom": John Selden and the Civil War' in *Reactions to the English Civil War* ed J.S. Morrill (1982) 137–61
- *Natural Rights Theories: Their Origin and Development* (Cambridge 1979)
Twyne, Brian *Antiquitatis academiae Oxoniensis apologia* (Oxford 1608) 24405
Udall, William *The Historie of the Life and Death of Mary Stuart* (1624) 24508.7
Van Leeuwen, Henry G. *The Problem of Certainty in English Thought, 1630–1690* (The Hague 1963)
Van Norden, Linda 'The Elizabethan College of Antiquaries' (PH D University of California at Los Angeles 1946; microfilm on deposit at Bodleian Library, Oxford)
- 'Peiresc and the English Scholars' *Huntington Library Quarterly* 12 (1948–9) 369–89
- 'Sir Henry Spelman on the Chronology of the Elizabethan College of Antiquaries' *Huntington Library Quarterly* 13 (1949–50) 131–60
Venn, J., and J.A. Venn *Alumni Cantabrigienses* (Part I to 1751, 4 vols, Cambridge 1922–7)
Verstegan, Richard (alias Rowlands) *A Restitution of Decayed Intelligence* (Antwerp and London 1605) 21361
Vicars, John *Magnalia dei Anglicana. Or, Englands Parliamentary-Chronicle* (1646) v319
Vickers, B.W., ed *Essential Articles for the Study of Francis Bacon* (Hamden, Conn. 1968)
Vincent, Augustine *A Discoverie of Errours in the First Edition of the Catalogue of Nobility, Published by Ralph Brooke, Yorke Herald, 1619* (1622) 24756
Vossius, G.J. *G.J. Vossii et clarorum virorum ad eum epistolae* ed P. Colomesius (1690)
- *Opera* (6 vols, Amsterdam 1690–1701)
Ware, Sir James, ed *Two Histories of Ireland* (1633) 25067

Warnicke, Retha *William Lambarde, Elizabethan Antiquary, 1536–1601*
(1973)
Weisinger, H. 'Ideas of History during the Renaissance' *Journal of the History
of Ideas* 6 (1945) 415–35
Weiss, Roberto *The Renaissance Discovery of Classical Antiquity* (2nd ed,
Oxford 1988)
Whear, Degory *De ratione et methodo legendi historias dissertatio* (1623)
25325
– *Method and Order of Reading Both Civil and Ecclesiastical Histories* trans
Edmund Bohun (1685, 1694) w1592, w1593
– *Relectiones hyemales, de ratione & methodo legendi utrasque historias,
civiles et ecclesiasticas* (Oxford 1637) 25328
Wheeler, Thomas 'Bacon's Henry vii as a Machiavellian Prince' *Renaissance
Papers* (1957) 111–17
– 'The New Style of the Tudor Chroniclers' *Tennessee Studies in Literature*
7 (1962) 71–77
– 'The Purpose of Bacon's History of Henry the Seventh' *Studies in Philology*
54 (1957) 111–17
Whibley, Charles 'The Chroniclers and Historians of the Tudor Age' in his
Literary Studies (1919) 1–59
White, Howard B. 'The English Solomon: Francis Bacon on Henry vii' *Social
Research* 24 (1957) 457–81
White, Richard *Historiarum Britanniae libri (I–XI) ... cum notis antiquitatum
Britannicarum* (Arras and Douai 1597–1607)
Whitelocke, Bulstrode *Memorials of the English Affairs* (1682) w1986
Wilcox, Donald J. *The Measure of Times Past: Pre-Newtonian Chronologies
and the Rhetoric of Relative Time* (Chicago and London 1987)
Willey, Basil *The Seventeenth Century Background* (New York 1953)
Williams, F.B., Jr *Index of Dedications and Commendatory Verses in English
Books before 1641* (1962)
Willson, D.H. 'King James i and Anglo-Scottish Unity' in *Conflict in Stuart
England* ed W.A. Aitken and B.D. Henning (1960) 41–55
Wing, Donald *Short-Title Catalogue of Books Printed in England, Scotland,
Ireland, Wales, and British America and of English Books Printed in Other
Countries, 1641–1700* (3 vols, New York 1945–51)
Wood, Anthony *Athenae Oxonienses* ed P. Bliss (4 vols, 1813–20)
– *Fasti Oxonienses, or Annals of the University of Oxford* ed P. Bliss (2 vols,
1815–20)
Woolf, D.R. 'Edmund Bolton, Francis Bacon and the Making of the *Hypercri-
tica*, 1618–1621' *Bodleian Library Record* 11 no 3 (1983) 162–8
– 'Genre into Artifact: The Decline of the English Chronicle in the Sixteenth
Century' *Sixteenth Century Journal* 19 (1988) 321–54
– 'John Selden, John Borough, and Francis Bacon's *History of Henry vii*,
1621' *Huntington Library Quarterly* 47 (1984) 47–53
– 'The True Date and Authorship of Henry, Viscount Falkland's History of

the Life, Reign and Death of King Edward II' *Bodleian Library Record* 12 no 6 (1988) 440–52

Wootton, David *Paolo Sarpi: Between Renaissance and Enlightenment* (Cambridge 1983)

Wormius, Olaus *Olai Wormii et ad eum doctorum virorum epistolae* (2 vols, Copenhagen 1751)

Wright, C.E. 'The Dispersal of the Monastic Libraries and the Beginning of Anglo-Saxon Studies' *Transactions of the Cambridge Bibliographical Society* 1 (1949–53) 208–37

– 'The Elizabethan Society of Antiquaries and the Formation of the Cottonian Library' in *The English Library before 1700* ed Francis Wormald and C.E. Wright (1958) 176–212

Wright, Louis B. 'Heywood and the Popularizing of History' *Modern Language Notes* 43 (1928) 287–93

– *Middle-Class Culture in Elizabethan England* (Chapel Hill 1935)

Yates, F.A. 'Paolo Sarpi's "History of the Council of Trent" ' *Journal of the Warburg and Courtauld Institutes* 7 (1944) 123–43

Young, Patrick *Patricius Junius: Bibliothekar der Könige Jacob I, und Carl I von England* ed J. Kemke (Leipzig 1898)

Index

265. *See also* Historical interpretation; Elizabeth I; James I; Self-censorship

Chamberlain, John 294n53

Chance and contingency 5–6, 124–5, 127–8, 131, 262–3, 280n11

Chancery, court of 222

Charlemagne 226

Charles I, king xv, 164, 167, 175, 244; and court culture 163, 243, 323n7; historical writing under 243–7; personal rule of 182, 186; in post-1640 historiography 248–9, 250, 257, 260–1; as prince of Wales 112, 156–7, 239; trial and execution of 174, 328n44

Charles V, emperor 138

Charron, Pierre 133

Chelsea College 38, 109, 277n110

Chester, Robert 35

Chorography and topography 21, 116, 201, 274n54, 303n42. *See also* Geography

Christina, queen of Sweden 206

Chroniclers, medieval 201; Asser 212; Bede 18, 42, 57, 86, 192, 212; Eadmer 207, 236; Robert Fabian 245; Gildas 195, 204, 253; Henry Knighton 236; Matthew Paris 39, 206, 303n49; Ranulf Higden (*Polychronicon*) 245; Roger Hoveden 39, 59; Thomas of Walsingham 23, 291n18; William of Malmesbury 57, 192, 212, 236, 252; William of Newburgh 57, 279n127

Chronicles 65, 118, 154; collections of 205, 238, 264; criticism of 39, 57, 65, 139, 142, 192–3, 232, 320n92; decline of 14, 192, 243, 283n48; distinguished from histories 57, 66–7, 152, 246, 284n55

Chronology 47, 171, 188, 209; use of Olympiad 67, 188. *See also* Beroaldus; Scaliger, Joseph; Selden, John

Chrysostom, Saint John 171, 226

Church history 35, 37–44, 226

Cicero, Marcus Tullius 172; his definition of history 10, 17, 107, 144; influence in Renaissance 17, 24, 150, 271n22

Civic humanism. *See* Humanism

Civil War, English, and Interregnum, historical writing during 247–61

Clapham, John 56–8, 63, 66, 68, 70, 75–6, 95, 159, 201

Claxton, William 22–3

Climate and history 203, 313n12

Cnut, king 179

Cochrane, Eric 246

Coins, discovery and collection of 18, 220, 241; numismatic study of 242; use of as historical source 68, 194–5, 197

Coke, Edward, Sir, chief justice 24, 30, 34, 86, 179, 196, 320n86; and chronicles 27–8, 39, 236; controversy with Parsons 38–40, 292n28; historical sense of 25–9, 62, 215, 251, 274n66

Coke, John, Sir, secretary of state 23, 191, 192, 196

College of Arms. *See* Heralds

Colman, Morgan 63–4

Common-law mind 25–9, 61. *See also* Ancient constitution; Custom; Law

Commynes, Philippe de 70, 142, 165

Conjecture 136, 202

Conquest theory 181, 289n38. *See also* Norman Conquest

Consensus in history writing xiv; establishment of in sixteenth century 31–3, 141; dissolution of

66006